The Football Game I'll Never Forget

The Football Game I'll Never Forget

100 NFL STARS' STORIES

as told to the editors of *Football Digest*

**SELECTED BY
CHRIS McDONELL**

FIREFLY BOOKS

A FIREFLY BOOK

Published by Firefly Books Ltd.

Articles copyright © 2004 Century Publishing Company
Introduction copyright © 2004 Chris McDonell

Second printing, 2011

Publisher Cataloging-in-Publication Data (U.S.)

The football game I'll never forget : 100 NFL stars' stories / selected by Chris McDonell.
[224] p. : col. photos. ; cm.
Includes index.
Summary: Collection of 100 personal accounts by NFL players and coaches from the 1950s to today.
ISBN 1-55297-850-8 (pbk.)
1. Football – Biography – Anecdotes. 2. Football players. 3. National Football League.
I. McDonell, Chris. II. Title.
796.332/64 21   GV954.M446 2004

National Library of Canada Cataloguing in Publication Data

McDonell, Chris
    The football game I'll never forget : 100 NFL stars' stories / Chris McDonell.
Includes index.
ISBN 1-55297-850-8
    1. National Football League. 2. Football players--United States--Anecdotes.
I. Title.

GV939.A1M33 2004   796.332'64   C2004-902567-8

Published in the United States in 2004 by
Firefly Books (U.S.) Inc.
P.O. Box 1338, Ellicott Station
Buffalo, New York 14205

Published in Canada in 2004 by
Firefly Books Ltd.
66 Leek Crescent
Richmond Hill, Ontario L4B 1H1

Cover and interior design by Christine Gilham

Printed in China

The Publisher gratefully acknowledges the financial support for our publishing program by the Government of Canada through the Canada Book Fund as administered by the Department of Canadian Heritage.

Title page:

In a classic portrait, Pro Football Hall of Fame end and halfback Elroy "Crazylegs" Hirsch takes flight.

To Sue Gordon, and Isaac, Tara and Quinn McDonell-Gordon, for their continuous love and support.

TABLE OF CONTENTS

INTRODUCTION

We hold our breath as the defensive back and wide receiver vault into the air with outstretched arms.

Time freezes when the quarterback ducks beneath the arms of an onrushing lineman. Will it be a sack or a successful scramble?

The kicker, with a mighty sweep of his foot, sends the ball toward the uprights as the clock runs out. The running back makes a sharp cut toward the end zone, as the linebacker reaches out to make the tackle. A precious few seconds or inches can make all the difference between winning and losing.

But no matter the outcome, the emotional highs and lows are what draw us to watch, to care. These stories bring out those same feelings. Reading them, we're pulled out of the stands, or off the couch, and onto the field. The accounts in *The Football Game I'll Never Forget* come directly from the players and coaches themselves, and in their own words.

Professional football has evolved into a tightly structured, highly specialized game. The two-way player is dead, as old-fashioned a concept as the leather helmet. The 300-pound lineman is now the norm, as is the 15-member coaching staff. Yet in most ways, football remains today as it was 70 years ago, when the National Football League began to tweak old college rules for a more entertaining match. The rise of the specialist player hasn't diminished the purpose of football. He still needs to move the ball over the goal line, and prevent his opponent from doing likewise.

So when the editors of *Football Digest* gather stories for their monthly feature, "The Game I'll Never Forget," it doesn't matter whether they get a narrative from a veteran Hall of Famer like "Crazylegs" Hirsch or a current star's recounting of last season's Super Bowl. The players all speak the same language: football. And in this book, a pleasing mix of players from across the generations offers much to appeal to fans of every age.

Game stories are told from the perspective of every position on the field, as well as from the sideline vantage point, thanks to a handful of successful coaches, such as Don Shula. Quarterbacks—such as John Elway, Joe Namath and Roger Staubach—dominate on these pages, as they do on the playing field; but not at the expense of others. Wide receivers, such as Steve Largent and Charlie Joiner; running backs, such as Earl Campbell and Tony Dorsett; and kickers, such as Mark Mosely and Nick Lowery, also find the spotlight here.

There are plenty of voices from the defense as well. Safeties, among them Ken Houston; tackles like Merlin Olsen; and defensive ends, such as Jack Youngblood, share their most memorable stories. Also included are guards like Mike Munchak, linebackers like Dave Wilcox, tight ends, defensive backs, halfbacks and fullbacks . . . and the roster is complete.

What kind of game stands out in a player's outstanding career? Not surprisingly, championship games and Super Bowls are chosen by many. Reaching the top is a sweet reward that makes all the years of sweat, pain and endless practice feel meaningful and worthwhile. Likewise, defeat at the pinnacle of success can sting with a lasting venom. As unsavory as it can be to rehash profound disappointment, some of the men in these pages choose to discuss a momentous loss—revealing particular honesty and strength of character.

Lighter moments also abound. "Hacksaw" Reynolds and John Matuszak were almost as notorious for their antics off the field as on. Don Meredith recalls a game when his Dallas Cowboys played the Detroit Lions; how and why Meredith does *not* get on the field for the whole game is as humble—and hilarious—a tale as you're likely to hear from anyone involved in pro sports.

Sometimes it can be a seminal moment that stands out. Gale Sayers, the legendary Chicago Bears running back, reflects on the importance of a great personal effort during a seesaw battle against Minnesota in his rookie season. Jan Stenerud, the first pure placekicker to enter the Hall of Fame, vividly recalls his first professional game, an exhibition-season blowout for Kansas City.

Stenerud is not alone in defining as a personal highlight a game that has faded—

for the rest of us—into the darker recesses of memory. Alongside the dozens of famous games recalled in this book are others that are delightfully obscure.

This collection of stories will refresh old memories and create new ones, quicken the pulse, and remind us why we've always loved the game. Enjoy.

—*Chris McDonell*

In the last minute of the 1981 NFC Championship Game, San Francisco wide receiver Dwight Clark hauls in a Joe Montana pass for the winning touchdown in the 49ers' 28-27 victory over the Dallas Cowboys. Montana's eyewitness account of the game—including the reason he didn't even see "The Catch"—is one of the 100 stories in *The Football Game I'll Never Forget*.

There are few times when a man can look back and say truthfully, "I won that game. Without me we would have lost."

OCTOBER 7, 1962
GREEN BAY PACKERS 9, DETROIT LIONS 7
LAMBEAU FIELD, GREEN BAY, WISCONSIN

SCORING

GB	3	0	3	3	**9**
DET	0	7	0	0	**7**

GB	Hornung, 15-yard field goal
DET	Lewis, 6-yard run (Walker kick)
GB	Hornung, 15-yard field goal
GB	Hornung, 27-yard field goal

TEAM STATISTICS

	GB	DET
First Downs	19	12
Rushes-Yards	34-129	27-107
Passing Yards	198	92
Passes	18-28-2	11-26-1
Punts-Average	2-40.0	6-45.5
Fumbles-Lost	2-2	0-0
Penalties-Yards	6-67	3-47

INDIVIDUAL STATISTICS

Rushing

GB	Gros 1 rush for minus 2 yards; Hornung 10-37; R. Kramer 1-minus 4; Moore 1-minus 1; Starr 1-4; Taylor 20-95
DET	Lewis 12-30; Pietrosante 8-19; Plum 7-58

Passing

GB	Hornung 0 completions, 1 attempt, 0 yards, 1 interception; Moore 0-1-0-1; Starr 18-26-198-0
DET	Plum 11-26-107-1

Receiving

GB	Dowler 3 receptions for 45 yards; Hornung 2-10; Kramer 2-26; McGee 5-69; Moore 3-23; Taylor 3-25
DET	Barr 2-12; Cogdill 1-9; Gibbons 3-41; Lewis 3-13; Studstill 2-32

ATTENDANCE 38,669

I'm talking about team games now, especially the game of football where each man depends so much upon the other 10, and where the offense and defense are so dependent on each other.

But I can look back to one murky, muddy Sunday in Green Bay, Wisconsin, and truthfully feel that on that day a young fellow named Herb Adderley made the big difference in the ball game.

To set the stage for you, all I have to tell you is that it was October 7, 1962. The Green Bay Packers were the defending champions of professional football. We thought we were going to repeat. The Detroit Lions didn't think we should. We both thought this game would settle it.

We, the Packers, were off to a good start, a great start. We beat the Minnesota Vikings opening day 34-7, shut out the St. Louis Cardinals 17-0, and then just rolled over the tough Chicago Bears 49-0. One touchdown in three games! That's really defense, and we had one too: Willie Davis and Bill Quinlan at the ends; Dave Hanner and Henry Jordan at the tackles; Dan Currie, Ray Nitschke and Bill Forester at linebacker; and Jess Whittendon, Hank Gremminger, Willie Wood and myself the deep backs.

Detroit was just about as tough. They scored 119 points in their first three games in defeating the Pittsburgh Steelers, the San Francisco 49ers and the Baltimore Colts. On offense they had guys like Terry Barr, Pat Studstill, Gail Cogdill and Jim Gibbons to catch the ball, Nick Pietrosante and Dan Lewis to run it and Milt Plum to throw it. On defense they had Alex Karras, Roger Brown, Joe Schmidt, Wayne Walker, "Night Train" Lane, Yale Lary and Dick LeBeau.

We were the champions and they figured they could use us as a stepping stone to a championship of their own. There was no love lost between the Packers and the Lions. Every time we played in those days, it was with a little extra of that complete abandon

that Vince Lombardi liked to talk about. And after all those hard-fought games, with the Packers usually winning, a lot of bitterness developed between the two teams.

We knew it was going to be an alley fight and we knew that by beating the Lions we'd have a clear track at our third consecutive Western division title. They knew they had to stop us. Our game plan was very simple: smother them on defense and ram it down their throats on offense.

It started that way when our offense marched the ball over 70 yards right from the opening kickoff. Jimmy Taylor was going great and he got well over half of that yardage by himself. We were playing our game, keeping the ball and eating up the clock. But when we got down close, the Lions' defense really tightened up and Paul Hornung had to kick a 15-yard field goal.

We went back in and made them give up the ball, but then the Lions got the break that turned the game around. Bart Starr went back to pass, but our blocking broke down. Starr was hit, he fumbled and Karras recovered the ball on our 34-yard line. That gave the Lions a tremendous lift and Dan Lewis scored from just outside our five-yard line, six plays later. They went into the lead 7 to 3.

From then on we were like two beasts locked at each other's throats. Our offense was able to move the ball but twice we turned it over on mistakes. We thought we could fool the Lions by having Tom Moore throw the option pass, a Hornung specialty, but he underthrew Boyd Dowler and Yale Lary intercepted. Then later, after another long drive, Hornung threw one intended for our tight end, Ron Kramer, but he underthrew him and the ball sailed right into the arms of their outside linebacker, Carl Brettschneider.

In the third quarter, our offense started another drive from deep in our own territory. Looking back now, that was one of the keys to the game. We held their offense in check, but we couldn't make them turn the ball over, we couldn't force them into mistakes so we were always starting drives from deep in our territory.

Do that, especially playing the basic kind of ball control game we played, and any little mistake along the way can stop you. This time we got down to about the Lions' 7-yard line, but again we were stopped, so on the last play of the third quarter Hornung kicked another 15-yard field goal to close the gap to 7 to 6.

Now the game intensified. It was for blood. We kicked off, and for once we couldn't stop the Lions. They knew they needed some points. Even a field goal now would put us in a deep hole. They drove the ball down to our 34-yard line, but we tightened up and with nine minutes to go Wayne Walker missed a field goal from the 41.

We came off the field cheering for our offense: "Go! Go! Go! Get some points!" The whole bench was up. Starr threw one to Dowler for a first down. Then he hit Max McGee for another. We ran a couple and then he hit Ron Kramer for another first down. We had the ball down on the Lions' 40-yard line, but again we stalled. Hornung came in and tried one from the 47-yard line, but the ball was wide to the left. It had the distance, but from the right hash mark it went wide.

With six minutes left to play the Lions took the ball on their own 20. They had to move the ball to kill the clock. We had to stop them. They ran on first down for a couple of yards. They ran it again on second down, but got very little. On third and long, Plum completed a pass to his tight end Gibbons for a first down.

The clock was moving and again they started the pattern all over again. Run for a short gain. Run again, and again Plum gambled and put the ball in the air, and again he completed it to Gibbons for the first down.

Time was really getting short now. We were going to have to use our time-outs now just to save whatever time we could. The drizzle, which had been steady throughout the game, seemed to be getting heavier. They ran and ran again, and for the third time on third down Plum went back to pass. He must have thought we'd be looking for him to go to Gibbons again so this time he changed the pattern.

Barr came straight out at me. About 10 yards off the line of scrimmage, he cut to go to the sidelines. He tried to cut it a little too sharp, though, and his foot slipped on the wet field. He went down and there was that ball just hanging in the air in front of me. I didn't think. I just reacted. I took two steps up, caught it and started down the sidelines. I don't remember who caught me, but by the time they did it didn't matter. I was able to run it back about 40 yards to the Detroit 18-yard line. With only 33 seconds left Hornung came in and kicked his third field goal of the game. We won, 9 to 7.

We went on to a great season, finishing 13 and 1 in the regular season and beat the New York Giants for our second straight World Championship. Later on, Vince Lombardi told me that if it hadn't have been for my interception he would have never been able to write his book, *Run To Daylight*.

—*As told to Bob Billings*

He went down and there was that ball just hanging in the air in front of me.

Herb Adderley, shown above returning one of his 48 career interceptions, played for Green Bay for nine seasons (1961–69). The speedy cornerback won five NFL Championship Games and two Super Bowl rings with the Packers before he was traded to Dallas in 1970. Adderley completed three campaigns with the Cowboys, going to two more Super Bowls, including a victory in Super Bowl VI. He retired after the 1972 season and was inducted into the Pro Football Hall of Fame in 1980.

I have to go back to 1982 and my first regular-season game as a pro for my most unforgettable game. Not only were the

SEPTEMBER 12, 1982

LOS ANGELES RAIDERS 23, SAN FRANCISCO 49ERS 17

CANDLESTICK PARK, SAN FRANCISCO, CALIFORNIA

SCORING

LA	3	10	0	10	**23**
SF	0	14	3	0	**17**

LA	Bahr, 41-yard field goal
SF	Solomon, 18-yard pass from Montana (Wersching kick)
LA	Bahr, 42-yard field goal
SF	Clark, 41-yard pass from Montana (Wersching kick)
LA	Allen, 3-yard run (Bahr kick)
SF	Wersching, 22-yard field goal
LA	Christensen, 3-yard pass from Plunkett (Bahr kick)
LA	Bahr, 43-yard field goal

TEAM STATISTICS

	LA	SF
First Downs	17	18
Rushes-Yards	43-161	22-60
Passing Yards	94	192
Passes	10-20-2	21-41-1
Punts-Average	4-49.5	8-35.8
Fumbles-Lost	4-2	3-3
Penalties Yards	11-102	6-99

INDIVIDUAL STATISTICS

Rushing

LA Allen 23 rushes for 116 yards; King 9-33; Hawkins 7-15; Guy 1-7; Plunkett 2-minus 4; Christensen 1-minus 6

SF Moore 7-30; Easley 5-11; Cooper 6-8; Lawrence 2-6; Montana 2-5

Passing

LA Plunkett 10 completions, 20 attempts, 123 yards, 2 interceptions

SF Montana 21-41-244-1

Receiving

LA Allen 4 receptions for 64 yards, King 2-30, Branch 2-21, Christensen 2-8

SF Clark 6-106; Young 6-45; Moore 3-22; Nehemiah 2-26; Cooper 2-21; Solomon 1-18; Lawrence 1-6.

ATTENDANCE: 73,564

Raiders playing the defending Super Bowl champion 49ers in San Francisco, but also it was the first game back in the Bay Area for the Raiders, who had moved to Los Angeles after the 1981 season. I had been in some pressure games before at USC, so I wasn't nervous for this one.

I wanted to have a good *team* game; I wanted my efforts to have an effect on our victory. Looking back, I know that my efforts did help the team win, although there were a lot of guys who played their hearts out to win that day.

During the preseason, many of the guys on the team worked hard to get into shape for the game. Many had been with the franchise in Oakland, and there was that whole mess when the Raiders moved down to Los Angeles. Some of the guys were anticipating cheers or boos from the crowd, but they knew either way there would be a reaction.

Because there was so much being made about the Raiders returning to the Bay Area for this game, and because the 49ers were the defending NFL champions, there wasn't that much pressure put on me. I know there were people watching who wanted to see how I would do in the pros after the college career that I had, but I didn't feel as much pressure and tension that a lot of other rookies might have felt in that situation. That helped me a great deal.

The guys on our team were all professionals, and a lot of them had been through pressure situations before. But you could tell that this game against the 49ers was special. The season before, the Raiders didn't have a good season, and it was important for us to get off to a good start. The Raiders have never backed down from a challenge, and I think that everyone, from Al Davis on down, was glad that the first game would be against the defending champs *and* in the Bay Area. A good showing would put us in position to do well for the whole season.

The first quarter was played at midfield; we

had a field goal for the only score. But from the beginning you could tell that there was no love lost between the two teams. There was a lot of hitting going on in the trenches, and guys were popping each other pretty well, coming through the line on running plays. There were a couple of plays on the ground early on where I was popped pretty well, but all that did was help me to concentrate even harder and to focus on my job. I never thought that being a running back in the NFL would be an easy assignment. I'm always out there to play as hard, but as clean, as I can, and I expect that any defender I come up against will play the same way.

In the second quarter the 49ers started to get their offense into motion. Quarterback Joe Montana's favorite targets were Freddie Solomon and Dwight Clark, and he seemed to be finding them pretty well in that quarter. Their first touchdown, a pass from Montana to Solomon, gave them the lead and also seemed to give them a boost of confidence. But we came back and put a strong drive together that took off some of the edge they had gained. Kenny King had a key 20-yard reception in that drive, and I remember running out in front of him and blocking one of the 49ers linemen.

Chris Bahr hit a field goal at the end of that drive, which pulled us to within one. But Montana came back and directed another strong drive for them, from about the 20 to past midfield. Then he hit Clark with a pass that gave them a 14-6 lead with time running out in the half.

Right from the start, I knew that the Raiders were not a team to quit or to pass up any opportunity to pressure the other team. And the next drive really showed me that we were going to play hard until time ran out. We started a drive on our 20. Quarterback Jim Plunkett was cool, moving the team quickly and professionally. A big play for us was a pass-interference call against the 49ers that gave us the ball on their three-yard line. On the next play I scored my first NFL touchdown with a run up the middle to bring us within one again. Our front line really made that play happen because our guys drove the 49ers defensive line back and apart.

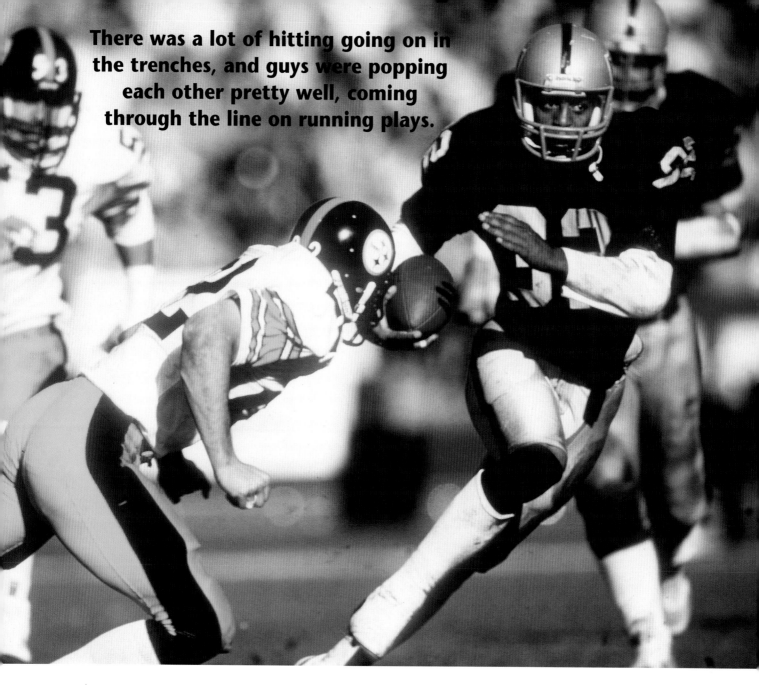

There was a lot of hitting going on in the trenches, and guys were popping each other pretty well, coming through the line on running plays.

At halftime, head coach Tom Flores kept stressing to our defense to put pressure on Montana, and they responded right from the start of the second half, forcing the 49ers to make mistakes. Our defense caused three fumbles and Montana was sacked five times at key spots.

The work done by our defense really keyed up our offense. Jim led another strong drive and the 49ers again were called for pass interference, giving us the ball on their three-yard line once more. This time Jim lobbed a pass to Todd Christensen and we had our first lead, 20-17. On our next drive, Chris Bahr hit another field goal for a 23-17 lead, and our defense played tough to make sure we maintained that lead. They allowed one field goal in the second half. We won 23-17.

It was a great feeling in the locker room because the entire team played tough and took the game away from them. Our defense put a lot of pressure on Montana and upset his rhythm, which is not an easy thing to do. Our offense was tough and the line helped me to have a great game. I ended up carrying the ball 23 times for more than 100 yards. I also caught four or five passes and led the team in yards receiving, so I was happy with my all-around performance, especially because we won the game.

I was fortunate to have a strong showing in my first professional game. The fact that we beat the world champs is something I'll never forget.

—As told to Barry Janoff

Running back **Marcus Allen** won the 1981 Heisman Trophy and was the NFL's 1982 rookie of the year. He played 17 pro seasons with the Los Angeles Raiders (1982–92) and the Kansas City Chiefs (1993–97), amassing career totals of 3,022 rushes for 12,243 yards and 123 touchdowns, along with 587 receptions for 5,411 yards and 23 touchdowns. A star high-school quarterback, he also completed 12 NFL passes for 284 yards and six more touchdowns. Allen, the Super Bowl XVIII MVP, entered the Pro Football Hall of Fame in 2003.

I played in a lot of games during my career—some were more intense and exciting than others. We didn't even win

JANUARY 22, 1984
LOS ANGELES RAIDERS 38, WASHINGTON REDSKINS 9
TAMPA STADIUM, TAMPA, FLORIDA

SCORING

LA	7	14	14	3	**38**
WAS	0	3	6	0	**9**

LA	Jensen, recovered blocked punt in end zone (Bahr kick)
LA	Branch, 12-yard pass from Plunkett (Bahr kick)
WAS	Moseley, 24-yard field goal
LA	Squirek, 5-yard interception return (Bahr kick)
WAS	Riggins, 1-yard run (kick blocked)
LA	Allen, 5-yard run (Bahr kick)
LA	Allen, 74-yard run (Bahr kick)
LA	Bahr, 21-yard field goal

TEAM STATISTICS	LA	WAS
First Downs	18	19
Rushes-Yards	33-231	32-90
Passing Yards	154	193
Passes	16-25-0	16-35-2
Punts-Average	7-43.0	8-32.0
Fumbles-Lost	3-2	1-1
Penalties-Yards	7-56	4-62

INDIVIDUAL STATISTICS

Rushing

LA	Allen 20 rushes for 191 yards; Pruitt 5-17; King 3-12; Willis 1-7; Hawkins 3-6; Plunkett 1-minus 2
WAS	Riggins 26-64; Theismann 3-18; J. Washington 3-8

Passing

LA	Plunkett 16 completions, 25 attempts, 172 yards, 0 interceptions
WAS	Theismann 16-35-243-2

Receiving

LA	Branch 6 receptions for 94 yards; Christensen 4-32; Hawkins 2-20; Allen 2-18; King 2-8
WAS	Didier 5-65; Brown 3-93; J. Washington 3-20; Giaquinto 2-21; Monk 1-26; Garrett 1-17; Riggins 1-1

ATTENDANCE: 72,920

all of the games that I consider to be some of the best I've played in. But when you play in the NFL, the goal is to get to the Super Bowl, and I did that twice—once with the Denver Broncos [Super Bowl XII] and once with the Los Angeles Raiders [Super Bowl XVIII]. Dallas beat us in the first one, but we beat Washington in the second one 38-9. So, based on results, winning the Super Bowl has to be a game I'll never forget.

I really didn't think about the hype leading up to the game. If you're a professional athlete, you're in the public eye. It's something you deal with the best way you can. It's not always easy, because I like my privacy. I like to be able to go out in public and have times when people don't recognize me.

There are a lot of distractions the week before the Super Bowl. The media want a story, and fans want to know everything that's happening, so there is a lot of commotion and distraction. But you focus on the game and the plays.

I made some major moves in between my two Super Bowl appearances. I went from Denver to the Cleveland Browns and then to the Raiders. I never doubted my skills as a player, but there were times when it seemed as if I wouldn't get back into a championship game. But Raiders owner Al Davis wanted me to play on his team, and that was a great boost of confidence. The team had some intense players—people liked to call them outlaws or renegades—but those guys were loyal to the team and dedicated to playing great football.

This was the first year the team played in Los Angeles, and that added fuel to the fire. Other teams wanted to beat us badly; they wanted to knock us off. But that was great for us; we wanted to be in that intense situation. We wanted to win every game, and we expected every team to come at us with everything. That fired us up, and we played great football—not as individuals with lots of talent—but as a talented, fiery team.

We won the division that season, then

beat Pittsburgh and Seattle in the playoffs to win the AFC title. At that point we were ready to take on any NFC team, but I guess there was a little extra surge knowing that we would play the Washington Redskins. They had won Super Bowl XVII and were the NFL's defending champs.

A lot of people knew that we had a team capable of winning the Super Bowl. Marcus Allen had come in the season before, and Jim Plunkett was having a great season, winning games for us in the clutch. On defense we had Howie Long, Mark Haynes, Lester Hayes, Matt Millen—guys who could hit hard and get the job done.

We had played Washington earlier in the year, and they beat us 37-35 in a game that wasn't a good defensive showing for either team. This time the defensive guys got together and vowed to play a tough game. With all the talk about how big and bad the Raiders were supposed to be, we knew the only place anything mattered was on the field. And that's where we wanted to get the job done.

If you look at the Super Bowl statistics you'll see that our defense was keyed up from start to finish. We shut them out in two quarters, allowed only a field goal in another and gave up only one touchdown. In the playoffs, we only gave up 33 points in three games. That's some playing.

Only a few plays really stand out for me, but that's because they were key plays in the final outcome. In the first quarter, special teams captain Derrick Jensen recovered a blocked punt in the end zone, which gave us our first score. In the second quarter Cliff Branch caught a tough pass from Plunkett to give us our second touchdown. In that quarter we put a lot of heat on Redskins quarterback Joe Theismann.

Near the end of the half Washington was on their 12, and they lined up for what looked like a short running play that would have run out the clock. But our defensive coach, Charlie Sumner, sent in Jack Squirek for Millen because Squirek was a bit better against pass plays. When we had played Washington earlier in the year they called a screen pass in a similar situation that went for 67 yards. This time I rushed right at

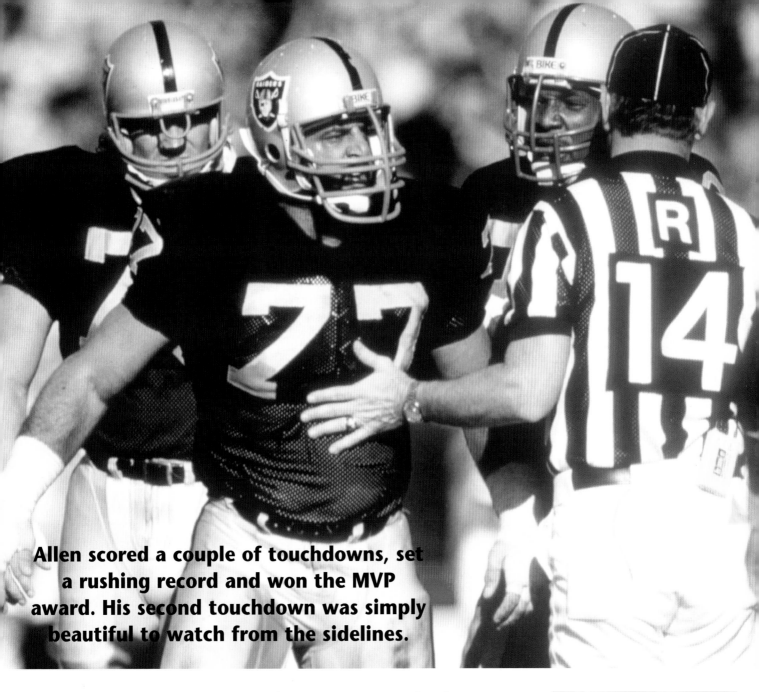

Allen scored a couple of touchdowns, set a rushing record and won the MVP award. His second touchdown was simply beautiful to watch from the sidelines.

Theismann, and he put up a soft pass over my arms. Squirek was in the right place at the right time—he intercepted it and went in for the touchdown.

We were very loud during halftime—we couldn't wait to get back on the field. However long halftime lasted, it was too long.

The offense really picked it up in the second half. Allen scored a couple of touchdowns, set a rushing record and won the MVP award. His second touchdown was simply beautiful to watch from the sidelines. We were on our 25 or 26, and he took a handoff from Plunkett and started to run wide. But then he cut back inside and left *everyone* behind—and I mean everyone. Even our guys couldn't keep up with him. He went 75 yards almost alone.

The locker room after the game was a madhouse. Al Davis later called us the greatest Raiders team ever. I don't feel a need to say anything like that—I knew that the hard work and sweat we put in all year ended up with us being the champs of the NFL.

You can play in great games and win great games and be on teams with great players, but there is a special feeling when you win the Super Bowl. I was on both sides—a team that didn't win the Super Bowl and a team that did. Let me tell you, if your goal is to be the best player you can be and the outcome is being on the best team in the NFL, that's what it's all about.

Winning the Super Bowl is special. It's something I'll never forget.

—*As told to Barry Janoff*

Defensive end/defensive tackle **Lyle Alzedo** first brought his aggressive approach to the Denver Broncos (1971–78), where he was part of the fabled "Orange Crush" defense. He won 1977's defensive player of the year honors and was voted All-Pro in 1977 and 1978. Alzedo was traded to the Cleveland Browns (1979–81) but is better remembered for his years with the Los Angeles Raiders (1982–85). He retired to a Hollywood career but the self-confessed steroid user succumbed to steroid-related health problems and died in 1991.

I felt like I was in my second career, playing with the Giants. So many great things happened with that team that

DECEMBER 24, 1989

NEW YORK GIANTS 34, LOS ANGELES RAIDERS 17

GIANTS STADIUM, EAST RUTHERFORD, NEW JERSEY

SCORING

NYG	7	10	10	7	**34**
LA	7	10	0	0	**17**

NYG	Meggett, 76-yard punt return (Nittmo kick)
LA	Horton, 1-yard pass from Beuerlein (Jaeger kick)
LA	Fernandez, 30-yard pass from Beuerlein (Jaeger kick)
NYG	Anderson, 1-yard run (Nittmo kick)
LA	Jaeger, 42-yard field goal
NYG	Nittmo, 28-yard field goal
NYG	Anderson, 1-yard run (Nittmo kick)
NYG	Nittmo, 21-yard field goal
NYG	Simms, 3-yard run (Nittmo kick)

TEAM STATISTICS	LA	NYG
First Downs	19	20
Rushes-Yards	23-82	38-116
Passing Yards	230	164
Passes	16-34-2	13-25-0
Punts-Average	5-40.8	5-41.2
Fumbles-Lost	4-1	4-1
Penalties-Yards	9-82	3-28

INDIVIDUAL STATISTICS

Rushing

LA   Jackson 10 rushes for 35 yards; Smith 7-24; Allen 2-13; Beuerlein 4-10

NYG   Anderson 23-74; Tillman 8-21; Carthon 6-18; Simms 1-3

Passing

LA   Beuerlein 16 completions, 34 attempts, 266 yards, 2 interceptions

NYG   Simms 13-25-169-0

Receiving

LA   Fernandez 6 receptions for 125 yards; Alexander 4-98; Gault 2-17; Jackson 2-14; Allen 1-11; Horton 1-1

NYG   Meggett 3-25; Mowatt 2-37; Cross 2-19; Anderson 2-16; Baker 1-17; Manuel 1-11; Carthon 1-9; Robinson 1-5

ATTENDANCE: 70,306

it's hard to pick out one or two games that were more special than others. I also had some great games when I played with the St. Louis Cardinals. I really feel like I was blessed when it came to my pro career.

Looking back, though, a game we played in 1989 against the Los Angeles Raiders seemed to bring together a lot of the positive things that happened to the Giants and me. It was on Christmas Eve, the last game of the season, and we needed a win to get into the playoffs. I also needed 51 yards rushing to go over 1,000 yards in one season for the first time in five years. We beat the Raiders 34-17 at home, which was a great way to pay our fans back for all their support. I also rushed for two touchdowns and 74 yards, which gave me 14 touchdowns and 1,023 yards rushing for the season.

The Raiders were a tough team, and they were playing exceptionally well under their head coach Art Shell. We knew they had a solid running game with Bo Jackson and Marcus Allen and a tough defense, and they gave up the sixth-fewest points in the AFC that season.

We had beaten Dallas the week before, which gave us an 11-4 record. Philadelphia had lost the week before and was 10-5, but they had beaten us twice during the season. If Philadelphia won and we lost, the Eagles would end up in first because they had beaten us in both games.

Head coach Bill Parcells didn't put any more or any less pressure on the team from week to week. Every game was equally important. Our game plans might change, but the ultimate goal was to play tough defense and tough offense and not to take any team lightly. I saw that happen: you think a team is soft, and they end up being a lot tougher than you ever expected. Bill Parcells was a winner because he believed in total preparation for every team.

The 1989 season was my fourth with New York, but it was the first where I felt the

running game was geared to my style. I didn't rush for a lot of yards on one play, but I carried the ball a lot and got the tough yards every time. With the Cardinals, when I was rushing for over 1,000 yards a season, I was averaging less than five yards per carry. That was my style.

In my first three seasons with the Giants the main man was Joe Morris, but he was injured and missed all of 1989. The running game became me and Maurice Carthon and Lewis Tillman. Maurice and I were big backs, and were hard to bring down. But we worked best in short-yardage situations.

When I first came into the league, and during the early 1980s, the Raiders had a reputation as being a tough, bruising team that would beat you any way it could. I think they lost their edge somewhat for a few seasons, but Art Shell had them playing the old style of Raiders football in 1989 and 1990, and they were a winning franchise again. We didn't want to be in a position of giving them a lead and having to chase them; we wanted to score and possibly get them off their game plan.

The game started off right for us when Dave Meggett returned a punt 76 yards for a touchdown early in the first quarter. However, the Raiders scored the next two touchdowns on passes from Steve Beuerlein, which gave them a 14-7 lead early in the second quarter.

The Raiders were playing tough ball to that point, but after they took that lead they scored only once the rest of the game. I think, after the second touchdown, our defensive guys got mad and decided to turn things up a couple of notches. Our defensive guys ended up with four sacks—two by Lawrence Taylor—and really shut down their running and passing games.

Our offense also got tough at that point, as if we knew we had to take charge of the game. Our quarterback, Phil Simms, directed a strong drive about mid-quarter, and I ended up tying the game when I busted in from the one. They scored a field goal a few minutes later, but we came back right at the end of the half to tie the game again on a field goal.

We weren't losing at the half, but I don't

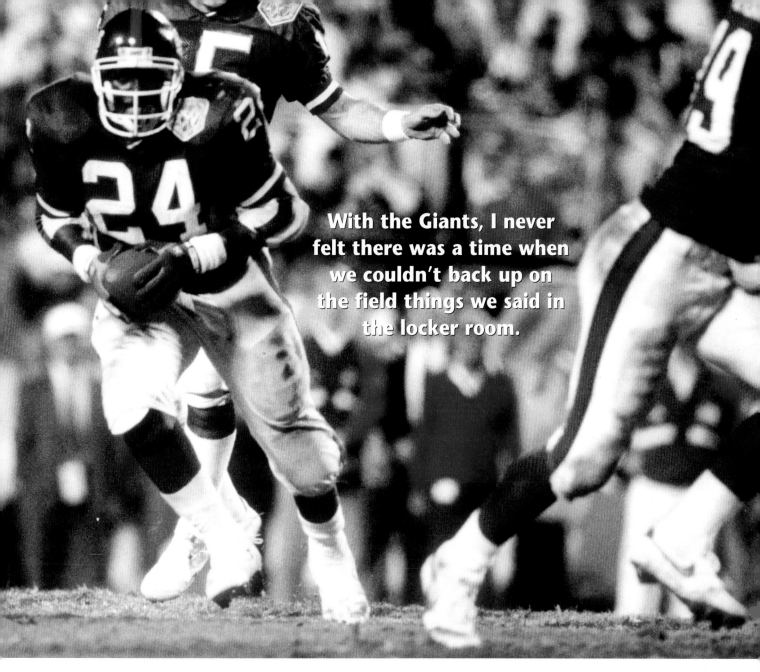

> **With the Giants, I never felt there was a time when we couldn't back up on the field things we said in the locker room.**

think we had played as well to that point as we wanted to. We didn't want to be in a situation where one turnover would decide the game; we wanted to go out in the second half and put points on the board and shut them down.

There were teams on which I had played where guys talked about doing this and that, and they got all fired up about it, but then they couldn't deliver on the field. With the Giants, I never felt there was a time when we couldn't back up on the field things we said in the locker room. There was an amazing team spirit and unity there, and that had a lot to do with the fact that the Giants were a winning football team.

Nothing much happened early in the third quarter, but then things came together for us. We had a good offensive drive, and about eight minutes into the quarter I scored to give us the lead. We scored again on a field goal a few minutes later, and in the fourth quarter Phil Simms ran in from a few yards out to give us another touchdown.

The game was played on December 24, and it was a terrific Christmas present for us and for our fans. The fact that we won and clinched first place in the division was my priority. Scoring two touchdowns and going over 1,000 yards rushing was an extra bonus. A lot of people didn't think I was capable of making the big plays anymore, but Bill Parcells and the Giants believed in me as much as I believed in myself. But it was the team's success that made it a game I won't forget.

—*As told to Barry Janoff*

St. Louis Cardinals rookie running back **Ottis Anderson** rushed a career-high 1,605 yards in 1979 and topped the 1,000-yard mark in five of his first six pro seasons. He was traded to the New York Giants early in the 1986 campaign. Although Anderson helped the Giants win Super Bowl XXI, he saw restricted action before busting loose again in 1989. He won Super Bowl XXV MVP honors after rushing 21 times for 102 yards. Anderson retired after the 1992 campaign with 10,273 career yards rushing and 3,062 yards receiving.

During the 2000 season, they started talking about the Baltimore Ravens having one of the greatest defenses ever. That got some people thinking about our Chicago Bears team in 1963.

The words "Chicago Bears" and "defense" always have gone together, but that year was something special. That may have been the best defense ever assembled; we allowed an average of about 10 points per game. And some of those points came from the other team returning an interception or two for a touchdown, not from our defense letting up.

George Allen was a huge part of our success; he was in charge of the defense that year. The problem we had with the Bears prior to 1963 was that Clark Shaughnessy was in charge for a while. He was an old man and was getting a little senile. When he was on offense that unit did real well, but George Halas switched him over to defense. He used all these Mickey Mouse defenses: switching here, switching there, jumping here, jumping there. He had us doing this, that and the other thing. What you need to do is throw all that stuff out and pick what you need. You need to simplify everything.

At defensive end, I could beat most offensive tackles in a 4-3 and put the heat on the quarterback. But Coach Shaughnessy had me going out and covering passes on some plays. Hell, I might go a full game and never make a tackle. When we would look at film, he sometimes wouldn't know whether to chew me out or not because he himself didn't know which defense we were supposed to be in.

When Allen took over the defense in 1963, we went to a basic 4-3. After that, we all knew what we were doing and we all just teed off and went. I wasn't out covering anybody. I was doing what I did best: teeing off on that quarterback.

We had some really good defensive players: Bill George, Larry Morris and Joe Fortunato were ferocious linebackers. Stan Jones was a terrific defensive tackle and Ed O'Bradovich was a good, young defensive end. Our secondary also was topnotch with Rosey Taylor, who led the league that year with nine interceptions.

Our offense was pretty good too. Billy Wade was our quarterback and Mike Ditka was our best receiver. Those guys didn't give the ball up—they didn't fumble it or throw interceptions. When they had to score, they'd score. Sometimes an offense will go in there, get off one play and fumble it away, and then the defense is forced to come out again. That's how defenses get tired quickly. But our offense would go in there and move the ball, which helped us on defense.

We lost one game all year and made it to the NFL Championship Game against the New York Giants. It was December 29 at Wrigley Field in Chicago, so you knew it was going to be cold. It must have been about eight degrees. I would have rather not played in it. Your hands and your feet got so cold that you couldn't keep them warm. But other than that, it didn't bother you.

The Giants came out and didn't seem to be fazed by the weather, scoring on a long drive in the first quarter to take the lead. Their quarterback, Y.A. Tittle, was getting up there in age by then, but he was still one of the best in the league. He sure looked good on that opening drive.

We went back to the sideline and said we couldn't let him do that to us all day. So we decided we were going to get after Y.A. In the first series we had played a basic defense, but then we started going after him. We were much more aggressive, blitzing extra guys. We hit him every chance we got. I don't know what the statistics were, but he got one beating. When you hit a quarterback as the ball is being thrown, that's just as good as a sack because those shots begin to take their toll.

Anyway, our offense turned around and did what I said it never would do: fumble. The Giants got the ball deep in our territory. If New York had scored another touchdown, we would have been in a big hole.

Tittle hit a receiver named Del Shofner right in his hands with a pass. I don't know if his hands were cold or what, but it bounced right off them. Hell, I could have caught that one. If he would have caught

---

DECEMBER 29, 1963
CHICAGO BEARS 14, NEW YORK GIANTS 10
WRIGLEY FIELD, CHICAGO, ILLINOIS

SCORING

CHI	7	0	7	0	**14**
NYG	7	3	0	0	**10**

NYG Gifford, 14-yard pass from Tittle (Chandler kick)
CHI Wade, 2-yard run (Jencks kick)
NYG Chandler, 13-yard field goal
CHI Wade, 1-yard run (Jencks kick)

TEAM STATISTICS

	CHI	NYG
First Downs	14	7
Rushes-Yards	31-93	38-128
Passing Yards	129	140
Passes	10-28-0	11-30-5
Punts-Average	7-41.0	4-43.3
Fumbles-Lost	2-1	2-2
Penalties-Yards	4-30	4-30

INDIVIDUAL STATISTICS

Rushing
CHI Bull 13 rushes for 42 yards; Galimore 7-12; Marconi 3-5; Wade 8-34
NYG King 9-39; Morrison 18-61; McElhenny 7-19; Webster 3-7; Tittle 1-2

Passing
CHI Wade 10 completions, 28 attempts, 138 yards, 0 interceptions
NYG Griffing 0-1-0-0; Tittle 11-29-147-5

Receiving
CHI Bull 1 reception for minus 5 yards; Ditka 3-38; Coia 1-22; Marconi 2-19
NYG Gifford 3-45; Morrison 3-18; Thomas 2-46; Webster 1-18; McElhenny 2-20

ATTENDANCE: 45,801

When you hit a quarterback as the ball is being thrown, that's just as good as a sack because those shots begin to take their toll.

that pass, the Giants would have been in command, and I think they would have won. But that's what kind of a season it was for us. We got just about every break.

Instead of the Giants mounting a big lead, we intercepted a pass and ran it back inside their 10. Then we scored to tie the game. They took a 10-7 lead into the locker room at halftime, but that was it for them, as our defense came up big again in the third quarter. O'Bradovich intercepted a pass and brought it 10 yards to the Giants' 14. Then Wade eventually scored on a one-yard run to give us a 14-10 lead.

From there, we were in control. It kept getting colder, and we kept hitting Tittle. He took a real pounding that game. He never gave up, but he never had a chance either. We intercepted five passes that day and held on for the victory.

That win was really sweet for Bears fans because it was their first championship since the 1940s. They finally had a team they could brag about, thanks to a great defense.

—*As told to Chuck O'Donnell*

Defensive end **Doug Atkins** (81), above, spent his first two pro seasons (1953-54) with the Cleveland Browns, but after being traded to the Chicago Bears in 1955, he developed into one of football's best defensive performers of all time. The six-foot-eight, 257-pound Atkins was surprisingly agile, known for leapfrogging blockers when rushing the passer. He starred for the Bears for 12 years before completing his Pro Football Hall of Fame career with three strong seasons with the New Orleans Saints (1967-69).

There's a rite of passage for every player, a moment of truth when years of practice and preparation are left behind in the

SEPTEMBER 17, 1967
DETROIT LIONS 17, GREEN BAY PACKERS 17
LAMBEAU FIELD, GREEN BAY, WISCONSIN

SCORING

DET	10	7	0	0	**17**
GB	0	0	7	10	**17**

DET	Barney, 24-yard interception (Walker kick)
DET	Walker, 47-yard field goal
DET	Marsh, 3-yard run (Walker kick)
GB	Pitts, 3-yard run (Chandler kick)
GB	Pitts, 2-yard run (Chandler kick)
GB	Chandler, 28-yard field goal

TEAM STATISTICS

	DET	GB
First Downs	10	13
Rushes-Yards	37-192	20-43
Passing Yards	41	263
Passes	7-17-0	14-23-4
Punts-Average	7-45.6	4-43.0
Fumbles-Lost	1-1	1-1
Penalties-Yards	4-52	3-38

INDIVIDUAL STATISTICS

Rushing
DET   Farr 16 rushes for 95 yards; Marsh 16-86; Nowatzke 3-4; Watkins 2-7
GB   Anderson 2-1; Grabowski 10-36; Pitts 7-1; Wilson 1-5

Passing
DET   Plum 7 completions, 17 attempts, 41 yards, 0 interceptions
GB   Starr 14-23-321-4

Receiving
DET   Farr 1 reception for minus 2 yards; Henderson 1-9; Kramer 1-8; Malinchack 1-7; Studstill 3-19
GB   Anderson 1-14; Dale 4-109; Dowler 2-28; Fleming 1-9; Grabowski 3-69; Pitts 2-98; Wilson 1-minus 6

ATTENDANCE: 50,861

locker room. Standing in a stadium packed with thousands of screaming people, a man emerges with hands clenched and chinstrap buckled tight, ready to take the field for his first NFL game.

The hours leading up to that moment are about as nerve-wracking as any other life experience. You can pace, you can mutter to yourself, you can listen to rock and roll—you can try whatever you want to ease your mind as the game time approaches. But it feels like you have butterflies performing gymnastics in your stomach until that first play, until you can forget about the significance of the day and concentrate on simply playing football. That's how it was for me before my first NFL game, with the Detroit Lions in 1967. I was so nervous, I wasn't sure I would be able to play. My heart was pounding, my legs were like jelly and my eyes were glassy.

Making matters worse was that we were playing the defending Super Bowl champion Green Bay Packers, my favorite team when I was growing up. I used to idolize these guys. I used to read about them, watch them on television and root them on—and now I was going to have to play against them. Could I really do that?

Packers quarterback Bart Starr was one of my favorites. I admired him for his grace on the field and for his graciousness off of it. He was a real gentleman. I also was in awe of their defense. Before the game I got to meet the great Herb Adderley—he was a terrific cornerback—and I also met their other cornerback, Bob Jeter, who was a good one too. There I was, staring across the field at the likes of Ray Nitschke, Willie Wood, Forrest Gregg, Henry Jordan and Max McGee. These guys had just won the Super Bowl and some of them would end up in the Pro Football Hall of Fame. I was wondering if I would even make it through the day.

Although we weren't stocked with the kind of talent the Packers had, we had some

good players. Mel Farr finished the 1967 season with team highs in rushing yards [860] and receptions [39]. We had a strong defense that was led by linebackers Mike Lucci and Wayne Walker and defensive backs Dick LeBeau and Wayne Rasmussen. Our defense wound up yielding just 18 points per game. Under first-year coach Joe Schmidt, we finished 5-7-2 and climbed out of the basement in the Western Conference.

But all that came later—first I had to get through this game against the Packers. I wasn't comforted at all by the fact that I had had some success leading up to the game. As a cornerback at Jackson State, I had 26 interceptions in three seasons. The Lions then picked me in the second round of the draft and I had a few interceptions in the preseason. But as I looked out across legendary Lambeau Field that day, I knew none of that mattered.

My plan was to play conservatively; I didn't want to surrender a big play. I simply wanted to get my feet wet before trying to do anything too drastic.

But a funny thing happened early in the game. The Packers received the opening kickoff, and I then lined up against Boyd Dowler, a receiver who went about six-foot-five and 225 pounds. On one of the plays that first series, the ball was hiked to Starr and Dowler ran right at me. After about seven, eight or nine yards, he planted his feet, pivoted and cut toward the sideline.

I could see the out pattern developing, so I stopped backpedaling and broke to the spot Dowler was headed. Starr wanted to throw the ball to Dowler but he realized I had read the play. Starr's considerable instincts took over, and like a crafty pitcher, he tried to throw the ball low and away so that I wouldn't be able to get to it. I continued to close on Dowler. With each stride, I realized I was either going to break up the play or get burned for a long gain, possibly a touchdown. It was going to be do or die.

Finally, the moment of truth arrived. I cut inside of Dowler, and with my arms outstretched, I jumped off the ground and went for the ball. The whole world was moving in slow motion. On my way down, I

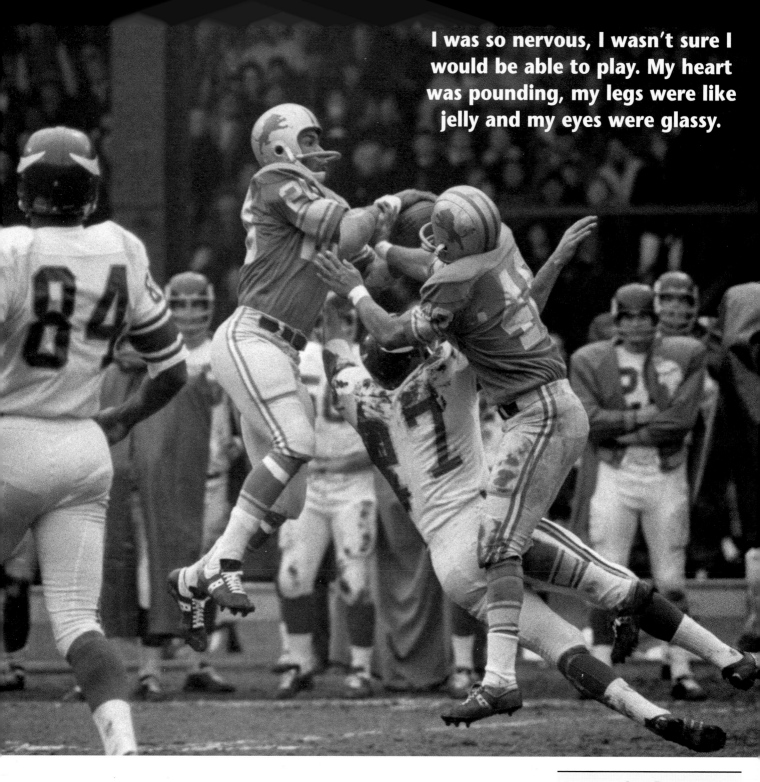

I was so nervous, I wasn't sure I would be able to play. My heart was pounding, my legs were like jelly and my eyes were glassy.

got my hands on the ball. I had it! I had intercepted my idol, Bart Starr.

But it wasn't time to celebrate quite yet. I hit the ground headfirst, rolled and got back on my feet. There were only 24 yards of empty grass between me and a touchdown. I don't know if I ever had run as fast as when I crossed the goal line. It was a tremendous feeling. The butterflies had been released—the anxiety was gone.

That play set the tone for us that day. We finished with a 17-17 tie, which was a huge moral victory for our team. It also sparked a season in which I had 10 interceptions, three of which I returned for touchdowns.

A few days before I was inducted into the Hall of Fame in 1992, I received a two-page telegram from Starr congratulating me. I don't think he remembered that day in 1967, but the ball he threw that I intercepted started it all.

—*As told to Chuck O'Donnell*

Cornerback **Lem Barney** played his entire 11-season NFL career for the Detroit Lions. Shown above making the 10th interception of his 1967 rookie season, Barney retired after the 1977 campaign with 56 interceptions for 1,077 yards. He returned seven of his pick-offs into the end zone, and gathered four more touchdowns on special teams. Barney entered the Pro Football Hall of Fame in 1992.

I have a lot of great memories from playing in the NFL, and I played in a lot of big games with the New York Giants. But

when I consider all the things that make a game great—excitement, tension, team play, outstanding performances and long-lasting memories—there is no doubt that our victory over the Denver Broncos in Super Bowl XXI was the most unforgettable game of my career.

I had been with the Giants since 1977, and we had some good teams and some bad teams during that time. During my first four seasons with the Giants, the team never played .500 ball. But we finished 9-7 in 1981. Then, when we were on the verge of contending, we regressed.

The turnaround for our team came in 1984, when Bill Parcells became head coach. The year before we were 3-12, which was the worst season since I had joined the team. But we were 9-7 in 1984. Most important, we began to respect ourselves, and other teams in the league began to respect us. We weren't just an easy win for the opposition; even in most of the games we lost, we played tough.

Guys like Lawrence Taylor, Harry Carson, Phil Simms and me had been with the team through the rough years. So there was a distinct change in attitude when we saw our hard work actually translate into victories. We made the playoffs in '84, beating the Los Angeles Rams before losing to the eventual Super Bowl XIX champion San Francisco 49ers. Then we had another good season in 1985, finishing at 10-6. But we lost to the Chicago Bears in the NFC divisional playoff, as the Bears went on to win Super Bowl XX.

I hated losing those games, just as I hate losing any game. But those playoff losses were a learning experience for the team. We knew what we had done wrong and we knew what we had to do to win. More than anything, it was a matter of developing a tougher mental attitude, which is what we did going into the 1986 season. Right from the first day of training camp, every player said to himself, "We will not lose. We will not do anything to beat ourselves, and we

will not allow any other team to beat us."

The entire '86 season was an amazing one for us. We had the best record in the league during the season, 14-2, and we got stronger in the playoffs. The two playoff games we won to get into the Super Bowl weren't even close: we beat the Niners, 49-3, and we beat the Washington Redskins, 17-0. We had a mission to accomplish and no team was going to stop us.

Before the Super Bowl there were a lot of distractions, which can be especially difficult for players who have never been in that situation before. But we handled ourselves very well. Our only thought was that we were one game away from becoming NFL champions.

The Rose Bowl, site of Super Bowl XXI, is a massive stadium, and even now it seems amazing that there were more than 100,000 people in the stands and so many millions watching on TV. On the field, just before the game, I wasn't thinking about that specifically, but a lot of related things did play on my mind. But my mental attitude had to be tough. I had to say to myself, "We came here to win a championship, and that's what we're going to do."

Even though all our players had that attitude, we played a bit too tentatively during the first half. The Broncos had a strong offense behind John Elway, and they had a tough defensive unit that was overshadowed by the offense.

Denver scored first on a field goal in the first five minutes. But we came back a few minutes later when Phil moved the team 78 yards and hit Zeke Mowatt with a six-yard touchdown pass. It was important for us to get that score because our offense had established itself early. The guys on the front line had a strong set of downs, and that was important because we knew their defenders would be keying on Phil and Joe Morris.

We were up 7-3, but Elway was hot that quarter and he led Denver on a drive that started at about their 40. He finished it off with a run from about the five to give them a 10-7 lead. We had the only score in the second quarter when George Martin sacked Elway in the end zone for a safety.

JANUARY 25, 1987
NEW YORK GIANTS 39, DENVER BRONCOS 20
ROSE BOWL, PASADENA, CALIFORNIA

SCORING

NYG	7	2	17	13	**39**
DB	10	0	0	10	**20**

DEN Karlis, 48-yard field goal
NYG Mowatt, 6-yard pass from Simms (Allegre kick)
DEN Elway, 4-yard run (Karlis kick)
NYG Safety, Elway sacked in end zone by Martin
NYG Bavaro, 13-yard pass from Simms (Allegre kick)
NYG Allegre, 21-yard field goal
NYG Morris, 1-yard run (Allegre kick)
NYG McConkey, 6-yard pass from Simms (Allegre kick)
DEN Karlis, 28-yard field goal
NYG Anderson, 2-yard run (kick failed)
DEN V. Johnson, 47-yard pass from Elway (Karlis kick)

TEAM STATISTICS

	DEN	NYG
First Downs	23	24
Rushes-Yards	19-52	38-136
Passing Yards	320	263
Passes	26-41-1	22-25-0
Punts-Average	2-41.0	3-46.0
Fumbles-Lost	2-0	0-0
Penalties-Yards	4-28	6-48

INDIVIDUAL STATISTICS

Rushing
DEN Lang 2 rushes for 2 yards; Elway 6-27; Winder 4-0; Willhite 4-19; Sewell 3-4
NYG Rouson 3-22; Simms 3-25; Morris 20-67; Anderson 2-1; Carthon 3-4; Rutledge 3-0; Galbreath 4-17

Passing
DEN Elway 22 completions, 37 attempts, 304 yards, 1 interception; Kubiak 4-4-48-0
NYG Simms 22-25-268-0

Receiving
DEN Lang 1 reception for 4 yards; Winder 4-34; Willhite 5-39; M. Jackson 3-51; Mobley 2-17; Sewell 2-12; V. Johnson 5-121; Watson 2-54; Sampson 2-20
NYG Rouson 1-23; Manuel 3-43; Bavaro 4-51; Morris 4-20; Robinson 3-62; Mowatt 1-6; Carthon 4-13; McConkey 2-50

ATTENDANCE: 101,063

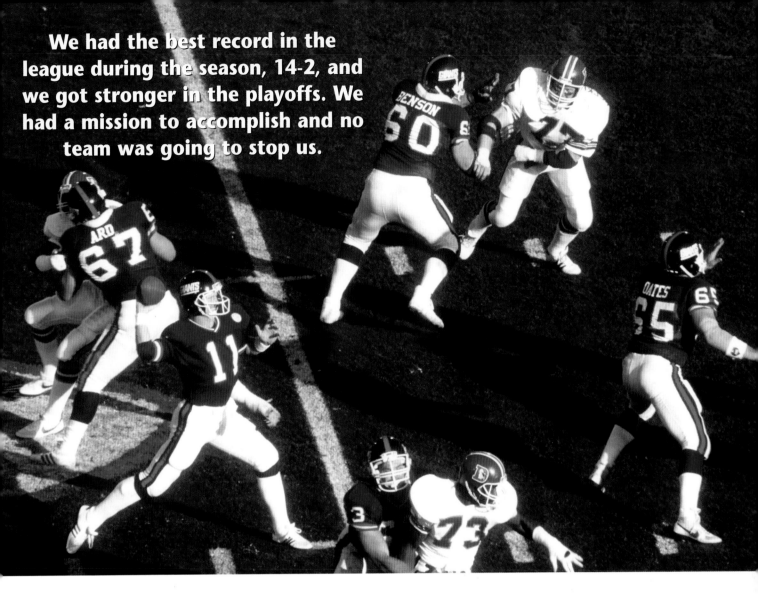

We had the best record in the league during the season, 14-2, and we got stronger in the playoffs. We had a mission to accomplish and no team was going to stop us.

Even though we were behind at the half, there wasn't a feeling in the locker room that we needed to make major changes. More than anything, we had to take charge of the game, as we had done in the playoff wins against the Niners and Redskins. We just came out as a team and said, "If we want this game, let's take control right now."

In the third quarter we played well both offensively and defensively. We called all the right plays and outscored them 17-0. The offensive line gave Phil all the protection he needed, and he had a super quarter. We went more than 60 yards and scored a touchdown within five minutes, and we put together strong back-to-back drives at the end of the quarter when we scored 10 points to take a 26-10 lead.

Even at that point, we knew that Denver could come right back behind Elway. If they scored two touchdowns, it would have been a 26-24 game. But we scored another touchdown with about four minutes gone in the quarter, which meant they needed three

touchdowns and a field goal to take the lead. They did score twice within the last six minutes, but we matched their touchdown drive and kept the game out of reach. The final score was 39-20.

We gave Parcells a Gatorade bath toward the end of the game, as we had done at the end of each of our victories that season. But I didn't really feel the excitement until the game was officially over. At that moment I felt a tremendous emotional rush, and a lot of things happened at once. Our guys were celebrating, fans were on the field, and photographers were trying to get their shots. Even in the locker room there was as much confusion as excitement with so many people running all over the place.

I was glad Phil was named MVP, and I was proud when he shared the award with the offensive line. Winning the Super Bowl was a team effort, and the game will always be my most memorable one because of that.

—*As told to Barry Janoff*

New York Giants offensive lineman **Brad Benson** (60) played, at various times, tackle, guard and center. He won a Super Bowl ring and his only Pro Bowl berth at the end of the 1986 campaign. When the six-foot-three, 270-pound lineman felt his game slip a little the following year—his ninth season (1978–87) in a Giants uniform—it was time for a change. Benson retired, on his own terms.

It may sound strange, but it was only seven or eight years ago that I first really began to comprehend the importance of

DECEMBER 28, 1958
BALTIMORE COLTS 23, NEW YORK GIANTS 17
YANKEE STADIUM, BRONX, NEW YORK

SCORING

BAL	7	7	0	3	6	**23**
NYG	3	0	7	7	0	**17**

NYG Summerall, 36-yard field goal
BAL Ameche, 2-yard run (Myhra kick)
BAL Berry, 15-yard pass from Unitas (Myhra kick)
NYG Triplett, 1 run (Summerall kick)
NYG Gifford, 15-yard pass from Conerly (Summerall kick)
BAL Myhra, 20-yard field goal
BAL Ameche, 1-yard run (no conversion attempt)

TEAM STATISTICS

	BAL	NYG
First Downs	27	10
Rushes-Yards	39-138	31-88
Passing Yards	322	178
Passes	26-40-1	12-18-0
Punts-Average	4-50.8	6-45.6
Fumbles-Lost	2-2	6-4
Penalties-Yards	3-15	2-22

INDIVIDUAL STATISTICS
Rushing
BAL Ameche 14 rushes for 65 yards; Dupre 11-30; Moore 8-23; Unitas 6-20
NYG Gifford 12-60; Webster 9-24; Triplett 5-12; Conerly 2-5; King 3-minus 13
Passing
BAL Unitas 26 completions, 40 attempts, 349 yards, 1 interception
NYG Conerly 10-14-187-0; Heinrich 2-4-13-0
Receiving
BAL Berry 12-176; Moore 6-101; Mutscheller 3-46; Ameche 3-17; Dupre 2-7
NYG Gifford 3-15; Rote 2-76; Schnelker 2-63; Webster 2-16; Triplett 2-15; MacAfee 1-15

ATTENDANCE: 64,185

the 1958 NFL Championship Game between my team, the Baltimore Colts, and the New York Giants. Simply put, it stood apart from any other game I ever participated in.

During my years as a wide receiver and later as a coach, we played in a lot of really big games. As a player, I had a lot of multiple-catch games. But it wasn't until someone asked me to do an article about that 1958 title game that I sat down and reflected on it. I kind of went back and researched it and talked to some people. It began to dawn on me that—without question—it was the high point of my whole career.

That two-minute drive to tie the ballgame at the end of regulation is particularly memorable. I've been coaching football for years, and I understand two-minute football as well as anyone. But it only recently dawned on me that a player doesn't ever catch three passes in a row on a two-minute drive. It just doesn't happen—but that's exactly what happened to me that day.

One of the greatest examples of John Unitas and I working and preparing together happened in that two-minute drive in the title game. The first play was one we had worked on together for four years. John and I spent time together after practice and talked football all the time.

We had a basic pattern: a 10-yard square-in. John and I would go over a checklist of things when we worked on plays by ourselves. One was what we would do on a 10-yard square if a linebacker walked out on me. We had an agreement that it would automatically adjust to a slant pattern; we called it a linebacker slant.

The Giants had never really shown this defense, but they did so on that first of those three passes to me. I came to the line, and one of their linebackers, Harland Svare, walked out on me.

There we were—the clock was running and we weren't in the huddle. Our ability to execute that play was based on four years of

preparation and talking football and going over things that we would do in case certain situations popped up. John picked up on it, I ran a slant, and we gained big yards.

I caught two more passes, then Steve Myhra came in and kicked a 20-yard field goal to tie the game at 17-17 and force overtime. No one even knew about overtime—I think it was a total surprise to everyone. I'll be willing to bet there wasn't one player on either team who knew what OT was.

By now, it was apparent that we were two evenly matched teams, especially defensively. Their defense and ours had finished 1-2 that season. Where we had the edge, though, was with Unitas at quarterback and with Lenny Moore, who was a weapon rushing or receiving.

The other advantage we had was the weather. Usually, if you're talking about a game on December 28 at Yankee Stadium, you're talking cold, wind and maybe even snow or freezing rain. But the conditions were perfect for our particular game plan. I think the temperature at the start of the game was in the 40s, the field was dry, and there was no wind.

I found out later that our coach, Weeb Eubank, had told Unitas he wanted him to throw, and throw a lot. Weeb felt like we were not going to make a living running against the Giants, so the plan was to put the ball in the air. The conditions were perfect for that.

Weeb was a great coach. Actually, the coaching was one of the most remarkable things that came out of that game. Vince Lombardi was in charge of New York's offense and Tom Landry headed its defense. We were up against two future legends. But Weeb was a match because, in my opinion, he was one of the top three coaches ever in the game.

Weeb's game plan was right on target. In overtime, we had a big play on a third-and-15 that we converted. About three or four plays later—I think we were inside the 20—we had a first down and we ran. The play didn't amount to much.

Then John drilled me on a slant pattern that put the ball on the eight-yard line. That was a big play. It now was first-and-goal.

We were not going to make a living running against the Giants, so the plan was to put the ball in the air. The conditions were perfect for that.

On the next play, we came out and ran the ball and got nothing, so the following play was critical. Unitas had been watching Giants safety Emlen Tunnell. He was lining up on our tight end, Jim Mutscheller; he was cheating to the inside. Johnny felt we could throw a flat zone pass to Jim, so that's what he called.

John said later that if Jim hadn't been open, he would have just thrown the ball away. But he was open—and he took it to the one-yard line. That was the key.

A lot of fans see a team get inside the 10 and say, "Oh, gee, that's a sure thing down there." Well, the closer you get, the more difficult it becomes to operate the passing game. And getting a running game going down there is extremely difficult, too.

But we were able to do it. Finally, Alan Ameche broke into the end zone on a one-yard run to end the historic game.

At the time, none of us had any real clue about the real significance of the game. I remember very vividly that after the game, we were outside Yankee Stadium near our buses and saw Bert Bell, the commissioner of the NFL, out there. He was talking to someone, and I was watching him. I could tell he was very emotional—he was crying. That kind of left a lasting impression on me.

It wasn't for several years that I began to realize what Bert Bell had realized. He knew something that day the rest of us didn't. That game was a huge turning point for the National Football League. Bert had been nursing the NFL along, and he knew it had grown up that day.

Today, you run into fans from all across the country who make the remark: "Oh, that game is what got me watching the NFL." The drama of that game obviously is something they'll never forget.

I know it was the game *I'll* never forget.

—As told to Chuck O'Donnell

Baltimore Colts end **Ray Berry**, above, leaps to snag a pass between two Los Angeles Rams defenders during his 1955 rookie season. Berry concluded his Pro Football Hall of Fame career with the Colts in 1967 after hauling in 631 career receptions, the most ever at the time. He also amassed 9,275 receiving yards and 68 touchdowns. Berry's 12 receptions on December 28, 1958 (the game he recounts here) remains the record for an NFL title game.

I have been in some very memorable games. Like our 1974 playoff game against Miami, for instance, when Ken "Snake"

JANUARY 9, 1977
OAKLAND RAIDERS 32, MINNESOTA VIKINGS 14
ROSE BOWL, PASADENA, CALIFORNIA

SCORING

OAK	0	16	3	13	**32**
MIN	0	0	7	7	**14**

OAK Mann, 24-yard field goal
OAK Caspar, 1-yard pass from Stabler (Mann kick)
OAK Banaszak, 1-yard run (kick failed)
OAK Mann, 40-yard field goal
MIN S. White, 8-yard pass from Tarkenton (Cox kick)
OAK Banaszak, 2-yard run (Mann kick)
OAK Brown, 75-yard interception return (kick failed)
MIN Voight, 13-yard pass from Lee (Cox kick)

TEAM STATISTICS

	OAK	MIN
First Downs	21	20
Rushes-Yards	52-266	26-71
Passing Yards	163	282
Passes	12-19-0	24-44-2
Punts-Average	5-32.4	7-37.9
Fumbles-Lost	0-0	1-1
Penalties-Yards	4-30	2-25

INDIVIDUAL STATISTICS

Rushing
OAK Davis 16 rushes for 137 yards; van Eeghen 18-73; Garrett 4-19; Banaszak 10-19; Ginn 2-9; Rae 2-9
MIN Foreman 17-44; McClanahan 3-3; Miller 2-4; Lee 1-4; S. White 1-7; S. Johnson 2-9

Passing
OAK Stabler 12 completions, 19 attempts, 1 yard, 0 interceptions; Rae 0-0-0-0
MIN Tarkenton 17-35-205-2; Lee 7-9-81-0

Receiving
OAK Casper 4 receptions for 70 yards; Biletnikoff 4-79; Garrett 1-11; Branch 3-20
MIN Foreman 5-62; Rashad 3-53; Miller 4-19; Voight 4-49; S. White 5-77; S. Johnson 3-26

ATTENDANCE: 103,438

Stabler threw the winning touchdown pass to Clarence Davis with only seconds remaining. Snake threw touchdown passes to four different receivers that day, and I caught one of them.

But the reason you play this game is to try to be the best, and we accomplished that goal during the 1976 season when we went all the way to beat Minnesota 32-14 in the Super Bowl. I was named the game's Most Valuable Player, which, I guess, helped make it even a little more meaningful. That, without a doubt, was the biggest game of my career.

I had a good day. Snake hit me with four passes for 79 yards and three of them set up touchdowns. But a number of our guys could have been the MVP; we had several outstanding performances that day. Clarence Davis ran for 137 yards. The offensive line, Art Shell and Gene Upshaw in particular, blocked the heck out of the Vikings. Snake did a super job of running the offense. And Willie Hall and Willie Brown had big interceptions. But the award went to me and I got to use a Thunderbird for a year.

It was my second chance to be on a Super Bowl winner. We lost to Green Bay 33-14 in Super Bowl II, in 1968 at Miami. The Packers had a great team, a great defense; but I felt going in we had a chance to beat them. I also knew things would have to go our way. They didn't.

I only caught two passes that day. I recall being confused about what patterns to run. We were up against a different class of player than what I was used to facing in the American Football League. Guys like Willie Wood, Herb Adderley and Ray Nitschke. The Packers had a very aggressive defense. Their defense was one of the best I have ever played against.

We were still in the game midway through the second quarter when Daryle Lamonica threw a touchdown pass to Bill Miller. That cut Green Bay's lead to 13-7. But we fumbled a punt near midfield just before the half and they turned it into a field goal and a 16-7

lead. That hurt. The final blow came in the fourth quarter when Lamonica tried to hit me with a pass. Adderley picked it off in the flat and returned it 60 yards for a touchdown to give the Packers a 33-7 lead.

I was only 24 then, so that loss didn't hurt that much, because I knew I would have a good chance to someday return to the Super Bowl with the Raiders. When we made it back two years ago, though, I was 33 and I knew it could be my last opportunity to be on a World Championship team. I was determined not to be a two-time Super Bowl loser.

I went into the Minnesota game with much more confidence than I had against Green Bay. I was experienced and, of course, much more knowledgeable. And I was more comfortable with the situation.

Minnesota had a veteran defense that played a basic 4-3-4, much the same as Green Bay did against us. In my position, all you have to do is run simple things, and that's exactly what I did all day.

We took the opening kickoff and drove deep into Minnesota territory, but we didn't get anything out of it when we missed a field goal.

Later in the quarter, punter Ray Guy had a kick blocked for the first time in his pro career and the Vikings had the ball on our three-yard line. But we got the ball back a couple of plays later when Minnesota fumbled.

Clarence Davis then got us going when he took off around the left side on a big 35-yard run. That got us out of the hole and we just kept driving to a field goal.

On our next possession, we moved the ball to the Minnesota six, where we had a third and three for a first down. I ran a slant-in and caught a pass from Snake for a first down at the one. With Minnesota's defense digging in for a goal-line stand, Snake dropped back on first down and flipped a touchdown pass to Dave Casper.

Later in the second quarter, we had a first down on the Vikings' 18 when Snake hit me again with a 17-yard gain. Pete Banaszak punched it in on the next play and we led 16-0.

We kicked another field goal for a 19-0 lead in the third quarter; then they scored

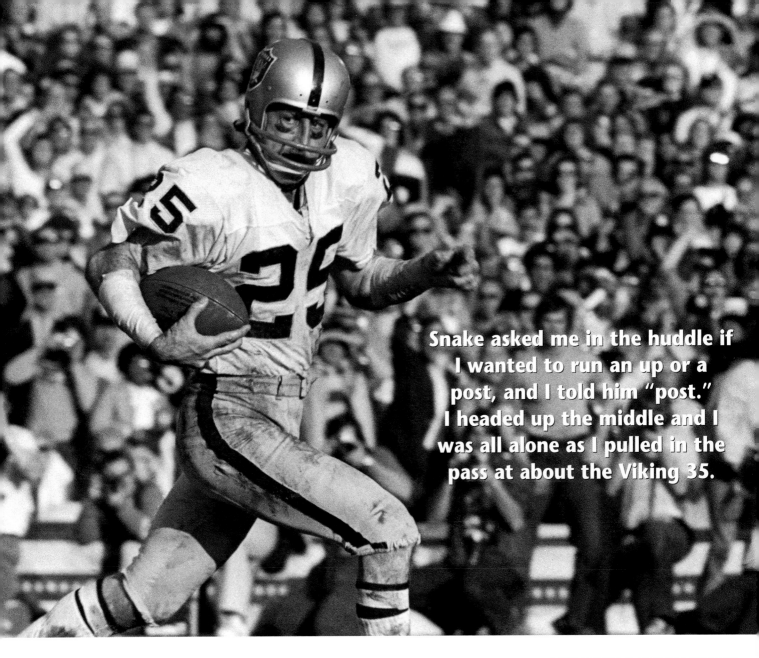

Snake asked me in the huddle if I wanted to run an up or a post, and I told him "post." I headed up the middle and I was all alone as I pulled in the pass at about the Viking 35.

late in the quarter, on a Fran Tarkenton pass to Sammy White, to pull within 19-7. We didn't have it won yet.

What I considered my biggest play of the game happened early in the fourth quarter when we had a third down at midfield. Snake asked me in the huddle if I wanted to run an up or a post, and I told him, "Post." I headed up the middle and I was all alone as I pulled in the pass at about the Viking 35. I knew I wasn't going to score; there's a little factor of speed. Also, their secondary guys had the angle on me. I made it to the two-yard line before Bobby Bryant caught me.

Banaszak scored and we were up 26-7. We put the game away a few minutes later when Willie Brown intercepted a Tarkenton pass and returned it 75 yards for a touchdown. Minnesota scored once more, but it was over by then.

It was an especially sweet win for Pete Banaszak, Willie Brown, Gene Upshaw and myself, because we were the only four players remaining from the 1968 Super Bowl team.

It was also odd the way the two Super Bowls paralleled each other. Against Green Bay, we fell behind 13-0, made it 16-7, and, with the score 26-7, Adderley returned that interception for a touchdown to give the Packers a 33-7 lead. We scored the last touchdown.

Against Minnesota, we led 19-0, the Vikings scored to make it 19-7, we went up 26-7, and Willie Brown's interception return made it 32-7. Then Minnesota scored the final touchdown. Had we made our last conversion, the score would have been identical.

Winning the Super Bowl was the ultimate.

—As told to Dave Payne

Oakland Raiders wide receiver **Fred Biletnikoff**, above, rambles downfield during Super Bowl XI. In the 1965 Gator Bowl—Biletnikoff's last college game—he caught 12 passes for four touchdowns and 192 yards to lead Florida State to an upset victory over Oklahoma. Raiders owner Al Davis immediately signed him to a contract, on the field under the goal posts. Biletnikoff starred for Oakland from 1965–78, accumulating 589 receptions for 8,974 yards and 76 touchdowns. He was inducted into the Pro Football Hall of Fame in 1988.

Playing this game of football for some 30 odd years, man and boy, can leave a fellow with an awful lot of memories. But the

game I'll really never forget, the prototype of all those storybook fast-minute finishes, was a game we played against the Kansas City Chiefs, October 24, 1965.

I was still with the Houston Oilers then, but I knew it wouldn't be for too long. We weren't doing too well that season, after years as one of the reigning powers of the American Football League.

The fans were getting down on everyone and they were especially down on me. I've noticed that the quarterback is always the first to get booed. They thought I was getting too long in the tooth and thought it was time to bring in a new pitcher.

And that's exactly what they did for this game against Kansas City. The youth movement was on and Don Trull was given the quarterback start against the Chiefs.

Well, it seemed that even youth was on the side of the Chiefs. They started Pete Beathard and by halftime they had an easy 17-0 lead. The only consolation I had sitting there on the bench was that Len Dawson was sitting this one out in favor of the youngsters too.

Apparently Houston's coaches soon got tired of youth because during halftime the coaches told me to get loosened up, that I was starting the second half at quarterback.

When I trotted out onto the field and into the huddle I heard one long chorus of boos. So the first time I laid my hands on the ball I dropped back and let it fly. I wanted to throw it right down some of those big mouths. Charlie Frazier was off and flying too, and we connected for a 66-yard touchdown play.

Our defense held. We got the ball back in real good field position. I tried one smash at that big Kansas City line and then I dropped back again. This time it was Ode Burrell in the clear and I hit him for six points, the play covering 49 yards overall.

We got the ball right back again and this time, just to change the pattern, we took the field in shorter bites. On the last one I hit our tight end, Willie Frazier, for 17 yards

and a touchdown. Bang, bang, bang, three touchdowns in four minutes.

With still 11 minutes left to play in the third quarter, we had rallied to take the lead 21-17. And still we weren't through. Our defense was just as hot as the offense and once again they stopped the explosive Chiefs. And once more we took the ball and marched it in. This time the payoff was a nine-yarder from me to Willie Frazier, our fourth touchdown of the quarter!

It looked like we might just run away with the game, except that the Kansas City coaches had seen as much youth as they wanted and sent Dawson into the game.

Like the cool veteran he is, Dawson didn't get excited. Instead, he brought the team back together, marched them upfield and narrowed the score a little with a 29-yard field goal.

The tide was still high for the Oilers though. We took the ball and brought it right back up the field. For the final nine yards, I found Bob McLeod for the touchdown. That made the score 35-20, and things were looking mighty cozy in Houston. Even my pals in the stands were cheering.

Dawson got a quick one right back, though. He hit his fullback, Curtis McClinton, with a little swing pass for a 40-yard touchdown play.

Trailing by 15, the Chiefs decided to go for a two-point conversion. Dawson rolled out, got outside the linebacker and then threw for the score when the cornerback had to come up to prevent him from running it in.

With a seven-point lead and just a few minutes left to play, we probably tried to play it a little too conservatively. We couldn't get the first down and had to give up the ball. With about a minute and half to go, Dawson hit Otis Taylor with an eight-yarder for the score.

The Kansas City coaches were forced to make a tough decision—go for an almost certain tie, or gamble for two points and the lead.

They went for the two points and made it. Now they had the lead—36-35.

We got a pretty good kickoff return and got the ball out-of-bounds to kill the clock, but when I huddled the boys up, that Kansas City goal looked a long ways off. It was only 60 yards, but it looked like a couple of miles.

OCTOBER 24, 1965
HOUSTON OILERS 38, KANSAS CITY CHIEFS 36
JEPPSEN STADIUM, HOUSTON, TEXAS

SCORING

HOU	0	0	28	10	**38**
KC	14	3	0	19	**36**

KC	McClinton, 48-yard run (Brooker kick)
KC	M. Hill, 8-yard run (Brooker kick)
KC	Brooker, 12-yard field goal
HOU	C. Frazier, 64-yard pass from Blanda (Spikes kick)
HOU	Burrell, 49-yard pass from Blanda (Spikes kick)
HOU	W. Frazier, 17-yard pass from Blanda (Spikes kick)
HOU	W. Frazier, 9-yard pass from Blanda (Spikes kick)
KC	Brooker, 29-yard field goal
HOU	McLeod, 9-yard pass from Blanda (Spikes kick)
KC	McClinton, 40-yard pass from Dawson (Wilson pass from Dawson)
KC	Taylor, 9-yard pass from Dawson (Beathard run)
HOU	Spikes, 18-yard field goal

TEAM STATISTICS

	HOU	KC
First Downs	21	32
Rushes-Yards	20-64	41-302
Passing Yards	302	240
Passes	22-43-0	17-42-4
Punts-Average	7-41.0	3-37.0
Fumbles-Lost	1-1	1-0
Penalties-Yards	7-63	10-107

INDIVIDUAL STATISTICS

Rushing

HOU	Spikes 5 rushes for 8 yards; Jackson 1-1; Tolar 2-1; Burrell 10-44; Trull 2-10
KC	Hill 17-130; McClinton 15-94; Beathard 7-66; Taylor 1-15; Dawson 1-minus 3

Passing

HOU	Trull 3 completions, 10 attempts, 12 yards, 0 interceptions; Blanda 19-33-290-0
KC	Beathard 11-32-157-3; Dawson 6-10-108-1

Receiving

HOU	W. Frazier 4 receptions for 48 yards; C. Frazier 3-75; Hennigan 3-36; McLeod 4-47; Burrell 5-87; Tolar 3-33
KC	Burford 5-75; Taylor 4-57; McClinton 7-48; Arbanas 2-33; Hill 2-21; Carolan 2-25

ATTENDANCE: 34,670

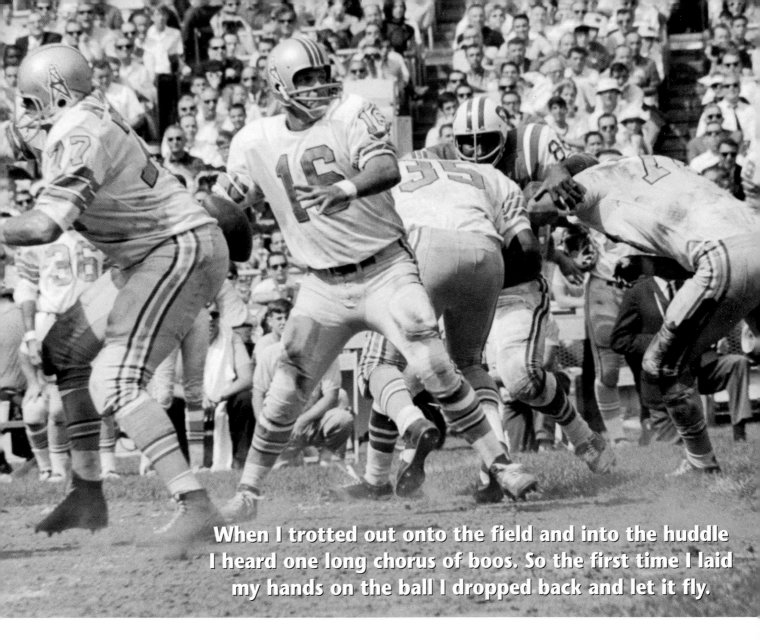

When I trotted out onto the field and into the huddle I heard one long chorus of boos. So the first time I laid my hands on the ball I dropped back and let it fly.

Those Kansas City safetymen were playing so deep they were almost offside for next Sunday's game. So I figured if they were going to give us the short stuff, we might as well take it. The main thing is not to get over-anxious yourself, because a team quickly reflects a quarterback's moods. That kind of stuff rubs off real easy.

And so does poise. So I acted like we had all the time in the world. I swung one out to Charlie Tolar, our fullback, for 17 yards.

Next I hit Burrell with a shortie for six yards, I went back to Tolar again, and this time we worked it for 12 yards. That gave us a first down on the Kansas City 27-yard line.

From that position it would have meant a field-goal try of about 35 yards to win, but I got cute and hit tight end Willie Frazier on a curl pattern down to the 9-yard line.

The clock was down to 17 seconds and Jack Spikes trotted out and booted one home to put us on top 38-36, a winner.

When I walked off that field, a thousand thoughts were racing through my head. One of them was that I could hang it up right there and never have a more satisfying moment or a greater day on which to do it.

I thought it was ironic that two old pros like Len Dawson and me, who had both been benched in favor of youth, should come off the bench and treat the fans to one of the grittiest, most exciting games ever played.

I also got a lot of satisfaction by serving up a big helping of crow to almost 35,000 fans who had been yelling for my scalp, and I made them enjoy eating every exciting morsel. They booed me when I came out, but now they were screaming their heads off.

Like I said, there's been a lot of games, but that's the one old George will never forget.

—As told to Bob Billings

Houston Oiler **George Blanda** (16), above, throws against the New York Jets in 1966. A remarkable quarterback and kicker, Blanda began his record 26-season, 340-game Pro Football Hall of Fame NFL career with the Chicago Bears (1949–58). He dressed for a single game with the Baltimore Colts in 1950 and played six seasons for the Oilers (1960–66) and nine (1967–75) for the Oakland Raiders. When he retired, Blanda had passed for 26,920 yards and 236 touchdowns, kicked 943 converts and 335 field goals and tallied 2,002 career points.

Having been with the Pittsburgh Steelers for my entire pro career, the games that stand out for me are the ones that were

DECEMBER 23, 1972
PITTSBURGH STEELERS 13, OAKLAND RAIDERS 7
THREE RIVERS STADIUM, PITTSBURGH, PENNSYLVANIA

SCORING

PIT	0	0	3	10	**13**
OAK	0	0	0	7	**7**

PIT	Gerela, 18-yard field goal
PIT	Gerela, 29-yard field goal
OAK	Stabler, 30-yard run (Blanda kick)
PIT	Harris, 60-yard pass from Bradshaw (Gerela kick)

TEAM STATISTICS	OAK	PIT
First Downs	13	13
Rushes-Yards	31-138	36-108
Passing Yards	78	144
Passes	12-30-2	11-25-1
Punts-Average	7-41.5	7-48.2
Fumbles-Lost	3-2	0-0
Penalties-Yards	2-15	1-5

INDIVIDUAL STATISTICS
Rushing
OAK   Hubbard 14 rushes for 44 yards; Smith 14-57; Davis 2-7; Stabler 1-30
PIT   Harris 18 rushes for 64 yards; Fuqua 16-25; Bradshaw 2-19
Passing
OAK   Lamonica 6 completions, 18 attempts, 45 yards, 2 interceptions; Stabler 6, 12, 57, 0 interceptions
PIT   Bradshaw 11, 25, 175, 1
Receiving
OAK   Chester 3 receptions for 40 yards; Biletnikoff 3-28; Smith 2-8; Banaszak 1-12; Siani 1-7; Jim Otto 1-5; Hubbard 1-2
PIT   Harris 5 receptions for 96 yards; Shanklin 3-55; Fuqua 1-11; McMakin 1-9; Young 1-4

ATTENDANCE: 50,350

team victories: the Super Bowl wins, the playoff wins, the games during the regular season where everyone played for the team. They're all important to me. As for the most memorable one, I think I'd have to go back to the playoffs in 1972 when the Steelers won their first ever playoff game, a 13-7 win over the Oakland Raiders. Not only was that *my* first playoff game, but it was also the first playoff game in the team's history.

There were outstanding individual efforts, but the key was that we never gave up; we never stopped playing the type of team game that had gotten us into the playoffs. Winning was important, but more important was the fact that that game raised the Steelers to a new level. We lost the next playoff game, but we had a taste for winning and we wanted more. We won our first Super Bowl a couple of seasons later, and I think it all began with that win against the Raiders.

Most people tend to remember that game for one play, the final play when Franco Harris caught a deflected pass and ran in for the winning touchdown. That was the "Immaculate Reception" game. But there was much more to the game than that play.

We won our division that season and had to face the Raiders in the opening round of the playoffs. The game was at our home field, on a Saturday, just a couple of days before Christmas. It turned out to be a good holiday for the team.

The Steelers and Raiders developed a great rivalry, but that was the first playoff meeting we had with them. Ken Stabler was their backup quarterback at the time, but he came into the game in the fourth quarter because Daryle Lamonica had to leave.

Most of the game was a defensive battle. They were able to shut down Franco and our running game at the line, and their secondary played tough against our receivers. Meanwhile, our defense was shutting down their attack. There was no scoring in the first half, but there was plenty

of action. Our guys were up for the Raiders and were hitting and blocking with great intensity. The scoring opportunities were very limited; the closest we came was late in the second quarter when coach Noll had our offensive unit go for a first down on fourth-and-one instead of trying for a field goal. I know he was angry with himself, because the Raiders stopped us.

Terry moved the offense in the third quarter and was able to hit his receivers with some key passes. On one series we got down to the Raiders' 11 and Roy Gerela hit a field goal to give us a 3-0 lead. At that point those three points looked mighty big. It was a game of minimal mistakes and maximum effort by both defenses. We still led, 3-0, going into the fourth quarter, and we could feel that we were in control of the situation.

With about five minutes to play, the Raiders had the ball and were trying to put a scoring drive together. Stabler had replaced Lamonica by this time, and he wasn't all that experienced, especially in pressure situations. As his confidence grew over the years, he killed us with some pressure passes. But that day we thought we had him contained. L.C. Greenwood broke through the Raiders offensive line and hit Stabler. Stabler fumbled and we recovered. A few plays later Gerela hit another field goal to put us up, 6-0, with less than four minutes to play.

The feeling on our sideline was that we could win the game if we just held them down. But three minutes can be a long time in the NFL. The Raiders had the ball with a couple of minutes left in the game and Stabler was mixing up his plays pretty well. Our defensive guys were dug in, trying to stop whatever they would attempt. But their coach, John Madden, was calling the right plays at the right time. At one point we had them on a fourth-and-one when they called a running play that went for a first down. Then they called a few pass plays that Stabler executed. One pass went to Mike Siani and put them down at our 30. Our defense lined up for a safety blitz on the next play to try to stop the pass.

However, Stabler not only got past the blitz, he ran in for the touchdown, which

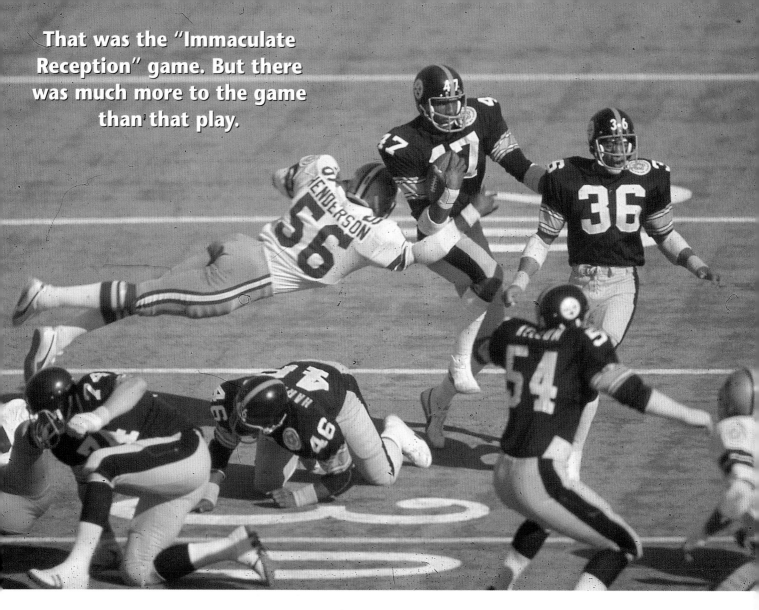

That was the "Immaculate Reception" game. But there was much more to the game than that play.

tied the score. Our only hope was to block the extra point, but Blanda put it up to give them a 7-6 lead with only about a minute and a half to play.

But the Steelers are a team that never quits. The Raiders' defense was still playing tough, but Terry moved our offense out to our 40. There were about 20 seconds to play and we had a fourth-and-10. A field goal would not have been enough, so at that point it would have to be a touchdown pass or nothing. That's when the fun began.

The original play was supposed to be a quick pass over the middle to Barry Pearson. Franco was hanging back to block, and then he would head upfield if the other receivers were covered. As it turned out, a couple of the Raiders defenders broke through our offensive line and Terry had to scramble. Pearson, his first target, was covered, so he threw a pass to "Frenchy" Fuqua. Jack Tatum hit Fuqua just as the ball got there, and it bounced off both of them and back toward

Franco. Franco told me later that he wasn't even supposed to be at the spot where he ended up on the field; he had moved to that spot to try to block for Frenchy.

Franco caught the ball at around the Raiders' 40 and headed toward the end zone still in stride. We were standing on the sideline not quite sure what had happened. But when we saw him running with the ball all we could do was jump up and down and yell, "Go! Go!" Even after he scored there was a lot of confusion as to exactly what had happened. A lot of us weren't even sure we had won until the refs signaled that the touchdown was good.

There was an incredible scene in the locker room afterwards. Even though we lost the next week, that win over the Raiders gave our club a tremendous boost. We had a lot of important wins after that, but I think that one was the game that set the pattern.

—As told to Barry Janoff

Cornerback **Mel Blount** (47) was a vaunted member of Pittsburgh's "Steel Curtain" defense, but early in his 14-season (1970-83) career, he also returned kickoffs. Blount entered the Pro Football Hall of Fame in 1989 with 57 career interceptions and 13 opponents' fumble recoveries. He won four Super Bowl rings and went to five Pro Bowls.

If there was one game that paved the way for our 1985 Super Bowl-winning season, it was a match-up against the big, bad

Los Angeles Raiders on November 4, 1984.

The Raiders, who were the defending Super Bowl champions and were 7-2 entering this game, came to town with their collection of rough guys. We were a good team, 6-3 when we took on the Raiders, but we were young, especially our offensive line. Still, we had great leaders in quarterback Jim McMahon and running back Walter Payton; they fired us up.

Numerous fights broke out during the game. McMahon suffered a lacerated kidney and was in so much pain that we barely could hear him calling the signals. People have said a lot of negative things about McMahon—that he wasn't a durable quarterback—but I remember him for the heart he showed in this game against the Raiders. McMahon's kidney injury was so severe that he ended up missing the rest of the '84 season. We were a young and impressionable group, and when we saw that kind of character, it kind of sealed our destiny to become a championship team.

People often mention linebacker Mike Singletary's intense eyes—but you should have seen Payton's eyes in the huddle. It's difficult to explain. When you looked at him, you saw an amazing competitive spirit, one that rubbed off on you. When you were exposed to Payton's intensity, you didn't want to let him down.

Other than staying after the Raiders and playing aggressively, we didn't have much of a game plan. We simply wanted to go out there and beat them up. Payton scored the first two touchdowns, on 18- and eight-yard runs, respectively, and by halftime we led 14-3. However, the Raiders rallied and shaved that advantage to 14-6 at 5:57 in the third quarter, when Chris Bahr connected on a 40-yard field goal.

When I was on the sideline, I never used to watch the defense work. Instead, I'd try to stay alert by talking to coaches and getting myself ready to go back on the field. As a result, I didn't realize how dominant our defense was that day against the Raiders. Our defense held L.A. to 75 yards rushing and 106 passing, and it had two fumble recoveries, three interceptions and nine sacks.

Back then, our defense would kick butt for three plays, and come out. The defense always was fresh, and that complemented our ball-control offense. The game against the Raiders was no different. We didn't pass very well that day, totaling 84 yards, but we did amass 175 rushing yards, 111 of which were collected by Payton.

Steve Fuller replaced McMahon in the second half, and the trash talking escalated. There were flare-ups everywhere. Keith Van Horne against Matt Millen, Kurt Becker against Howie Long, me against Bill Pickel.

We hung on and won the game 17-6, and that victory took us to a higher level. We gained a ton of confidence because we proved we could compete with the league's best teams. It was one thing to beat up on a team such as the Tampa Bay Buccaneers; it was quite another to topple the mighty Raiders.

Coach Mike Ditka really knew how to motivate us. Before every game, he'd tell us how the press and the fans were against us, and that we had a great opportunity to prove them wrong. That approach certainly worked against the Raiders.

And that game prepared us for 1985. Still, there are a lot of things about the Raiders match-up that I don't remember. That's probably because I spent most of the game getting knocked in the head.

—As told to John Nixon

NOVEMBER 4, 1984
CHICAGO BEARS 17, LOS ANGELES RAIDERS 6
SOLDIER FIELD, CHICAGO, ILLINOIS

SCORING

CHI	7	7	0	3	**17**
LA	0	3	3	0	**6**

CHI   Payton, 18-yard run (B. Thomas kick)
CHI   Payton, 8-yard run (B. Thomas kick)
LA   Bahr, 44-yard field goal
LA   Bahr, 40-yard field goal
CHI   B. Thomas, 29-yard field goal

TEAM STATISTICS	LA	CHI
First Downs	12	13
Rushes-Yards	23-75	47-175
Passing Yards	106	84
Passes	12-28-3	7-16-1
Punts-Average	5-44.4	7-41.1
Fumbles-Lost	4-2	2-0
Penalties-Yards	1-5	4-40

INDIVIDUAL STATISTICS
Rushing
LA   Wilson 1 rush for 3 yards; Allen 15-42; King 3-20; Humm 1-minus 2; Hawkins 3-12
CHI   Suhey 8-17; Payton 27-111; McMahon 3-10; C. Thomas 5-23; Fuller 4-14

Passing
LA   Wilson 7 completions, 19 attempts, 70 yards, 2 interceptions; Humm 4-7-56-1; Allen 1-2-38-0
CHI   McMahon 3-11-68-1; Fuller 4-5-27-0

Receiving
LA   Allen 4 receptions for 53 yards; Christensen 5-61; Williams 3-50
CHI   Gault 1-50; Suhey 1-11; Payton 3-15; Moorehead 2-19

ATTENDANCE: 59,858

We didn't have much of a game plan. We simply wanted to go out there and beat them up.

Mark Bortz was drafted as a defensive tackle but was soon switched to offense by the Chicago Bears. He played twelve seasons (1983–94) as a guard. The six-foot-six, 290-pound behemoth was named to two Pro Bowl games and started all 19 of the Bears' 18-1 1985 Super Bowl season. Bortz retired not long after suffering a season-ending knee injury in the twelfth game of the 1994 campaign.

TERRY BRADSHAW

1974 AFC CHAMPIONSHIP GAME

The Raiders had beaten us soundly in two previous meetings: 17-0 at Pittsburgh when Joe Gilliam was the quarterback and

DECEMBER 29, 1974
PITTSBURGH STEELERS 24, OAKLAND RAIDERS 13
OAKLAND COLISEUM, OAKLAND, CALIFORNIA

SCORING

PIT	0	3	0	21	**24**
OAK	3	0	7	3	**13**

OAK Blanda 46-yard field goal
PIT Gerela 23-yard field goal
OAK Branch 38-yard pass from Stabler (Blanda kick)
PIT Harris 8-yard run (Gerela kick)
PIT Swann 6-yard pass from Bradshaw (Gerela kick)
OAK Blanda 24-yard field goal
PIT Harris 21-yard run (kick failed)

TEAM STATISTICS	PIT	OAK
First Downs	20	15
Rushes-Yards	50-224	21-29
Passing Yards	81	249
Passes	8-17-1	19-36-3
Punts-Average	4-41.0	5-43.4
Fumbles-Lost	3-2	0-0
Penalties-Yards	4-30	5-60

INDIVIDUAL STATISTICS
Rushing
PIT Harris 29 rushes for 111 yards; Bleier 18-98; Bradshaw 3-15
OAK Davis 10-16; Banaszak 3-7; Hubbard 7-6; Stabler 1-0
Passing
PIT Bradshaw 8 completions, 17 attempts, 95 yards, 1 interception
OAK Stabler 19-36-271-3
Receiving
PIT Brown 2 receptions for 37 yards; Bleier 2-25; Swann 2-17; Stallworth 2-16
OAK Branch 9-186; Moore 4-32; Biletnikoff 3-45; Davis 2-8; Banaszak 1-0

ATTENDANCE: 53,515

fullback Franco Harris was hurting, and 33-14 in an opening round playoff game in Oakland the year before. And they were coming off a very emotional 28-26 win over Miami, a team that had beaten them two straight years in the AFC Championship Game.

Oakland was favored, naturally. But everyone in the Steelers organization, from the secretaries right up on through the players and coaching staff to the club owners, felt we were going to win this game. To win, you've got to have great desire, you've got to hate to lose, you've got to love the people you're playing with and you've got to love the game. All these things were in effect.

We started feeling we could beat Oakland after winning 32-14 against Buffalo. We had beaten the Bills with a balanced attack, something we had lacked through most of the season. We were awesome; our defense was superb and our offense was really moving.

We were excited to get this close to going to the Super Bowl. After struggling through the season, we were now just beginning to peak, which is the time to do it. The defense had the confidence in the offense, and vice versa. It was a unity like you've never seen. Even Coach Chuck Noll came out and said we were going to win, which is something he seldom does. He's normally a quiet, confident person who says very little.

We arrived in Oakland on a Friday night and went out to the Coliseum for a closed workout the next afternoon. We were all on edge.

I didn't have any problem going to sleep that evening, but in the middle of the night a light woke me up. Then I heard something in my room and realized it was a burglar. I didn't move—I froze. Sweat was pouring from my brow. I was lying so still I could hear myself breathing. I didn't want to get shot or anything like that. I was petrified. I wanted to look, but my better sense told me to lie there, pretend you're asleep, don't budge. Let him have whatever he wants.

When the burglar left, I jumped out of bed and looked out the door. I saw our wide receiver Lynn Swann and another person. They also had been robbed. So we chased the burglars and hollered, but they got away.

It was around 5 a.m. and I was wide awake. So I went down and had some coffee. I started thinking what a great year it would be for me to take the team to the Super Bowl after the comeback I had.

I still remembered the day after losing to Houston, when Chuck told me he was going to stick with me. That really gave me a lift. A quarterback can't play without confidence. All of us need a pat on the back, and I'd never gotten one in my five years as a Steeler.

It was a clear, cool day, around 50 degrees, perfect for a Championship Game.

The Raiders received the opening kickoff and our defense stopped them. But they got a break when Swann fumbled a punt and they recovered. They turned it into a field goal.

We got things moving on our second possession and drove to the Raiders three-yard line. But we didn't get anything out of it. We missed a short field goal. If nothing else, I was encouraged by the way we moved the ball.

We drove from midfield to the Raider six on our next possession, but again we couldn't punch it in. We settled for a Roy Gerela field goal for a 3-3 tie.

We moved it again the next time to Oakland's eight. On first down from that point, I threw what I thought was a touchdown pass to John Stallworth, but the umpire disallowed it. He said Stallworth was out of bounds. John was clearly in bounds; our films showed he was. A couple of plays later I tried to hit Stallworth again in the end zone and Willie Brown intercepted.

On our first play of the second half, things didn't improve. Rocky Bleier fumbled and Oakland got the ball on our 30. But our defense stopped them when Jack Ham intercepted a Ken Stabler pass.

The Raiders drove 80 yards to a touchdown later in the third quarter. Stabler threw a pass to Cliff Branch for the score.

The crowd was going crazy and we knew if we were going to make our move, it would definitely have to be now. On our second

It was so quiet in the Coliseum you could hear a pin drop.

play after the ensuing kickoff, Bleier busted over left tackle for 23 yards to the Oakland 32. That made me feel great. We were beginning to roll. A couple of plays later I completed a 13-yard pass to Stallworth to the eight-yard line. Franco ran it in on the next play and Gerela's conversion made it 10-10.

A few moments later, Ham came through again. He picked off another Stabler pass and ran it back 24 yards to the Raider nine. On third down, I threw a six-yard touchdown pass to Swann. When that happened, I knew that was the ball game. There was no way they were going to catch us. We all felt that way. It was so quiet in the Coliseum you could hear a pin drop.

The Raiders did throw a little scare into us when they later drove to our seven, but our defense stopped them and they had to settle for a Blanda field goal.

We put the game away with around a minute left. J.T. Thomas intercepted Stabler and ran back some 37 yards to the Raider 24. Two plays later Franco charged through a hole big enough for a Mack truck and ran for a 21-yard touchdown. That was it. We started thinking about the Super Bowl and the Minnesota Vikings.

We went on to beat the Vikings 16-6 in the Super Bowl, but that win wasn't nearly as big or emotional as the one over the Raiders. We had beaten Oakland on its home turf for the AFC Championship and that was super, just super.

—As told to Dave Payne

Terry Bradshaw quarterbacked the Pittsburgh Steelers to four Super Bowl victories, and was named Most Valuable Player in Super Bowls XIII and XIV. By the end of his Pro Football Hall of Fame career (1970–83), entirely with the Steelers, Bradshaw had completed 2,025 passes for 27,989 yards and 212 touchdowns. He also carried the ball for an additional 2,257 yards and 32 touchdowns.

My memory takes me back a long, long way to a chilly Friday evening in Boston. The date was November 6, 1964.

I was with the Patriots then and we had a good team. We had won the Eastern Division Championship of the American Football League the year before and we were looking to repeat. Up to then, though, we weren't doing too well. It was time to get something going and we would have to do it against the Houston Oilers, one of the toughest teams in the league.

Let me set it up for you as best I remember it. George Blanda was their quarterback, and we thought of him as an old pro even then. Most of us were young kids compared to him. And they had a little back, Charlie Tolar, who was about five-foot-five, who had to be the smallest guy who ever played fullback in the pros.

If you got yourself real low, and I mean real low, and thought you could give Charlie a real shot, you'd still end up trying to tackle the stripe on the top of his helmet. Blanda used to use him a lot on quick traps and lates and most of the time, screened off by all those big bodies, you couldn't even see him until he was past you.

That's how he scored their first touchdown. It was a short plunge, but I don't think any of us ever saw him. Blanda had marched them down in one of those really masterful drives, when an offense really gets a rhythm going and they keep hitting you—bang, bang, bang—and you're never ready.

That seemed to wake us up though, because for the rest of the first half we really took over, both on offense and defense. Babe Parilli marched the team down on a long drive for a touchdown and then every time we forced the Oilers to punt they came back down and got a couple of field goals by Gino Cappelletti.

We went into the locker room with a cozy little six-point lead thinking we were really in control of the game. But we weren't. The old pro Blanda hit us quick and it hurt. We blew the coverage and Willie Frazier, the tight end, was all alone up the middle. It was

just one of those plays where you say to yourself, "Oh, my God," and watch the guy's backside and heels as he runs 80 yards for a touchdown.

The lead came back to us, though, when Babe drove the team deep into Oilers territory. We had to settle for Cappelletti's third field goal when the drive stalled out, but we were up by two.

Blanda wasn't about to let that stand. Shortly after the fourth quarter opened he hit Charlie Frazier with a scoring pass from about 40 yards out.

We were a wild blitzing team in those days. We used to blitz about 70 percent of the time, and used all kinds of unorthodox defenses and stunts. The old man had caught us again. Now they were five points on top.

Back came our offense though, and for the sixth time the lead changed hands when Parilli bootlegged the ball over from a first down on the Oilers 10-yard line.

Our best wasn't quite good enough. We made a goal line stand to keep them out of the end zone, but Blanda kicked an easy 10-yard field goal to put them back on top with less than a minute to go in the ball game.

They kicked off and sent it deep, challenging us to run it back. Actually it was the smart thing to do when you consider the odds against a long runback, and they didn't want to put us in a position where a couple of completions would give us a shot at the winning field goal.

I can still remember standing there on the sidelines pulling my darndest for a long runback, but it wasn't to be. When Babe and the offense took over we had 45 seconds and one time-out left. And we had to go about 80 yards. It looked hopeless, but that didn't stop me from praying for a miracle.

On first down Parilli completed a sideline pass to Cappelletti for about 10 yards. But my heart almost popped right out of my mouth when the ball was almost intercepted. His next pass was again almost intercepted, which shortened my life by another couple of months. Now there were only 25 seconds left.

He was right on target the next time, though, and hit Cappelletti at about the 40 and he went out of bounds to stop the clock.

NOVEMBER 6, 1964
BOSTON PATRIOTS 25, HOUSTON OILERS 24
FENWAY PARK, BOSTON, MASSACHUSETTS

SCORING

BOS	7	6	3	9	**25**
HOU	7	0	7	10	**24**

HOU Tolar, 2-yard run (Blanda kick)
BOS Parilli, 1-yard run (Cappelletti kick)
BOS Cappelletti, 25-yard field goal
BOS Cappelletti, 33-yard field goal
HOU W. Frazier, 80-yard pass from Blanda (Blanda kick)
BOS Cappelletti, 22-yard field goal
HOU C. Frazier, 38-yard pass from Blanda (Blanda kick)
BOS Parilli, 5-yard run (pass failed)
HOU Blanda, 10-yard field goal
BOS Cappelletti, 41-yard field goal

TEAM STATISTICS	BOS	HOU
First Downs	21	22
Rushes-Yards	37-193	23-84
Passing Yards	257	329
Passes	14-29-1	21-45-1
Punts-Average	5-41.0	3-37.0
Fumbles-lost	1-1	0-0
Penalties-Yards	3-25	2-20

INDIVIDUAL STATISTICS
Rushing
BOS Garron 23 rushes for 91 yards; Burton 6-6; Parilli 8-96
HOU Tolar 14-57; Blanks 9-27
Passing
BOS Parilli 14 completions, 29 attempts, 256 yards, 1 interception
HOU Blanda 20-44-328-1; Trull 1-1-1-0
Receiving
BOS Graham 8 receptions for 167 yards; Cappelletti 2-37; Romeo 2-31; Garron 2-21
HOU C. Frazier 9-143; W. Frazier 2-102; Blanks 3-37; Tolar 3-0; Jancik 1-14; Hennigan 2-32; Smith 1-1

ATTENDANCE: 28,161

It looked hopeless, but that didn't stop me from praying for a miracle.

Linebacker **Nick Buoniconti** split his 14-season NFL career between the Boston Patriots (1962–68) and the Miami Dolphins (1969–76). He was named All-AFL/AFC eight times. Buoniconti won two championship rings in three consecutive Super Bowl appearances (1971–73) with the Dolphins. Frequently heralded as one of the top linebackers of all time, he entered the Pro Football Hall of Fame in 2001.

We still needed another 25 yards or so to be in position for a field goal with a reasonable chance of success and when he missed on his next two passes it looked like we were going down the drain.

With only 10 seconds left the Babe dropped back again. He was almost buried under a terrific rush. But somehow he got away and started doing the only thing he could, run upfield. I was running the sidelines right along with him and he was finally forced out of bounds at the Oilers' 35-yard line and they killed the clock with one second showing.

Now it was easy.

Cappelletti calmly lined it up and kicked through the winning field goal from the Oilers' 42. Actually the ball was still in the air when the gun sounded to end the game.

Maybe I was young, but I'll never forget that.

—*As told to Bob Billings*

Saturday I could barely walk. I tried to jog a little at practice, but it almost crumpled up on me. The knee was swollen and it

SEPTEMBER 19, 1971
CHICAGO BEARS 17, PITTSBURGH STEELERS 15
SOLDIER FIELD, CHICAGO, ILLINOIS

SCORING

CHI	0	3	0	14	**17**
PIT	0	6	6	3	**15**

PIT	Pearson, 6-yard fumble recovery (kick failed)
CHI	Percival, 33-yard field goal
PIT	Gerela, 32-yard field goal
PIT	Gerela, 29-yard field goal
PIT	Gerela, 42-yard field goal
CHI	Brupbacher, 30-yard fumble recovery (Percival kick)
CHI	Farmer, 8-yard pass from Nix (Percival kick)

TEAM STATISTICS

	CHI	PIT
First Downs	8	15
Rushes-Yards	21-45	43-223
Passing Yards	96	129
Passes	16-29-1	10-24-4
Punts-Average	8-42.6	5-47.4
Fumbles-Lost	3-3	5-3
Penalties-Yards	6-60	6-64

INDIVIDUAL STATISTICS
Rushing
CHI Grabowski 8 rushes for 13 yards; Concannon 1-0; Wallace 1-0; Shy 9-19; Nix 2-13
PIT Fuqua 17-114; Pearson 7-14; Bradshaw 2-4; Shanklin 1-2; Bankston 16-89

Passing
CHI Concannon 15 completions, 26 attempts, 116 yards, 1 interception; Nix 1-3-8-0
PIT Bradshaw 10-24-129-4

Receiving
CHI Grabowski 3 receptions for 16 yards; Farmer 4-59; Gordon 1-9; Wallace 4-20; Shy 3-16; Tucker 1-4
PIT Bankston 2-4; Fuqua 2-12; Shanklin 6-113

ATTENDANCE: 55,049

hurt like hell. All that night I just dozed and kept waking up. I lay there flat on my back, afraid to get up, afraid to try and put any kind of weight on it.

I didn't know what was going to happen and I was scared. Our team doctor, Dr. Ted Fox, operated on the knee in January, but there were some complications. I hadn't done a thing all through camp. The exhibition season came and went. Fox told me I was trying to do too much; but you just can't stand around while everyone else is working. You don't even feel like part of the team.

Game day came and it felt a little better. And the weather was on my side. It was a misty, rainy day. That Astroturf in Soldier Field was miserable stuff. You plant your foot to make a cut or make a block or tackle and your foot stops—bang—just like that. But with the mist and dampness putting a thin coating on the field, we could get a little slide instead of those knee-shuddering stops.

The early birds took the field. We're the boys who shag the balls for the kickers, Bobby Joe Green, our punter, and Mac Percival, our placekicker. On the Bears, we like to keep it a defensive players' prerogative. It brings us a little closer together.

So I was out there throwing the ball around and shagging kicks and fooling around, but mostly worrying about my knee. It felt pretty good running forward, and even running backwards it felt all right.

I went back in the locker room and told Fox the pain seemed to go away once I got it warm and loose. We taped it up and I went out to play the Pittsburgh Steelers in the opening game of the 1971 season.

Everyone wants to win that first game. It sets you up in a positive mental attitude right away and gets you looking forward to the next game instead of looking backward and asking yourself, "Why?" You worked hard just to get this far, and if you blow it you feel like all that work was wasted and

you have to start all over again.

Pittsburgh had a good team, a young team, an improving team. They had good young quarterbacks in Terry Bradshaw and Terry Hanratty, some good running backs in John Fuqua, Preston Pearson and Warren Bankston, and a real tough defense.

It was a slugfest from the opening kickoff. The Steelers thought they were contenders for the division title and they acted like it. The Bears—well, we were the Bears, playing a very physical game, our kind of game.

Our defense was really up. I don't see how we could have really played much better. We made a few mistakes, but nothing really major. And, most important, we were forcing, getting the turnovers, taking the ball away from the Steelers and giving it to our offense in good field position.

I intercepted one pass on a screen play but it was nullified because we were offside. On the very next play Bradshaw threw one over the middle and I guess he wasn't reading the defense right because I grabbed that one too. I grabbed another one later in the game and just missed a fourth when I slipped.

We seemed to have Bradshaw confused all day. One series we'd play man-to-man. The next we'd go zone. Then we'd go combination zone and man-to-man and then we'd blitz every play. We tried to keep him guessing, keep him off balance and not give him a chance to pick up any tendencies.

But going into the fourth quarter we were still behind 14-3. Our offense just couldn't get anything going. We never gave up, but the clock kept ticking off the seconds. It was getting awfully fine now. We punted again and knew they were going to try and eat as much of that clock as possible.

They ran an end sweep with Fuqua. Big Ed O'Bradovich, our defensive end, hit him high and hard and knocked the ball loose. Bru scooped it up and ran about 30 yards for the score. That made it 14-10. But now we had to give them the ball.

That score really set the defense on fire. We really smelled blood, but there were only about two minutes left. As we were standing along the sidelines for the kickoff, our coach Abe Gibron told me they'd probably try to

That score really set the defense on fire. We smelled blood, but there were only about two minutes left.

kill the clock with some trap plays. He told me if I could see it coming to go ahead and blitz. We might force another fumble.

We kept them inside their own 30-yard line on the kickoff return and I knew Bradshaw wasn't going to throw the ball if he could help it.

I had one of my intuitive visions. While they were still in the huddle I could see the play.

They tried to run a trap. Their center, Ray Mansfield, moved to his left to block our tackle, Bill Staley, and I shot right up the hole. For a split second I thought I could get

the handoff. I hit Bankston just as hard as I could, trying to drive right through him, the instant he touched the ball.

It popped loose and we got it. Kent Nix came off the bench and threw it in for the winning touchdown.

That was so satisfying I can't begin to express it. The day before the game I couldn't walk—then to have it come out like that . . .

—*As told to Bob Billings*

Chicago Bear **Dick Butkus** (51), above, makes one of his 22 career interceptions. The six-foot-three, 245-pound middle linebacker also recovered 25 career fumbles. Although Chicago posted only two winning seasons during Butkus' illustrious career (1965–73) with the Bears, he was voted All-NFL six times and went to eight consecutive Pro Bowls. Butkus was elected to the Pro Football Hall of Fame in 1979.

Earl Campbell was discovered, and "Luv Ya Blue" was born, on November 20, 1978, against the Miami Dolphins. It was the

twelfth game of my rookie season.

In college, I would hear *Monday Night Football* broadcasters Frank Gifford, Howard Cosell and Don Meredith praise a particular lineman or running back. I couldn't believe that in 1978 I was going to have a chance to hear those guys mention Earl Campbell's name. After visualizing and dreaming about it for so many years, I got the chance to be on *Monday Night Football*.

Before each game, the Houston Oilers running backs would come out earlier than most of the players. My legs were so big that it took time to get them warmed up. While sitting in the end zone, stretching, I noticed there weren't many people in the stands.

But later, when my name was called during the introductions, I ran into the Astrodome and didn't see an empty seat. Still, after the whistle blows, you forget about the crowd.

For some reason, I felt a burst of energy in my body once the game started. That might have been because it was *Monday Night Football*, and I wanted to kick it up a gear. It was the night that vaulted my career into something special.

This was an important game for both teams. The Oilers were 7-4, chasing the Pittsburgh Steelers for the AFC Central title and our first playoff game in nine years. Miami was 8-3 and battling the New England Patriots for first place in the AFC East.

Miami scored a touchdown on its first possession, driving 82 yards. But we answered with a 70-yard touchdown drive of our own; I went into the end zone from the one-yard line.

Our defense proceeded to stop the Dolphins. We scored again, this time on a 15-yard pass from Dan Pastorini to Mike Barber to give us a 14-7 lead in the second quarter. Miami tied the game at 14-14 just before the end of the half after driving 59 yards for a touchdown.

The first half ended with all the scores coming from long drives. The game didn't look like a defensive battle. Instead, I think

both offenses were completely sharp that night. During the entire game, it appeared as if Earl Campbell was playing Miami quarterback Bob Griese.

I had always been a Griese fan. I would sit on my helmet on the sidelines and watch that guy pick apart defensive backs. Miami didn't have a running game, but it had a heck of a passing game.

The Houston Oilers offense, on the other hand, was built to go straight ahead because of this guy named Earl in the backfield. We would hit you for four yards, then you might throw us for a loss of three, but we'd come right back.

We didn't think the Dolphins defense was as strong as our offense. In particular, we felt we could run right against Miami behind right guard Ed Fisher and tackle Conway Hayman. The Dolphins had one guy who couldn't take us on one-on-one: linebacker Steve Towle.

We started the second half by marching 63 yards and scoring on my six-yard TD run to give us a 21-14 lead. Soon after that, however, Griese directed an 89-yard scoring drive to tie the game again. He was amazing. The Dolphins even took a 23-21 lead in the fourth quarter, sacking Pastorini in the end zone for a safety.

My third touchdown was a 12-yard run, which came midway through the fourth quarter after I bulldogged a Miami defender near the end zone. I just lowered my shoulder and lunged for the flag in the corner of the end zone. The touchdown put us up 28-23.

Miami started to drive again, but Griese was intercepted by linebacker Steve Kiner. A clipping penalty moved the ball back to our own seven-yard line. Time was critical, as we had a five-point edge with just more than three minutes left.

Running back Tim Wilson and I combined on four straight running plays to give us a first down at our own 19-yard line with two minutes left.

That's when Pastorini said to me in the huddle, "Earl, we only need two yards at a time." Then Wilson turned to me and said, "Earl, that corner keeps coming to the inside. I'll kick him out so you can go outside."

The play developed as planned. A burst of

NOVEMBER 20, 1978
HOUSTON OILERS 35, MIAMI DOLPHINS 30
ASTRODOME, HOUSTON, TEXAS

SCORING

HOU	7	7	7	14	**35**
MIA	7	7	7	9	**30**

MIA   Moore, 10-yard pass from Griese (Yepremian kick)
HOU   Campbell, 1-yard run (Fritsch kick)
HOU   Barber, 15-yard pass from Pastorini (Fritsch kick)
MIA   Williams, 1-yard run (Yepremian kick)
HOU   Campbell, 6-yard run (Fritsch kick)
MIA   L. Harris, 1-yard run (Yepremian kick)
MIA   Safety, Pastorini tackled in end zone
HOU   Campbell, 12-yard run (Fritsch kick)
HOU   Campbell, 81-yard run (Fritsch kick)
MIA   Cefalo, 11-yard pass from Griese (Yepremian kick)

TEAM STATISTICS	MIA	HOU
First Downs	27	23
Rushes-Yards	32-127	42-265
Passing Yards	320	141
Passes	23-33-1	10-16-1
Punts-Average	5-46.4	4-45.2
Fumbles-Lost	2-1	0-0
Penalties-Yards	9-96	8-58

INDIVIDUAL STATISTICS
Rushing
MIA   Williams 18 rushes for 73 yards; L. Harris 12-51; Moore 1-3; Griese 1-0
HOU   Campbell 28-199; Coleman 2-9; T. Wilson 10-35; Renfro 1-9; Barber 1-13

Passing
MIA   Griese 23 completions, 33 attempts, 349 yards, 1 interception
HOU   Pastorini 10-16-156-1

Receiving
MIA   L. Harris 5 receptions for 25 yards; Moore 3-84; Williams 2-20; D. Harris 4-79; Bulaich 4-46; Tillman 3-45; Rather 1-39; Cefalo 1-11
HOU   Barber 3-56; Renfro 2-24; Burrough 2-37; Caster 2-31; Coleman 1-8

ATTENDANCE: 50,209

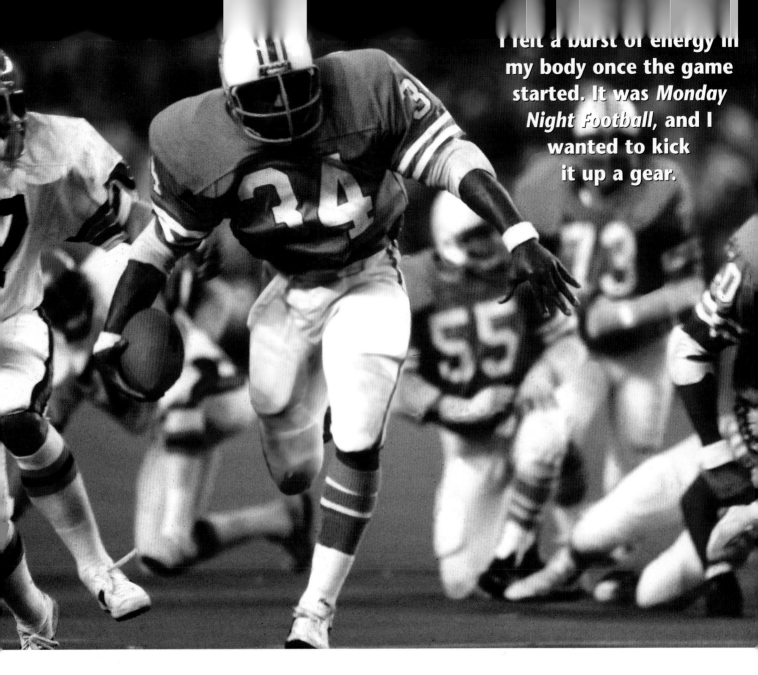

I felt a burst of energy in my body once the game started. It was Monday Night Football, and I wanted to kick it up a gear.

energy carried me, and I outran the defensive backs. Towle lunged for me with his right hand just as I looked over my shoulder and saw him. I dipped my left shoulder, and that was the end of it. I moved down the sidelines, then stepped into the end zone after an 81-yard run.

After I came to the sidelines, I went to the bench. With all the noise in the Astrodome, Coach Bum Phillips shouted, "E.C., can you hear me?"

I said, "Yes, sir."

"You've got 199 yards," Bum said. "You need one more yard for 200. You wanna go back into the game?"

I said, "No, sir. I think Ronnie Coleman should play." When I came to the Oilers, I took Ronnie's position as the team's starting fullback. I wouldn't rub it in so that the crowd would yell louder.

There wasn't much time left, but Griese only needed five plays to score again. Then, however, time ran out. Houston 35, Miami 30. Walking across the field, my first thought was whether my mother had watched the game from her home in Tyler, Texas. I found out later that she had seen it.

I struggled back to the locker room; I was so tired that the trainer helped me take off my uniform. Then I collapsed under a cold shower. I didn't fall asleep that night until 3 a.m. because I was wondering how I had done and how I'd look in the films.

That Miami game forced me to perform at the caliber of a Brown, Payton or Dorsett. I thank God for Howard Cosell, Don Meredith and Frank Gifford. Cosell helped make me big.

—*As told to John Nixon*

Running back **Earl Campbell** (34), above, rushed the ball 9,407 yards and scored 74 touchdowns in his eight-season Pro Football Hall of Fame NFL career. Campbell won the 1977 Heisman Trophy while starring for the University of Texas, then joined the Houston Oilers in 1978. He hit a career high with 1,934 yards rushing in 1980, including four games with at least 200 yards. Campbell was traded to the New Orleans Saints six games into the 1984 campaign and retired after the 1985 season.

1987 NFC DIVISIONAL PLAYOFF GAME

A memorable game for me is one in which the entire team plays well and we're successful in reaching our goal: winning

JANUARY 9, 1988

MINNESOTA VIKINGS 36, SAN FRANCISCO 49ERS 24

CANDLESTICK PARK, SAN FRANCISCO, CALIFORNIA

SCORING

MIN	3	17	10	6	**36**
SF	3	0	14	7	**24**

MIN	Nelson, 21-yard field goal
SF	Wersching, 43-yard field goal
MIN	Hilton, 7-yard pass from Wilson (Nelson kick)
MIN	Nelson, 23-yard field goal
MIN	Rutland, 45-yard interception return (Nelson kick)
SF	Fuller, 48-yard interception return (Wersching kick)
MIN	Jones, 5-yard pass from Wilson (Nelson kick)
SF	Young, 5-yard run (Wersching kick)
MIN	Nelson, 40-yard field goal
MIN	Nelson, 46-yard field goal
SF	Frank, 16-yard pass from Young (Wersching kick)
MIN	Nelson, 23-yard field goal

TEAM STATISTICS

	MIN	SF
First Downs	22	17
Rushes-Yards	34-117	18-115
Passing Yards	280	243
Passes	20-34-1	24-44-2
Punts-Average	5-36.0	6-41.0
Fumbles-Lost	0-0	1-0
Penalties-Yards	2-20	8-75

INDIVIDUAL STATISTICS

Rushing

MIN	Nelson 11 rushes for 42 yards; Wilson 6-30; Carter 1-30; Anderson 7-9, Rice 6-8; Dozier 3-minus 4
SF	Young 6-72; Montana 3-20; Craig 7-17; Rathman 1-12; Cribbs 1-minus 6

Passing

MIN	Wilson 20 completions, 34 attempts, 298 yards, 1 interception
SF	Montana 12-26-109-1; Young 12-17-158-1; Sydney 0-1-0-0

Receiving

MIN	Carter 10 receptions for 227 yards; Rice 4-39; Nelson 2-17; Hilton 1-7; Jones 1-5; Lewis 1-5; Anderson 1-minus 2
SF	Craig 9-78; Wilson 4-50; Rice 3-28; Taylor 2-48; Rathman 2-18; Frank 1-16; Clark 1-13; Cribbs 1-7; Jones 1-7

ATTENDANCE: 62,547

the game. I've had some unforgettable games in my career, but I guess the biggest one so far was the NFC divisional playoff game against the 49ers when we beat them in San Francisco. We went into the game as 10- or 11-point underdogs and ended up beating them by 12 points.

The great thing about the game was that it was a total team victory. Our offense was strong all day, and our defensive guys kept them in check. At one point, we even chased Joe Montana out of the game.

San Francisco had a great season, 13-2 if I remember. People were picking them to make it to the Super Bowl, and I'm sure a lot of people figured that a home game against Minnesota wouldn't be too hard for them to handle. We were only 8-7 that year, but the key thing was that we had a team of hungry guys who went all out to win.

The week prior to the game, we did our homework and studied game films. Our plan was to be aggressive, to air it out and put San Francisco's secondary to the test. Our head coach Jerry Burns and offensive coordinator Bob Schnelker came up with the right game plan.

We had a great group of receivers—Steve Jordan, Leo Lewis, Hassan Jones and Darrin Nelson—but, to be honest, going into the playoffs we were frustrated because we felt we hadn't been getting the ball enough. I was only getting the opportunity to catch two or three passes per game. I was vocal about it. I went to coach Burns and coach Schnelker, because they're the ones who make those decisions. I told them, "Get me the ball. I'm not afraid to take a hit."

A receiver likes to catch more than two passes a game. I'm not looking to catch all of them, but it should be more than two. I know what I'm capable of. In our first playoff game we beat New Orleans 44-10. I had six receptions and I returned a punt 84 yards for a touchdown. Against San Francisco, I had 10 catches for 227 yards.

I'm not bragging, but I always felt I was capable of playing like that. When we got into the playoffs, I was aggressive in the huddle and aggressive in running my routes. I wasn't about to be stopped, and I didn't think that any of the San Francisco defensive backs *could* stop me.

It had rained in San Francisco prior to the game, and the field was wet and slick in spots. I ended up jamming my left shoulder into the ground on one play. But a lot of guys were playing hurt. In the playoffs, everything becomes intensified. You try to rise above it.

We might have set the tone for the game on our first drive. We took the opening kickoff and went about 80 yards in 15 plays. I caught two passes on that drive, but San Francisco kept us out of the end zone and we went ahead on a field goal. In the second quarter, I caught two more passes in a 70-yard drive that ended up with Wade Wilson throwing a touchdown pass to Carl Hilton. The key in that drive was a pass-interference call against 49ers cornerback Tory Nixon, which wiped out an interception by 49ers safety Ronnie Lott.

To that point, my receptions had been for short gains: 10, 11, 12 yards. About midway through the second quarter, we were on another offensive drive when Wilson hit me with a pass and I ended up going 63 yards. We put up another field goal on that drive, and we were up 20-3 at the half.

It seemed as if the coaches didn't want to make too many changes in the locker room. Our defensive guys had kept San Francisco from scoring a touchdown, and the offense had put together some strong drives. The only thing that was a bit frustrating was that we had to take the field goals instead of scoring touchdowns on a couple of long drives.

The Niners scored a touchdown on an interception return about two minutes into the second half, which made the score 20-10. But we came back right after that, going from about our 30 on a drive that ended with a touchdown. In that series, I had one reception for about 15 yards but I rushed for 30 yards on a reverse play, my only running play of the game.

Our offensive was strong all day, and our defensive guys kept them in check. At one point, we even chased Joe Montana out of the game.

The 49ers weren't about to quit, though, and they came back to score a touchdown. But the thing I remember most about that game is that we came back again and again to maintain the lead. We took the kickoff after they scored, and on the first play I out-leaped 49ers cornerback Tim McKyer to grab a 40-yard pass from Wilson. We got another field goal out of that drive and had two more in the fourth quarter.

It was a great feeling when the game was over. The crowd was quiet, but the guys on the team were overwhelmed with a variety of emotions. I knew I had a lot of catches and a lot of yards, but my immediate reaction was a rush of joy because we were headed to the NFC Championship Game. Unfortunately, we lost, but that game against the 49ers is one I'll never forget.

—As told to Barry Janoff

Wide receiver **Anthony Carter** spent three seasons in the USFL after completing an All-America college career in 1982. He joined the Minnesota Vikings in 1985, and posted 478 receptions for 7,615 yards and 52 touchdowns before he was traded to Detroit after the 1993 campaign. Carter retired after catching only 8 passes in 7 games combined over the 1994 and 1995 seasons with the Lions.

I was fortunate to play on two Super Bowl championship teams with the Pittsburgh Steelers, and both of those games are

unforgettable for me. Super Bowl XIII against the Dallas Cowboys will always be special to me, but because of the difficulty that teams in any sport have defending their title, our win over the Los Angeles Rams in Super Bowl XIV is my most unforgettable game.

Any player will tell you that after you win a title, all the other teams in the league play you a lot tougher the following season. Everyone wants to knock off the champs. That's exactly what happened to us during the 1979 season. The Steelers were the big game for every team we faced that year.

What makes our victory in Super Bowl XIV so special is that it capped off a very strong season for us. We won our division with a 12-4 record, but Houston was right on our tails all year. They finished at 11-5, and we ended up meeting them in the AFC Championship Game. Before we even got to that point, though, we had to play 16 tough games during the season, and then we had to beat Miami in the divisional playoffs.

The Houston game was especially tough. Looking back, though, the fact that the Oilers played so hard prepared us mentally and physically to meet the Rams in the Super Bowl. A lot of people told us before the Houston game, "You'll beat them, no problem." But the Oilers *were* a problem. Our lead was only 17-10 at the half, and they were within three points early in the fourth quarter. But we outscored them 10-0 the rest of the game for the 27-13 victory.

The Rams were a surprise team in the Super Bowl that year. Many people were expecting another Pittsburgh-Dallas game. But the Rams knocked off the Cowboys in the divisional playoffs, 21-19, and then they beat Tampa Bay 9-0 in the NFC Championship Game. Again, many people told us before the Super Bowl, "You'll beat the Rams, no problem."

But the Rams had a strong team. The game was played in the Rose Bowl in Pasadena, California, so it was like a home

game for them. Also, we were the team that was expected to win. Of course, the Rams wanted to win the game, but the pressure to win was on the Steelers, not the Rams.

As a linebacker, my job was to stop their running game and the medium- to long-range passes that their quarterback, Vince Ferragamo, might throw. Going into the game, we knew we had the offensive power to score points. On defense, we had to shut down Ferragamo, wide receivers Preston Dennard and Drew Hill and running backs Wendell Tyler and Cullen Bryant.

Coach Chuck Noll wanted us to establish ourselves early in the game on offense and defense, and the offense did its part when it drove down for a field goal to open the scoring. We had the passing lanes covered on the Rams' next possession, so Ferragamo and Rams Head Coach Ray Malavasi decided to move the ball on the ground. Tyler caught a short dump-off pass, then ran around left end for about 40 yards to get them inside our 15. They ate up small chunks of yardage after that, and eventually Bryant scored from the one-yard line to give them the lead, 7-3.

Bradshaw directed a strong drive in the second quarter, and Franco Harris finished it off by taking a pitchout and running in from the one to give us the lead again. Our defensive plan at that point was to prevent them from knocking off a big gain. We had them stopped long, but Ferragamo was content to keep their offense moving with short gainers on the ground or with short passes just under our secondary coverage. After our touchdown, they moved about 65 yards to our 15, and Frank Corral kicked a field goal to tie the score, 10-10.

Bradshaw had a pass intercepted by safety Dave Elmendorf with about three minutes to play, and they converted that into a field goal that gave them a 13-10 lead at the half.

The crowd was buzzing as the teams left the field, mainly because the Rams had played us so tough during the half. We didn't need to do anything drastic in the second half, but the talk in the locker room mainly focused on getting back to doing the things that had earned us a spot in the title game. We had to keep playing tough on defense,

---

JANUARY 20, 1980
PITTSBURGH STEELERS 31, LOS ANGELES RAMS 19
ROSE BOWL, PASADENA, CALIFORNIA

SCORING

PIT	3	7	7	14	**31**
LA	7	6	6	0	**19**

PIT   Bahr, 41-yard field goal
LA   Bryant, 1-yard run (Corral kick)
PIT   Harris, 1-yard run (Bahr kick)
LA   Corral, 31-yard field goal
LA   Corral, 45-yard field goal
PIT   Swann, 47-yard pass from Bradshaw (Bahr kick)
LA   Smith, 24-yard pass from McCutcheon (kick failed)
PIT   Stallworth, 73-yard pass from Bradshaw (Bahr kick)
PIT   Harris, 1-yard run (Bahr kick)

TEAM STATISTICS	LA	PIT
First Downs	16	19
Rushes-Yards	29-107	37-84
Passing Yards	194	309
Passes	16-26-1	14-21-3
Punts-Average	5-44.0	2-42.0
Fumbles-Lost	0-0	0-0
Penalties-Yards	2-26	6-65

INDIVIDUAL STATISTICS
Rushing
LA   Tyler 17 rushes for 60 yards; Bryant 6-30; McCutcheon 5-10; Ferragamo 1-7
PIT   Harris 20-46; Bleier 10-25; Bradshaw 3-9; Thornton 4-4
Passing
LA   Ferragamo 15 completions, 25 attempts, 212 yards, 1 interception; McCutcheon 1-1-24-0
PIT   Bradshaw 14-21-309-3
Receiving
LA   Bryant 3 receptions for 21 yards; Waddy 3-75; Tyler 3-20; Dennard 2-32; Nelson 2-20; D. Hill 1-28; Smith 1-24; McCutcheon 1-16
PIT   Swann 5-79; Stallworth 3-121; Harris 3-66; Cunningham 2-21; Thornton 1-22

ATTENDANCE: 103,985

The crowd was buzzing as the teams left the field, mainly because the Rams had played us so tough during the half.

and the offense had to open up and play more aggressively.

It took our offense about five plays to score in the second half, with the big play being a 47-yard pass play from Bradshaw to Swann that gave us the lead. The Rams weren't about to quit, though, and Ferragamo came right back to lead them in for a touchdown. They had two big plays on that drive: a 50-yard pass to Billy Waddy and an option pass from running back Lawrence McCutcheon to Ron Smith for the score.

Our defensive players were wondering what we had to do to stop them. But that touchdown was a turning point for us on defense. We knew that the offense would score more points, so we just went out there determined not to let them score again.

We took control of the game in the fourth quarter. The defense shut down the Rams, and Bradshaw took charge on offense. The biggest play of the quarter—and probably of the game—was a 73-yard pass from Bradshaw to John Stallworth for the go-ahead touchdown. That put a burden on the Rams offense to come right back and score again. We knew if we could stop them on their next possession, it would provide as big a boost as the touchdown had.

Ferragamo moved them down to our 35, but Lambert intercepted Ferragamo's pass. Bradshaw threw a big pass to Stallworth, and Harris ran in from the one to give us another touchdown.

Bradshaw was named the MVP of the game, but it was a total team effort that earned us the win. I was one of the younger players on the team at that time, but I felt I was a key part of winning the championship.

—As told to Barry Janoff

Linebacker **Robin Cole** (56) was a member of Pittsburgh's famed "Steel Curtain" defense, helping the Steelers prevail in Super Bowls XIII and XIV. He played 11 seasons in Pittsburgh (1977-87), part of five AFC Central Division winners, and on only two teams that finished with losing records. The day after the Steelers released Cole, the New York Jets picked up the six-foot-two, 229-pound linebacker for the 1988 campaign.

I've been fortunate enough to use my God-given talent to play in the NFL. As a member of the San Francisco 49ers, I've

been in many big games. Of those, the one that stands out the most was Super Bowl XIX, when we defeated the Miami Dolphins, 38-16.

That game stands out for me because it was a great effort by the entire team. Joe Montana was named MVP, and I scored three touchdowns, but the whole team contributed to the victory. The team worked all season to get into the Super Bowl, and when we did get there—and we won—we achieved our ultimate goal.

We lost the NFC Championship Game the previous season to Washington, but we had a solid season prior to that loss, so many people thought we would have a good season in 1984 as well. But I don't think that even coach Bill Walsh would have predicted the type of season we ended up having.

We lost only once during the year, to the Pittsburgh Steelers. In the playoffs, we played two strong games, beating the Giants 21-10 and the Bears 23-0 to reach the Super Bowl. At that point, we were 17-1, and our confidence was extremely high.

The Super Bowl was played in Stanford Stadium, near San Francisco, so it was like playing a home game for us. But extra pressure was put on us to win because we had the home-field advantage.

Going into the Super Bowl we were as concerned about stopping Miami's quarterback Dan Marino as we were with our own offensive output. We knew we could score points, especially with Joe Montana, but Marino was a scoring machine. Therefore, much of coach Walsh's pregame planning was aimed at stopping Miami's offense and, in particular, Marino.

We were all relaxed during the week leading up to the game, mainly because we were at home, but also because we were confident in what we could do. But when I ran onto the field, I felt a surge of electricity throughout my body. It was an incredible feeling. I think all the guys felt a bit nervous as we waited for the game to begin, but that passed once it started.

People expected a high-scoring game, and it certainly started that way. Miami scored a field goal and a touchdown and we scored a touchdown in the first quarter. At that point, it seemed that the game was going to resemble a great heavyweight fight, with one side punching and the other side counterpunching.

Joe connected with running back Carl Monroe in the first quarter on a 33-yard pass play, which finished a scoring drive that began on our 20-yard line. That threw Miami's defense off a bit because they were concentrating on our heavy hitters—Freddie Solomon, Wendell Tyler, Dwight Clark and me. But Marino came right back on the next set of downs, working without a huddle and leading the Dolphins down the field as if they were in a two-minute drill. The only word I can think of to describe the action is amazing. It was amazing being on the field with Joe leading us downfield, and it was equally amazing standing on the sidelines watching Marino lead them.

We were trailing 10-7 after the first gun, but we took charge in the second quarter, both on offense and defense. We had good field position at about midfield on a drive early in the quarter. Dwight Clark had a key reception in that drive, and we were inside the 10 when Joe called my number and hit me with a pass in the end zone. That gave us a 14-10 lead.

Joe led us downfield and scored from six yards out later in the quarter to give us a 21-10 lead. We began another drive toward the end of the quarter, which began at just our side of the 50. Joe was in total command by then, and he moved us inside Miami's five. Then he called my number on a straight run up the middle from the two, and I scored through a big hole opened up by our offensive linemen. Actually, it was more than a "run." Later I saw a picture of that touchdown, and it looked as if I was airborne for the entire play.

Miami added a couple of field goals in the second quarter, but we were up by 12 points at the half. There was a tremendous amount of energy in the locker room. We felt that if we kept up the pressure, we could win the game. That sounds simple, but when you're dealing

---

**JANUARY 20, 1985
SAN FRANCISCO 49ERS 38, MIAMI
DOLPHINS 16
STANFORD STADIUM, PALO ALTO, CALIFORNIA**

SCORING

SF	7	21	10	0	**38**
MIA	10	6	0	0	**16**

MIA   von Schamann, 37-yard field goal
SF   Monroe, 33-yard pass from Montana (Wersching kick)
MIA   D. Johnson, 2-yard pass from Marino (von Schamann kick)
SF   Craig, 8-yard pass from Montana (Wersching kick)
SF   Montana, 6-yard run (Wersching kick)
SF   Craig, 2-yard run (Wersching kick)
MIA   von Schamann, 31-yard field goal
MIA   von Schamann, 30-yard field goal
SF   Wersching, 27-yard field goal
SF   Craig, 16-yard pass from Montana (Wersching kick)

TEAM STATISTICS

	MIA	SF
First Downs	19	31
Rushes-Yards	9-25	40-211
Passing Yards	289	326
Passes	29-50-2	24-35-0
Punts-Average	6-39.0	3-33.0
Fumbles-Lost	1-0	2-2
Penalties-Yards	1-10	2-10

INDIVIDUAL STATISTICS

Rushing
MIA   Bennett 3 rushes for 7 yards; Nathan 5-18; Marino 1-0
SF   Tyler 13-65; Craig 15-58; Montana 5-59; Harmon 5-20; Cooper 1-4; Solomon 1-5

Passing
MIA   Marino 29 completions, 50 attempts, 318 yards, 2 interceptions
SF   Montana 24-35-331-0

Receiving
MIA   Nathan 10 receptions for 83 yards; D. Johnson 3-28; Clayton 6-92; Duper 1-11; Rose 6-73; Moore 2-17; Cefalo 1-14
SF   Tyler 4-70; D. Clark 6-77; Craig 7-77; Monroe 1-33; Francis 5-60; Solomon 1-14

ATTENDANCE: 84,059

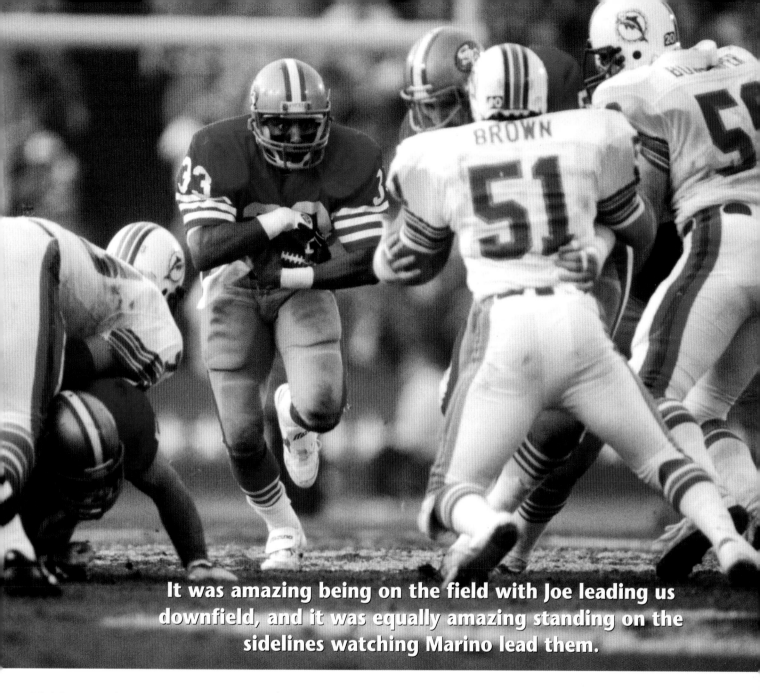

It was amazing being on the field with Joe leading us downfield, and it was equally amazing standing on the sidelines watching Marino lead them.

with Marino nothing is simple. We knew he could get them right back in the game.

Our defense took over early in the third quarter and sacked Marino three times. I got the feeling that Marino was listening for footsteps after that. They didn't score for the rest of the game, and we blew it open in the third quarter with 10 more points. Ray Wersching kicked a field goal, and then I scored a touchdown on a 16-yard pass play from Joe that capped a 70-yard drive.

We didn't want to celebrate until the game was officially over, but I could tell we had them beaten going into the fourth quarter. We held possession of the ball just long enough to maintain control of the game, and our defense was shutting down Marino all over the field.

By the time the game ended, it seemed as if 84,000 people were on the field celebrating with us. I hadn't been with the 49ers when they won Super Bowl XVI, so this was a first-time experience for me.

Joe had a super game and was named MVP. People have asked me whether I thought I should have won the award, but Joe deserved it. He was the main man. I'm more of a team player. My role was to play the angles, take advantage of scoring opportunities and to help us win the game. I did my job, and we were champions of the NFL. Knowing that I played a key role in the victory made the game unforgettable for me.

—As told to Barry Janoff

In Super Bowl XIX, above, running back **Roger Craig** (33) carries the ball on his way to a record-setting three-touchdown performance. In 1985, Craig became the first player in NFL history to gain more than 1,000 yards rushing and 1,000 yards receiving in the same season. He was a major contributor to three San Francisco 49ers Super Bowl victories in eight seasons (1983–90) as a 49er. He played for the Los Angeles Raiders in 1991, then joined the Minnesota Vikings for two seasons before retiring.

Some people have called it "the greatest game ever played." Others have called it the most exciting. It was the longest game

DECEMBER 25, 1971
MIAMI DOLPHINS 27, KANSAS CITY CHIEFS 24
ARROWHEAD STADIUM, KANSAS CITY,
MISSOURI

SCORING

MIA	0	10	7	7	0	3	**27**
KC	10	0	7	7	0	0	**24**

KC   Stenerud, 24-yard field goal
KC   Podolak, 7-yard pass from Dawson (Stenerud kick)
MIA Csonka, 1-yard run (Yepremian kick)
MIA Yepremian, 14-yard field goal
KC   Otis, 1-yard run (Stenerud kick)
MIA Kiick, 1-yard run (Yepremian kick)
KC   Podolak, 3-yard run (Stenerud kick)
MIA Fleming, 5-yard pass from Griese (Yepremian kick)
MIA Yepremian, 37-yard field goal

TEAM STATISTICS	MIA	KC
First Downs	22	23
Rushes-Yards	42-144	44-213
Passing Yards	263	238
Passes	2-20-35	2-18-26
Punts-Average	6-40.0	2-51.0
Fumbles-Lost	0	2
Penalties-Yards	26	44

INDIVIDUAL STATISTICS
Rushing
MIA Kiick 15 rushes for 56 yards; Csonka 24-86;
       Griese 2-9; Warfield 2-minus 7
KC   Hayes 22-100; Podolak 17-85; Wright 2-15; Otis
       3-13
Passing
MIA Griese 20 completions, 35 attempts, 263 yards,
       2 interceptions
KC   Dawson 18-26-246-1
Receiving
MIA Warfield 7 receptions for 140 yards; Fleming
       4-37; Kiick 3-24; Twilley 5-58; Mandich 1-4
KC   Podolak 8-110; Hayes 3-6; Wright 3-104; Taylor
       3-12; Frazier 1-14

ATTENDANCE: 50,374

ever played, and it held the nation spellbound on a Christmas Day when it should have been nothing more than a diversion. It was also the game I'll never forget.

And that's saying a lot, because I was around a long time—college and pro, about 20 years. I was fortunate to always play with good teams and there were a lot of big games. Then there were the two Super Bowls. The first was the first Super Bowl ever played. It was against the Green Bay Packers. The second was against the Minnesota Vikings. Surely these were the most important games I ever played in.

But the game that has burned itself the deepest into my memory was the now famous sudden-death, six-quarter Christmas Day game against the Miami Dolphins.

There was something about this game right from the beginning that set it apart from any other game I've ever been in. I've never been in another game when the players unashamedly and openly prayed on the sidelines.

It was the most exciting game I've ever been involved in. The Chiefs seemed to take control at times but the Dolphins always came back. At one point, with only seconds left, and Jan Stenerud, the best placekicker in football, lining up a straight-on 31-yard field goal, they seemed to have conceded defeat.

Somehow he missed. There was a terrific cheer from the Miami bench in the otherwise quiet stadium. A moment ago they had conceded the victory to us and now they were given new life. We were shocked. For a few minutes we didn't believe it had happened, but we didn't give up.

Going into the game, we were ready. We started very strongly and broke on top. The first time we got the ball we held it for seven minutes and then Stenerud kicked a 24-yard field goal.

Again our defense smothered the Dolphins and again we marched the ball. On the eighth play of the drive I threw a little swing screen to Podolak and we led 10-0.

We had the game under control. Everything we did, we did right. On offense our execution was exact and stunning. On defense we were aggressive and determined. But for some unknown reason we let it slip away.

Just as we had dominated the first part of the first half, now the Dolphin offense dominated the second half. Bob Griese engineered a great drive and Larry Csonka crashed into the end zone from the one to put them right back in the game.

They got the ball right back and raced the clock down the field. With time running out, Garo Yepremian kicked a 14-yard field goal to tie the score.

Once again we took control and marched the ball in for a touchdown, with Jim Otis, our tough short-yardage back getting the final yard. But this time Miami seemed determined not to let us pull away.

Back they came with almost a duplicate of our drive with Jim Kiick going over from the one. Now we were entering the final quarter, the time when mistakes magnify and one break can mean the ball game.

We still stuck to our game plan: control the ball and don't force it. It paid off again when Podolak scored his second touchdown of the game with a short burst over tackle. But Miami hadn't given up yet. With about two minutes to go Griese hit Marv Fleming, his tight end, with a five-yard hook in the end zone and we had a tie ball game.

There was no doubt in my mind that we were going to pull it out. I just sensed it as I watched the teams line up for the kickoff.

The ball went to Podolak, a tremendous workhorse for us all day. He started up the middle. Our blocking wedge cleared out the first men down and he cut to the outside at about the 30. With a burst of desperate speed Curtis Johnson caught up to Ed and made a saving tackle, but not before he reached the Dolphins' 22-yard line, a dazzling clutch kickoff return of 78 yards.

We ran the ball for three plays and got the time down to only 35 remaining seconds. We could feel victory. But somehow it didn't come. Stenerud missed. Miami ran off what

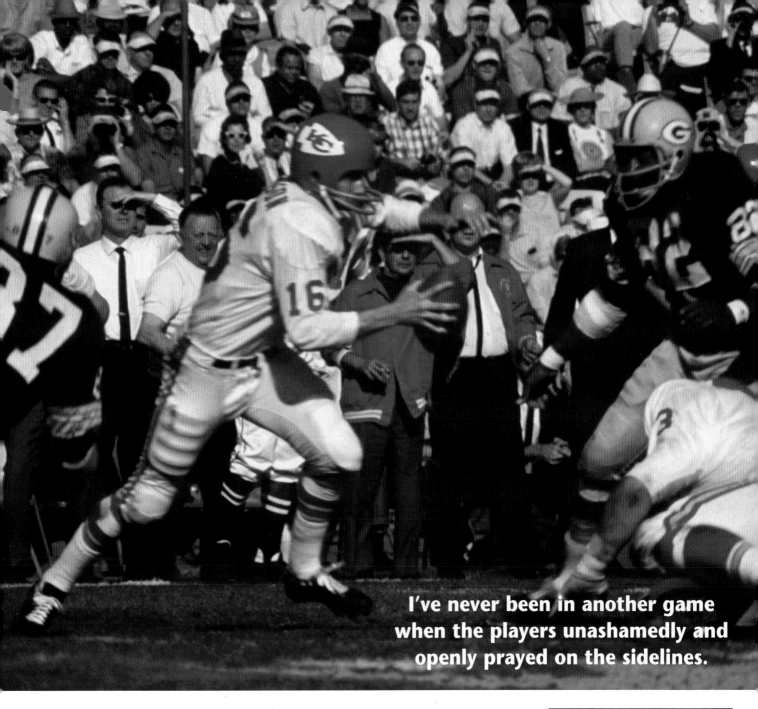

I've never been in another game when the players unashamedly and openly prayed on the sidelines.

was left of the clock and punted.

The Chiefs won the toss to receive the kickoff to start the sudden death. We caught a second break when the Dolphins were offside after kicking the first one into the end zone. Podolak ran the second one out to our 46. We worked the ball carefully down to the Dolphins 35 and Stenerud came in to try a 42-yard field goal, well within his effective range. But it was blocked and the ball rolled dead on the Miami 24.

Now what had been a game of grinding offense became a battle of pit-slugging defenses. Neither team had punted for four quarters but now it became a punting duel. Almost half the sixth quarter went by. The players on the field were still struggling,

bone tired but determined.

Then the nightmare. The play flowed to the right, but Csonka blasted back on the trap to the left. Our defense was completely fooled. He ran for 29 yards deep into our territory. It was the break the Dolphins had been praying for. Yepremian came in and kicked a 37-yard field goal to end the longest game in pro football history at 82 minutes and 40 seconds.

The Dolphins jumped and cheered in that stunned, silent stadium. A few Chiefs cried, but no one said a word. It was a game we'd all remember forever.

—As told to Bob Billings

Kansas City Chiefs quarterback **Len Dawson** (16), above, runs the ball against Green Bay in Super Bowl I. The Packers prevailed but Dawson led the Chiefs to victory in Super Bowl IV. He began his pro career as a backup with the Pittsburgh Steelers (1957–59) and Cleveland Browns (1960–61) before earning a starting position in 1962 with the Dallas Texans. After 13 seasons with Kansas City (1963–75), Dawson retired with 28,711 passing yards for 239 touchdowns. He entered the Pro Football Hall of Fame in 1987.

When you ask me if there is an unforgettable game in my football career, I have to look back and say that I've been

fortunate enough to play in a lot of memorable games. When you're a player you think *every* game is important. As a coach you try to win every game, but you're able to put them into perspective.

As a player, the games that really stand out now are the NFL championship with Chicago in '63 [a 14-10 victory over the New York Giants], and Super Bowl VI with Dallas in '71 [a 24-3 victory over the Miami Dolphins]. But I think the game that has the most significance for me is the Chicago victory in Super Bowl XX against New England, mainly because I was head coach of the Bears.

When you climb the ladder from being a player to being an assistant coach and then a head coach, as I have, you realize certain games are more significant to you as a coach than as a player. Winning Super Bowl XX, for example, was a team effort; the whole team worked together for the win. As the head coach, that win was a reflection on my efforts.

There was a good feeling about the team that whole season. The entire staff thought the team could accomplish a lot of things. Everything just seemed to go our way. We ended up losing only one game that season, 38-24 in Miami during the last month of the season. By that time, we had won 12 games, so the important thing was to keep the team sharp for the playoffs, which we did.

We had played New England the second week of the season in Chicago and beat them 20-7. Despite the difference in our records—the Patriots went 11-5—we weren't about to take them lightly. They won three tough games in the playoffs—all on the road—to get into the Super Bowl. They had players who knew how to win games under pressure.

There were a lot of specific things we wanted to accomplish going into the game. However, we knew that if we could score points early, our defense would make it very difficult for them to mount any kind of

sustained offense. It worked out that way for us, and the final score was definitely in our favor.

The key to the game may have been the first quarter. New England came out and scored on its first possession. But we came right back on our next possession and took control. We ended up going about 59 or 60 yards in seven plays, and Kevin Butler kicked a field goal to tie the score. Standing on the sidelines, I could feel that our guys had the momentum.

I remember in the locker room the day before the game, defensive tackle Dan Hampton stood up and said, "Either we're going to get Super Bowl rings, or the guys we're playing are going to get them. Let's make sure *we* get them." That was the feeling the whole game, a sort of take-no-prisoners attitude.

With about a minute and a half to play in the quarter, Butler hit another field goal to give us the lead. Then our defense got the ball back almost immediately, and we ended up putting together a two-play drive from about their 15-yard line that ended with Matt Suhey scoring on an 11-yard run. We had the Patriots back on their heels at that point, and I don't think we ever let them get any solid footing after that.

The players were getting pumped up on the sideline. We were up by only 10 at the quarter, but I could feel that the guys were hungry. The defensive guys were pumped up; the guys on offense were pumped up. Hey, I was pacing up and down too, because I could feel that all the energy we had was going in a positive direction.

We put another 10 points on the board in the second quarter on two massive drives. Quarterback Jim McMahon scored on a short run after the offensive unit went about 55 yards in nine plays. Then, toward the end of the half, we started a drive that ended up going about 70 yards, with Butler kicking a field goal with no time left in the half.

We had a good lead at the half, but the main thing we stressed in the locker room was the fact that the Patriots could put points on the board in a hurry. If they could

---

JANUARY 26, 1986

CHICAGO BEARS 46, NEW ENGLAND PATRIOTS 10

LOUISIANA SUPERDOME, NEW ORLEANS, LOUISIANA

SCORING

CHI	13	10	21	2	**46**
NE	3	0	0	7	**10**

NE	Franklin, 37-yard field goal
CHI	Butler, 28-yard field goal
CHI	Butler, 24-yard field goal
CHI	Suhey, 11-yard run (Butler kick)
CHI	McMahon, 2-yard run (Butler kick)
CHI	Butler, 24-yard field goal
CHI	McMahon, 1-yard run (Butler kick)
CHI	Phillips, 28-yard interception return (Butler kick)
CHI	Perry, 1-yard run (Butler kick)
NE	Fryar, 8-yard pass from Grogan (Franklin kick)
CHI	Safety, Grogan sacked in end zone by Waechter

TEAM STATISTICS	CHI	NE
First Downs	23	12
Rushes-Yards	49-167	11-7
Passing Yards	241	116
Passes	12-24-0	17-36-2
Punts-Average	4-43.0	6-44.0
Fumbles-Lost	3-2	5-5
Penalties-Yards	6-35	5-35

INDIVIDUAL STATISTICS

Rushing

CHI	Payton 22 rushes for 61 yards; Suhey 11-52; McMahon 5-14; Thomas 2-8; Gentry 3-15; Perry 1-1; Fuller 1-1; Sanders 4-15
NE	Collins 3-4; Grogan 1-3; Weathers 1-3; James 5-1; Hawthorne 1-minus 4

Passing

CHI	McMahon 12 completions, 20 attempts, 256 yards, 0 interceptions; Fuller 0-4-0-0
NE	Eason 0-6-0-0; Grogan 17-30-177-2

Receiving

CHI	Gault 4 receptions for 129 yards; Moorehead 2-22; Thomas 1-4; Suhey 1-24; Gentry 2-41; Margerum 2-36
NE	Morgan 7-70; Starring 2-39; Fryar 2-24; Collins 2-19; Ramsey 2-16; James 1-6; Weathers 1-3

ATTENDANCE: 73,818

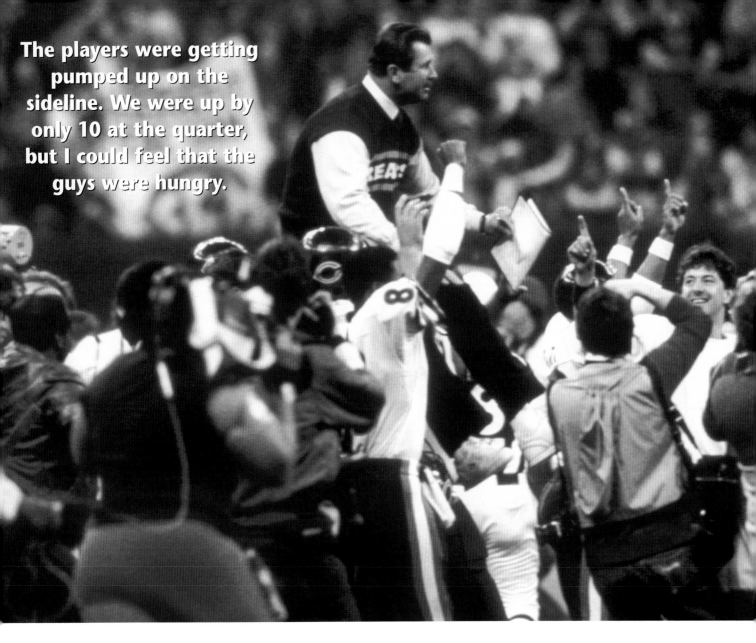

The players were getting pumped up on the sideline. We were up by only 10 at the quarter, but I could feel that the guys were hungry.

come out and put a couple of scoring drives together, they're back in it.

In the third quarter we put the game out of reach with three touchdowns. That may have been as close to a perfect 15 minutes of football as you would ever want to see, especially in a game that important. McMahon scored the first touchdown at the end of a drive that started on our four. Reggie Phillips intercepted a pass about a minute later and scored. A couple of minutes after that, we sent defensive tackle William Perry in as a back and he scored from the one.

I know there were some people who complained later that we were rubbing the Patriots' noses into the dirt because we used Perry as a back when the score was already one-sided. But I'm not concerned about what people think. We weren't trying to show up the Patriots. If you're on the other guy's one-

yard line—I don't care what the score is— you're going to try for the touchdown. The decision was to use Perry, and it turned out to be a good one.

The Bears are a tough team. We try to go out and take care of business every game. That year, we went out and did the things we wanted to do on offense and defense. The Super Bowl capped off an amazing year, which made me feel special as head coach.

I played in this league for a dozen years before I became an assistant coach. I know that as a player you have a lot of thoughts about succeeding as an individual. You can't do anything about that. Even now, I don't begrudge the players for that. But when you become the coach, you do things for the team. Winning the Super Bowl against the Patriots meant that we were successful as a team.

—As told to Barry Janoff

Chicago coach **Mike Ditka**, above, is carried off the field after the Bears' Super Bowl XX victory. The first tight end elected to the Pro Football Hall of Fame (1988), Ditka starred for the Bears (1961–66), Philadelphia Eagles (1967–68) and Dallas Cowboys (1969–72). He remained with Dallas as an assistant coach until Chicago hired him for the head position in 1982. Over 11 seasons (1982–92), he compiled a 106-62 win-loss record. Ditka also coached the New Orleans Saints (1997–99).

Winning a championship has to be the highlight of any player's career. I played on two NFC championship teams with

JANUARY 15, 1978
DALLAS COWBOYS 27, DENVER BRONCOS 10
LOUISIANA SUPERDOME, NEW ORLEANS, LOUISIANA

SCORING

DAL	10	3	7	7	**27**
DEN	0	0	10	0	**10**

DAL Dorsett, 3-yard run (Herrera kick)
DAL Herrera, 35-yard field goal
DAL Herrera, 43-yard field goal
DEN Turner, 47-yard field goal
DAL Johnson, 45-yard pass from Staubach (Herrera kick)
DEN Lytle, 1-yard run (Turner kick)
DAL Richards, 29-yard pass from Newhouse (Herrera kick)

TEAM STATISTICS	DAL	DEN
First Downs	17	11
Rushes-Yards	38-143	29-121
Passing Yards	182	35
Passes	19-28-0	8-25-4
Punts-Average	5-41.6	4-38.2
Fumbles-Lost	6-2	4-4
Penalties-Yards	12-94	8-60

INDIVIDUAL STATISTICS
Rushing
DAL Dorsett 15 rushes for 66 yards; Newhouse 14-55; White 1-13; D. Pearson 3-11; Staubach 3-6; Laidlaw 1-1; Johnson 1-minus 9
DEN Lytle 10-35; Armstrong 7-27; Weese 3-26; Jensen 1-16; Keyworth 5-9; Perrin 3-8
Passing
DAL Staubach 17 completions, 25 attempts, 183 yards, 0 interceptions; White 1-2-5-0; Newhouse 1-1-29-0
DEN Morton 4-15-39-4; Weese 4-10-22-0
Receiving
DAL P. Pearson 5 receptions for 37 yards; DuPree 4-66; Newhouse 3-1; Johnson 2-53; Richards 2-38; Dorsett 2-11; D. Pearson 1-13
DEN Dolbin 2-24; Odoms 2-9; Moses 1-21; Upchurch 1-9; Jensen 1-5; Perrin 1-7

ATTENDANCE: 75,583

Dallas and five division-winning teams, and there were a lot of memorable games along the way. But the highlight has to be winning Super Bowl XII with the Cowboys after we won the division title and the NFC title, all in my rookie season.

Going into my first NFL season, I had hoped that I could help the Cowboys accomplish a lot of things. But at that point, it was hard to imagine that things would work out as well for me in the pros as they had in college. When I was with the University of Pittsburgh, we won the Sugar Bowl and a national title, and I won the Heisman Trophy. When Dallas selected me in the first round of the 1977 draft, I was excited because the Cowboys were a championship-caliber team.

My initial thoughts, of course, were not about winning the Super Bowl; the first thing I had to do was work hard and prove to coach Tom Landry that I deserved a spot on his squad. I actually began the season playing behind Preston Pearson, but I got a shot at starting on a regular basis around midseason, and I made the most of it.

I had a good season—I rushed for 12 touchdowns and more than 1,000 yards. Playing with the best and against the best brought out the best in me. But there were a lot of key people on that squad, from the coaches on down, which is why the team had such a great year. We won the division, then beat Chicago in the division playoffs and Minnesota in the NFC Championship Game. The offense and defense really thrived on the pressure of the playoffs. We ended up outscoring the Bears and the Vikings by a combined total of 60-13, then we beat the Broncos in the Super Bowl 27-10, so it was a great time for everyone on the team.

I wouldn't say we were overconfident going into the Super Bowl, but we did have a lot of confidence in the things we could accomplish as a team. Of course, we weren't about to underestimate Denver at all. That would have been a fatal mistake. They had the best record in the AFC—12-2, and they beat Pittsburgh and the Raiders in two tough playoff games. Also, we had played them in the last month of the season, and Dallas won 14-6, so we knew firsthand that they were a tough team.

It was important for us to establish our offense and defense early on. Also, I wanted to get the ball and run some plays early just to get some dirt on my uniform. You do a lot of scrimmaging and watch a lot of game films prior to the Super Bowl, but it's not the same as actually taking a handoff from Roger Staubach in a game and trying to elude the other team's defense.

A lot of the guys were trying to act cool, but I could tell that everyone on the team could feel the electricity in the air. It's hard to ignore all the hoopla, especially when you're standing on the sidelines waiting for the game to start and 75,000 people are yelling and screaming. As a player, I always felt the best thing to do was to turn all that yelling into positive energy so that I could actually get a boost out of it.

Our defensive guys set the mood in the first quarter when Randy White tackled Denver quarterback Craig Morton for an 11-yard loss, stopping one of their first drives. Later on, Morton was intercepted by Randy Hughes, which gave us a first down on Denver's 25. Roger fired a bullet to Billy Joe DuPree, which put us on the 12. Then we ran a few successive plays on the ground, and I finished the drive when I scored from the three.

It was a tremendous feeling to run off the field having just scored the first touchdown in the Super Bowl. Guys were coming over to congratulate me, and I remember feeling sky-high as far as my emotions and confidence level were concerned. But my focus remained on the game. We ended up scoring on field goals in the first and second quarters, and our defense kept them in check, so we led 13-0 at the half. Halftime basically was a time to talk about playing up our strengths on offense and defense. Even during the regular season, the aim of the coaches was to go with our strengths and to take advantage of the other team's weaknesses.

It's hard to ignore all the hoopla, especially when you're standing on the sidelines waiting for the game to start and 75,000 people are yelling and screaming.

Denver scored on a field goal in the third quarter, but Roger led us on a scoring drive that ended with a 45-yard pass play to Butch Johnson. Denver then came back for a touchdown, which made the score 20-10.

In the fourth quarter, we had another scoring drive that ended with an option play that we rarely used. We were on about Denver's 30. Roger handed off to fullback Robert Newhouse, who ran to his left, then threw a pass to Golden Richards for a touchdown. Right then I knew that playing for the Cowboys was not only going to be rewarding, but also very interesting. This was an organization that was determined to find ways to win, and I knew I would be a key part of that.

It was an amazing season, and winning the Super Bowl culminated a great rookie year for me. Playing in the Super Bowl is just an unbelievable feeling—it's something that every player in the league aims for, and I was fortunate to have been in two of them with the Cowboys. Winning Super Bowl XII certainly was a game I'll never forget.

—As told to Barry Janoff

Dallas Cowboys running back **Tony Dorsett** (33), above, carries the ball in a 1985 game against the San Francisco 49ers. Dorsett, the 1976 Heisman Trophy winner, had eight NFL seasons with better than 1,000 yards rushing, peaking with 1,646 in 1981. He spent the majority of his Pro Football Hall of Fame career with Dallas (1977–87) and a season (1988) with the Denver Broncos. Dorsett retired with 2,936 carries for 12,739 yards and 77 touchdowns, along with 398 receptions for 3,554 yards and 13 touchdowns.

Every time two teams take the field there's a lot happening under the surface. I call it the game within the game.

DECEMBER 27, 1969
MINNESOTA VIKINGS 23, LOS ANGELES RAMS 20
METROPOLITAN STADIUM, BLOOMINGTON, MINNESOTA

SCORING

MIN	7	0	7	9	**23**
LA	7	10	0	3	**20**

LA	Klein, 3-yard pass from Gabriel (Gossett kick)
MIN	Osborn, 1-yard run (Cox kick)
LA	Gossett, 20-yard field goal
LA	Truax, 2-yard pass from Gabriel (Gossett kick)
MIN	Osborn, 1-yard run (Cox kick)
LA	Gossett, 27-yard field goal
MIN	Kapp, 2-yard rush (Cox kick)
MIN	Safety, Gabriel tackled in end zone by Eller

TEAM STATISTICS

	LA	MIN
First Downs	19	18
Rushes-Yards	30-126	29-97
Passing Yards	150	196
Passes	22-32-1	12-19-2
Punts-Average	3-36.3	3-39.3
Fumbles-Lost	1-0	3-1
Penalties-Yards	4-37	4-36

INDIVIDUAL STATISTICS

Rushing
LA   L. Smith 11 rushes for 60 yards; Josephson 10-16; Gabriel 4-26; Ellison 4-22; Mason 1-2
MIN   Osborn 13-30; Brown 8-22; Kapp 7-42; Reed 1-3

Passing
LA   Gabriel 22 completions, 32 attempts, 150 yards, 1 interception
MIN   Kapp 12-19-196-2

Receiving
LA   Josephson 7 receptions for 41 yards; L. Smith 6-36; Truax 5-47; Tucker 3-23; Klein 1-3
MIN   Washington 4-90; Henderson 4-68; Brown 2-18; Reed 2-18

ATTENDANCE: 47,900

It's like there are little mental chess matches being played all over the field on every play. Maybe a quarterback has picked up on a safety's coverage tendencies and is waiting for just the right time during the game to exploit him for a touchdown pass. Or maybe a linebacker has timed a quarterback's cadence and then uses that knowledge for a surprise blitz on a crucial third-down play. They're subtle, but when they're added up, winning these little chess matches can result in a victory.

I won one of these little mental games in a 1969 playoff game against the Los Angeles Rams, and it helped us win the bigger game and eventually get to Super Bowl IV.

In those days people called us "the Purple People Eaters"; our defensive front four—me, Jim Marshall, Alan Page and Gary Larsen—was one of the best of all time.

The key to our success as a unit was that we really understood how each of us was crucial to the success of the others. In other words, our success was predicated on the other guys doing their jobs. Alan was quick off the ball and could make a great rush up the middle and crush the pocket. Marshall could apply hard pressure from the outside coming from the backside of a right-handed quarterback. Larsen was our safety valve. Not only could he pass rush, but he was great at skirting out to break up a screen pass or tackle a quarterback who might be trying to scramble out of the pocket. I liked to try and push the lineman into the quarterback. When I couldn't outmuscle an offensive lineman, I would use my quickness to go around him.

Teams couldn't concentrate on just one of the Purple People Eaters. Otherwise, the others would dominate. And rarely could they contain all of us.

We had a strong regular season that year under coach Bud Grant, winning 12 in a row in between losing our season opener and finale. Our defense led the league in several categories, including fewest first downs, net passing yards allowed and points allowed. The offense had a good year too. With quarterback Joe Kapp leading the way, we led the league with 379 points scored.

In the NFL Conference Playoffs, we hosted the Los Angeles Rams on a typically frigid day in Bloomington. The Rams had won their first 11 games of the year before dropping their final three. Their coach, George Allen, had put together a great ball-control offense led by quarterback Roman Gabriel. He had a fantastic offensive line in front of him, including Charlie Corwan, Tom Mack, Joe Scibelli and Ken Iman.

But on that frigid day, I had the misfortune of having to line up against Bob Brown on every play. Brown may have been the first of the 300-pound linemen. He was listed at 275 pounds, but I'm sure he was bigger. And he didn't just like to block you or keep you away from his quarterback. That wasn't enough for Bob. He had a different attitude than most offensive linemen. He wanted to hit you and inflict pain and pound you and beat you down. There were plays where if you'd slip and you were out of a play, most offensive linemen would just let up, but not Bob. If you let your guard down for just a second, he would pound on you. He had no mercy.

Sometimes I used my quickness to beat a lineman and sometimes I used my strength and just overpowered a lineman, but with Brown I had to use my entire gamut of moves. I knew it was going to be a long afternoon.

And as the afternoon went on, Brown and the Rams were controlling the line of scrimmage. On touchdowns by tight ends Bob Klein and Bill Truax, and a field goal by Bruce Gossett, the Rams built a 17-7 lead by halftime. We cut the lead to three points in the third quarter on a one-yard touchdown run by Dave Osborn. Things didn't look good for us when Gossett hit another field goal in the fourth quarter, but luckily our quarterback didn't know the meaning of the word quit. Kapp scored on a two-yard run to give us our first lead.

Then it was my turn to win the little game inside the game.

Earlier in the game, the Rams had success with a play in which Gabriel did a little roll

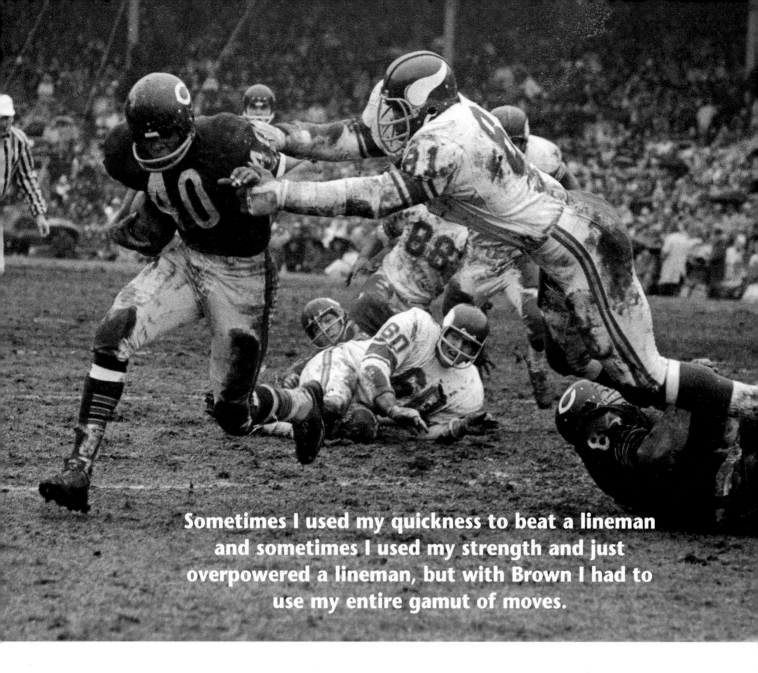

Sometimes I used my quickness to beat a lineman and sometimes I used my strength and just overpowered a lineman, but with Brown I had to use my entire gamut of moves.

out to my side. Brown let me come up the inside and sealed me off, allowing Gabriel to get outside. He had a ton of time to find an open receiver, although he also could have easily run the ball for a big gain.

After that, in the back of my mind, I kept waiting for them to run that play again. When they got the ball deep in their territory late in the game, I had a feeling they were going to that play.

Sure enough, they did. I saw it developing, but I knew I had to rush in a way that wouldn't let on that I had guessed the play. I took Brown upfield, but maintained my leverage and didn't widen my stance. I took him a little bit inside. Gabriel read the block and thought I was falling for the play again. He tried to come around us, but I knew what was coming.

I got free from Brown, and my momentum carried me right into Gabriel. He was big, about 220 pounds, so he wasn't the kind of quarterback you could tackle with one hand or just push down. But with my momentum carrying me, I hit him square and took him down in the end zone for a safety. That made the score 23-20.

Not only did we widen our lead, but we got the ball back. By the time the Rams got possession again, they had little time to mount a serious threat.

I had won the mind game. We had won the game. They were both the games I'll never forget.

—*As told to Chuck O'Donnell*

Minnesota Vikings' defensive end **Carl Eller** (81), above, dives at Chicago Bears running back Gale Sayers (40) on December 10, 1967. Eller played 15 seasons (1964–78) for the Vikes before finishing his career with one campaign (1979) for the Seattle Seahawks. The six-foot-six, 250-pound lineman took four unsuccessful trips to the Super Bowl but won respect for his pass-rushing and run-stopping skills. Eller was voted All-Pro five times, named to six Pro Bowl rosters and inducted into the Pro Football Hall of Fame in 2004.

The most memorable games, for me, are the ones in which the entire team comes together, plays together and proves just

JANUARY 11, 1987
DENVER BRONCOS 23, CLEVELAND BROWNS 20
MUNICIPAL STADIUM, CLEVELAND, OHIO

SCORING

DEN	0	10	3	7	3	**23**
CLE	7	3	0	10	0	**20**

CLE Fontenot, 6-yard pass from Kosar (Moseley kick)
DEN Karlis, 19-yard field goal
DEN Willhite, 1-yard run (Karlis kick)
CLE Mosley, 29-yard field goal
DEN Karlis, 26-yard field goal
CLE Moseley, 24-yard field goal
CLE Brennan, 48-yard pass from Kosar (Moseley kick)
DEN Karlis, 33-yard field goal

TEAM STATISTICS

	DEN	CLE
First Downs	22	17
Rushes-Yards	37-149	33-100
Passing Yards	225	256
Passes	22-38-1	18-32-2
Punts-Average	7-37.6	6-43.2
Fumbles-Lost	2-0	3-1
Penalties-Yards	6-39	9-76

INDIVIDUAL STATISTICS

Rushing
DEN Elway 4 rushes for 56 yards; Winder 26-83; Lang 3-9; Willhite 3-0; Sewell 1-1
CLE Mack 26-94; Kosar 4-3; Fontenot 3-3

Passing
DEN Elway 22 completions, 38 attempts, 244 yards, 1 interception
CLE Kosar 18-32-259-2

Receiving
DEN Watson 3 receptions for 55 yards; Sewell 3-47; Mobley 3-36; Johnson 3-25; Winder 3-2; M. Jackson 2-25; Kay 2-23; Willhite 2-20; Sampson 1-10; Lang 1-1
CLE Fontenot 7-66; Brennan 4-72; Langhorne 2-35; Mack 2-20; Weathers 1-42; Slaughter 1-20; Byner 1-4

ATTENDANCE: 79,937

how great the Denver Broncos organization is. I set very high standards for myself, and I set high standards for this team. When I feel in my heart that those standards have been met, it's a very satisfying feeling.

There have been several games in which the Broncos have displayed a combination of guts and class—games in which we played hard as a team and then, afterwards, were able to sit down and say, "Wow, that was a great showing by our team." The one that immediately comes to mind is the 1986 AFC Championship Game against the Cleveland Browns that put us into Super Bowl XXI. We beat the Browns in Cleveland 23-20 in overtime, and the way we played as a team makes that game stand out for me.

We had a good year in 1986 and won the AFC West with an 11-5 record. That was the same mark we had in 1985, but we didn't make the playoffs that year. So there was a determined effort from everyone on the team to not only win the division but to win the conference title as well. We also had been in the playoffs in 1983 and 1984, but we were eliminated early each year. Everyone on the team, from coach Dan Reeves on down, felt the team we had in 1986 could go all the way. There were some rough weeks along the way, but there was a feeling throughout the season that this team could make a special impact on the NFL.

We played against New England in the divisional playoffs, and they played an extremely tough game against us. We ended up winning 22-17, and that game brought us together physically and mentally even more than we had been before. But still, I don't know if anything really prepares you to go into Cleveland to face Bernie Kosar and 80,000 fans.

We matched up very well against the Browns, so everyone knew that it was going to be a tough, physical game. The feeling going into the game was that if we played solid, intelligent football, kept our mistakes

to a minimum and focused our attention on doing the things that got us into the championship game, we would come away with a victory.

There were a lot of heroes on our team that day. Our kicker, Rich Karlis, had a great game, as did Rulon Jones, Sammy Winder and coach Reeves. It was the type of game where everyone contributed to the effort and then shared in the victory. Fans remember our last two drives—one at the end of the game that led to our game-tying touchdown and one in overtime that led to the game-winning field goal. Those stand out for me as well, but there were key plays throughout the game that reinforced for me the feeling that we would win.

In the second quarter, when we were down 7-0, our offensive line opened up a lot of holes so that we could run some key plays on the ground. And our defensive guys played a consistent game and held the Browns to just 10 points after three quarters. But Bernie got his team moving in the fourth quarter, and they scored on a field goal and a touchdown to take a 20-13 lead with less than six minutes to play.

After scoring their last touchdown, the Browns put us in a deep hole when the kickoff was downed on our 2-yard line. From that point until we eventually won the game, everyone on our team played All-Pro football. The plan was to score, of course, but equally important was to prevent Cleveland from getting the ball back. Bernie is a great quarterback, and his offense is explosive, so we didn't want to break our backs to score a touchdown only to have them come back onto the field to negate our efforts.

I was very excited during that final drive—maybe too excited. I wanted to do everything right away, to get it all done very quickly. Coach Reeves called a time-out at one point just to talk to me, to direct my energy. We mixed up our running and passing plays very well on that drive, which kept Cleveland's defense back on its heels. We used Sammy Winder as a running back and receiver on consecutive plays, and we kept the ball moving to several different receivers, which enabled us to advance to the Browns' 40

I remember being very excited during that final drive—maybe too excited.

when the two-minute warning came.

We got stalled at the 40 and actually were moved back to the 48 when I was sacked. We had a third-and-18, and we called a release-66 pass play, which put tight end Orson Mobley over the middle about 10 yards out as the primary receiver. But Cleveland strong safety Ray Ellis was playing deep, so I went to wide receiver Mark Jackson instead and picked up about 20 yards. Wide receiver Steve Sewell caught a tough pass to move us down to the 14 with about a minute to play, then I ran for about nine yards to put us on the five. We went back to Mark on the next play when he ended up one-on-one with a safety in the end zone.

It was funny in a way because after having been so intense throughout the drive, I remember thinking to myself as I threw the pass to Mark, "No problem," like it was a scrimmage game. When he caught it, though, I think I yelled louder than the 80,000 fans combined had done all day.

Cleveland didn't score during the final half-minute, but they got the ball to start the overtime. They had a third-and-two on their 38, and Rulon Jones and Karl Mecklenburg made sure they stayed there when they stuffed Cleveland running back Herman Fontenot at the line. We got the ball on our 25, then moved to Cleveland's 48 on a great pass play with Mobley. A couple of plays later I was pushed out of the pocket, but I hit Steve Watson with a pass that put us on Cleveland's 22.

After three short running plays we had a fourth-and-three. Rich Karlis got the call, and as he came running onto the field I remember yelling to him, "Just like in practice." I was partially blocked on the sidelines when he kicked the ball, and honestly, I thought he had missed it. But I knew immediately from the reaction of our guys and the reaction of the crowd that we had won the game. That was a great feeling—one that I'll never forget.

—*As told to Barry Janoff*

John Elway quarterbacked the Denver Broncos for 16 seasons (1983–98), passing for 51,475 yards and 300 touchdowns and rushing for 3,410 yards and 33 touchdowns. Elway and the Broncos came up short in three Super Bowl trips in the 1980s, but finally won the big game in January 1998. Proving the win was no fluke, a year later Elway earned MVP honors in the last game of his career, guiding the Broncos to victory in Super Bowl XXXIII. He entered the Pro Football Hall of Fame in 2004.

1979 NFC DIVISIONAL PLAYOFF GAME

The game I'll never forget happened during the 1979 playoffs when I was with the Los Angeles Rams. We beat the Dallas

Cowboys in the NFC Divisional Playoffs 21-19, and went all the way to the Super Bowl.

We were underdogs because the game was to be played in Dallas, but what I remember as being more important is that the Cowboys didn't seem to have any respect for us. We won the NFC West Division that year, but we only had a 9-7 record. Dallas had beaten us pretty badly during the regular season, so it was easy to feel that the Cowboys were fired up and ready to beat us again.

There were a couple of keys to that game for us: We threw a new defense at the Cowboys, which kept their offense pretty well contained; and we were the team that made the big plays instead of the Cowboys.

Our offense had some injuries going into the game, but we knew we could put enough points on the board to win. On the defensive side, defensive coordinator Bud Carson set up the "Seven-Up" defense. We knew how strong Dallas' quarterback, Roger Staubach, was out of the shotgun, so the plan was to play seven defensive backs against him, instead of our usual four defensive backs and three linebackers.

I don't remember Staubach's exact numbers, but I know he had only about 140 or 150 yards passing with one touchdown. Throwing out of the shotgun, I think he completed only five passes for 40 or 50 yards.

Our guys on offense were ready for this game right from the start. But I think the fact that our defense was playing so tough inspired the offensive unit to play even tougher. Actually, the first quarter wasn't what you would call high-quality football. We didn't score, and Dallas' only points came when Randy White sacked me in the end zone for a safety. We put a strong drive together in the second quarter, however, that led to our first touchdown. We were back inside our own 10-yard line and drove 92 yards to score. Wendell Tyler had two big plays in that drive: a 36-yard run and the touchdown on a 32-yard pass play.

Dallas drove downfield a couple of minutes later and ended up with a field goal, but we came back and scored another touchdown less than a minute later. That drive began on our 30, and it went bang-bang-bang-bang—four plays, three of which were passes, including the touchdown aerial to Ron Smith.

We were leading by nine points at the half, 14-5, which isn't much when you're playing an explosive team such as Dallas. But in the locker room at the half, we felt that our offense was heating up and knew that our defense had held the Cowboys without a touchdown. This was only the sixth start of my NFL career, so the chemistry between my receivers and me was still developing. Throwing the two touchdown passes in the second quarter, though, was a definite morale booster for me.

Although our defense was containing them for the most part, the Cowboys put a strong drive together about five minutes into the second half that led to a touchdown. Ron Springs ran the ball in from the one-yard line, but the key play was a pass interference call against linebacker Jim Youngblood, which put the ball on the one.

We were still leading going into the fourth quarter, but I knew that we had to generate some more points. Unfortunately, Dallas scored next to take the lead. Safety Cliff Harris intercepted my pass, and then Staubach led Dallas on a 60-yard drive in which he completed passes to at least four different receivers. Jay Saldi was his primary target during the drive, though, and Staubach hit him in the end zone to give them the lead.

We were down by five with about three minutes to play. I knew Dallas could almost taste the victory, especially since the Cowboys had beaten us so decisively during the regular season and in a playoff game the previous year. We decided to go for one big play at that point, aiming for at least a big gain, if not a touchdown. We had a first down right at midfield. Wide receiver Billy Waddy lined up wide to the right, then cut over the middle of the Cowboys' zone, about 20 yards deep. I saw that he was open and

---

DECEMBER 30, 1979
LOS ANGELES RAMS 21, DALLAS COWBOYS 19
TEXAS STADIUM, IRVING, TEXAS

SCORING

LA	0	14	0	7	**21**
DAL	2	3	7	7	**19**

DAL	Safety, Ferragamo tackled in end zone by R. White
LA	Tyler 32-yard pass from Ferragamo (Corral kick)
DAL	Septien 33-yard field goal
LA	R. Smith, 43-yard pass from Ferragamo (Corral kick)
DAL	Springs 1-yard run (Septien kick)
DAL	Saldi 2-yard pass from Staubach (Septien kick)
LA	Waddy 50-yard pass from Ferragamo (Corral kick)

TEAM STATISTICS

	LA	DAL
First Downs	16	16
Rushes-Yards	39-159	34-156
Passing Yards	202	124
Passes	9-21-2	12-29-1
Punts-Average	5-40.6	8-36.8
Fumbles-Lost	0-0	0-0
Penalties-Yards	6-44	7-55

INDIVIDUAL STATISTICS

Rushing

LA	Tyler 19 rushes for 82 yards; Bryant 17-67; Cromwell 1-7; Waddy 1-3; Ferragamo 1-0
DAL	Dorsett 19-87; DuPree 1-27; Newhouse 7-21; Springs 5-20; Staubach 1-3; P. Pearson 1-minus 2

Passing

LA	Ferragamo 9 completions, 21 attempts, 210 yards, 2 interceptions
DAL	Staubach 12-28-124-1; Spring 0-1-0-0

Receiving

LA	Waddy 3 receptions for 97 yards; Smith 2-55; Tyler 2-40; Dennard 1-15; Bryant 1-3
DAL	D. Pearson 3-61; DuPree 2-26; Saldi 2-17; P. Pearson 2-15; Johnson 1-3; Springs 1-2; Hill 1-0

ATTENDANCE: 64,792

We were down by five with about three minutes to play. I knew Dallas could almost taste the victory.

threw a pass that he caught right at his belt buckle. He then curved to his right and headed down the sideline for the touchdown.

Waddy was a secondary receiver on that play. I got great protection from our offensive line, and when I stepped up into the pocket I had time to look over the entire field and see Waddy break open across the middle. After I threw it, it seemed like someone got a hand on the ball and tipped it. I later found out that Dallas tackle Harvey Martin had tipped it, but he didn't slow it down, so Waddy didn't have too much difficulty catching the pass.

That drive, which turned out to be for the winning touchdown, covered 50 yards in just one play. The Dallas fans were stunned, I'm sure, because you know that they're used to seeing Staubach and the Cowboys, not the opposing team, make those kinds of plays to win. We held them scoreless the remaining two minutes to finally pull out a big win against Dallas. After the game, Dallas coach Tom Landry said: "Los Angeles made the big plays. That was the game."

That game was important to the Rams as a team, and to me as a player. People gave us a lot more respect after that. We were a championship team, and I had proven my ability to win under pressure.

—*As told to Barry Janoff*

Los Angeles Rams quarterback **Vince Ferragamo** (15), above, hands off the ball to running back Lawrence McCutcheon en route to a 9-0 victory over the Tampa Bay Buccaneers in the 1979 NFC Championship Game. Ferragamo played seven seasons for the Rams (1977–84), one (1985) for the Buffalo Bills and three games (1986) for the Green Bay Packers. He retired with 902 career completions for 11,336 yards and 76 touchdowns.

We won our first two games of the 1976 season over Kansas City and Tampa Bay on the road. That was encouraging since we

had gone 2-12 the year before. But we knew our first real test was coming up against the St. Louis Cardinals in San Diego.

The Cardinals also had won their two opening games and they were the defending champions of their division, the NFC Central. They were coming in with a real explosive offense and, considering our defense was still young and inexperienced, we figured we would have to score a lot of points to win. This was going to be a basketball game and we were going to have to reach a hundred before them. Their quarterback, Jim Hart, had one of the best arms around, was well protected and had some good receivers and backs to go to that season.

Judging by St. Louis' defense, we were confident there were some things we could do against them. We knew we could take advantage of their coverages by running certain motion plays. Our game plan was sound, which was nothing unusual since Bill Walsh was our offensive coordinator. He's an outstanding coach.

We didn't waste any time going after them. On the first play from scrimmage, I hit Charlie Joiner over the middle at about our 40. He spun to the outside, received a great block from guard Doug Wilkerson and ran to the 13 for a 59-yard play. Don Woods scored on the next play on an unbelievable run.

That was important to us. The first series of downs, I believe, are the most important in a game. If you can get a good jump on a team, why not take it? I like to keep a defense as off-balance as possible, and the sooner the better.

We missed the conversion and St. Louis came back to get 10 points on a Hart touchdown pass and a field goal by Jim Bakken.

We regained the lead, 13-10, on the first play of the second quarter when Rickey Young capped a long drive with a three-yard touchdown run. St. Louis fumbled the following kickoff and we recovered on their 30. I threw a scoring pass to Joiner on the next play to put us in front 19-10. Both touchdowns came within 14 seconds.

I threw two more touchdown passes to Dwight McDonald, covering 44 and 18 yards, before the half. We ended up with four touchdowns in the second quarter. It was Dwight's first game back since being placed on waivers late in the preseason. He was brought back after an injury to receiver Gary Garrison.

We led 33-10 at the half, but Hart came back with a touchdown pass midway through the third quarter to put the Cardinals back in it. Toni Fritsch gave us a little more cushion with a long field goal later in the quarter.

Midway through the final quarter, we put the game away when I rolled right on a third down option play and threw a one-yard touchdown pass to tight end Pat Curran. It was Pat's first scoring reception in his two seasons with us. He only had a couple of touchdown catches in his previous six seasons with the Rams. He told me after the game that if I had decided to run the ball in, he would have tackled me.

It turned out to be one of my best passing days with the Chargers. I completed 15 of 18 attempts; two of the incompletions were dropped and I relaxed on the other when I had the receiver open. Going 18-for-18 would have been nice.

I had a better day than Hart, but it was no great satisfaction to me. After all, he wasn't playing defense against me nor was I playing defense against him. I was just happy we'd won and that I was able to contribute with a good day. And it was fun seeing things we'd worked on during the week work out so well during the game.

—As told to Dave Payne

SEPTEMBER 26, 1976
SAN DIEGO CHARGERS 43, ST. LOUIS CARDINALS 24
SAN DIEGO STADIUM, SAN DIEGO, CALIFORNIA

SCORING

SD	6	27	3	7	**43**
STL	10	0	7	7	**24**

SD — Woods, 13-yard run (kick failed)
STL — Cain, 14-yard pass from Hart (Bakken kick)
STL — Bakken, 32-yard field goal
SD — Young, 3-yard run (Fritsch kick)
SD — Joiner, 30-yard pass from Fouts (kick failed)
SD — McDonald, 44-yard pass from Fouts (Fritsch kick)
SD — McDonald, 18-yard pass from Fouts (Fritsch kick)
STL — Morris, 11-yard pass from Hart (Bakken kick)
SD — Fritsch, 39-yard field goal
SD — Curran, 1-yard pass from Fouts (Fritsch kick)
STL — Morris, 1-yard run (Bakken kick)

TEAM STATISTICS

	STL	SD
First Downs	22	24
Rushes-Yards	26-124	45-206
Passing Yards	240	245
Passes	20-33-1	15-18-0
Punts-Average	3-36.7	4-35.3
Fumbles-Lost	4-4	2-0
Penalties-Yards	5-20	5-54

INDIVIDUAL STATISTICS
Rushing
STL — Metcalf 11 rushes for 40 yards; Jones 4-36; Latin 2-29; Otis 8-16; W. Morris 2-3; Hart 1-0
SD — Young 10-72; Woods, 13-60; Matthews 9-29; M. Morris 6-21; Scarber 6-20; Fouts 1-4
Passing
STL — Hart 20 completions, 33 attempts, 1 interception, 240 yards
SD — Fouts 15-18-0-259
Receiving
STL — Cain 6 receptions for 98 yards; Harris 6-71; W. Morris 4-34; Metcalf 2-11; Latin 1-15; Tiley 1-11
SD — Joiner 5-134; McDonald 3-73; Young 3-27; Curran 2-13; Woods 2-12

ATTENDANCE: 40,372

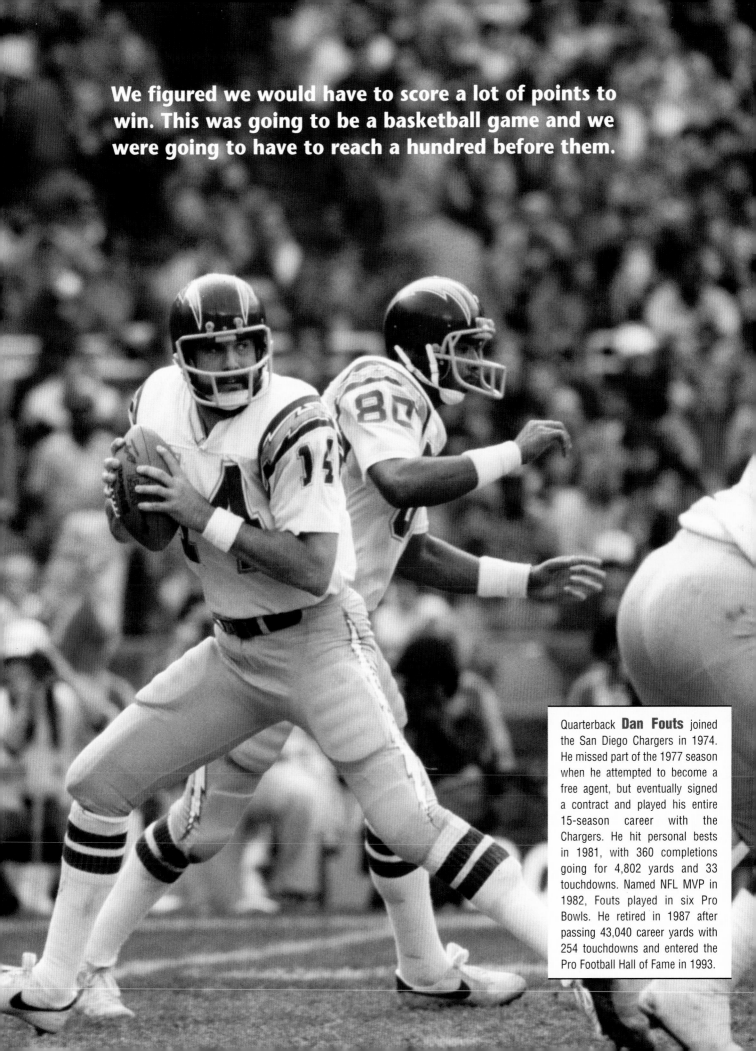

We figured we would have to score a lot of points to win. This was going to be a basketball game and we were going to have to reach a hundred before them.

Quarterback **Dan Fouts** joined the San Diego Chargers in 1974. He missed part of the 1977 season when he attempted to become a free agent, but eventually signed a contract and played his entire 15-season career with the Chargers. He hit personal bests in 1981, with 360 completions going for 4,802 yards and 33 touchdowns. Named NFL MVP in 1982, Fouts played in six Pro Bowls. He retired in 1987 after passing 43,040 career yards with 254 touchdowns and entered the Pro Football Hall of Fame in 1993.

If you had seen as many losses as I did with the Los Angeles Rams—if you had experienced as many lows as I did, if you

DECEMBER 17, 1967

LOS ANGELES RAMS 34, BALTIMORE COLTS 10

MEMORIAL COLISEUM, LOS ANGELES, CALIFORNIA

SCORING

LA	3	14	3	14	**34**
BAL	7	0	0	3	**10**

LA Gossett, 47-yard field goal
BAL Richardson, 12-yard pass from Unitas (Michaels kick)
LA Snow, 80-yard pass from Gabriel (Gossett kick)
LA Casey, 23-yard pass from Gabriel (Gossett kick)
LA Gossett, 23-yard field goal
BAL Michaels, 14-yard field goal
LA Truax, 9-yard pass from Gabriel (Gossett kick)
LA Bass, 2-yard run (Gossett kick)

TEAM STATISTICS

	LA	BAL
First Downs	16	18
Rushes-Yards	29-71	27-104
Passing Yards	257	158
Passes	18-22-0	19-31-2
Punts-Average	5-39.4	4-47.0
Fumbles-Lost	2-1	0-0
Penalties-Yards	5-46	4-21

INDIVIDUAL STATISTICS

Rushing
LA Bass 12 rushes for 36 yards; Josephson 9-20; Mason 8-15
BAL Lorick 13-39; Hill 2-20; Matte 9-24; Moore 1-6; Unitas 2-15

Passing
LA Gabriel 18 completions, 22 attempt, 257 yards, 0 interceptions
BAL Unitas 19-31-206-2

Receiving
LA Bass 4 receptions for 27 yards; Casey 4-78; Josephson 1-4; Snow 1-80; Truax 5-51; Mason 3-17
BAL Berry 1-11; Lorick 2-12; Matte 2-13; Mackey 5-72; Moore 3-29; Richardson 5-57; Hill 1-12

ATTENDANCE: 77,277

had been as buried on the depth chart as I was—you would have been as shocked as I was to be playing the Baltimore Colts in the last game of the 1967 season for the right to go to the playoffs.

Needless to say, it was a long road to that game. In my first five years with the Rams we never had a winning season, and I was a backup receiver, a backup tight end and a backup quarterback. The 1962 season was my first in Los Angeles; we had a young guy named Ron Miller and a veteran named Zeke Bratkowski playing quarterback. The next year the Rams brought in Terry Baker, a Heisman Trophy winner from Oregon State. Then they imported Bill Munson, a big-time quarterback from Utah State. After that, they drafted Billy Anderson, another hotshot quarterback.

They were experimenting with a new quarterback every year, and here I was just sitting and waiting for the chance to play. Things got so bad that before the 1965 season, I asked to be traded to the expansion Atlanta Falcons so I could be closer to my home in North Carolina. Then I signed with the Oakland Raiders of the fledgling AFL and was going to join them after playing out my option with the Rams in 1966.

But when George Allen came in to coach the Rams in '66, he made me the quarterback. He also made us winners. After seven straight years of losing, we had an 8-6 record that season.

Things really took off in 1967. With a nice mix of veterans and youngsters, we lost just one of our first 12 games. Les Josephson, in his fourth year, led the team with 800 rushing yards; Dick Bass, a 30-year-old veteran, added 627 more yards on the ground; big flanker Bernie Casey led the team with 53 receptions; and Jack Snow, who was just coming into his own, finished with 28 catches.

In the trenches, we were tough on both sides of the ball. Jack Pardee, Tony Guillory and Tom Mack were all tough as nails; they were the type of guys you needed on your team if you were going to be successful. And, of course, there was our defensive line, the one that struck such terror into opponents that it became known as "the Fearsome Foursome." Together, Deacon Jones, Lamar Lundy, Roger Brown and Merlin Olsen could change the entire face of a game with a clothesline of a running back or one blindside blast to a quarterback.

With two games left in the 1967 regular season and the Coastal Division title on the line, we faced a must-win situation against Vince Lombardi's Green Bay Packers. Casey ran a perfect corner route from a wing position, and I hit him with the touchdown pass that gave us the win and sent us against the coastal rival Colts in what would turn out to be the game I'll never forget.

Looking up and down their lineup, we knew we were in for a game. The Colts had leadership in coach Don Shula, running back Lenny Moore and quarterback John Unitas. They had athleticism in running back Tom Matte and receiver Willie Richardson. And they had toughness in linebacker Mike Curtis and rookie end Bubba Smith.

They also had depth, which they would need. Receivers Ray Berry and Jimmy Orr went down with injuries, while behemoth offensive tackle Jim Parker retired midway through the year. But Richardson and Alex Hawkins filled in for Berry and Orr, and Sam Ball was thrust into action in Parker's spot. All the while, the Colts continued to win. In fact, they were 11-0-2 entering this final game. We were 10-1-2, so the team that won this game would go to the playoffs.

The teams felt each other out for the first quarter or so, like two heavyweights in a title bout. But after the Colts mounted a 7-3 lead after one quarter, that changed. We took over on our 20 after Baltimore kicker Lou Michaels missed a field goal. On the first play, we called a play-action pass; it worked perfectly. The line did a great job of buying me some time, the backs sold the fake and Snow ran a good route. He was behind the defense when I heaved the ball about 60 yards and into his arms. He took it the rest of the way untouched for a touchdown.

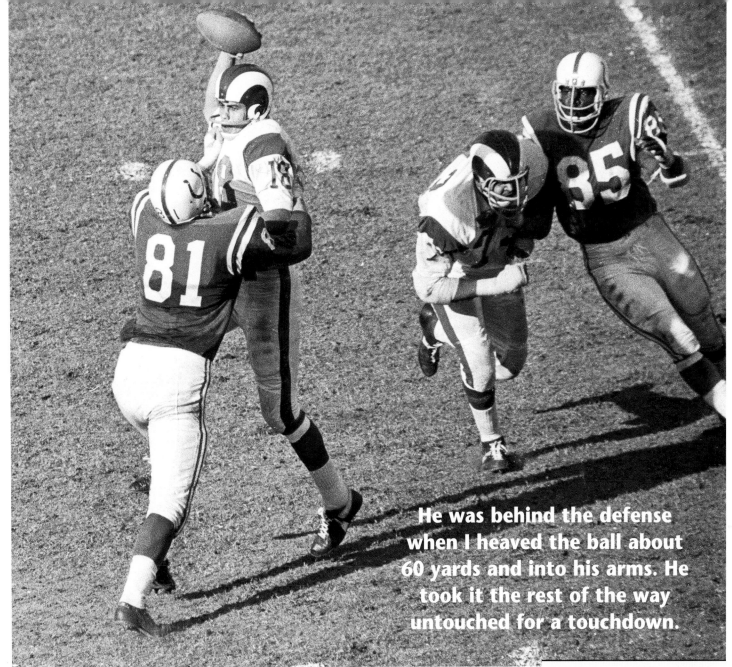

He was behind the defense when I heaved the ball about 60 yards and into his arms. He took it the rest of the way untouched for a touchdown.

We scored 14 unanswered points in the second quarter, taking control of the game. But our sudden surge wasn't all the offense's doing. The defense helped us build on that lead when Deacon forced Unitas into throwing a wobbly pass that we intercepted. Using some quick-hit pass plays, we drove the ball down into Colts territory and scored on a 23-yard pass to Casey, which gave us a 17-7 lead at the half.

When the third quarter began, I felt as if our defense wasn't going to let them score and that our offense still had a few touchdowns left in us. Linebacker Pardee helped set up a field goal with another interception of Unitas, and after the Colts trimmed our edge to 20-10 with a field goal of their own, we broke the game open. In the fourth quarter, we drove the ball 67 yards downfield, hitting paydirt when I connected with Bill Truax on a nine-yard TD pass.

And when it came time to put the game away, it was fitting that it was our defense that set up our offense. Getting stronger as the day wore on, the defense sacked Unitas three times in four downs. When we took over on downs, we had the ball at our own four-yard line. We drove the ball down the field, and Bass scored on a two-yard run to give us a 34-10 victory and send the 77,000 fans in the Coliseum home happy.

After all those years of losing, after the years of embarrassment and torment, I could hardly believe we were headed to the playoffs.

—*As told to Chuck O'Donnell*

Los Angeles Rams quarterback **Roman Gabriel** (18), above, faces pressure from the Baltimore Colts on December 17, 1965. Gabriel played 11 seasons (1962–72) for the Rams before he was traded to Philadelphia. He posted career highs with the Eagles in 1973, when he led the league in passing yards (3,219) and completions (270) and tied with Dallas' Roger Staubach in touchdown passes (23). Gabriel retired after the 1977 campaign, ranking among the top ten quarterbacks of all time, with 4,498 passing attempts, 2,368 completions, 29,444 passing yards and 201 touchdowns.

Everyone who played in the 1958 championship game, I suppose, is expected to select that game as the most

OCTOBER 7, 1962
NEW YORK GIANTS 31, ST. LOUIS
CARDINALS 14
BUSCH STADIUM, ST. LOUIS, MISSOURI

SCORING

NYG	7	14	7	3	**31**
STL	7	7	0	0	**14**

STL Crow, 7-yard run (Perry kick)
NYG Shofner, 6-yard pass from Tittle (Chandler kick)
STL Crow, 1-yard run (Perry kick)
NYG Webster, 1-yard run (Chandler kick)
NYG Lynch, fell on blocked punt in end zone (Chandler kick)
NYG Tittle, 21-yard run (Chandler kick)
NYG Chandler, 35-yard field goal

TEAM STATISTICS	NYG	STL
First Downs	21	15
Rushes-Yards	31-105	27-104
Passing Yards	231	120
Passes	20-34-1	12-25-2
Punts-Average	4-30.5	6-35.3
Fumbles-Lost	1-1	1-0
Penalties-Yards	6-40	4-47

INDIVIDUAL STATISTICS
Rushing
NYG King 7 rushes for 24 yards; Webster 13-23; Counts 4-31; Morrison 4-1; Tittle 1-21; Guglielmi 2-5
STL Crow 12-47; Gautt 13-57
Passing
NYG Tittle 16 completions, 26 attempts, 190 yards, 1 interception; Guglielmi 4-8-47-0
STL Etcheverry 4-10-50-2; Crow 1-1-57-0; Johnson 7-14-57-0
Receiving
NYG Gifford 6 receptions for 97 yards; Webster 5-33; Shofner 4-41; Walton 2-21; Thomas 1-18; Counts 1-15; King 1-12
STL Conrad 6-105; Gautt 2-30; Anderson 2-7; Crow 1-15; Randle 1-7

ATTENDANCE: 20,627

outstanding of his career. It's regarded as *the* game, the greatest game ever played—the Baltimore Colts and the New York Giants in the first sudden-death championship game in pro football history, December 28, 1958.

That was a game that supposedly had everything, exciting offense, great defense, with the Giants putting up a tremendous goal line stand in the third quarter when we were down 14 to 3. Then we came back to take the lead, and I had the pleasure of scoring that touchdown. Then there was the drive John Unitas engineered, the length of the field with under two minutes to play.

My memories of that game, though, really aren't all that glowing. I scored a touchdown, sure, but I also fumbled twice and in the late stages of the game I was stopped inches short of a first down on third and four. If we would have made that first down we probably would have been able to kill the clock or run out enough of it so there would have been no Colt drive in the closing minutes. I'll always feel that I made that first down, that my forward progress got the ball past that end stick. But when the referee spotted the ball and they measured, we were inches short. We argued that they had moved the ball back a good half yard, but it was a futile argument.

Those are some of the reasons why that game arouses negative thoughts in me, and I just didn't think it was as great a game as people said it was. Both teams just made too many mistakes, to my way of thinking.

No, it wasn't that one. For me, the game I'll never forget was an obscure game several years later; a kind of nothing game, really. As a matter of fact, I'd be just about willing to bet that of all the fellows who played in it, I'm probably the only one who remembers anything about it, and I remember it for a very personal reason.

But first, a little history is necessary to understand why this game stands out in my mind.

In 1959 the Giants were Eastern Division champions again and in the title game we found ourselves in a rematch with the Colts. This time no one called it the greatest game ever played. It was close going into the last quarter, but then we made so many mistakes the Colts won it easily.

The following year the Eagles climbed over us to win the division championship. I was hurt. A brain concussion and a knee operation made it look like it was all over for me. I laid out the 1961 season while my teammates were winning the division title again but losing the championship game to the Green Bay Packers.

All that year I had been working hard trying to get it together again and I had made enough progress where I felt justified in trying to come back. When training camp opened I was there and they moved me from running back to flanker so there would be less pounding and wear and tear on the old frame.

I hung on through the camp, playing behind Aaron Thomas and I thought maybe a few others too. Until you've been through it you never really know just how much you can slip backwards in a year. I wasn't even sure if I was making the team because I could still perform, or if they were keeping me around for old time's sake.

During the exhibition season I didn't get to play a lot because the coaches said they wanted to look at rookies. That didn't make me feel too good, but after they cut the rookies I still wasn't getting in much playing time. When the league schedule started I was playing even less than I had in the preseason. That really bothered me.

We got off to a good start in our first three games, but my game time was down to nothing. I didn't even get in against the Steelers. I was really depressed that day. I was debating with myself whether or not to just pack it up and call it a career. I felt so empty. For years I had been such a big part of the team and I just couldn't face the prospect of sitting on the bench because they wanted to be nice to me and carry me on the roster as a reward. I really didn't feel I was part of the team anymore. It was a traumatic moment in my life, to come to the end just like that.

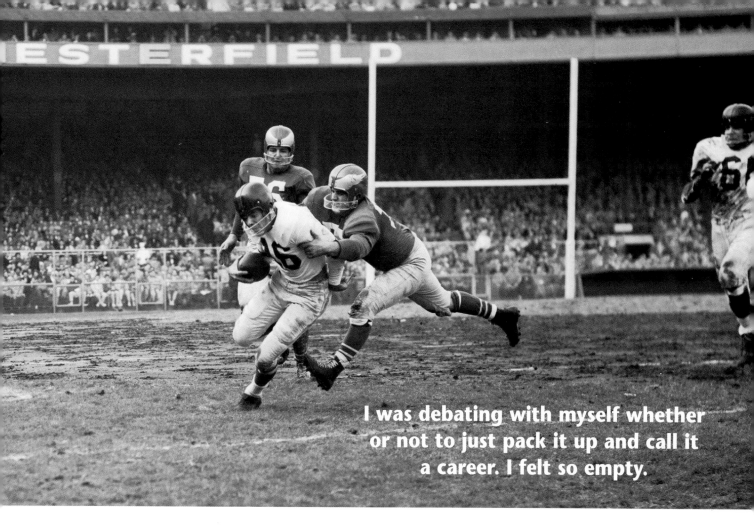

I was debating with myself whether or not to just pack it up and call it a career. I felt so empty.

Before I made my decision, though, Joe Walton, our tight end, came up with a bad knee. Thomas was moved to his spot and I was put in at flanker. It felt real good to be back, but the real test would come on Sunday against the St. Louis Cardinals. When you get a few years on you, your body sometimes gets balky about doing what your mind is telling it to do.

It was early in the season, our fourth game, on October 7, 1962, but it was the whole season for me.

I don't remember the whole game anymore, just the good parts. They got off to an early lead on a touchdown run by John David Crow, but Y.A. Tittle hit our great split end, Del Shofner, with a touchdown pass. They took the lead again when Don Chandler had to punt from deep in our territory. He didn't catch it quite right and the ball hit his blocker, Mickey Walker, square in the backside to set them up.

Tittle brought us right down the field again. First he hit Shofner, then me, then Shofner, then me again to set it up on the Cardinal 13-yard line.

I was up against Pat Fischer, the Cardinals' cornerback—one of the toughest, grittiest little guys ever to play the game. Fischer was a real battler who'd use every trick he could think of to beat you. One of his favorite tactics was to get right up on the line of scrimmage and hand fight you right there. That's right, bump and run, only he was doing it before anyone else even knew what it was.

From the 13-yard line, Tittle threw for me again. I put a good move on Pat and when he tried to recover he tripped me. The ball was thrown way too high and way too wide to be caught, but it was still a clear case of interference. The foul gave us a first down on the one, and fullback Alex Webster took it across to tie the score.

We really won the game with 11 seconds to go in the first half when Sam Huff broke through and blocked a punt Dick Lynch recovered for the go-ahead touchdown. The second half, our defense put us in complete control of the game. They held the Cardinals scoreless.

It ended up an easy 31 to 14 victory and as I said at the beginning, everyone else has probably forgotten about it by this time. But not me. That's the game that showed everyone I could come back.

—As told to Bob Billings

New York Giants halfback **Frank Gifford**, above, is hauled down by Philadelphia Eagle Jess Richardson in a 1954 match-up. Gifford also starred at wide receiver and defensive back during his Pro Football Hall of Fame career. He was with the Giants from 1952 to 1964, played in seven Pro Bowls and was the 1956 NFL player of the year. He went on to a long and successful broadcasting career, most notably with 27 seasons at *Monday Night Football*.

One of my strong suits as the quarterback of the Miami Dolphins was preparation. I would pore over game films and dissect

NOVEMBER 24, 1977
MIAMI DOLPHINS 55, ST. LOUIS CARDINALS 14
BUSCH MEMORIAL STADIUM, ST. LOUIS, MISSOURI

SCORING

MIA	14	14	20	7	**55**
STL	7	0	0	7	**14**

MIA	N. Moore, 4-yard pass from Griese (Yepremian kick)
MIA	D. Harris, 7-yard pass from Griese (Yepremian kick)
STL	Metcalf, 1-yard run (Bakken kick)
MIA	N. Moore, 9-yard pass from Griese (Yepremian kick)
MIA	N. Moore, 28-yard pass from Griese (Yepremian kick)
MIA	Davis, 17-yard pass from Griese (kick failed)
MIA	Tillman, 37-yard pass from Griese (Yepremian kick)
MIA	L. Harris, 4-yard run (Yepremian kick)
STL	Harris, 19-yard pass from Hart (Bakken kick)
MIA	Malone, 4-yard run (Yepremian kick)

TEAM STATISTICS

	MIA	STL
First Downs	34	13
Rushes-Yards	55-295	22-54
Passing Yards	208	156
Passes	17-25-1	16-29-1
Punts-Average	2-37.0	5-32.8
Fumbles-Lost	1-0	4-2
Penalties-Yards	6-47	8-65

INDIVIDUAL STATISTICS
Rushing

MIA	L. Harris 18 rushes for 76 yards; Davis 20-104; N. Moore 1-6; Malone 8-64; Bulaich 1-13; Nottingham 6-21; T. Anderson 1-11
STL	Hart 1-0; Morris 4-1; Metcalf 9-28; Jones 4-14; Otis 4-11

Passing

MIA	Griese 15 completions, 23 attempts, 207 yards, 1 interception; Strock 2-2-12-0
STL	Hart 15-28-167-1; Donckers 1-1-3-0

Receiving

MIA	N. Moore 7 receptions for 68 yards; Davis 3-62; Mandich 1-15; D. Harris 2-20; Tillman 1-37; Bulaich 1-5; Solomon 1-3; McCreary 1-9
STL	Gray 1-5; Cain 2-43; I. Harris 4-41; Morris 4-39; Metcalf 1-8; Otis 1-9; Jones 3-25

ATTENDANCE: 50,269

defenses. I knew every tendency of a defense going into a game. So when I had only four days to prepare for a Thanksgiving Day game against the St. Louis Cardinals in 1977, I thought I was in for big trouble.

We were coming off a really one-sided loss in Cincinnati on Sunday—I mean, we got *destroyed*. We were going in to play the Cardinals, who at that time had a high-scoring offense. Their quarterback, Jim Hart, really could put a lot of points up on the board. What an arm. He had a lot of guys to go to in that offense, too, guys like Mel Gray and Terry Metcalf. They won so many close games that season, they got the nickname "the Kardiac Kids."

It was my 11th year in the league, and I knew I was going to have to draw on my experience and wing it for us to have a chance. But coming off a big loss, having only four days to prepare, knowing we were going to have to score a lot of points to keep pace with their offense, and having to go into St. Louis as underdogs on a holiday, I was expecting the worst. So the fact that we went into St. Louis and blew out the Cardinals—while I put up the best single-game passing numbers of my career—really made it the game I'll never forget.

It turned out to be one of those days when everything went right—I wish I could have bottled it. On our first possession, we called the right play and I threw a touchdown pass to wide receiver Nat Moore. I knew we couldn't let up. I got the guys together on the sideline and told them not to let up and to keep scoring. The next time we got the ball, I connected with wide receiver Duriel Harris for another touchdown. At that point, I knew we were in for a big day but I came back to the sideline and again told the offense not to let up. I kept telling them, "That's not enough. That's not enough." I hit Moore for two more touchdowns, and all of a sudden we had a huge lead.

The touchdown I threw to Andre Tillman

in the third quarter really was a fitting ending to my day. I came up to the line and looked over the defense. I saw that the strong safety was head-up on the tight end, the free safety was up close to the line, and they had their cornerbacks man-on-man and lined up on our wide receivers' inside shoulders, I said to myself: "This is definitely going to be a blitz. I'm going to have to get rid of the ball in a hurry." So I checked off. I wanted to get the tight end, Tillman, open down the field. All I needed was for the blocking to hold up just long enough for me to get the throw off, and we would have at least a big gainer, if not a touchdown. I checked off, the blocking held up fine, and Tillman made a nice play to get open for a long touchdown.

We kept scoring and scoring, and at the end of three quarters we'd scored 48 points. I was a little embarrassed, but considering their record and how many points they'd been scoring, we didn't feel safe until the end of the third quarter. I finally went to our coach, Don Shula, and told him to get our backup quarterback, Don Strock, some snaps. By that point I had thrown six touchdown passes. Someone came over and told me that the NFL single-game record for touchdown passes was seven, but I wasn't interested in going for it; I told Shula to put Strock in. We ended up winning 55-14. I never would have guessed before the game that I was going to have that kind of success, but everything went right.

Much like everything went right for us during the 1972 season, five years before. Sure, that game against the Cardinals was the most memorable from a personal stand-point, but Super Bowl VII was a close second.

I went down in the fifth week of that season with an ankle injury, and Earl Morrall stepped in and did a fantastic job. We won the next nine regular-season games and the first round of the playoffs behind him. In the AFC Championship Game, we were tied 7-7 with the Pittsburgh Steelers. Don Shula put me in after I had missed 10 games, and we ended up winning 21-17.

I got the start in the Super Bowl against the Washington Redskins. Everything was on the line—the perfect season, the NFL title.

It was my 11th year in the league, and I knew I was going to have to draw on my experience and wing it for us to have a chance.

We ended up winning 14-7. I hit Howard Tilley with a touchdown pass, and our defense just played unbelievably.

Super Bowl VIII also was a great memory for me, although I didn't have to throw the ball much; I completed six of my seven pass attempts. About the best thing I did that day was hand the ball off to Larry Csonka. We just controlled the ball and the game. With Csonka, Mercury Morris and Jim Kiick running so well, there was no sense in passing the ball. We didn't need to.

Our offensive linemen—guys like Jim Langer, Larry Little and Bob Kuechenberg—just dominated the line of scrimmage against the Minnesota Vikings' "Purple People Eaters." Before the game, everyone was talking about Minnesota's defensive line, guys like Jim Marshall and Allan Page. If you look at it, our line was probably the heart of our team; our whole attack was structured around it. We ended up winning the game 24-7, but the score didn't really sum up how one-sided the game was.

—*As told to Chuck O'Donnell*

Miami Dolphins quarterback **Bob Griese** (12), above, is shown steering his team to victory in Super Bowl VII, with running back Larry Csonka (39) moving to his right. Griese, one of the steadiest and most efficient quarterbacks of all time, also led the Dolphins to victory in Super Bowl VIII. The two championships were highlights in his 14-season (1967–80) Pro Football Hall of Fame career in Miami. Griese retired with 25,092 passing yards and 192 touchdowns.

There are three games I consider memorable in my career. They were played in succession in the 1976 season; they

SEPTEMBER 26, 1976
NEW ENGLAND PATRIOTS 30, PITTSBURGH STEELERS 27
THREE RIVERS STADIUM, PITTSBURGH, PENNSYLVANIA

SCORING

NE	6	3	14	7	**30**
PIT	7	6	7	7	**27**

PIT Harris, 3-yard run (Gerela kick)
NE Smith, 42-yard field goal
NE Smith, 40-yard field goal
PIT Gerela, 32-yard field goal
NE Smith, 26-yard field goal
PIT Gerela, 41-yard field goal
PIT Harris, 2-yard run (Gerela kick)
NE Francis, 38-yard pass from Grogan (Smith kick)
NE Stingley, 58-yard pass from Grogan (Smith kick)
NE Grogan, 6-yard run (Smith kick)
PIT Grossman, 11-yard pass from Bradshaw (Gerela kick)

TEAM STATISTICS

	NE	PIT
First Downs	18	24
Rushes-Yards	40-142	37-169
Passing Yards	257	291
Passes	13-32-2	20-39-0
Punts-Average	5-41.8	5-44.6
Fumbles-Lost	4-2	7-6
Penalties-Yards	4-52	8-70

INDIVIDUAL STATISTICS
Rushing
NE Cunningham 18 rushes for 45 yards; Johnson 12-39; Grogan 4-33; Calhoun 5-24; Stingley 1-1
PIT Harris 19-78; Bleier 11-49; Bradshaw 6-42; Walden 1-0
Passing
NE Grogan 13 completions, 32 attempts, 257 yards, 2 interceptions
PIT Bradshaw 20-39-0-291
Receiving
NE Francis 6 receptions for 139 yards; Cunningham 3-29; Stingley 2-72; Johnson 2-17
PIT Grossman 7-67; Lewis 5-95; Swann 4-97; Bleier 4-32

ATTENDANCE: 47,379

were very big for me and the New England Patriots.

We were a young team coming off a 3-11 record in 1975 and, although we knew we had a lot of talent, we weren't really sure how good we were. We went 3-3 in preseason and we seemed to have pretty good momentum going into our first league game with Baltimore after having beaten Philadelphia, 27-7. But Baltimore beat us 27-13 at home and that left us wondering if we were in for another disastrous year, especially when our next three games were against Miami, Pittsburgh and Oakland, all playoff clubs from the previous season.

Our whole team had a horrible day against Baltimore. I threw a bunch of interceptions, and I remember the talk being in Boston that maybe quarterback Jim Plunkett shouldn't have been traded.

The night before the Miami game, offensive guard Tommy Neville called a team meeting to clear the air. If anyone had anything to say, they could say it then. I don't know how much that meeting had to do with bringing our team together, but we went out the next day and did a job on Miami. We were behind 7-6 in the second quarter when I ran 13 yards for a touchdown and we went on to win, 30-14. I threw three touchdown passes in the game, two of them to running back Andy Johnson.

We still weren't quite sure where we stood. We had lost to Baltimore and we had beaten Miami at home, so what did that mean? We knew our next game—at Pittsburgh—might give us a pretty good idea if we were as bad as the Baltimore loss might have indicated or as good as we played against the Dolphins.

The Pittsburgh game has to be the single most important game in my career. We were going in against the defending Super Bowl champions and we were about as high as you could get. It was like our Super Bowl.

I didn't particularly have a good first half—we had opportunities to score touchdowns, but we instead had to settle for three field goals by John Smith. Franco Harris scored a touchdown for Pittsburgh and Roy Gerela kicked a couple of field goals to give them a 13-9 halftime lead. Our defense really did a good job keeping us in the game. They were hitting as hard as I've ever seen them hit—Pittsburgh fumbled seven times and we recovered six of them.

It didn't look good when Harris scored again in the third quarter to give the Steelers a 20-9 lead. That meant we were going to have to score two touchdowns against the best defense in the league while holding one of the best offenses to nothing to take the lead.

The biggest play in the game for us came later in the quarter when we gambled on a fourth-and-one on the Steelers' 38-yard line. I faked a handoff up the middle and threw a touchdown pass to tight end Russ Francis. That really turned the tide. The momentum suddenly swung our way.

We took the lead a short time later when I hit wide receiver Stanley Morgan with a 58-yard touchdown pass. We made it three consecutive touchdowns when I ran one in from six yards in the fourth quarter for a 30-20 lead. We were having a ball.

Pittsburgh came back to score, but that was it. They did throw a little scare into us when Gerela missed a 48-yard field goal attempt on the last play of the game. New England had won 30-27 for its first win ever over the Steelers.

Our locker room was wild after the game. Mr. Sullivan [William H. Sullivan, Jr.], the Pats' president, came up to me and said, "The Patriots have arrived; this is a good football team." He gave me a cigar and I still have it at home in my den. That was a real thrill for me.

Oakland was coming to New England the following week, which was fine with us. After having beaten Miami and Pittsburgh, we felt we could beat anyone.

We expected a tough game with the Raiders, but it didn't turn out that way. We took it to them in every way—our defense stopped them and, offensively, we had 468 total yards. I threw two touchdown passes

We were going to have to score two touchdowns against the best defense in the league while holding one of the best offenses to nothing to take the lead.

and ran two in, and fullback Sam Cunningham barely missed 200 total yards. He had 101 yards rushing and 94 yards receiving.

We went on to tie Baltimore for the division title with an 11-3 record and made the playoffs as the American Conference's wild-card team. Going from 3-11 in '75 to 11-3 in '76 was one of the biggest turnarounds ever by an NFL team from one season to the next.

We lost in the first round of the playoffs to Oakland, in a game we should have won. But that still couldn't take away from the great season we had nor the memory of those three games early in the season, especially the win over Pittsburgh.

—As told to Dave Payne

Steve Grogan was a New England Patriots quarterback for 16 years (1975–90). In 1979, he posted his most productive season; he was the NFL's leading rushing quarterback with 368 yards (and two touchdowns) and passed for 3,286 yards and 28 touchdowns. Grogan's 182 career passing touchdowns remain a Patriots franchise record. He retired with 26,882 yards passing, and 2,176 yards and 35 touchdowns rushing.

I don't like to compare one game to another and say that one is more memorable. I liked to feel that the next

JANUARY 21, 1979
PITTSBURGH STEELERS 35, DALLAS COWBOYS 31
ORANGE BOWL, MIAMI, FLORIDA

SCORING

PIT	7	14	0	14	**35**
DAL	7	7	3	14	**31**

PIT   Stallworth, 28-yard pass from Bradshaw (Gerela kick)
DAL   Hill, 39-yard pass from Staubach (Septien kick)
DAL   Hegman, 37-yard fumble return (Septien kick)
PIT   Stallworth, 75-yard pass from Bradshaw (Gerela kick)
PIT   Bleier, 7-yard pass from Bradshaw (Gerela kick)
DAL   Septien, 27-yard field goal
PIT   F. Harris, 22-yard run (Gerela kick)
PIT   Swann, 18-yard pass from Bradshaw (Gerela kick)
DAL   DuPree, 7-yard pass from Staubach (Septien kick)
DAL   B. Johnson, 4-yard pass from Staubach (Septien kick)

TEAM STATISTICS	PIT	DAL
First Downs	19	20
Rushes-Yards	24-66	32-141
Passing Yards	291	176
Passes	17-30-1	17-30-1
Punts-Average	3-43.0	5-39.6
Fumbles-Lost	2-2	3-2
Penalties-Yards	5-35	9-89

INDIVIDUAL STATISTICS
Rushing
PIT   Harris 20 rushes for 68 yards; Bleier 2-3; Bradshaw 2-minus 5
DAL   Dorsett 15-96; Staubach 4-37; Laidlaw 3-12; P. Pearson 1-6; Newhouse 8-3; D. Pearson 1-minus 13
Passing
PIT   Bradshaw 17 completions, 30 attempts, 318 yards, 1 interception
DAL   Staubach 17-30-228-1
Receiving
PIT   Swann 7 receptions for 124 yards; Stallworth 3-115; Grossman 3-29; Bell 2-21; Harris 1-22; Bleier 1-7
DAL   Dorsett 5-44; D. Pearson 4-73; Hill 2-49; B. Johnson 2-30; DuPree 2-17; P. Pearson 2-15

ATTENDANCE: 78,656

game I was going to play in was my most important one. But I think the most intense game I've ever been in was Super Bowl XIII, when the Steelers beat the Dallas Cowboys. I don't want to take anything away from the other games I've been in, but for excitement and intensity that one stands out.

I can't point to one thing or another and say that's what made it so exciting. Two strong teams were on the field that day, each with so many great players. The Steelers had won a pair of Super Bowl games [IX and X] at that point and we really wanted to win again. Dallas was the defending champ, and I think that had a great deal to do with the intensity I mentioned.

The Steelers had a great team in the '70s, especially during the years we won the Super Bowls. We had a lot of players I hold a great deal of respect for. We had the type of guys who didn't like to quit no matter what the odds. They had the desire to be number one.

We won our division that season with the best record in the league, 14-2, then beat Denver and Houston in the playoffs. Our offense and defense really were clicking and we beat them by a combined total of about 50 points. I mean, we really were rolling.

During the time between our AFC championship win against Houston and the Super Bowl, all you heard or read about was how great the Super Bowl was going to be, about what a great match-up the game was. A lot of it, I guess, was typical of any Super Bowl, because, after all, the winner is the champion of the entire league.

But there was something special about this particular game; even the players felt that way. Because both teams were so strong and so evenly matched, and because there was such a strong rivalry between the two teams, the players felt that whichever team did win really would have earned the title of champion. I think that more than usual both teams really looked forward to the game because we knew it would be something special.

It was hard not to notice the excitement and intensity in the air. Usually you don't notice it or you try not to be affected by it, but there were 80,000 people in the Orange Bowl that day and the electricity was just amazing.

We scored first, in the first quarter, when Terry Bradshaw passed to John Stallworth. On that play John was all alone in the end zone because Dallas had three defenders covering Lynn Swann. The whole play had been set up when John Banaszak recovered a Dallas fumble for us.

Dallas scored the next two touchdowns, one on a pass from Roger Staubach and the other when Bradshaw fumbled after he was hit. But we came right back to tie the score when Terry hit Stallworth with his second touchdown pass.

Toward the end of the second quarter Mel Blount intercepted a pass from Staubach. As our offense moved onto the field we knew that taking the lead at the half would be very important. The game had been so even to that point and we knew that taking the lead would really give us a boost.

Bradshaw hit Swann with two passes on the drive and I ran for nine yards on a trap play. Then, with about 25 seconds left in the half, Bradshaw completed a pass to Rocky Bleier to give us the lead.

I think one of the plays that most people tend to remember about the game came in the third quarter. Dallas had moved the ball down to our 10 and had a third-and-three situation. Jackie Smith came in for Dallas and it seemed as if they were going to run the ball. Instead, Staubach faked the run and threw a pass to Smith, who had gotten open in the end zone.

The pass hit Smith on the numbers, but fell incomplete. Smith had a great career in the NFL, but that was one play I'm sure he would have wanted to do over.

There was about 10 minutes to play in the fourth quarter and the game was still close. We were leading by four, with the ball at midfield, when Bradshaw threw a pass to Swann down the right sideline. Benny Barnes was covering Swann and both of them fell as the pass came down. At first it was ruled an incomplete pass by one

Staubach threw two touchdown passes to bring them within four points. They had the momentum and it seemed as if we could to nothing to prevent them from scoring.

of the officials. But another official, Fred Swearingen, called it pass interference on Dallas to give us a first down on their 23.

A few plays later I ran for 22 yards on another trap play to extend our lead. Nineteen seconds later we scored again to give us a 35-17 lead.

I remember standing on the sideline and yelling at our defense to hold Dallas down. We had worked hard and I felt we had earned a victory. There was about eight minutes to go and a lot of our guys were celebrating as though the game was over. But I've been around too long—especially in games against Dallas—and knew that they had a history of coming back. I wasn't about to celebrate yet.

It's hard to describe the next few minutes, but Staubach threw two touchdown passes to bring them within four points. They had the momentum and it seemed as if we could do nothing to prevent them from scoring. Fortunately, Rocky Bleier recovered an onside kick for us as time was running out. That's when I said to myself, "We won."

I'm really not conscious of what I've done on the field as an individual. But I am proud of what the Steelers have accomplished as a team. I'm very proud of the four Super Bowls we won. That about sums up everything else.

—As told to Barry Janoff

Pittsburgh Steelers running back **Franco Harris** (32), above, cuts through the Dallas Cowboys defense during Super Bowl XIII. He won his fourth Super Bowl ring the following season, when he was MVP of Super Bowl XIX. Harris, the 1972 AFC rookie of the year, racked up a franchise-record 11,950 rushing yards over a dozen seasons (1972–83) with the Steelers. He concluded his Pro Football Hall of Fame career in 1984 with the Seattle Seahawks.

Looking back over my career there were good games, great games and games that shouldn't be remembered. I've been

DECEMBER 24, 1988
HOUSTON OILERS 24, CLEVELAND BROWNS 23
MUNICIPAL STADIUM, CLEVELAND, OHIO

SCORING

HOU	0	14	0	10	**24**
CLE	3	6	7	7	**23**

CLE	Bahr, 33-yard field goal
HOU	Pinkett, 14-yard pass from Moon (Zendejas kick)
HOU	Pinkett, 16-yard run (Zendejas kick)
CLE	Bahr, 26-yard field goal
CLE	Bahr, 28-yard field goal
CLE	Slaughter, 14-yard pass from Pagel (Bahr kick)
HOU	White, 1-yard run (Zendejas kick)
HOU	Zendejas, 49-yard field goal
CLE	Slaughter, 2-yard pass from Pagel (Bahr kick)

TEAM STATISTICS

	HOU	CLE
First Downs	19	19
Rushes-Yards	35-129	26-68
Passing Yards	205	192
Passes	16-26-3	19-28-1
Punts-Average	3-37.7	3-35.5
Fumbles-Lost	2-0	1-1
Penalties-Yards	13-118	9-75

INDIVIDUAL STATISTICS

Rushing

HOU	Pinkett 14 rushes for 82 yards; White 12-30; Moon 6-16; Highsmith 2-3; Givins 1-minus 2
CLE	Byner 9-57; Mack 12-14; Strock 1-0; Pagel 1-minus 1; Fontenot 3-minus 2

Passing

HOU	Moon 16 completions, 26 attempts, 213 yards, 3 interceptions
CLE	Pagel 17-25-179-1; Strock 2-3-13-0

Receiving

HOU	Hill 5 receptions for 73 yards; Jeffires 3-52; Duncan 2-33; Pinkett 2-24; J. Williams 1-14; Givins 1-8; Highsmith 1-8; White 1-1
CLE	Slaughter 5-58; Langhorne 6-57; Brennan 2-34; Weathers 2-27; Byner 3-10; Mack 1-6

ATTENDANCE: 75,896

fortunate because the Oilers were such an explosive team that we seemed to have a lot of exciting games that are memorable. Probably the game that stands out for me was a playoff victory over the Browns in Cleveland in 1988. That was a tough game that could have gone either way.

Going in we were the underdogs, mainly because we had to travel to Cleveland. But Browns quarterback Bernie Kosar was injured and didn't play, so that was one thing that worked in our favor.

I joined the Oilers in 1985, and we had a couple of losing seasons before we started to turn it around in 1987. The Browns had won the AFC Central Division title in 1985, 1986 and 1987, so they were established as the team to beat if you wanted to get anywhere. We tied Cleveland with a 10-6 record in 1988, but that was the season that the Cincinnati Bengals won the division title and the AFC championship before losing to the San Francisco 49ers in Super Bowl XXIII. With the Pittsburgh Steelers also in the Central, there's a great division rivalry. Every team wants to beat the other, not just to get into the playoffs but also because there is a tremendous amount of pride involved.

We had made the playoffs in 1987, and we beat Seattle in overtime in the wild-card game, but then we got bumped out by Denver in the next game. We had a taste of winning in the playoffs that season, but it was frustrating. When we made the playoffs in 1988 it was because everyone on the team had worked hard to get there. With the tie-breakers and other ways they figure it out, we finished in third even though we had the same record as Cleveland. That meant we had to travel to Cleveland for our playoff game.

It was cold that day, and the field was pretty solid. Both teams already had some players banged up, but even guys with minor injuries could hurt themselves further if they hit the turf too hard.

Our defensive guys had to adjust their

game plan somewhat because Kosar was out and Mike Pagel was the Browns' starting quarterback. Kosar has been their main guy for a lot of years, and teams act differently when they're being guided by a quarterback they're not used to. Also, our offensive guys had several goals to accomplish. We scored 427 points that season, which I think was the second most in the league, and what we wanted to do against Cleveland was to get our passing game going and also get our running game in gear.

We ended up doing that because Warren had a strong passing game, although he didn't even reach 300 yards passing. As a wideout, I would have liked to see more passes, but I had five catches that day, and a lot of other guys had receptions. It also helped that running back Alan Pinkett had a strong game.

We didn't do much on offense in the first quarter, and the Browns were up 3-0. Then Warren moved us on a few good drives, including one at the end of the quarter and into the second quarter that ended with a pass to Pinkett coming out of the backfield for a touchdown. We got the ball right back on a turnover off the kickoff, which put us down near their goal line, and Pinkett busted a couple of tackles and went into the end zone from about 16 yards out. That gave us our second touchdown within a span of 20 seconds. The Browns had the next three scores, including two field goals in the second quarter and a touchdown pass from Pagel to Webster Slaughter in the third, which gave them a 16-14 lead.

One of the problems of playing aggressive offense and defense, which we did then and in later years, is that the refs will call a lot of penalties. That day we were penalized for more than 100 yards, which tended to stall some of our offensive drives. But Warren is a gutsy clutch player, and he kept drives alive with his arm.

Early in the fourth quarter we moved down inside Cleveland's 5-yard line and then scored to regain the lead. About 10 minutes later, Tony Zendejas hit a field goal from way out to give us a 24-16 lead with less than two minutes to play. Pagel had been knocked out of the game for a couple of plays earlier on,

One of the problems of playing aggressive offense and defense is that the refs will call a lot of penalties.

and I think it was Don Strock who came in for a short stint. But Pagel was there for the two-minute drill, and he did a great job of moving them. Our defensive guys were playing them tough, but they went down the field in about a minute, and Pagel hit Slaughter with a pass to bring them to within a point.

They tried an onside kick, but we got the ball with less than 30 seconds to play and managed to run a few plays and run out the clock.

It wasn't the Super Bowl or the AFC championship, but it was a great moral victory for us, because it showed we could beat the teams we needed to beat under pressure situations. Even though we lost to Buffalo the next week, we were able to shake some of the negative baggage that was with us for a few seasons prior to that.

It may not have been my best game as far as stats, but there was certainly a feeling that the team came together as a unit and played very well on the road. That's something you don't tend to forget.

—*As told to Barry Janoff*

Houston Oilers wide receiver **Drew Hill**, above left, catches the football as Buffalo Bills defensive back Lonnie Smith closes in. Hill was primarily a kickoff return specialist during five seasons (1979–84) with the Los Angeles Rams before he was traded to the Oilers. Over nine campaigns (1985–93) in Houston, he tallied more than 1,000 reception yards five times. Hill retired with 634 career receptions for 9,831 yards and 60 touchdowns.

1950 NFL CHAMPIONSHIP GAME

It was stifling hot in that tunnel. There didn't seem to be any breeze from off Lake Michigan. Most of it, though, was nerves.

DECEMBER 24, 1950
CLEVELAND BROWNS 30, LOS ANGELES RAMS 28
MUNICIPAL STADIUM, CLEVELAND, OHIO

SCORING

CLE	7	6	7	10	**30**
LA	14	0	14	0	**28**

LA   Davis, 82-yard pass from Waterfield (Waterfield kick)
LA   Hoerner, 3-yard run (Waterfield kick)
CLE Jones, 31-yard pass from Graham (Groza kick)
CLE Lavelli, 35-yard pass from Graham (conversion pass failed)
CLE Lavelli, 39-yard pass from Graham (Groza kick)
LA   Hoerner, 1-yard run (Waterfield kick)
LA   Brink, 6-yard fumble return (Waterfield kick)
CLE Bumgardner, 14-yard pass from Graham (Groza kick)
CLE Groza, 16-yard field goal

TEAM STATISTICS	CLE	LA
First Downs	22	22
Rushes-Yards	25-112	36-106
Passing Yards	298	312
Passes	22-33-1	18-32-4
Punts-Average	5-38.2	4-50.3
Fumbles-Lost	3-3	0-0
Penalties-Yards	3-25	4-48

INDIVIDUAL STATISTICS
Rushing
CLE Graham 12-99; Motley 6-9; Jones 2-4; Bumgardner 5-2; Lavelli 1-2
LA   Hoerner 24 rushes for 86 yards; Smith 4-11; Davis 6-6; Waterfield 1-2; Pasquariello 1-1
Passing
CLE Graham 22-32-298-1; James 1-0-0-0
LA   Waterfield 18 completions, 31 attempts, 312 yards, 4 interceptions; Van Brocklin 1-0-0-0
Receiving
CLE Lavelli 11-128; Jones 4-80; Bumgardner 4-48; Gillorn 1-29; Speedie 1-17; Motley 1-minus 2
LA   Fears 9 receptions for 138 yards; Davis 6-80; Hirsh 4-42; Smith 3-46

ATTENDANCE: 29,751

I was never so scared in my life. I had spent the last few years wearing a different kind of uniform and here it was August of 1946 and I was a member of the College All-Stars going up against the world professional champions, the Los Angeles Rams.

After a couple of years away from the game, you have to wonder if you can still do it. It's the doubt in the back of your mind, the lack of deep-down confidence. And I had two things to prove. I was drafted by the Rams, that's when they were the Cleveland Rams, but I chose to go into professional football with the Chicago Rockets of the brand new All-America Conference.

I had to prove to myself that I could make it with the best and prove to the Rams that they shouldn't have let me get away.

That's what was running through my mind standing in that tunnel in Soldier Field and then I felt someone give me a little shove and I started to move and I was out on that field running under the goal posts and up the field.

The whole stadium was darkened except for the spotlight I was running in. I could hear the cheers, but I couldn't feel my feet touch the turf. I just seemed to be floating along. That was the most moving, greatest thrill I've ever experienced in football.

The game itself was quite a thrill too. We beat the Rams, 16-0. I broke one long run for a touchdown and caught a pass from our quarterback, Otto Graham, for another. That gave me all the confidence I needed. And a few years later I found myself with the Rams preparing for the 1950 World Championship game with the Cleveland Browns, the game I'll never forget.

This was a game that sports fans had waited four years to see. The Cleveland Browns had completely dominated the All-America Conference, winning that championship every year. They had fellows like quarterback Otto Graham, great ends in Mac Speedie and Dante Lavelli, and Marion Motley at fullback.

Lou Groza played left tackle and kicked field goals. And Horace Gillom came in to punt, every fan in the country knew their lineup practically by heart: Dub Jones, Abe Gibron, Frank Gatski, Bill Willis, Rex Bumgardner, Lou Rymkus, Weldon Humble, Alex Agase.

The Rams were not without some heroes of their own. We had not one, but two great quarterbacks. Bob Waterfield was a passer and did our punting and place kicking, and Van Brocklin kept the air alive with footballs. The two usually split the games, each playing alternate quarters.

To catch the ball we had Tom Fears. He led the league in receiving, and there was Jack Zilly and myself. This was my first year with the Rams, who converted me from a running back to a wide receiver.

The Browns kicked off and we put the ball in play from our own 18. Waterfield came right out winging. On the first play of the game he circled Glenn Davis of the backfield and down the left sideline. He arched it high and Davis caught it on about the 45 and outran the Browns into the end zone for an 82-yard touchdown.

From then on the two teams hammered and clawed at one another as if their lives were at stake. Graham came back and hit Jones with a 31-yard pass for a touchdown. We put together an 80-yard march in eight plays with big Dick Hoerner hammering over from the three.

In the second quarter the Browns got their second touchdown on a 35-yard Graham to Lavelli pass. We got what looked like a big break when the center snap on the extra point was bad and the Browns couldn't convert.

They went ahead for the first time in the game when Lavelli again got free deep and Graham hit him with a 39-yard bomb.

We went to work again. We got it down to the Browns eight-yard line and then just kept giving it to Hoerner until he got it in.

Whatever sun there was was long gone by now and the wind off Lake Erie was whistling through the stadium. The field was slipperier and icier every minute. Then we caught our second big break of the game.

> I could hear the cheers, but I couldn't feel my feet touch the turf. I just seemed to be floating along.

Graham tossed Motley a pitchout, but he was hemmed in and had nowhere to go. He tried to reverse his field, but he slipped, and as he slipped he was hit hard while he was off-balance. He went down and the ball rolled free. Our tackle Larry Brink picked it up on a clean bounce and ran it into the end zone.

Now we had an eight-point lead with just a quarter left to play. Then Graham put together a masterful march and found Rex Bumgardner all alone in the end zone from 14 yards out.

We got the ball with a couple of minutes to play and still nursing a one-point lead. With only a minute and 48 seconds to play, Waterfield punted to the Browns 31-yard line.

I was sent in to play in the deep secondary because we knew that Graham had to throw the ball. But when a field is that slippery, all the advantage is with offense. The defensive linemen can't get a good rush, and the receivers, who know where they're going, can leave their defenders flat-footed.

Graham dropped back three times and in succession he hit Bumgardner, Jones and then Bumgardner again. With 20 seconds left on the clock and the ball on the Rams 11-yard line, Groza stepped back and kicked a 16-yard field goal to beat us 30-28.

It was a great game, well played and hard fought. I still say it was one of the greatest games ever played. I'm glad I was part of it. It's one I'll never forget.

—As told to Bob Billings

In the 1951 Championship game (Los Angeles 24, Cleveland 17), above, Rams end **"Crazylegs" Hirsch** (40) reaches for a pass before being tackled by Cliff Lewis (62) of the Browns. Hirsch earned his nickname for his powerful but unorthodox running style. Originally a halfback, he started his Pro Football Hall of Fame career with the AAFC's Chicago Rockets (1946–48) before joining the Rams. Hirsch retired after the 1957 campaign with 387 receptions for 7,029 yards and 60 touchdowns.

My unforgettable game was December 19, 1971, against San Diego, when I still played for the Houston Oilers. But I have

DECEMBER 19, 1971
HOUSTON OILERS 49, SAN DIEGO CHARGERS 33
ASTRODOME, HOUSTON, TEXAS

SCORING

HOU	0	7	28	14	**49**
SD	0	23	7	3	**33**

SD Queen, 4-yard run (Partee kick)
SD Partee, 50-yard field goal
HOU Joiner, 14-yard pass from Campbell (Moseley kick)
SD Queen, 5-yard run (Partee kick)
SD Babich, 27-yard fumble return (kick failed)
HOU Holmes, 1-yard run (Moseley kick)
SD Burns, 1-yard run (Partee kick)
HOU Burrough, 62-yard pass from Pastorini (Moseley kick)
HOU Houston, 35-yard interception return (Moseley kick)
HOU Houston, 29-yard interception return (Moseley kick)
SD Partee, 20-yard field goal
HOU Holmes, 2-yard run (Moseley kick)
HOU Atkins, 25-yard interception return (Moseley kick)

TEAM STATISTICS

	HOU	SD
First Downs	22	20
Rushes-Yards	32-135	31-88
Passing Yards	220	147
Passes	15-23-3	12-29-3
Punts-Average	3-36.3	5-45.0
Fumbles-Lost	4-2	3-1
Penalties-Yards	7-81	6-89

INDIVIDUAL STATISTICS
Rushing
HOU Holmes 16 rushes for 92 yards; Campbell 13-38; Pastorini 1-3; Hopkins 1-2; Walsh 1-0
SD Queen 13-53; Burns 8-20; Garrett 9-17; Dicus 1-minus 2
Passing
HOU Pastorini 14 completions, 22 attempts, 212 yards, 3 interceptions; Campbell 1-1-14-0
SD Hadl 12-29-147-3
Receiving
HOU Burrough 4 receptions for 122 yards; Joiner 3-34; Beime 1-29; Holmes 3-23; Campbell 1-12; Walsh 1-6
SD LeVias 5-68; Garrison 1-31; Norman 2-30; Queen 1-6; Dicus 1-7; Burns 1-4; Garrett 1-1

ATTENDANCE: 35,359

to go back one week before that, to the last road game of the '71 season, for an unforgettable moment.

We were in Buffalo December 12 to play the Bills. I had a vivid dream the night before. I dreamed I picked off a pass and scored with it to win the game.

You don't normally talk about things like that, but this dream was so real I felt I had to tell some of our guys. Most of them knew about it by the time we'd eaten our pregame meal. When we had nearly finished eating, the two broadcasters and two writers traveling with the team walked into the room for a cup of coffee. They sat at my table, so I told them, too. When the dream came true a few hours later, they had a lot to talk and write about.

That afternoon, in the third quarter, I intercepted a pass and took it back 17 yards for a touchdown. The score gave us a 13-0 lead. We eventually won, 20-14. That touchdown on an interception also was my seventh in five seasons, and tied me with Herb Adderley and Erich Barnes for the NFL career record.

Going into our last game, December 19 at the Houston Astrodome—the one game I'll never forget—I needed one interception touchdown to break the league record. I admit I was thinking numbers. But after the game started, it didn't look like the Chargers would have to throw much. They were up on us, 23-7, by halftime.

We started coming back in the third quarter. Robert Holmes scored for us, but they got the touchdown back and it was 30-14. Then Dan Pastorini—he was a rookie that year—hit Ken Burrough with a 62-yard touchdown. Their lead was down to 30-21, so they couldn't sit on the ball.

John Hadl was throwing on their next series. We were in a zone coverage—I've forgotten which one—when he threw a little out pass. I took off after the ball, caught it and ran 35 yards for a touchdown. Nobody was close enough to touch me.

Mark Moseley converted for the third time in that third quarter. When we kicked off, we were down only 30-28. Hadl went back and threw on first down, only about eight seconds of clock time after we had scored. He was looking for the tight end. I saw the ball, got in front of it on their 29 and intercepted. You think touchdown when you steal a pass, but I knew right away this one would be harder than the first one. There was a crowd. I got some great blocks, though. Once I was free, only one man had a shot at me: Mike Garrett. He gave it a good effort and tried to block me out a step or two before I scored. I barely got across.

The two touchdowns gave me nine scores on interceptions and enabled me to break the NFL career record [since broken]. I hope Adderley wasn't upset about losing his record. But Herb has a bunch of Super Bowl rings. I never played in a Super Bowl. Given a choice between the record and a Super Bowl ring, I'd take the ring.

Those two touchdowns on interceptions gave me four for the 1971 season, another league record, and also tied the record of two in one game.

What counted at the time was that we had a 35-30 lead after that fourth touchdown in one period. We built it up to 42-33 in the fourth quarter. Then Bob Atkins, our free safety, intercepted Hadl and ran 25 yards for another touchdown. That made the final score 49-33. Bob's touchdown tied the league record for most scores on interceptions by one team in one game—three.

I remember some of what went on that day. Lots of the rest has been told to me. One of my teammates, Ron Billingsley, and I collided early in the game. I was dizzy and had a cut above one eye, so they took me out. I recall our team doctor, Gary Freeman, putting about six stitches into the cut. I remember Allen Aldridge and Linzy Cole picking me up after the second touchdown. There's a bunch I've forgotten. I couldn't tune into everything after the head blow.

It was a big win for us. It closed our season with three straight wins. I doubt there were any hard feelings on the other side after we came from so far back to win it. John and I

I took off after the ball, caught it and ran 35 yards for a touchdown. Nobody was close enough to touch me.

didn't see each other again until we made the Pro Bowl a few years later. He was with Los Angeles then. I was with Washington. We sat down and had a good laugh about the interceptions.

Sid Gillman was the coach of the Chargers in 1971. When he came to the Oilers in 1973, one of the first things he did was trade me. I don't feel my day in 1971 made him dislike me. I'm told he's not that type of person.

I'm convinced that day against the Chargers helped my career. You hear coaches talk about steady play, and how a defensive back who covers well is doing a great job even if he never intercepts a pass. They

say he gets no interceptions because quarterbacks won't throw on him.

No matter how much is said on the subject, I think interceptions build a reputation. Coaches seem to like men who come through with big plays. The coaches put a label on you and remember you.

Looking back on that day, I remember thinking, "This is so easy." I was wrong. I didn't make a single interception the next year, 1972, after getting 25 my first five seasons. And after those nine touchdowns in those five seasons, including the two on consecutive plays, I never had another one.

—*As told to Hal Lundren*

Washington Redskins' defensive back **Ken Houston** (27) knocks away a pass intended for San Francisco 49er O.J. Simpson (32) in a 1978 game. Houston, the NFL's premier strong safety of the 1970s, joined the Houston Oilers in 1967. He was traded to Washington in 1973. Houston played in 11 Pro Bowls before retiring after the 1980 season. He entered the Pro Football Hall of Fame in 1986.

Playing in the NFL is exciting; something different always happens. Things could have been more exciting during the years

**DECEMBER 31, 1989
PITTSBURGH STEELERS 26, HOUSTON OILERS 23
ASTRODOME, HOUSTON, TEXAS**

SCORING

PIT	7	3	3	10	3	**26**
HOU	0	6	3	14	0	**23**

PIT Worley, 9-yard run (Anderson kick)
HOU Zendejas, 26-yard field goal
HOU Zendejas, 35-yard field goal
PIT Anderson, 25-yard field goal
HOU Zendejas, 26-yard field goal
PIT Anderson, 30-yard field goal
PIT Anderson, 48-yard field goal
HOU Givins, 18-yard pass from Moon (Zendejas kick)
HOU Givins, 9-yard pass from Moon (Zendejas kick)
PIT Hoge, 2-yard run (Anderson kick)
PIT Anderson, 50-yard field goal

TEAM STATISTICS	PIT	HOU
First Downs	17	22
Rushes-Yards	30-177	25-65
Passing Yards	112	315
Passes	15-33-0	29-48-0
Punts-Average	6-25.0	4-33.0
Fumbles-Lost	1-1	3-2
Penalties-Yards	5-40	8-45

INDIVIDUAL STATISTICS
Rushing
PIT Hoge 17 rushes for 100 yards; Worley 11-54; Stone 1-22; Brister 1-1
HOU Pinkett 8-26; White 7-13; Moon 3-12; Rozier 5-12; Highsmith 2-2
Passing
PIT Brister 15 completions, 33 attempts, 177 yards, 0 interceptions
HOU Moon 29-48-315-0
Receiving
PIT Worley 4 receptions for 23 yards; Mularkey 3-40; Hoge 3-26; Lipps 3-24; Stock 1-7; Hill 1-7
HOU Givins 11-136; Hill 6-98; Pinkett 3-24; Highsmith 3-21; Jefferies 3-16; Duncan 2-15; Rozier 1-5

ATTENDANCE: 59,406

we were losing more games than we won, but it always was interesting nonetheless. We got that winning feeling back in 1989, though, and it made almost the entire season unforgettable. The one game that really stands out has to be the overtime victory against the Oilers in Houston in the playoffs. I'll remember that one for a long time to come.

The season began very poorly for us. We lost to Cleveland and Cincinnati and were outscored 92-10. A lot of people wrote us off at that point, and it was very frustrating because I knew we were a better team than that. The third week, we played a strong game and beat Minnesota, which boosted our morale sky-high. One win—it was amazing. Everything changes when you win; everything seems a bit better.

We played Houston twice during the season and lost both times. The first game, in Houston, was a 27-0 blowout. We couldn't focus offensively or defensively in that game, and the Oilers pretty much did what they wanted. A few weeks later we played them in Pittsburgh. We played a much better game, but they still came out on top, 23-16.

The ironic thing is that after we lost that second game to Houston, we won our last three games of the season. That set up the wild-card game against the Oilers in Houston. Actually, we had won five of our final six games, so we were seeing things fall into place.

People talk about Houston's advantage at home but we didn't pay much attention to it. We figured that it was the playoffs and anything could happen. The key was to play our best game, get the other guys to make mistakes and score some points.

The fact that we had come so far during the season helped us a great deal in preparing for the Oilers. I remember our coach, Chuck Noll, calling our season "stranger than fiction." We watched our game films and ran through our plays the week before the playoff game, and everyone seemed to have the same

feeling: We can win this game. The attitude on the squad was great. It was the playoffs, our key guys were healthy and we were peaking at the right time.

Houston was in a bit of a slump then, which may have meant more than they let on. They were blasted by Cincinnati the next to last week of the season, 61-7, and we kept hearing stories about infighting on the team. You really have to leave those things aside when you're focusing on the upcoming game, but the situation did give us something else to focus upon. Early in the season Houston was the hot team, and we were losing; now we had our confidence, and they seemed to be having problems.

Their place, the Astrodome, is loud, and the fans certainly are vocal. There was a lot of energy in the air—a lot of electricity. We had a young team, but some of the guys had been through the playoffs before, and, of course, coach Noll was a master at this sort of thing.

What the coach stressed the week prior to the playoff game was to run our plays, keep them off balance on defense and focus on our strengths. We weren't a high-scoring team, but quarterback Bubby Brister could put points on the board, and fullback Merrill Hoge was capable of breaking open plays on the ground. We weren't there to pull off a lot of trick plays. Steelers football is tough, hard-nosed football; it's meeting the other guy head on and knocking him down, getting yards and scoring points.

We scored first, which is exactly what we wanted to do. It was quiet on the field until about 10 minutes into the game, and then we moved down to about their nine or 10. Bubby handed the ball to rookie running back Tim Worley, and he went in.

Houston put in a couple of field goals in the second quarter, and Gary Anderson put one in for us to give us a 10-6 lead at the half. No one knew it then, but Gary was about to have a fantastic game—probably one that *he'll* never forget.

I think the key things we talked about in the locker room were, on offense, getting the line to open up some more holes and keeping their defensive guys pushed back. Our defensive guys were doing a great job on quarterback Warren Moon, and our secondary guys were doing a great job on their receivers. But Coach Noll kept reminding us that they were explosive and that Moon could bust open the game with two or three long passes to guys like Drew Hill, Ernest Givins and Alonzo Highsmith.

Each team had a field goal in the third, so we still had a 13-9 lead after three quarters. In the fourth quarter, though, they really turned on the juice. There aren't many quarterbacks in the league who can turn on a switch and take control of a game almost at will, but Moon is one of those guys who can. He moved them down inside our 20 a few minutes into the quarter, then hit Givins with a pass that he took in for a score. That tied the score at 16—Anderson had kicked a field goal earlier in the quarter—but standing on the sidelines, it was as if all their fans had been turned loose at once when Givins scored.

That touchdown got their offensive guys pumped up. On their next set of downs, Moon moved them inside our 10, then hit Givins again with a touchdown pass. They hadn't led all day, and that touchdown gave them a seven-point lead, 23-16.

Bubby led the offense onto the field with a lot of class and style—Steelers class and style. He had the energy flowing, and each of us felt that we could put together a scoring drive. We were just short of our 20 and needed a touchdown to tie. We had been in a similar situation when we played Houston during the 1988 season, and we went about 80 yards to win by three points with time running out. So we knew that we were capable of going 80 yards to score.

Merrill ended up with 100 yards rushing that day, and he had a couple of key runs in that drive. The guys on the offensive line knew that we had to work double time to get the job done, and we really rose up to the occasion. We drove down inside their five with less than a minute to play, and Merrill went over for the tying score.

The score pumped us up and seemed to take a lot of steam out of their players. We won the toss and received the ball in overtime, but Houston stopped our drive and got the ball back. Our guys went out looking to make a big defensive play, and they did that right away. Houston had the ball on our 45, and Moon pitched the ball left to running back Lorenzo White. A bunch of our guys were right on top of him, and cornerback Ronnie Woodson popped him and forced a fumble, then recovered the ball.

We lined up for a field goal, but they

Steelers football is tough, hard-nosed football; it's meeting the other guy head on and knocking him down, getting yards and scoring points.

called time to put some pressure on Gary. But he was cool; he knew what he had to do. When he put his foot into the ball, it was so sweet to watch it sail between the goal posts. There were a few moments when the ball seemed to be traveling in slow motion. After it went through, there was a great burst of electricity from our guys. It was a great win, a very satisfying win. We lost the next week to Denver 24-23 in the AFC divisional playoffs, but I was very proud of the way we played those two games. We could have given up after the first two games of the season, but we came back to play exciting football. I'll never forget that.

—*As told to Barry Janoff*

Offensive tackle **Tunch Ilkin** played 13 seasons (1980–92) for the Pittsburgh Steelers. Born in Istanbul, Turkey, Ilkin moved to the United States with his family when he was two years old. He graduated from Indiana State University with a degree in broadcasting before being drafted by the Steelers. Ilkin was named to both the 1988 and 1989 Pro Bowl rosters. He played a single game for the 1993 Green Bay Packers before retiring to a broadcasting career.

I was in a number of so-called "big" games with Philadelphia, but the one that stands out for me was in 1979, when the Eagles

beat the Cowboys in Dallas. From a team point of view more than a personal one, that victory gave us an emotional and physical boost of confidence. After that game, every man on the team—from the coaches on down the roster—felt that if we could beat the Cowboys on their home field, then we were capable of beating any team in the league.

Prior to the victory, the Eagles hadn't won a game in Dallas in 13 years. That was a psychological block that helped to keep us from becoming the best team in the division. In our minds, Dallas was number one. They were the team that we had to aim for every year if we wanted to win our division.

Dallas had been to the Super Bowl the previous two seasons and many were picking them to go again. They had a way of improving every season, and if they lost a player to injury, or if someone didn't do well, there was another player ready to come in.

The Eagles had been through some rough seasons during the 1960s and '70s, but the previous season we were 9-7 and made the playoffs for the first time since winning the NFL championship in 1960. We lost in the opening round, but that gave our guys a taste for winning and a real desire to do better.

I remember coming into training camp for the '79 season and coach Dick Vermeil talking to us about the goals he had set for the year. One of them was to beat Dallas at least once, if not on their home field, then on ours. So by the time we played Dallas, the game had been building up for us for four months.

Actually, looking back, that might have hurt us somewhat. We had won six of our first seven games, but then lost three in a row just prior to the Dallas game. We were 6-4, and with Dallas and Washington in our division, it looked as if it would be an uphill battle just to make the playoffs.

The game was also important in other ways. It was a Monday night game and being nationally televised, which added to its aura and mystique. Everyone was ready

physically and mentally. We hadn't beaten them in Dallas for so long, but we put all that behind us.

The game started off badly for us. Roger Staubach had a great talent for being able to move his team down the field. It was still the first minute of the game when Dallas scored the opening touchdown. Some of our guys probably felt like saying, "Oh, no, here we go one more time." It could have been a long day for us.

The important thing is that we didn't give up; we didn't roll over for Dallas. We came right back and put pressure on their defense. The turning point came when we attempted a long field goal and missed. But the Cowboys were called offside, so instead of it being fourth-and-six it became fourth-and-one. Coach Vermeil decided to go for the first down.

We were on their 32. We called for a play-action fake, which started off with a fake handoff to one of our backs. Instead, I threw a pass to Harold Carmichael, which he ran in for the touchdown. It was 7-7 following the conversion, which helped to swing the momentum in our favor.

After the touchdown, I could see a definite change in our team. We loosened up a bit and got down to our game plan. Unfortunately, things didn't exactly go according to plan. Their defensive line broke through and sacked me. I injured my wrist and had to be taken into the locker room for X-rays. Our backup quarterback was John Walton, who had seen limited action. But he came in and threw a touchdown pass to Charlie Smith. After that, Tony Franklin kicked a field goal to give us a 17-7 lead at the half. I'm sorry I missed seeing that field goal, because it was something like a 58- or 59-yarder.

In the locker room at the half, a good deal of our talk dealt with improving our running game. We were a ball-control team and we liked to get a lot of yards on the ground and use up as much of the clock as possible. I think we had only 10 yards rushing in the first half, but with a 10-point lead we were able to mix things up a bit. I think we finished with 170 yards rushing for the game, so almost all of that came in the second half.

We scored another touchdown to boost

NOVEMBER 12, 1979
PHILADELPHIA EAGLES 31, DALLAS
COWBOYS 21
TEXAS STADIUM, IRVING, TEXAS

SCORING

PHI	7	10	7	7	**31**
DAL	7	0	0	14	**21**

DAL Hill, 48-yard pass from Staubach (Septien kick)
PHI Carmichael, 32-yard pass from Jaworski (Franklin kick)
PHI Smith, 29-yard pass from Walton (Franklin kick)
PHI Franklin, 59-yard field goal
PHI Carmichael, 13-yard pass from Jaworski (Franklin kick)
DAL Hill, 75-yard pass from Staubach (Septien kick)
DAL DuPree, 5-yard pass from Staubach (Septien kick)
PHI Montgomery, 37-yard run (Franklin kick)

TEAM STATISTICS

	PHI	DAL
First Downs	17	17
Rushes-Yards	38-170	27-123
Passing Yards	158	285
Passes	14-35-0	19-35-1
Punts-Average	8-39.0	7-40.6
Fumbles-Lost	0-0	2-2
Penalties-Yards	3-28	4-25

INDIVIDUAL STATISTICS
Rushing
PHI Montgomery 25 rushes for 127 yards; Harris 5-26; Giammona 4-11; Jaworski 1-4; Barnes 2-3; Campfield 1-minus 1
DAL Dorsett 13-53; Staubach 4-31; Newhouse 5-16; Laidlaw 3-12; Springs 1-6; Pearson 1-5

Passing
PHI Jaworski 12 completions, 29 attempts, 145 yards, 0 interceptions; Walton 2-6-41-0
DAL Staubach 17-28-308-0; White 2-6-14-1; Springs 0-1-0-0

Receiving
PHI Carmichael 4 receptions for 69 yards; Smith 4-54; Krepfle 1-24; Montgomery 2-19; Campfield 1-12; Harris 2-8
DAL Hill 7-213; Dorsett 7-64; Springs 2-22; Laidlaw 1-12; Drew Pearson 1-6; DuPree 1-5

ATTENDANCE: 62,417

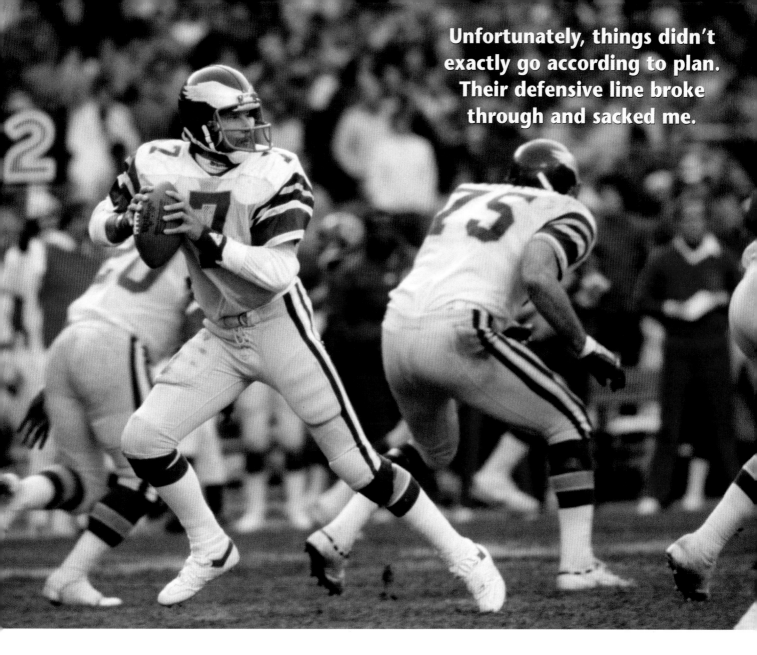

Unfortunately, things didn't exactly go according to plan. Their defensive line broke through and sacked me.

the lead to 24-7. But we weren't able to relax, because we had seen Dallas come back too many times. As it turned out, Staubach gave us a scare in the fourth quarter. Our defense was digging in, but the Cowboys seem to play on another level when they're losing and time is running out. When they go into their two-minute offense, it seems as if no team can stop them.

With less than six minutes to play, Dallas scored to make it 24-14, then scored again a couple of minutes later to make it 24-21. The fans were going crazy, and the Dallas players were getting pumped up even higher.

We got the ball back with a couple of minutes to play, and had a couple of key first downs, which enabled us to run the clock down. We thought about going long on a pass play, but stayed on the ground, since we were moving the ball so well. Finally, we

were inside their 40 with about a minute to play. We were close to field-goal range, but that would have given us only a six-point lead. Dallas still could have scored a touchdown and extra point to win.

We were on the 37 when we called a running play for Wilbert Montgomery, who went around left end, broke past their secondary and ran in for the touchdown. It was a great feeling when he scored.

If you're looking at stats, that game against Dallas wasn't my best. But the victory was important to the entire team. We gained a great deal of confidence as a team from the win, especially because everything seemed to be going against us. But we were able to take control and maintain control against one of the NFL's top teams, which is why I'll never forget that victory.

—As told to Barry Janoff

Quarterback **Ron Jaworski** had his best season in 1980, when he passed for 3,529 yards and 27 touchdowns and led the Philadelphia Eagles into Super Bowl XV. Unfortunately, the Oakland Raiders prevailed. Jaworski played three seasons (1974–76) with the Los Angeles Rams, ten years (1977–86) with the Eagles and single campaigns with the Miami Dolphins (1988) and Kansas City Chiefs (1989). He retired with 2,187 completions that went for 28,190 yards and 179 touchdowns.

When I think back over my career, the most memorable game I played in is one that probably was unforgettable to a lot of

people. It was on a steamy night in Miami during the AFC playoffs in January 1982 that my San Diego Chargers pulled out a 41-38 win against the favored Dolphins. If you remember—and, really, who doesn't?—there were lead changes and heroics, and an overtime finish that would have been perfect for a Hollywood script.

Back then I was playing with one of the greatest offenses ever assembled. Our official name was Chargers, but everyone called us "Air Coryell" in honor of our coach, Don Coryell. He was the architect of our offense. Underneath that mean frown was a great coach and one of the greatest offensive minds the game has ever known. He was a real player's coach.

Quarterback Dan Fouts was the trigger man. He had a quick delivery, and he could really gun it in there when he had to. In the backfield we had guys like Chuck Muncie and James Brooks. Our tight end was Kellen Winslow, an All-Pro; he was backed up by a couple of young, talented guys, Pete Holohan and Eric Sievers. Alongside me at wide receiver was Wes Chandler. Even our offensive line—with guys like tackle Russ Washington, center Don Macek and guard Ed White—was awesome.

We were a team that truly was together, a very cohesive group, and that's really a credit to Coryell. He had us believing we could score every time we got the ball. Before we went into a game, we were guessing how many *plays* it would take us to score, not how many *possessions* or how many *quarters*. As a group, I would say our offensive players were the best of all time.

The 1981 regular season was great for us. In the opener against the Cleveland Browns, I had a career-high 191 receiving yards. In week two, I had 166 receiving yards against the Detroit Lions. We ended up winning the AFC West for the third straight year.

We drew the Dolphins in the first round of the playoffs. They'd enjoyed a pretty good

season themselves—in fact, they'd gone 11-4-1 to our 10-6.

The game was so exciting that it went by like a blur. But I'll always remember the heat and humidity of that night, and, more important, how we raced out to a 24-0 lead after the first quarter and thought we were in line for a rout.

How wrong we were. The turning point for the Dolphins was when they lifted quarterback David Woodley and put in Don Strock. He really sparked their passing game, getting the ball to guys like Nat Moore and Duriel Harris. You've got to give Strock credit: He pitched them right back into the game.

Miami made it a close game late in the second quarter on a hook-and-lateral play. Strock threw downfield to Harris; out of nowhere, Harris pitched the ball to running back Tony Nathan, who was streaking down the sideline. No one in the building saw that play coming—it was one of the greatest gimmick plays I've ever seen. Nathan carried the lateral 25 yards into the end zone, and suddenly we were sitting in the locker room with only a seven-point lead.

The second half was even more of a blur than the first. The teams just went back and forth scoring touchdowns. The heat on the field really was taking its toll on the defenses. Neither defense had much of a chance in the second half, especially the secondaries. I remember being able to get open on just about every play.

I'll never forget the magic Fouts and Winslow had between them that night. Winslow had to leave the field from exhaustion a few times, but he kept coming back. He was just heroic. Not only did he have a divisional-playoff–record 13 receptions, but he blocked an Uwe von Schamann 43-yard field-goal attempt with four seconds left in regulation to force overtime. Fouts also had an awesome game. Inside the huddle, you could tell by the look in his eyes that he was thriving on the competition. He was not going to let us lose that game.

My big moment came in overtime. The Dolphins had a two-deep rotation in the secondary. My job was to read it and find some room in the middle. Danny hit me

JANUARY 2, 1982
SAN DIEGO CHARGERS 41, MIAMI DOLPHINS 38
ORANGE BOWL, MIAMI, FLORIDA

SCORING

SD	24	0	7	7	3	**41**
MIA	0	17	14	7	0	**38**

SD	Benirschke, 32-yard field goal
SD	Chandler, 56-yard punt return (Benirschke kick)
SD	Muncie, 1-yard run (Benirschke kick)
SD	Brooks, 8-yard pass from Fouts (Benirschke kick)
MIA	von Schamann, 34-yard field goal
MIA	Rose, 1-yard pass from Strock (von Schamann kick)
MIA	Nathan, 40-yard pass from Strock (von Schamann kick)
MIA	Rose, 15-yard pass from Strock (von Schamann kick)
SD	Winslow, 25-yard pass from Fouts (Benirschke kick)
MIA	Hardy, 50-yard pass from Strock (von Schamann kick)
MIA	Nathan, 12-yard run (von Schamann kick)
SD	Brooks, 9-yard pass from Fouts (Benirschke kick)
SD	Benirschke, 29-yard field goal

TEAM STATISTICS

	SD	MIA
First Downs	33	25
Rushes-Yards	29-149	28-78
Passing Yards	433	417
Passes	33-54-1	30-47-2
Punts-Average	4-40.3	5-42.0
Fumbles-Lost	3-3	2-1
Penalties-Yards	8-45	7-44

INDIVIDUAL STATISTICS
Rushing
SD   Muncie 24 rushes for 120 yards; Brooks 3-19; Fouts 2-10
MIA   Nathan 14-48; Woodley 1-10; Hill 3-8; Vigorito 1-6; Franklin 9-6

Passing
SD   Fouts 33 completions, 53 attempts, 433 yards, 1 interception; Muncie 0-1-0-0
MIA   Strock 28-42-397-1; Woodley 2-5-20-1

Receiving
SD   Winslow 13 receptions for 166 yards; Joiner 7-108; Chandler 6-106; Brooks 4-31; Muncie 2-5; Scales 1-17
MIA   Nathan 8-108; Harris 6-106; Hardy 5-89; Rose 4-37; Cefalo 3-62; Vigorito 2-12; Hill 2-3

ATTENDANCE: 73,735

We raced out to a 24-0 lead after the first quarter and thought we were in line for a rout. How wrong we were.

perfectly around Miami's 10-yard line. I was worried about fumbling down there, so I immediately ran to get out of bounds. Rolf Benirschke came in and ended the game with a 29-yard field goal. From a team standpoint, it was the game I'll never forget.

From a personal standpoint, there's another game. It came in the final week of the 1980 season. Beat the Denver Broncos, and we win the AFC West and make the playoffs; lose, and we're watching the postseason from home. We hadn't made the playoffs in some time, so it was an especially big game.

We went into the game banged up at wide receiver. John Jefferson, a true star, was out, as were a few others. I ended up getting knocked out of the game twice. The first time, I pulled

a muscle in my thigh; I went back into the locker room, the trainers worked on my leg, and I came back out. A few plays later, I got hit by Broncos linebacker Tom Jackson and required 12 stitches in my chin. But, again, I had to keep playing because we had so few receivers.

Eventually, I caught a fourth-quarter touchdown pass to win the game. The play was called "Charlie 10 flat go": I had to run a quick slant, make another move outside, and then hit the post seam. Fouts just hit me perfectly. To get knocked out of the game twice, and get up to score the touchdown that won the game and sent us to the playoffs, truly was an amazing moment.

—As told to Chuck O'Donnell

When wide receiver **Charlie Joiner** retired after the 1986 season, he had amassed 750 career receptions (a league record, since broken) for 12,146 yards and 65 touchdowns. Joiner made his NFL debut with the Houston Oilers in 1969 out of Grambling State. Traded to the Cincinnati Bengals midway through the 1972 season, he blossomed after joining the San Diego Chargers in 1976. Joiner appeared in three Pro Bowls over the next five campaigns and was inducted into the Pro Football Hall of Fame in 1996.

1977 NFC DIVISIONAL PLAYOFF GAME

I was fortunate during my career with the Dallas Cowboys to have played in a number of unforgettable games. But on a

personal level, as far as performance goes, the one that really stands out for me was a playoff victory over the Chicago Bears in 1977.

Dallas went on to win the Super Bowl that season and I remember that win and a few others as being emotionally memorable. But as I said, based on my performance, that game against the Bears is the one I won't forget. Everything seemed to come together for me that day, both mentally and physically. Looking back, I wish I could have played every game in my career the same way I played that one.

In 1975 we had a good team and we went to the Super Bowl. But Pittsburgh's team that year was really tough and they just beat us by four points, 21-17.

The next season a lot of people were picking us to go all the way, and we really felt like we could, too. We won our division during the season, which was something we hadn't done for a couple of years. Actually, I think that was the first time we had come in first in the division since I joined the team. So we were feeling good about the playoffs because of that.

This is something that's obvious to anyone who knows the NFL, but other teams really get hyped up when they play the Cowboys. I mean, they *really* wanted to beat us. And that was good, in a way, because it kept us on our toes.

Anyway, we had to face Los Angeles in the 1976 divisional playoffs in Dallas. And they came in and beat us by a couple of points! I don't think we were looking past them and on to the NFC championship; we always played—or we tried to play—one game at a time. They simply beat us.

This is all leading up to the 1977 season, because we came in more determined than ever to win the Super Bowl. We won our division again and met Chicago in the divisionals, also at our home stadium.

I don't think Chicago had beaten Dallas since 1971. But the Bears got in as a wild-card team and we weren't about to take them

lightly, mainly because of a guy on their team named Walter Payton. I'd seen him run over and through and around the best defenses. But I was determined that he wasn't going to do that to us.

The reason this game stands out for me is because of the stats I had that day: 14 unassisted tackles, four quarterback traps, three quarterback sacks and three blocked passes. It seemed like I couldn't do anything wrong. I was just making all the right moves and doing all the right things, like I had just read a textbook on how to play defensive end and was able to follow all the instructions exactly as they had been written. It was just a great physical performance for me.

Their quarterback, Bob Avellini, wasn't the best of scramblers and we kept forcing him out of the pocket. During the game their offensive line tried double- and triple-teaming me, but I was still able to do my job.

I saw my role with the Cowboys as being a leader. I like my actions to speak for themselves. So when I put an effort into doing something I like to feel that my actions will lead others into performing better. And that game I put in a great deal of effort.

We won that game 37-7 and I like to feel it was the defense that spurred on the offense. In fact, we held Chicago without a touchdown until about midway through the last quarter, while our offense was scoring in every quarter. The turning point, if there was one, came in the first quarter when we held Chicago to something like eight or nine plays from scrimmage while our offense was scoring a touchdown on a 75- or 80-yard drive. We pretty much took command right there.

Roger Staubach was having a good day for us at quarterback, though I've seen him have much better days. Tony Dorsett had a couple of touchdowns for us rushing. I think our offensive unit ended up with almost 400 yards and a lot of that was in the first half. We were up by 17 points at the half and by 34 after three, so we really were in control of things.

I was proud of my performance that day, even though it was a blowout, and some of the other guys had good games as well. Tony had like 85 yards rushing, Robert Newhouse had about 80 and Charlie Waters had three

---

DECEMBER 24, 1977
DALLAS COWBOYS 37, CHICAGO BEARS 7
TEXAS STADIUM, IRVING, TEXAS

SCORING

DAL	7	10	17	3	**37**
CHI	0	0	0	7	**7**

DAL Dennison, 2-yard run (Herrera kick)
DAL DuPree, 28-yard pass from Staubach (Herrera kick)
DAL Herrera, 21-yard field goal
DAL Dorsett, 22-yard run (Herrera kick)
DAL Herrera, 31-yard field goal
DAL Dorsett, 7-yard run (Herrera kick)
DAL Herrera, 27-yard field goal
CHI Schubert, 34-yard pass from Avellini (Thomas kick)

TEAM STATISTICS	CHI	DAL
First Downs	15	20
Rushes-Yards	27-81	48-233
Passing Yards	143	132
Passes	15-25-4	8-13-1
Punts-Average	6-43.4	3-37.0
Fumbles-Lost	3-3	2-2
Penalties-Yards	4-43	3-35

INDIVIDUAL STATISTICS
Rushing
CHI Payton 19 rushes for 60 yards; Harper 5-11; Earl 2-6; Avellini 1-4
DAL Dorsett 17-85; Newhouse 16-80; Dennison 8-40; Staubach 4-25; Brinson 3-3

Passing
CHI Avellini 15 completions, 25 attempts, 177 yards, 4 interceptions
DAL Staubach 8-13-134-1

Receiving
CHI Schubert 5 receptions for 69 yards; Payton 3-33; Scott 3-29; Latta 2-25; Earl 1-15; Latta 1-6
DAL D. Pearson 2-38; Dorsett 2-37; DuPree 1-28; Newhouse 1-13; Richards 1-12; Brinson 1-6

ATTENDANCE: 62,920

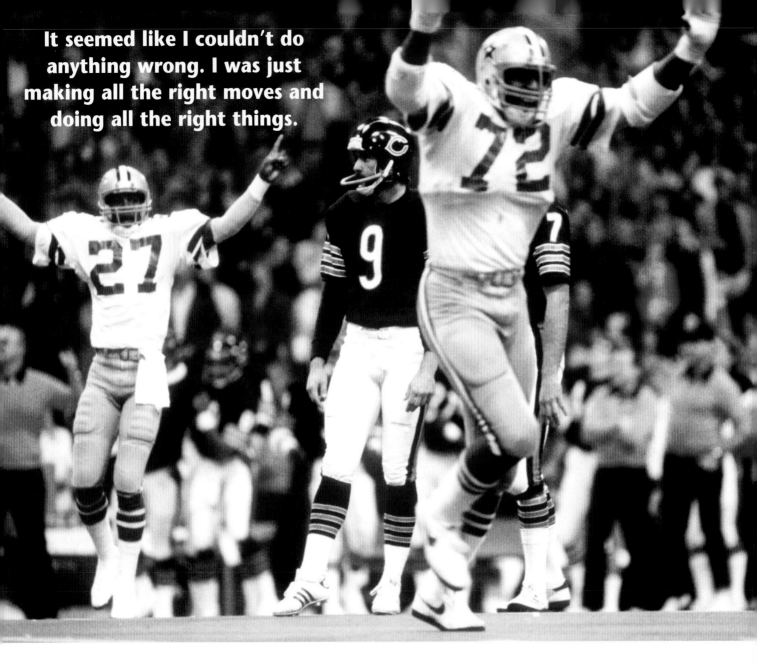

It seemed like I couldn't do anything wrong. I was just making all the right moves and doing all the right things.

interceptions, which I think was a record for a playoff game.

No one received any extra pats on the back after the game, but we all knew we had done well. It wasn't until later that I looked back and thought that it was one of the best games I'd ever played.

The next week we played Minnesota for the NFC title. I was ready to have another good game and I did, as it turned out, with eight solo tackles and four assists. I think our defense stopped the Vikings for just 60 yards rushing with no touchdowns. We won that game 23-6 and then went on to beat Denver in Super Bowl XII.

The Chicago game probably was my best performance, but the one that stands out as far as emotions go was the "Hail Mary" game against Minnesota during the 1975 playoffs.

We were in Minnesota and trailing 14-10 with less than half a minute to play when Staubach tossed a pass toward the end zone that Drew Pearson caught with defenders hanging all over him.

I remember standing on the sidelines and it was cold and we were losing. And I was thinking, "Well, that's it for this season." But when Drew caught the pass for the winning touchdown it was like it suddenly got 50 degrees warmer. Unfortunately, that was the year we lost to Pittsburgh in the Super Bowl, but that win over the Vikes was one I'll never forget. Emotionally, that ranks as the best game I've been in. But for a physical performance, the playoff win against Chicago is my most memorable experience.

—*As told to Barry Janoff*

Six-foot-nine, 265-pound defensive end **Ed "Too Tall" Jones** (72), above, was not only big, but also fast. Jones menaced opposing quarterbacks for 15 seasons (1974–89) with the Dallas Cowboys. Drafted number one out of Tennessee State, where the Tigers lost only one game in his three seasons with them, Jones played in three Pro Bowls and three Super Bowls, winning one title ring. He retired after 224 games, with 57.5 recorded sacks and countless passes swatted down.

SONNY JURGENSEN

Not all philosophers would make good quarterbacks, but every good quarterback I ever met somehow developed a pretty wide

OCTOBER 29, 1961
PHILADELPHIA EAGLES 27, WASHINGTON
REDSKINS 24
D.C. STADIUM, WASHINGTON, D.C.

SCORING

PHI	7	7	3	10	**27**
WAS	7	10	0	7	**24**

WAS Horner, 3-yard pass from Snead (Aveni kick)
PHI Retzlaff, 46-yard pass from Jurgensen (Walston kick)
WAS Bosseler, 3-yard run (Aveni kick)
WAS Aveni, 52-yard field goal
PHI Tetzlaff, 11-yard pass from Jurgensen (Walston kick)
PHI Walston, 13-yard field goal
PHI Walston, 33-yard field goal
WAS Cunningham, 7-yard pass from Snead (Aveni kick)
PHI McDonald, 41-yard pass from Jurgensen (Walston kick)

TEAM STATISTICS	PHI	WAS
First Downs	19	17
Rushes-Yards	15-12	28-77
Passing Yards	413	258
Passes	27-41-1	21-31-2
Punts-Average	3-50.0	4-36.0
Fumbles-Lost	3-2	1-1
Penalties-Yards	3-45	9-95

INDIVIDUAL STATISTICS
Rushing
PHI Peaks 5 rushes for minus 8 yards; Barnes 6-3; Jurgensen 2-minus 5; Brown 2-minus 2
WAS Bosseler 11-39; Horner 7-7; Snead 6-1; James 1-29; Cunningham 1-1; Sommer 2-0
Passing
PHI Jurgensen 27 completions, 41 attempts, 436 yards, 1 interception
WAS Snead 21-31-296-2
Receiving
PHI Barner 3 receptions for 32 yards; Walston 4-53; Retslaff 7-125; McDonald 7-141; Peaks 4-68; Brown 1-12; Lucas 1-5
WAS Osborne 2-19; Horner 4-48; Dugan 6-82; James 3-82; Anderson 2-28; Bosseler 3-30; Cunningham 1-7

ATTENDANCE: 31,066

philosophical streak. You have to learn to live with those fumbles and interceptions, your own mistakes and everyone else's. You have to learn to take victory in stride and defeat without losing your optimism.

Speaking personally, I suppose that I, in a way, have the reputation of being maybe a little more philosophical than most quarterbacks. Well, chalk that up to the hard, adventurous football life I've led, and maybe that's why it's kind of hard to pin me down on that *one* game I'll never forget.

If pressed real close, maybe I'd pick two games, two games that we won in the last couple of seconds.

The first was a game we played way back in 1961. I was with the Philadelphia Eagles then and we were playing the Washington Redskins. The Eagles were one great team, the defending world champions of professional football. The season before we defeated the Green Bay Packers, 17-13, to win the crown. Norm Van Brocklin was our quarterback that year, but he retired and I took over.

We had a 5-1 record going into that game and had great ambitions of winning our second straight championship. It was also a game that started to make a philosopher out of me.

We seemed to be coming from behind all day. They scored, then we scored. Then we fumbled on our own 24 to hand them an easy touchdown, and they added a field goal before Pete Retzlaff got free for his second touchdown catch.

As I remember that game now, we had almost no ground game. I think we wound up with minus rushing yardage. That's something that does things to a quarterback's philosophy too. So I wound up, if you'll pardon the pun, and just kept throwing most of the time.

Bobby Walston kicked a couple of field goals in the second half and his second one gave us our first lead, 20-17 late in the fourth

quarter. I was praying for the defense to hold, but with less than a minute to play Norm Snead threw a touchdown pass.

When you're down with only seconds to play you have to hope beyond hope for a long kickoff return. But the Skins kicked it almost out of the end zone, so there we were with 80 yards to go and about 50 seconds to do it in.

But like I said, you have to have confidence and optimism. I went into that huddle with the attitude that we had all the time in the world. The rest of the team must have believed me because we went right to work.

I hit Walston with two straight to move the ball down to the Redskins' 41—bang, bang—just like that. I missed the next one and now we were down to just about 20 seconds to play. I knew I needed one more completion for a good shot at a tying field goal, but figured I had enough time to still go for the win.

Tommy McDonald, a fiery little competitor out of Oklahoma, thought we could still do it too. So with that kind of positive thinking, we did it.

Tommy said they were playing him tight to the outside so he ran a slant toward the post to draw the cornerback and safety man over and then broke quickly back toward the flag. I just laid it up there and let him run under it. He caught it around the 10 and would have run through a wall to get it into the end zone, and there were only something like 13 seconds remaining on the clock when the referee threw up his hands.

That was one big game because it was an important game and anytime you pull one out in the closing seconds it's a big thrill. That's what we did to Dallas one year, too.

This time I was playing with the Washington Redskins. It was the second-to-last game of the 1966 season. It was a crazy season for us. The week before we beat the New York Giants, 72-41, to set all kinds of records for scoring. But the previous game, we could score only three points against the Cleveland Browns.

Just a couple of weeks before that, the Cowboys beat us 31-30. They drove from their own three-yard line to our 13 after all their time-outs had been used up and then

I just laid it up there and let him run under it. He caught it around the 10 and would have run through a wall to get it into the end zone.

kicked a field goal for the victory. So we had some evening up to do.

We went into the fourth quarter all tied up at 17 apiece. Then it all broke loose. Dane Reeves broke free on a run of almost 70 yards to put them on top. We came right back and I hit Jerry Smith with a pass for the tying touchdown.

Dallas brought it right back and took the lead on a short run by Don Perkins. Again, confidence and optimism paid off and I hit Charley Taylor with a bomb of about 65 yards to tie the score again.

Our defense came through and stopped the Cowboys, who had to punt with just a couple of minutes left to play. I spread everybody out and gave the ball to A.D. Whitfield a couple of times. Whitfield was a former Cowboy and all that stuff you hear

about how guys like to show up the team that traded them—well, you can believe it.

A few runs by Whitfield, a couple of passes and we had good field position. Running the ball had forced the Cowboys to use up all three of their time-outs and now we had it down close to their 20.

I just took my time standing there watching that clock run down second by second and talking to the referee, telling him what a terrible position I'd be in if he was giving me bad information on the time remaining. When it got down to eight seconds I called time-out. In came Charlie Gogolak and he kicked it right through.

That, I figured, would give the Cowboys something to philosophize over.

—As told to Bob Billings

Quarterback **Sonny Jurgensen** entered the Pro Football Hall of Fame after passing for more than 1,000 yards in 11 of his 18 NFL campaigns (1957–74). He played his first seven seasons for the Philadelphia Eagles before he was dealt to the Washington Redskins in 1964. Jurgensen's best season came in 1967, when he completed 288 passes for 3,747 yards and 31 touchdowns. He surpassed 3,000 yards five different years and, in total, tallied 2,433 completions for 32,224 yards and 255 touchdowns.

I remember playing in a lot of exciting games—wins as well as losses—but my best game as a pro was against the Houston

SEPTEMBER 24, 1989
BUFFALO BILLS 47, HOUSTON OILERS 41
ASTRODOME, HOUSTON, TEXAS

SCORING

BUF	10	10	7	14	6	**47**
HOU	7	3	14	17	0	**41**

BUF   Norwood, 43-yard field goal
HOU   Moon, 1-yard run (Zendejas kick)
BUF   Thomas, 6-yard pass from Kelly (Norwood kick)
BUF   Norwood, 26-yard field goal
HOU   Zendejas, 26-yard field goal
BUF   Kelso, 76-yard blocked field goal return (Norwood kick)
BUF   Beebe, 63-yard pass from Kelly (Norwood kick)
HOU   Highsmith, 4-yard run (Zendejas kick)
HOU   Dishman, 7-yard blocked punt return (Zendejas kick)
BUF   Reed, 78-yard pass from Kelly (Norwood kick)
HOU   Givins, 26-yard pass from Moon (Zendejas kick)
HOU   White, 1-yard run (Zendejas kick)
BUF   Thomas, 26-yard pass from Kelly (Norwood kick)
HOU   Zendejas, 52-yard field goal
BUF   Reed, 28-yard pass from Kelly

TEAM STATISTICS	BUF	HOU
First Downs	23	33
Rushes-Yards	24-112	39-131
Passing Yards	337	311
Passes	17-29-1	28-42-2
Punts-Average	3-28.0	1-55.0
Fumbles-Lost	1-0	1-0
Penalties-Yards	13-84	10-59

INDIVIDUAL STATISTICS

Rushing
BUF   Thomas 12 rushes for 58 yards; Kelly 3-43; Kinnebrew 9-11
HOU   Highsmith 12-58; Moon 5-36; Pinkett 12-26; White 8-11

Passing
BUF   Kelly 17 completions, 29 attempts, 363 yards, 1 interception
HOU   Moon 28-42-338-2

Receiving
BUF   Reed 5 receptions for 135 yards; Johnson 5-86; Thomas 3-37; Metzelaars 2-36; Beebe 1-63; McKeller 1-6
HOU   Duncan 6-69; Jeffires 6-57; Givins 4-65; Highsmith 4-47; Hill 3-58; Pinkett 2-13; Harris 1-13; White 1-11; Mrosko 1-5

ATTENDANCE: 57,278

Oilers in 1989. It was the third game of the season and we had to travel to Houston, where the Oilers are always tough. But we beat them 47-41 in overtime, which said a lot to me about the team and about our players.

The key for us coming into the season was to play tough, aggressive football. We won the division in 1988 and beat Houston in the opening round of the playoffs, but then we lost to Cincinnati in the AFC Championship Game, 21-10. A lot of the guys felt that we really didn't represent ourselves and the team properly. The Bengals had a good team, but we knew we were capable of playing better than we had.

We wanted to come out strong early in 1989 to establish ourselves. We beat the Dolphins in Miami in the first week, but lost at home to Denver in the second week. That loss hurt more than many others because it was our home opener—the fans were revved up, and the team was ready to play well. We came up flat, though.

In the week prior to the Houston game, the talk among the players was that we wouldn't give up, that we would play solid football from start to finish. We watched game films and paid attention to their "special" tactics. We knew Houston would play a tough game, but we weren't about to be intimidated. If any rough stuff happened, we could handle ourselves—and give it out as well as take it.

I played my first two professional seasons in Houston with the USFL Gamblers. Of course, the fans who were cheering me on when I played there and led the team to some success were now booing me because I was on the opposing side. The Astrodome is a tough place to play, and a lot of that has to do with the fans there.

We opened up the scoring with a field goal by Scott Norwood from just inside the 50. They scored a touchdown when Warren Moon drove them down to about our one and then ran the ball in on a quarterback keeper. We put together a solid drive in the

last couple of minutes of the quarter, and Thurman Thomas ran a short out route and caught a six-yard pass for our first touchdown.

It was too early at that point to feel that anything special was happening, but I could tell that it was going to be a high-scoring game rather than a defensive game. The touch on the ball felt right, and our guys were running their plays.

The second quarter was relatively quiet, with just a couple of field goals. But late in the quarter, they were on about our 25 with time running out. They were lined up for a field goal, but someone on our defensive line blocked the kick. Mark Kelso picked up the ball and ran it back for a touchdown with no time showing on the clock.

That play got us hyped up in the locker room during the half. I knew that they would come out and put some points on the board, especially with Warren throwing passes. I think the feeling was that if we could maintain the type of offensive and defensive pressure we had been applying during the first half, we would come out with a win.

We talked about running deep patterns right away to catch their defense a step or two behind. A few minutes into the quarter, we were about on our 40, and I sent Don Beebe on a slant pattern. He got behind his defensive man—he was a rookie so there was only single coverage on him—and I hit him with a pass that ended up going about 60 yards for a touchdown.

We had a 17-point lead, but they went on a drive that put them inside our five. They went in on the ground from there. Then, with less than a minute to play in the quarter, we had to punt from deep in our territory, from inside the 10. One of their guys blocked the punt and ran it in.

We took the opening kickoff, and on the first play we sent Andre Reed long. He is one of the fastest receivers I've ever seen. He split the defense, opened up the secondary and caught a bomb that went for a 78-yard pass play.

Moon put together back-to-back drives after that on which they scored twice—one on a pass to Ernest Givins, and then on a long drive

If any rough stuff happened, we could handle ourselves—and give it out as well as take it.

that went down to our one, where Lorenzo White ran it in. We were down 38-34 at that point, and their players and fans must have felt as if they had the momentum. But we came back to take the lead when I hit Thomas with a touchdown pass from about the 25.

We were up by three with less than a minute to play, but they had moved to about midfield, then lined up for a field goal. I was on the sidelines with our offensive guys and the coaches, and we all watched the ball take off and head straight through the uprights. When something like that happens, all you can do for the moment is take a deep breath and get ready to take the field again.

Houston won the toss and elected to receive in overtime. Moon moved them to about our 40, where Tony Zendejas went in to

try for the game-winning field goal. But Ray Bentley blocked it. However, we got called for being offside, and Zendejas had another shot from five yards closer. This time his kick went wide left, and we got the ball back.

Before our offensive guys ran out, we got together and said, "No mistakes. No mistakes." We moved the ball down inside their 30. Reed was double-covered, as he had been for most of the game, but he told me in the huddle that he felt he could split the defense as he had done before. He caught the pass, broke a tackle and went in for the winning touchdown.

That was a great game because we scored so many points when we had to. We really got the job done.

—As told to Barry Janoff

Pro Football Hall of Fame quarterback **Jim Kelly** led the Buffalo Bills to four Super Bowls (1990–93) without winning. After two stellar seasons with the USFL's Houston Gamblers, Kelly began his 11-season (1986–96) NFL career with the Bills. He went to his first of four Pro Bowls in 1987. In 1991, Kelly hit personal bests when he threw 304 completions for 3,844 yards and 33 touchdowns, taking the Bills to a second consecutive 13-3 season. He retired with 2,874 career completions for 35,467 yards and 237 touchdowns.

The Falcons had a good season in 1991, one of the best since I'd joined the team in 1978. We were very focused going into the

campaign—we knew we had the personnel to get the job done, and we were determined to show that we could play with the top teams in the league.

The four years before that were very dry. We hadn't won more than five games in any of those seasons, and there were times when I knew that we were better than 3-13 or 5-11. So it got very frustrating.

Going into 1991, there was just a different feeling on the team, as if we knew that we had the right guys in the right places to get things moving. It wasn't as if we were going to blow out every other team, but we knew that if we could win nine or 10 games we had a good shot at making the playoffs.

We were in a very tough division—San Francisco, New Orleans and Los Angeles were solid teams with top coaches. The Rams didn't have a good season overall in 1991, but you can't take them for granted. Part of the coaches' plan—coach Jerry Glanville and the others—was to have a solid showing in our division. If we could go 4-2 or 5-1, we had a good shot at winning four or five games among our other 10.

As it turned out, we won five of the six games in our division, and most of those stand out as memorable games for me. We beat the Saints in New Orleans, and we took both games against the 49ers. The first victory is the one that really stands out because it was in San Francisco, and it came at a time when we hadn't proved what we could do, either to ourselves or to the rest of the league. Beating the 49ers told the other teams that they had to respect us because we respected ourselves.

That first game against San Francisco was the sixth game of the season, and it came a week after we had been rocked at home by New Orleans, 27-6. We were 2-3 at that point, and a loss would have put us in a deep hole. But we put together a strong game, beat them 39-34 and went 8-3 the rest of the season to earn a spot in the playoffs.

As an offensive lineman, I wanted to accomplish two key things in that game: protect our quarterback, Chris Miller, and open up holes for our backs. The offensive line did both things that day—Chris was not sacked even once, and Steve Broussard rushed for over 100 yards.

Teams playing us knew enough about our game plan and about the quality of our receivers to realize that we were going to throw the ball a lot. But we knew going in that if we could establish a ground game, it would keep San Francisco's defense honest. They would have to respect our running game, and that would enable our receivers—guys like Andre Rison and Michael Haynes—to have a bit more room to roam.

None of this planning would have meant anything if we couldn't make it work on the field. Chris came out throwing, and we were inside San Francisco's 30 right away. Then he connected with Michael for our first touchdown.

Our defensive guys shut down 49ers quarterback Steve Young, and about two minutes later we were inside the San Francisco 10. This time, Chris and Andre hooked up for a touchdown that gave us a 14-0 lead less than five minutes into the game.

Our offensive and defensive guys were pumped up at that point. But, being a veteran of so many battles, I knew that it was far too early to put this one in the win column, especially against an explosive team such as San Francisco. But we kept our momentum going, and we had another solid drive late in the opening quarter that carried over into the second quarter. Norm Johnson kicked a field goal a few seconds into the second quarter, putting us up 17-0.

Norm had a great day—I think he had four field goals—including two in the fourth quarter when San Francisco had battled all the way back to take the lead. He also had three extra points, so he accounted for 15 points that day.

San Francisco's defense ran a lot of blitzes at us, using guys from their secondary, but our offensive line did a great job to nullify

---

OCTOBER 13, 1991
ATLANTA FALCONS 39, SAN FRANCISCO 49ERS 34
ATLANTA-FULTON COUNTY STADIUM, ATLANTA, GEORGIA

SCORING

ATL	14	6	13	6	**39**
SF	0	14	13	7	**34**

ATL	Haynes, 27-yard pass from Miller (Johnson kick)
ATL	Rison, 7-yard pass from Miller (Johnson kick)
ATL	Johnson, 29-yard field goal
SF	Young, 6-yard run (Cofer kick)
ATL	Johnson, 43-yard field goal
SF	Taylor, 54-yard pass from Young (Cofer kick)
SF	Rice, 57-yard pass from Young (kick failed)
ATL	Sanders, 100-yard kickoff return (Johnson kick)
SF	Sydney, 5-yard run (Cofer kick)
ATL	Rison, 1-yard pass from Miller (snap fumbled, no PAT)
SF	Young, 7-yard run (Cofer kick)
ATL	Johnson, 44-yard field goal
ATL	Johnson, 30-yard field goal

TEAM STATISTICS

	SF	ATL
First Downs	24	19
Rushes-Yards	25-94	27-160
Passing Yards	348	208
Passes	22-38-3	16-28-0
Punts-Average	2-31.0	2-47.0
Fumbles-Lost	3-1	1-0
Penalties-Yards	5-35	7-62

INDIVIDUAL STATISTICS

Rushing

SF	Young 11 rushes for 68 yards; Henderson 7-12; Rathman 3-11; Carter 1-6; Sydney 3-minus 3
ATL	Broussard 10-104; Pegram 10-35; Chaffey 3-11; Rozier 2-9; Miller 2-1

Passing

SF	Young 22 completions, 38 attempts, 348 yards, 3 interceptions
ATL	Miller 16-28-208-0

Receiving

SF	Rice 7 receptions for 138 yards; Taylor 3-80; Williams 3-46; Sydney 3-12; Sherrard 2-38; Rathman 2-13; Beach 1-20; Carter 1-1
ATL	Rison 6-69; Haynes 5-94; Pritchard 3-37; Colling 1-9; Pegram 1-minus 1

ATTENDANCE: 57,343

It felt like a heavyweight fight, where the two big guys are slugging away.

that. Their offensive guys were getting fired up at this point, and Young brought them back into it by the half. He ran in for one score and connected with John Taylor on an amazing 54-yard pass play. Watching that one from the sidelines, I remember thinking that someone was going to catch Taylor before he scored. But he got in, and we were leading 20-14 at the half.

We didn't need to make too many major adjustments for the second half. The talk in the locker room mainly focused on stopping Young and on keeping our running and passing game in synch. We still felt as if we had the momentum, but we knew that Young would come out smoking.

A few minutes into the third quarter, Young and Jerry Rice connected on a touchdown play that was longer than the one Young had with Taylor. But they missed the point after, which left the score 20-20. On the following kickoff, Deion Sanders took the ball on the goal line and blew through everyone for a 100-yard touchdown.

At that point, it felt like a heavyweight fight, where the two big guys are slugging away. They scored another touchdown, and we scored another one, and it was 33-27 in our favor after three quarters. They scored another touchdown early in the fourth quarter, which gave them a 34-33 lead. Players on our sidelines were getting mad—we wanted to put them away. The defensive guys did their part, and San Francisco was shut out the rest of the game. On offense, we put together a couple of solid drives, both of which ended with Norm Johnson hitting a field goal, to give us the victory.

When we ran off the field, it was a tremendous feeling. It wasn't as if we had won the Super Bowl, but it felt like a very big playoff game. We had tested ourselves, and we had won.

—As told to Barry Janoff

Atlanta offensive tackle **Mike Kenn** (78), above right, blocks 49ers defensive end Pierce Holt. Kenn completed a remarkable 251-game 17-season (1978–94) career with the Falcons. Six-foot-seven and 280 pounds, he suffered only one major injury, when he missed five games with a knee injury in 1985. Since the Falcons never got through the divisional playoffs throughout his career, Kenn got relatively little time in the national spotlight. But he made the 1978 All-Rookie Team and played in his fifth consecutive Pro Bowl Game in 1984.

There are two games I consider the most memorable and important to me in my career; both were against Dallas. To win

the Eastern Division of the NFC you had to beat Dallas, and the Cowboys became a very big rival for the Redskins, especially during George Allen's years as head coach. 1971 to 1977.

It was always a lot of fun going against the Cowboys' defense. They had one of the very finest defenses in the league with people such as Bob Lilly, Lee Roy Jordan and Cliff Harris, and you had to execute with precision to beat them. They were big and physical, but overpowering you wasn't their game. It took a thinking man to beat Coach Tom Landry's defense. They would always be prepared to stop what you do best. Before the game, you had to actually chart yourself and attempt to guess what they would try to do to stop you. If you would make a big play against the Cowboys, seldom could you run the same play successfully in the same game. They adjusted very well. You had to stay a step ahead of them. It was like playing a chess game against Landry.

The biggest of the two Dallas games I remember in my career was the 1972 championship game. We won our division that year and Dallas made the playoffs as a wild card. We finished with an 11-3 record and they were 10-4. We split during the season; we beat them 20-16 in Dallas and they beat us 13-0 at RFK. In the opening round of the playoffs, we defeated Green Bay, 16-3, and Dallas came from behind to beat the 49ers, 30-28. That set up the title game in Washington.

I remember not being able to sleep the night before the game. I got up around six o'clock that morning—it was New Year's Eve day—and went down to the restaurant to get a cup of coffee. I picked up the paper and there was a statement by Landry that read, "One of the things that gives us an edge is that Roger Staubach is a better athlete than Kilmer." He shouldn't have said that. That comment had me on edge the rest of the day—it was a four o'clock game and I

couldn't wait to get at the Cowboys. I was bound and determined to prove to Landry and everyone else that I was a better athlete than Staubach, at least on that day. And I was—I completed 14 of 18 passes for 194 yards and two touchdowns, and I believe Roger completed only nine. The line play made a big difference, I must admit. I received good protection while our defense seemed to be chasing poor Roger all day.

Curt Knight gave us a 3-0 lead with a second-quarter field goal and we made it 10-0 when I hit Charley Taylor with a 15-yard touchdown pass. The touchdown was set up earlier when I hooked up with Charley on a 41-yard pass play. We were going after Charlie Waters at left corner. He was a young player who had beaten out Herb Adderley for the job that season.

Dallas moved deep into our territory later in the half and probably would have scored a touchdown had Calvin Hill not overthrown Walt Garrison in the end zone with a pass. Dallas ended up settling for a field goal for its only points of the day. Our defense really did a job on them.

Waters broke his arm in the third quarter and was replaced by Mark Washington. We continued to exploit that area and we iced the game in the fourth quarter when I threw a 45-yard touchdown pass to Taylor. We played pretty conservatively on offense the rest of the way. We added nine more points on three field goals by Knight.

It was a great victory for me personally because, after Sonny Jurgensen was hurt near the middle of the season and I took over, the newspapers were saying the Redskins wouldn't go anywhere with me at quarterback. It was a pleasure to face those reporters after the Dallas game and say, "Fellas, you were wrong about Billy Kilmer."

The other Dallas game that was important to me was the first time we played them in 1975. It was the year after Sonny was forced into retirement and, again, it was being written that the Redskins couldn't win without Sonny. I was getting a little sick and tired of hearing and reading that stuff.

We were 4-2 going into the game with Dallas at RFK. I threw a couple of early

---

DECEMBER 31, 1972
DALLAS COWBOYS 3, WASHINGTON REDSKINS 26
RFK STADIUM, WASHINGTON, D.C.

SCORING

DAL	0	3	0	0	**3**
WAS	0	10	0	16	**26**

WAS Knight, 18-yard field goal
WAS Taylor, 15-yard pass from Kilmer (Knight kick)
DAL Fritsch, 35-yard field goal
WAS Taylor, 45-yard pass from Kilmer (Knight kick)
WAS Knight, 39-yard field goal
WAS Knight, 46-yard field goal
WAS Knight, 45-yard field goal

TEAM STATISTICS

	DAL	WAS
First Downs	8	16
Rushes-Yards	21-96	44-122
Passing Yards	73	194
Passes	9-21-0	14-18-0
Punts-Average	7-43.1	4-36.0
Fumbles-Lost	1-1	2-1
Penalties-Yards	4-30	4-38

INDIVIDUAL STATISTICS

Rushing
DAL Staubach 5 rushes for 59 yards; Hill 9-22; Garrison 7-15
WAS Brown 30-88; Harraway 11-19; Kilmer 3-15

Passing
DAL Staubach 9 completions, 20 attempts, 0 interceptions, 98 yards; Hill 0-1-0-0
WAS Kilmer 14-18-194-0

Receiving
DAL Sellers 2 receptions for 29 yards; Garrison 2-18; Hill 2-11; Parks 1-21; Alworth 1-15; Ditka 1-4
WAS Taylor 7-146; Harraway 3-13; Jefferson 2-19; Brown 2-16

ATTENDANCE: 53,129

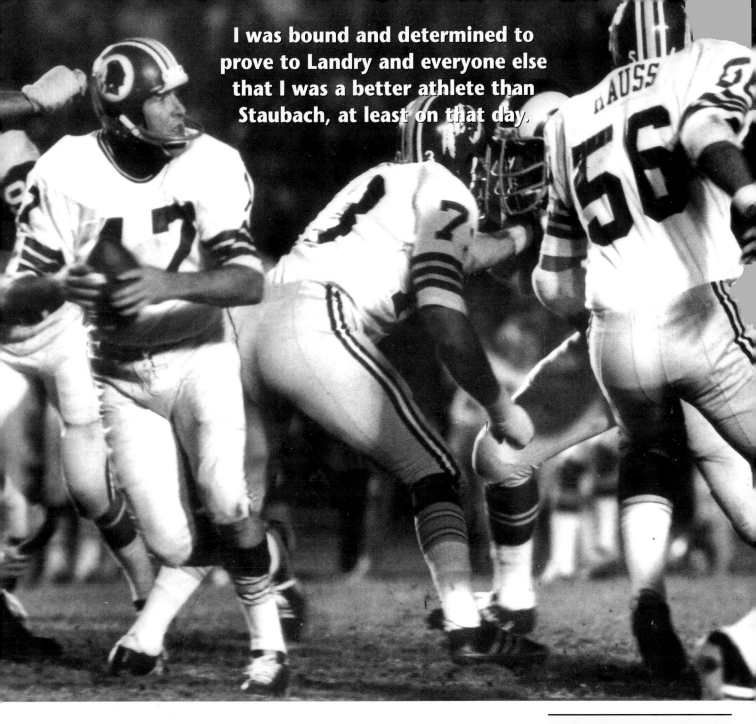

I was bound and determined to prove to Landry and everyone else that I was a better athlete than Staubach, at least on that day.

interceptions and the crowd was all over me. The boos must have been bouncing off the White House. It was a seesaw game and the crowd was unbelievable—they would boo me when things went wrong and cheer me when things went right. They were really on a boo-yea string, a real rollercoaster ride.

The score was tied late in the game when I threw my fourth interception of the day and Cliff Harris ran it in for a touchdown. The boos were like thunder. But I brought the team back and I threw a pass to Jerry Smith to tie it up and send the game into overtime. Now the cheers were deafening.

In the overtime, Kenny Houston intercepted a Staubach pass and ran it back to inside the Cowboys' 30. We moved the ball down to around the 20 and, on a third-and-seven situation, I threw a play-action pass to Taylor and he ran it to the one. I sneaked over from there and we had ourselves a pretty exciting 30-24 win.

The crowd, of course, was now on my side. I think they had finally accepted the fact that Billy Kilmer did have what it took to pull out a win in the last minute, that the Redskins could win with Billy. That game probably did more than any other to establish me in the hearts of the people in Washington, especially the press.

—*As told to Dave Payne*

Billy Kilmer began his 16-season NFL career playing more at halfback than quarterback. Over four seasons with the San Francisco 49ers, he tallied 15 touchdowns and 1,411 yards rushing and receiving while picking up only 2 touchdowns and 643 yards passing. Kilmer went to the New Orleans Saints in the 1967 expansion draft and established himself as a starting quarterback. Traded to Washington in 1971, he retired after the 1978 campaign with 1,585 completions for 20,495 yards and 152 touchdowns.

Picking a most memorable game is a little like asking a dad to choose his favorite child. He loves them all the same.

DECEMBER 2, 1979
LOS ANGELES RAMS 27, MINNESOTA VIKINGS 21
MEMORIAL COLISEUM, LOS ANGELES, CALIFORNIA

SCORING

MIN	7	7	0	7	0	**21**
LA	7	7	7	0	6	**27**

LA	Harris, 31-yard blocked punt (Corral kick)
MIN	LeCount, 36-yard pass from Kramer (Danmeier kick)
MIN	White, 6-yard pass from Kramer (Danmeier kick)
LA	Bryant, 2-yard run (Corral kick)
LA	Dennard, 41-yard pass from Lee (Corral kick)
MIN	Rashad, 22-yard pass from Kramer (Danmeier kick)
LA	Cromwell, 5-yard run (no conversion attempt)

TEAM STATISTICS

	MIN	LA
First Downs	26	14
Rushes-Yards	38-141	38-126
Passing Yards	268	174
Passes	21-42-3	12-25-2
Punts-Average	7-39.0	10-40.0
Fumbles-Lost	1-1	3-1
Penalties-Yards	7-65	9-90

INDIVIDUAL STATISTICS

Rushing

MIN	Young 16 rushes for 70 yards; Brown 18-52, Kramer 2-15; McClanahan 1-2; R. Miller 1-2
LA	Bryant 14-44; McCutcheon 7-39; Tyler 13-36, Ferragamo 1-2; Lee 2-0; Cromwell 1-5

Passing

MIN	Kramer 21 completions, 42 attempts, 297 yards, 3 interceptions
LA	Lee 7-14-161-1; Ferragamo 4-10-22-1; Clark 1-1-30-0

Receiving

MIN	Rashad 6 receptions for 102 yards; Brown 5-56; S. White 4-55; Young 3-27; LeCount 1-36; Tucker 1-8; Voigt 1-13
LA	Smith 3-99; Tyler 3-17; Dennard 2-57; Waddy 1-5; McCutcheon 1-9; Young 1-6

ATTENDANCE: 56,700

But when I look back, I'd have to start with my first game in the NFL, in 1964. I was as raw as a rookie could be, but the Washington Redskins threw me right into the starting lineup against the reigning champion Cleveland Browns. I ended up intercepting Frank Ryan twice, but that wasn't the only reason it was special. It was great because I was actually sharing the same field with Jim Brown, who was, as far as I'm concerned, the greatest running back of all time. And I played against a lot of them, so I should know.

Then, as a member of the Minnesota Vikings, there was the 1969 Western Conference playoff game against the Los Angeles Rams. We were losing 17-7 at halftime, then came out and took over the game and won. I don't remember how I played—I may have had a great game or a bad one—but from a team standpoint, it was memorable. It was one of those frigid Minnesota days, which we always tried to use to our advantage. The players on the opposing team would always come off the field and go running to their heaters. Our coach, Bud Grant, told us to stay involved in the game. Eventually, the Rams grew cold, and Joe Kapp led our offense down the field for the winning score late in the game.

But I guess the game against the Rams in 1979, when I broke the all-time interceptions record, is one that really stands out.

Emlen Tunnell's record must have stood for 20 years, but when I broke it, I could truthfully say, "Well, I have something no one else has ever done before." And you think about all the football players who have come through the league—all the great defensive backs who have come through the league—and I had more interceptions than any of them. So, yes, that stands out.

Frankly, I wasn't sure I was going to break the record. At the end of the 1977 season, I had 78 career interceptions, which put me one behind Tunnell's record. However, in 1978 I didn't intercept a pass for the first time in my career. By 1979, I was going into my 16th season knowing that I was getting up there in age.

I tied the record early in the season against the Detroit Lions. I don't remember a lot of the interceptions during my career, but that was one of the best ones I ever had. I cut in front of Gene Washington—he was a wide receiver for the Lions—and I just laid right about a foot off the ground and picked it up.

But as the season dragged on, I couldn't get the record breaker. When we went into Los Angeles in week 14, I wasn't sure I'd ever get it.

Through the years, I was able to get a lot of interceptions, in part because I played on such a great defense. Up front, we had the famous "Purple People Eaters" with Jim Marshall, Carl Eller, Alan Page and Gary Larsen. You couldn't run on them, and if you tried to pass, you better have gotten rid of it in a hurry. Nobody really noticed our linebackers, but we had some great ones: Matt Blair, Wally Hilgenberg, Amos Martin, Fred McNeill and Jeff Siemon. They really set the front four up to succeed.

Our secret was to try to disguise our defenses so the quarterback didn't know what we were going to do until the ball was snapped. We tried to keep him off-balance all the time.

Our front seven were so fantastic that I could focus a little more on defending the pass. I always tried to be in a place where the quarterback didn't expect to find a free safety. Maybe I'd be over here for one play, over there for another and over there for yet another. I knew how much ground I could cover, and I would try to lure the quarterback into a trap, lure him into throwing into my area by making him think a particular receiver was going to be open. Then I could close in on the ball.

I always knew I couldn't make my move for the ball until it was in the air. Back there, you have to be careful not to react to a quarterback's pump fake and commit too early. The other guys in the secondary are counting on you to be back there for help.

Speaking of help—help in setting the

It seems I always caught the hard ones and dropped the ones that were right in my hands, but I wasn't going to drop this pass. It was sweet.

record, that is—I finally got it in Los Angeles. On the last play of the first half, Rams quarterback Vince Ferragamo went back to pass and threw the ball right down the middle of the field. He was trying to get the ball to tight end Charlie Young, but he overthrew him. It may have tipped off Young's finger—I'm not sure—but it came right to me. I caught it, and finally passed Tunnell.

I thought it was pretty ironic that the interception that gave me the record was one of the easiest I ever had. All I had to do was stand there and catch it. It seems I always caught the hard ones and dropped the ones

that were right in my hands, but I wasn't going to drop this pass. It was sweet.

In the second half, I got another one— number 81—against my former teammate Bob Lee. That came on the next-to-last play of regulation time. (We ended up losing 27-21 in overtime.)

Those turned out to be the final two interceptions of my career, as I retired after the season. I don't know how I would have felt if I had retired tied for the record. But thanks to those interceptions in Los Angeles, I'll never have to know.

—As told to Chuck O'Donnell

Washington Redskin **Paul Krause** (26), above, breaks up a pass intended for Dallas Cowboy Bob Hayes (22) in 1967. After four seasons (1964–67) with Washington, Krause went to the Minnesota Vikings in a trade. He started four Super Bowls at safety with the Vikes but failed to win a ring. Krause retired in 1979 after 16 pro seasons and entered the Pro Football Hall of Fame in 1998. He remains the NFL's all-time leader with 81 career interceptions.

My greatest game took place in 1983, when the Seattle Seahawks made the playoffs for the first time. We had a new head coach in

Chuck Knox and a rookie running back from Penn State named Curt Warner, whom we drafted in the first round. Warner gained 1,449 yards on the ground his first year.

We were 9-7 that season and slipped into the playoffs as a wild-card team. Our first playoff game resulted in a 31-7 win over the Denver Broncos at home. The Miami Dolphins were next, in the divisional playoffs; they had tied the Los Angeles Raiders for the best record in the AFC at 12-4. It also was Dan Marino's rookie season for Miami. He was firing touchdown passes left and right to receivers Mark Clayton and Mark Duper.

We had to travel to Miami and play in the Orange Bowl, as obvious underdogs. The weather was overcast, misting throughout the game. It definitely was Seattle weather, not Miami weather. That was a good omen for our team. As we took the field, we felt that light mist coming down, and it continued for most of the game.

Playing in a 3-4 scheme, Miami was a light defensive team across the front. The Dolphins weren't very big. We felt that with the size of our two big tight ends—Pete Metzelaars and Charlie Young—and our offensive line, we could pound away at the Dolphins defense, protect the football and win a low-scoring game. We had an extremely solid defensive unit.

We started out by running the ball; we really didn't throw it very often. The score went back and forth throughout the game, but we managed to gain a 14-13 lead after three quarters. Nevertheless, as the fourth quarter began, I still hadn't touched the football.

When Norm Johnson kicked a 27-yard field goal with 11 minutes left in the game, we went up 17-13. After a couple of changes of possession, we got the ball back and simply tried to control the clock and nurse our four-point lead. Less than five minutes remained in the contest.

Miami started blitzing its strong safety, Glenn Blackwood, on every play to slow our running game and put pressure on quarterback Dave Krieg when he did throw. I told Krieg that if the Dolphins blitzed the strong safety again on a pass play, I would run a quick post instead of a quick out. Sure enough, we threw on first down and there came Blackwood, blitzing away.

I ran the quick post, and Krieg threw the ball behind me. It was intercepted by Miami cornerback Gerald Small and returned to our 10-yard line. Miami scored three plays later.

We now were behind 20-17 with three minutes and 43 seconds left and were forced to play catch-up in a noisy stadium. On the third play from the line of scrimmage, I grabbed a 16-yard pass that put us at Miami's 42; it was my first catch of the game. The clock then was stopped while the chains were moved.

Krieg went to me again when I ran a corner route after breaking off a post pattern. There was double coverage, but I caught the ball along the right sideline, a 40-yard reception that got us to Miami's two. Warner scored on the next play, and we went up 24-20 with a little less than two minutes remaining.

Miami fumbled the ensuing kickoff, and we recovered. Four plays later, Johnson's 37-yard field goal gave us a 27-20 lead. The Dolphins fumbled the kickoff again, then Krieg ran out the clock.

We upset the Dolphins in the playoffs—and in their home stadium. For those reasons, that was my greatest game as a Seahawk.

—As told to John Nixon

DECEMBER 31, 1983
SEATTLE SEAHAWKS 27, MIAMI DOLPHINS 20
ORANGE BOWL, MIAMI, FLORIDA

SCORING

SEA	0	7	7	13	**27**
MIA	0	13	0	7	**20**

MIA   Johnson, 19-yard pass from Marino (kick failed)
SEA   Bryant, 6-yard pass from Krieg (Johnson kick)
MIA   Duper, 32-yard pass from Marino (von Schamann kick)
SEA   Warner, 1-yard run (Johnson kick)
SEA   Johnson, 27-yard field goal
MIA   Bennett, 2-yard run (von Schamann kick)
SEA   Warner, 2-yard run (Johnson kick)
SEA   Johnson, 27-yard field goal

TEAM STATISTICS	SEA	MIA
First Downs	21	21
Rushes-Yards	42-151	30-128
Passing Yards	183	193
Passes	15-29-1	15-26-2
Punts-Average	4-38.0	4-35.5
Fumbles-Lost	0-0	3-3
Penalties-Yards	2-15	5-30

INDIVIDUAL STATISTICS
Rushing
SEA   Warner 29 rushes for 113 yards; Bryant 5-22; Krieg 4-minus 5; Hughes 4-21
MIA   Nathan 8-19; Franklin 6-28; Bennett 7-31; Overstreet 9-50
Passing
SEA   Krieg 15 completions, 28 attempts, 192 yards, 1 interception; Zom 0-1-0-0
MIA   Marino 15-25-193-2; Clayton 0-1-0-0
Receiving
SEA   Johns 4 receptions for 60 yards; Bryant 2-12; Warner 5-38; Doomink 2-26; Largent 2-56
MIA   Duper 9-117; Nathan 1-6; Johnson 2-29; Rose 1-15; Moore 2-26

ATTENDANCE: 71,032

If the Dolphins blitzed the strong safety again on a pass play, I would run a quick post instead of a quick out. Sure enough, we threw on first down and there came Blackwood, blitzing away.

At the end of the 1989 season, Seattle Seahawks 14-year veteran wide receiver **Steve Largent** retired, holding NFL career records for receptions (819), receiving yards (13,089), touchdowns (100), consecutive games with a reception (177), 50-catch seasons (10) and 1,000-yard receiving seasons (8). While those records have fallen, Largent earned a spot in the Pro Football Hall of Fame and remains a Seattle franchise leader. He has been an Oklahoma delegate in the U.S. House of Representatives since 1994.

SEPTEMBER 16, 1950

That's easy. The game I'll never forget is the first game we ever played in the National Football League. It was the

opening game of the 1950 championship season, but it was more than that, way more. Opening games have their own kind of tension and expectation surrounding them, but this game went way, way beyond anything like that. This game had the intensity and atmosphere of a championship game, and a grudge championship game at that.

For four years the Browns had been the champions of the All-America Football Conference. Now that conference was dissolved and we were merged into the NFL. For four years we had won the AAFC championship. But that didn't count for much in the NFL cities. There they said things like, "Champions of what?" and called us "cheese champions," and said that we'd lose 10 games a year if we had to play the established powers of the older league.

Now we were ready to find out. The Eagles were a great team. They had a powerful running game and they took a great deal of pride in their famed five-four defense. In those days many players still went both ways, and it seemed there, too, the Eagles were outstanding, with two-way players like Pete Pihos, Chuck Bednarik, Bucko Kilroy, George Muha and Russ Craft, one of the finest defensive backs who ever played.

So this was to be a battle of champions—the Browns, four-time champions of the All-America Football Conference, against the Eagles, the two-time champions of the NFL. To set this game off even further it was scheduled for Saturday night, September 16, 1950, in Philadelphia's Municipal Stadium, the day before the rest of the league opened the season. Some 72,000 fans jammed into the stadium, but we Cleveland players could feel the eyes of every football fan in the country on us.

We had waited four years for this game. Every year we had asked for a game with the NFL Champion to determine who was the real ruler of pro football, but every year we were brushed off. Now we looked for vindication. In a way, we were playing for our honor.

Our quarterback, Otto Graham, had one of his greatest days. He threw nearly forty passes, and completed better than two-thirds of them for almost 350 yards and three touchdowns—and scored another one himself.

That Eagle five-four defense might have been extremely tough to run against, but Graham just picked it apart. In the first half, he threw often to our backs, Rex Bumgardner, Dub Jones and Marion Motley, and that really opened things up for the ends, Mac Speedie and me.

Bednarik told me later that their coach, old Greasy Neale, was muttering at halftime, "We can't watch those ends. They're like spiders. As soon as you tackle one the other gets the ball and is off and away."

The Eagles got on the board first with a field goal. Near the end of the quarter, Jones, from his flanker spot, outran the linebacker who was trying to cover him, and Graham hit him with a pass for a touchdown. The play covered 59 yards.

Our defense probably won the game for us when they made a goal-line stand after the Eagles had driven to a first down at the three-yard line. We took over on the two and Graham went right to work. He hit Jones, Speedie and Motley, and finished off the last 26 yards with a toss to me.

I can still picture Bednarik and Alex Wojciechowicz running, trying to catch me, hollering and swearing. That sent us into the locker room ahead, 14-3.

We wrapped it up early in the third quarter. We took the kickoff and Graham completed seven straight passes, including one to me for more than 30 yards. He missed one, but then made it eight out of nine by hitting Speedie from 13 yards out for the score.

Down now 21-3, the Eagles took out their number-one quarterback, one-eyed Tommy Thompson, and replaced him with Bill Mackrides. He got them into the end zone when he hit Pihos from 17 yards away on the first play of the fourth quarter.

There was a lot left in Otto's arm, though. We drove down to the Eagles' 25-yard line, and I managed to get in the way of another

---

SEPTEMBER 16, 1950
CLEVELAND BROWNS 35, PHILADELPHIA EAGLES 10
MUNICIPAL STADIUM, PHILADELPHIA, PENNSYLVANIA

SCORING

CLE	7	7	7	14	**35**
PHI	3	0	0	7	**10**

PHI Patton, 15-yard field goal
CLE Jones, 59-yard pass from Graham (Groza kick)
CLE Lavelli, 26-yard pass from Graham (Groza kick)
CLE Speedie, 13-yard pass from Graham (Groza kick)
PHI Pihos, 17-yard pass from Mackrides (Patton kick)
CLE Graham, 1-yard run (Groza kick)
CLE Bumgardner, 2-yard run (Groza kick)

TEAM STATISTICS

	CLE	PHI
First Downs	23	24
Rushes-Yards	24-141	44-148
Passing Yards	346	118
Passes	21-38-2	11-32-3
Punts-Average	5-39.8	6-40.3
Fumbles-Lost	3-2	3-2
Penalties-Yards	12-98	3-45

INDIVIDUAL STATISTICS
Rushing
CLE Bumgardner 4 rushes for 18 yards; Graham 3-3; Jones 6-72; Motley 11-48
PHI Craft 4-28; Mackrides 2-2; Myers 5-12; Palmer 2-2; Scott 13-46; Thompson 1-1; Ziegler 17-57
Passing
CLE Graham 21 completions, 38 attempts, 346 yards, 2 interceptions
PHI Mackrides 3-8-45-1; Thompson 8-24-73-2
Receiving
CLE Bumgardner 3 receptions for 37 yards; Jones 5-98; Lavelli 4-76; Motley 2-26; Speedie 7-109
PHI Ferrante 3-24; Myers 2-29; Pihos 4-51; Ziegler 2-14

ATTENDANCE: 71,237

Every year we had asked for a game with the NFL Champion to determine who was the real ruler of pro football, but every year we were brushed off. Now we looked for vindication.

toss, this one good for about 25 yards. From there, we kept it on the ground, with Otto going the final yard.

Our fifth and last touchdown came after Warren Lahr intercepted a pass on our 36. Dub Jones broke loose for a 57-yard run, and Bumgardner carried it the final couple of yards.

There was pandemonium outside our locker room. About 25,000 of our fans had come down from Cleveland to see the game and they surrounded our team bus. I decided to walk back to the hotel, about two miles. I beat the bus by a long ways.

What a party there was in that hotel that night, the Philadelphia blue laws notwithstanding. I doubt if there has ever been a time since when fans and players were so close.

We went back to Cleveland the next day and waiting for us was something else we could be proud of. The press had asked Bert Bell, Commissioner of the NFL, what he thought of the game.

"The Browns are the greatest football club I ever saw," he said.

—As told to Bob Billings

Pro Football Hall of Fame end **Dante "Gluefingers" Lavelli**, above left, joined the Cleveland Browns in 1946. He was the AAFC's top receiver as a rookie and was All-AAFC in 1946 and 1947. In 1950, the Browns moved to the NFL and Lavelli caught a then-record 11 passes in a 30-28 NFL title game victory. Lavelli started in three of the first five Pro Bowl games played. He retired after the 1956 campaign having caught 386 passes for 6,488 yards and 62 touchdowns.

I played 18 seasons in the NFL, so I remember a lot of games. Some of them were good, some not so good. One that

stands out was against the New York Giants in 1988.

It was the last game of the season, and there was a great deal riding on the outcome for both teams. We already had been eliminated from the playoffs, but we were 7-7-1 going into the game and wanted to finish the season with a winning record. They were battling for first place and a playoff spot, and the way the season came down, a victory would put them into the playoffs and a loss would keep them out.

There was always a love-hate rivalry with the Giants when I was with the Jets. It wasn't a personal thing—they had a lot of great seasons, and I respected a lot of the guys there, some of whom I was very friendly with—but when two teams are in the same city, a rivalry is going to happen.

Going into the game, everyone on the team was loose but excited. We were coming off a big victory against the Indianapolis Colts, and a couple of weeks earlier we had beaten Miami in a big game. It was a little late in the season to make the playoffs, but you play for pride, and you play hard for the team. It wasn't difficult to get motivated for that game. We don't play the Giants that often during the regular season, so it was exciting to be going head to head with them. Both teams play at Giants Stadium, so it was going to be a special game for the fans as well. There were about 70,000 people there, and I remember a wave of yelling and screaming that started before the opening kickoff and didn't seem to end until the game was over.

As a kicker, I got to spend a lot of time on the sidelines, and I spent a lot of time talking to the other guys and getting a feel for what's happening. That day there was a lot of electricity on our bench. All the guys felt that if we weren't getting into the playoffs, this would be the playoffs for us. As it turned out, the guys on offense had a great game, but the guys on defense had a Super Bowl game. I

think we had eight sacks, and a lot of guys on offense and defense just let it all hang out.

The Giants came out pumped up, but it might have been a situation where they were too tense, like they had thought about the situation too much and put too much pressure on themselves. Our guys were up, but it was a looser feeling, and it showed throughout the first half. I had a couple of field goals, and Mickey Shuler caught a touchdown pass from Ken O'Brien. We weren't overpowering them, but we were playing solid football, and they seemed to be . . . well, not struggling so much as playing just off their game. I think, again, that it was that they had put too much pressure on themselves. Every play became a big thing to them, and it seemed no one wanted to make even the slightest mistake, as if any one mistake might be the thing that cost them the game.

We were up 13-7 at halftime, and we were feeling pretty good in the locker room, but I've been in a lot of games where emotions and fortunes go back and forth so many times during the day that you lose track. That's what makes pro football such an exciting thing for me: Every game is different, and every set of downs in each game brings a variety of emotions.

We came out loose after the half, and we got on the board again when we got inside their 10 and Freeman McNeil went in for the touchdown. We played them tough in the third quarter, but they put together a drive toward the end of the quarter and got inside our 10. Then Phil Simms hit Stephen Baker with a pass for a touchdown with less than a minute to play.

The score was still 20-14 late in the fourth quarter. Our defensive guys kept them from sustaining any drives, and after each set of downs they'd come to the sidelines pumped up. The Giants were too good a team to keep down, though, and Simms led them on a tough drive that put them inside our 10 again. Then Simms hooked up with Lionel Manuel, who caught a touchdown pass to tie the game. Their kicker, Paul McFadden, came out and hit the extra point to give them the lead.

There wasn't much time to play at that point, and in other situations and on other

There wasn't even a moment of doubt that we could still go out there and win the thing.

days there might have been the feeling on our side that, well, we played our best, but it wasn't meant to be. However, there wasn't even a moment of doubt that we could still go out there and win the thing.

After the Giants scored, Bobby Humphrey took the kickoff and blew through the Giants coverage. He just seemed to outrace everyone else, and he ended up going about 35 yards to put the ball at midfield. Their defense played it very tight, but O'Brien was determined to get into the end zone. He moved our offense down to about the Giants five, then he found Al Toon in the corner of the end zone for the touchdown. I hit the point after with about 30 seconds left to play. They still had some time, but our defensive guys covered them and put the game away for us.

Both teams were hit with a mixture of emotions when time ran out. We felt as if a huge weight had been lifted from our shoulders because we were able to take on the Giants and play them tough. Our guys were overjoyed, and their guys, naturally, were dejected. The fans must have felt that mixture of emotions, but I would think that our fans must have felt, if not vindicated, at least elated. Personally, I felt good not just because we beat the Giants or because I had a part in the victory, but because it was a solid victory for the team.

There were other games when the Jets played well under pressure or played beyond expectations. The game against the Giants was memorable because it was a victory for the team. We ended the season on a positive note, which certainly made the offseason a whole lot nicer.

—As told to Barry Janoff

Kicker **Pat Leahy** holds the New York Jets' franchise records for field goals (304) and points (1,470). Amazingly, Leahy did not play college football and was a virtual walk-on in his rookie year. His 18-season (1974–91) career was highlighted by a 121-point year in 1985, and he scored more than 100 points six different times. Leahy also posted six seasons with a 100 per cent convert conversion rate, including his last two campaigns, when he was the NFL's oldest active player.

The Buffalo Bills teams I coached in the early 1990s were—and I know this term is probably overused—the most resilient

bunch of individuals ever put together on an athletic field. And I think our playoff game against the Houston Oilers in January 1993 was the quintessential example of the resiliency of that team.

We came out that day at Rich Stadium and just played terribly. Going into that game, our starting quarterback, Jim Kelly, and our best linebacker, Cornelius Bennett, didn't suit up because of injuries. In addition, running back Thurman Thomas had to come out of the game with injuries of his own.

So without those vital players, we were getting crushed. You hope to come out for the second half and turn things around a little, but in the first series of the second half, we threw an interception that the Oilers returned for a touchdown. We were down 35-3, and people in the stadium were leaving and those at home were clicking the game off their television sets.

Because of a miskick following that score, the ball hit one of our front five on the kickoff return team and bounced back to the Oilers. It looked like more of the same for us. But somehow we recovered the ball in the scramble, and we had good field position. We went on and scored a touchdown.

We decided to go for an onside kick, which we recovered. We scored again—and suddenly, we had some momentum going. We were starting to get the big breaks we needed.

Frank Reich, playing in place of Kelly, did a great job of getting us back into that game. He kept finding Andre Reed open; they were connecting on pass after pass. We'd get the ball back and—boom—we'd score again. We'd get the ball and—boom—another score. In a period of seven minutes, we scored four touchdowns.

That type of play was typical of the Bills back then. To come back after losing the Super Bowl—after losing one and losing another and fighting to come back—well, I think that team showed a lot of character over the years.

One key to our resiliency was that the players were very close to each other. They really cared about each other as human beings. We had some great players but some of the lesser-known names were just as crucial to whatever success we had.

And these guys were playing great as we stormed all the way back and took a 38-35 lead over the Oilers. But the Oilers had a great team too. Jack Pardee was an excellent coach, and with Warren Moon at the controls of that run-and-shoot offense, a defense had to be ready to play.

After we took the lead, Houston put on a go-down-the-field drive. It looked as if the Oilers were going to score a touchdown and win. We couldn't stop them—Moon was finding his receivers.

The Oilers got down deep into our territory, but one of the least-remembered plays of the game was made by defensive end Phil Hansen. They threw a screen pass that looked like it would go for a touchdown. Hansen had rushed the passer, was chop-blocked, and hit the ground. But Hansen got back onto his feet in the blink of an eye, somehow got downfield, and dove to make a game-saving, shoestring tackle at the seven-yard line. That forced the Oilers to settle for a score-tying field goal, which sent the game into overtime.

The team that wins the coin toss in overtime usually wins, and it went in Houston's favor. I was hoping that Moon and company wouldn't pick up where they had left off and drive down the field. But finally, our defense came up with the big play we needed: We got an interception down at about their 30-yard line.

We figured we would just nurse the ball and get into field-goal position. Eventually, Steve Christie came in and kicked a 32-yard, game-winning field goal.

We went on to the Super Bowl again that year, facing the Dallas Cowboys in Super Bowl XXVII. We didn't win, but just getting there was a real testament to our fortitude and heart. These guys never quit—they never gave up. Beating the Oilers in the playoffs was proof of that.

—As told to Chuck O'Donnell

JANUARY 3, 1993
BUFFALO BILLS 41, HOUSTON OILERS 38
RICH STADIUM, BUFFALO, NEW YORK

SCORING

BUF	3	0	28	7	3	**41**
HOU	7	21	7	3	0	**38**

HOU   Jeffires, 3-yard pass from Moon (Del Greco kick)
BUF   Christie, 36-yard field goal
HOU   Slaughter, 7-yard pass from Moon (Del Greco kick)
HOU   Duncan, 26-yard pass from Moon (Del Greco kick)
HOU   Jeffires, 27-yard pass from Moon (Del Greco kick)
HOU   McDowell, 58-yard interception return (Del Greco kick)
BUF   Davis, 1-yard run (Christie kick)
BUF   Beebe, 38-yard pass from Reich (Christie kick)
BUF   Reed, 26-yard pass from Reich (Christie kick)
BUF   Reed, 18-yard pass from Reich (Christie kick)
BUF   Reed, 17-yard pass from Reich (Christie kick)
HOU   Del Greco, 26-yard field goal
BUF   Christie, 32-yard field goal

TEAM STATISTICS

	HOU	BUF
First Downs	27	19
Rushes-Yards	22-82	26-98
Passing Yards	347	268
Passes	36-50-2	21-34-1
Punts-Average	2-24.5	2-35.0
Fumbles-Lost	2-0	0-0
Penalties-Yards	4-30	4-30

INDIVIDUAL STATISTICS

Rushing
HOU   White 19 rushes for 75 yards; Moon 2-7; Montgomery 1-0
BUF   Davis 13-68; Thomas 11-26; Gardner 1-5; Rich 1-minus 1

Passing
HOU   Moon 36 completions, 50 attempts, 371 yards, 2 interceptions
BUF   Reich 21-34-289-1

Receiving
HOU   Givens 9 receptions for 117 yards; Jeffires 8-98; Slaughter 8-73; Duncan 8-57; Harris 2-15; White 1-11
BUF   Reed 8-136; Beebe 4-64; Metzelaars 3-43; Davis 2-25; Lofton 2-24; Thomas 2-minus 3

ATTENDANCE: 75,141

We were down 35-3, and people in the stadium were leaving and those at home were clicking the game off their television sets.

Pro Football Hall of Fame coach **Marv Levy** led the Buffalo Bills to six AFC Eastern Division titles and an unprecedented four consecutive Super Bowls. After 15 years coaching college football, he was an NFL assistant for four seasons (Philadelphia Eagles, 1969; Los Angeles Rams, 1970; Washington Redskins, 1971–72). Levy won two Grey Cups as head coach of the Canadian Football League's Montreal Alouettes (1973–77) and steered the United States Football League's Chicago Blitz (1985) before rejoining the NFL for a dozen years with Buffalo (1986–97).

When you've just lost a Super Bowl, there isn't anything anyone can say to you. After our Pittsburgh Steelers lost to the Dallas

Cowboys in Super Bowl XXX, people were like, "Hey, man, glad you made it an interesting game." You want to pause because you're not sure how to take that. What do you say?

I know that a lot of the Super Bowls are blowouts, but we expected to win. Unless they were handing out runner-up trophies, second place just wasn't good enough for us. We were thrilled that people were happy and got their money's worth, but we wanted to win the ballgame. I'm sure, if I had been a spectator and had been sitting at home watching on television, that probably would have been my viewpoint. But as a player, you don't look at it that way.

As I said, we expected to beat Dallas. In the second half, Dallas had 61 yards of total offense to our 201 yards. You look back at that and say, "How does a team beat you when all they have is 61 yards total offense for 30 minutes of the game?"

Long before that, though, a lot of people were asking a different question: "How did the Steelers make it to the Super Bowl?" Cornerback Rod Woodson was hurt in the opener, and midway through the season we were just 4-4. A lot of people wondered if we were even a playoff team.

Rod was one of our leaders on the defense, so when he went down, a lot of people were like, "Oh, my gosh, Rod Woodson is hurt. You talk about going to the Super Bowl? How are you going to get it done?"

Now you had to go into team meetings and hear, "Listen, we're going to miss Woody. I'm going to miss Woody as much as you guys will. But, hey, it's time now for everybody to step their game up. We don't have time to sit around and wonder, if we had him . . . If, if, if. We have games to play. Regardless of whether we like it or not, Woody isn't going to play. We have guys in the back that have to step it up, and we have guys in the front that need to step it up, including even linemen. We need to step it up because we're trusting a

younger player to get back there and play that position, so we have to get off the ball and not give the quarterback all day long to pick those guys apart."

Everyone did a great job of doing that. You almost felt like you had to baby-sit a lot of these guys, but one of the nice things was that we had more than one leader. Once Woody went down, a lot of people looked to safety Carnell Lake for leadership. Then there were our linebackers: me, Kevin Greene, Levon Kirkland, Chad Brown, Jason Gildon. You're looking at a bunch of Pro Bowlers—we had a slew of players who could step it up at any time.

We got together and said, "Hey, we'll give you all the help we can give you, just as long as we talk." It looked bleak, but we used to tell each other, "Nobody has faith in us but us. Nobody believes in the Pittsburgh Steelers except the 53 guys out on the field right now."

We probably became a lot closer than we had been the season before, in 1994. After losing in the AFC Championship Game in '94, a lot of guys stayed around and worked out together. But then when we lost Rod, we were like, "Strike one. What's next?"

Things started to work out, though. Guys started gelling, and Woody gave advice on what to do and not to do. It was good to have him around, even though he wasn't playing. He could give players ideas about what was going on, what to expect.

The Cowboys had a great team that season. They had the biggest offensive line in the league, featuring Nate Newton and Erik Williams. We, meanwhile, probably had one of the smallest defensive lines, and we depended on our speed. Our defensive coaches—Dom Capers, Marvin Lewis, and Dick LeBeau—did a great job. When I mention those names today, we're talking about head coaches and the most highly respected defensive coordinators.

They made sure we were prepared, sometimes to the point where it was annoying and we would have to say, "Hey, we've got it. Now get out of the huddle." I spent more time in practice telling Marvin Lewis, "Will you stay out of my huddle? If we

---

JANUARY 28, 1996
DALLAS COWBOYS 27, PITTSBURGH STEELERS 17
SUN DEVIL STADIUM, TEMPE, ARIZONA

SCORING

DAL	10	3	7	7	**27**
PIT	0	7	0	10	**17**

DAL	Boniol, 42-yard field goal
DAL	Novacek, 3-yard pass from Aikman (Boniol kick)
DAL	Boniol, 35-yard field goal
PIT	Thigpen, 6-yard pass from O'Donnell (N. Johnson kick)
DAL	E. Smith, 1-yard run (Boniol kick)
PIT	N. Johnson, 46-yard field goal
PIT	Morris, 1-yard run (N. Johnson kick)
DAL	E. Smith, 4-yard run (Boniol kick)

TEAM STATISTICS	DAL	PIT
First Downs	15	25
Rushies-Yards	25-56	31-103
Passing Yards	198	207
Passes	15-23-0	28-49-3
Punts-Average	5-38.0	4-45.0
Fumbles-Lost	0-0	2-0
Penalties-Yards	5-25	2-15

INDIVIDUAL STATISTICS

Rushing

DAL	E. Smith 18 rushes for 49 yards; Aikman 4-minus 3; Johnston 2-8; K. Williams 1-2
PIT	Morris 19-73; Pegram 6-15; Stewart 4-15; O'Donnell 1-0; Williams 1-0

Passing

DAL	Aikman 15 completions, 23 attempts, 209 yards, 0 interceptions
PIT	O'Donnell 28-49-239-3

Receiving

DAL	Irvin 5 receptions for 76 yards; Novacek 5-50; K. Williams 2-29; Sanders 1-47; Johnston 1-4
PIT	Hastings 10-98; Mills 8-78; Thigpen 3-19; Morris 3-18; Holliday 2-19; J. Williams 2-7

ATTENDANCE: 76,347

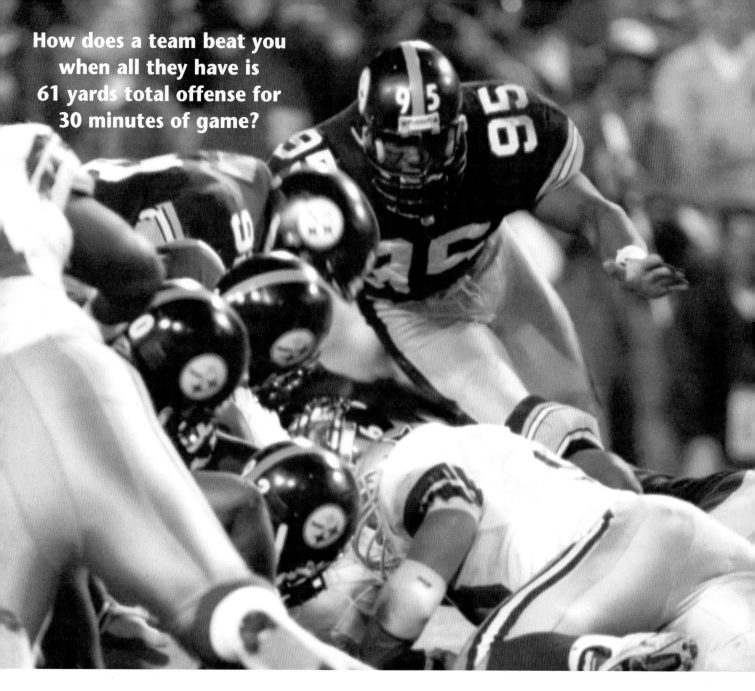

How does a team beat you when all they have is 61 yards total offense for 30 minutes of game?

screw up something, you can come out here, pull your hair out, stand on your head. Until then, will you stay out of our huddle?"

Obviously, we were well prepared for the Cowboys in Super Bowl XXX. And like I said, we dominated the second half. We were losing 20-7 after three quarters, but we narrowed it to 20-17 in the final quarter. What's more, we had the momentum.

But the whole game turned on the two interceptions Neil O'Donnell threw in the second half. That was the whole game right there, especially the second interception late in the fourth quarter. The Cowboys returned it down near the goal line and then scored, giving them a 27-17 lead. That was it.

Amazingly, O'Donnell had led the league in the regular season in '95 with the fewest interceptions per attempt. Part of you wants to kill him, and part of you says, "That's just part of the game." You look back and say, "Man, most people only get one chance to come here—one chance at it." In my case, unless I end up in the league as a coach or something, that was my one chance.

But as I revisit that season, there are fond memories. We came together as a team, fought, and never gave up. Everybody gave everything they had. When the game was over, I looked in the guys' eyes. Some people were crying. To me, that said enough. These guys wanted it as much as I did. Everybody laid it on the line, and that's all you can ask.

—*As told to Chuck O'Donnell*

Quickness, brute force and intensity defined the career of linebacker **Greg Lloyd** (95), above. He went to five consecutive Pro Bowls (1991–95) during his 10 seasons (1988–97) with the Pittsburgh Steelers. An intimidating and punishing pass rusher, Lloyd notched 10 quarterback sacks in 1994, a personal best; he retired with 54.5 career sacks. Released by the Steelers after a broken ankle never healed properly, Lloyd completed his career in 1998 with the Carolina Panthers.

I wasn't even sure we were going to have enough players to play Super Bowl XVI. I had gotten to the Pontiac Silverdome early,

JANUARY 24, 1982
SAN FRANCISCO 49ERS 26, CINCINNATI
BENGALS 21
PONTIAC SILVERDOME, PONTIAC, MICHIGAN

SCORING

SF	7	13	0	6	**26**
CIN	0	0	7	14	**21**

SF	Montana, 1-yard run (Wersching kick)
SF	Cooper, 11-yard pass from Montana (Wersching kick)
SF	Wersching, 22-yard field goal
SF	Wersching, 26-yard field goal
CIN	Anderson, 5-yard run (Breech kick)
CIN	Ross, 4-yard pass from Anderson (Breech kick)
SF	Wersching, 40-yard field goal
SF	Wersching, 23-yard field goal
CIN	Ross, 3-yard pass from Anderson (Breech kick)

TEAM STATISTICS	CIN	SF
First Downs	24	20
Rushes-Yards	24-72	40-127
Passing Yards	300	157
Passes	25-34-2	14-22-0
Punts-Average	3-43.7	4-46.3
Fumbles-Lost	2-2	2-1
Penalties-Yards	8-57	8-65

INDIVIDUAL STATISTICS
Rushing

CIN	Johnson 14 rushes for 36 yards; Alexander 5-17; Anderson 4-15; A. Griffin 1-4
SF	Patton 17-55; Cooper 9-34; Montana 6-18; Ring 5-17; Davis 2-5; Clark 1-minus 2

Passing

CIN	Anderson 25 completions, 34 attempts, 300 yards, 2 interceptions
SF	Montana 14-22-157-0

Receiving

CIN	Ross 11 receptions for 104 yards; Collinsworth 5-107; Curtis 3-42; Kreider 2-36; Johnson 2-8; Alexander 2-3
SF	Solomon 4-52; Clark 4-45; Cooper 2-15; Wilson 1-22; Young 1-14; Patton 1-6; Ring 1-3

ATTENDANCE: 81,270

but a lot of the other San Francisco 49ers were stuck in traffic on a bus from the hotel. Hours before the game, Vice President George Bush's motorcade was trying to get to the Silverdome, and that caused a big traffic jam.

Most of my teammates didn't make it to the stadium until 40 minutes before the game was supposed to start. I think it was a blessing in disguise; instead of getting nervous and concentrating too much on the game against the Cincinnati Bengals, it offered a distraction. We were making light of the situation and having fun with it. When everyone arrived and got suited up, we went out and won our first Super Bowl, 26-21. It was the game I'll never forget.

In 1981 we had a bunch of players from a bunch of different backgrounds. We had rejects, veterans no other teams wanted, rookies—we just came together from all places of the world. Joe Montana was in his first year as starting quarterback. We had Freddie Dean on defense, who the San Diego Chargers didn't want anymore and traded to us. We had Jack Reynolds, who the Los Angeles Rams didn't want anymore. We had guys like Dwight Clark, who was a low-round draft pick. We had gutsy guys like Paul Hofer, a running back coming off surgery. I was one of three rookies in the secondary, along with Carlton Williamson and Eric Wright. We just all came together and went to war for each other every Sunday.

The team did start out shakily that year; we were 1-2 going into our fourth game. But then we got on a roll, winning seven games in a row and really starting to build some momentum. However, even as we started winning and the team was beginning to gel, we weren't getting our due. We just weren't getting any respect. *Monday Night Football* was a big thing with our team. The program would run the weekend's NFL highlights on TV, and it never showed our team. Our coach, Bill Walsh, made that a point for us to rally around, and it got louder each week. We

wound up the regular season at 13-3.

The road to the Super Bowl, of course, was highlighted by "The Catch." When Clark made that leaping, game-winning catch against the Dallas Cowboys in the NFC Championship Game, my heart stopped. Wright then made a great defensive play to stop Drew Pearson from scoring at the end of the game.

We were going to Super Bowl XVI, and *still* no one believed in us—even though we had beaten Cincinnati earlier in the season. Everyone was saying that the consequences were too high, that Bengals quarterback Ken Anderson was too good, that our young secondary wouldn't be able to perform under the pressure.

Well, at first it looked like they were absolutely correct. Our return man, Amos Lawrence, fumbled the opening kickoff. Right off the bat, Cincinnati had the ball in scoring position. But then Dwight Hicks—a veteran who had stuck it out through some lean years in San Francisco—made an interception. That just showed what kind of confidence we had on our team. When Dwight made that big play, it really got us going.

With Dwight's interception setting the tone, we were able to contain their big players. Anderson wasn't able to throw the ball deep down the field to guys like Isaac Curtis and Cris Collinsworth. We were also keying on their big running back, Pete Johnson. We took a 20-0 halftime lead, and after that we just tried to play sound "situational football." We would let them move the ball somewhat—they actually outgained us in that game—but their offense was burning up time trying to score, and our offense would burn up time running the ball. You never know: Maybe we eliminated a series of downs that the Bengals could have done something with. If Anderson had had four more plays, maybe they would have won.

For me, one of the greatest moments was our goal-line stand late in the third quarter. You would think that with guys like Johnson and Charles Alexander—with their sheer size—they could get in from two or three yards out. I mean, they were *massive* running backs. But we had a lot of things go right for us.

We had rejects, veterans no other team wanted, rookies—we just came together from all places of the world.

On the first two plays, they gave the ball to Johnson. Goal-line defense is about beating your opponent to the punch and establishing position, and that's what we did, stopping him short of the goal line both times. On third down they threw a pass in the flat to Alexander. This time Dan Bunz came up and made a great open-field tackle. They went for it on fourth down, giving the ball to Johnson again. But again Bunz, this time with Reynolds, was there to stuff him. If you look at every play on that stand, we beat them to the punch. We drew a new line of scrimmage each time.

Wright made an interception at the end of the game to clinch the win. He was instrumental in my maturing as a person and as a player. Wright had our first interception

that year in a preseason game against Seattle, and he wound up with our last one when it counted most. That was one of the moments I'll never forget. That's football. That's life. To start from where we started and to finish like that was beautiful.

The guys were able to grow from that moment; the win really set the tone for what the Niners were going to be. We created a feeling that everyone was counting on everyone else, and that you couldn't let the team down. It took everyone on that team to win the Super Bowl. I now know that in life, if you bring a bunch of people together for a common goal, anything can happen.

—*As told to Chuck O'Donnell*

San Francisco 49er **Ronnie Lott** (42), above, runs back an interception in the 1989 NFC Championship Game. Lott made 63 career interceptions on his way to the Pro Football Hall of Fame. During his first 10 pro seasons (1981–90) with the 49ers, he won four Super Bowl rings. After attending four Pro Bowls as a cornerback, Lott switched positions in 1985; he went to six more Pro Bowls at safety. He played for the Los Angeles Raiders (1991–92) and New York Jets (1993–94) before retiring to a broadcasting career.

NICK "DR. TOE" LOWERY

DECEMBER 2, 1984

All players have their good games and bad games, games they want to remember and others they want to forget. As a kicker, I

DECEMBER 2, 1984
KANSAS CITY CHIEFS 16, DENVER BRONCOS 13
ARROWHEAD STADIUM, KANSAS CITY, MISSOURI

SCORING

KC	0	7	0	9	**16**
DEN	7	3	3	0	**13**

DEN	Watson, 48-yard pass from Elway (Karlis kick)
DEN	Karlis, 22-yard field goal
KC	Carson, 24-yard pass from Kenney (Lowery kick)
DEN	Karlis, 37-yard field goal
KC	Lowery, 46-yard field goal
KC	Lowery, 28-yard field goal
KC	Lowery, 42-yard field goal

TEAM STATISTICS

	DEN	KC
First Downs	17	17
Rushes-Yards	34-145	27-93
Passing Yards	164	225
Passes	16-36-1	20-38-1
Punts-Average	8-31.0	7-40.9
Fumbles-Lost	2-2	5-2
Penalties-Yards	2-10	3-61

INDIVIDUAL STATISTICS
Rushing
DEN   Winder 25 rushes for 96 yards; Elway 3-24; Wilhite 4-23; Parros 2-2
KC   Heard 22-84; Lacy 3-10; Gunter 1-1; Kenney 1-minus 2
Passing
DEN   Elway 16 completions, 36 attempts, 183 yards, 1 interception
KC   Kenney 20-38-281-1
Receiving
DEN   Watson 4 receptions for 89 yards; Wilhite 6-50; Winder 2-8; Sampson 1-9, Alexander 1-5; Johnson 1-5; Wright 1-17
KC   Carson 7-126; Paige 2-46; Marshall 1-29; Brown 4-16; Lacy 1-4; Heard 4-49; Arnold 1-11

ATTENDANCE: 38,494

like to think that I remember all the games I've been in. But the ones that stand out are games where my team has won because of a field goal, or lost because I missed a field goal.

The game I'll never forget is one that Kansas City played in 1984 in which we upset the Denver Broncos. We played them in Kansas City and we were in last place. They were in first place in the AFC West, tied with Seattle. We were 5-8 at the time and people figured the game wouldn't even be close. Denver was beating everyone and needed a win to stay in first place. We were playing for pride, because I think we were already out of the playoffs.

But pride can be a big factor, especially when you're playing in front of your hometown fans. You want to show them that you haven't given up. And everyone on the squad wants to prove that you can play together and win as a team.

We had lost four in a row going into the Denver game and it would have been very easy for us to give up. We were in last place in what I felt was the toughest division in the league. Going into the season, we felt confident that we could challenge for first place. But the Raiders, Denver and Seattle all started very strong. We had some good games early in the season but nothing outstanding, and we were 5-4 before losing those four games in a row.

As I said, at that point we could have given up. But the whole week before the Denver game the feeling was that we *could* beat the Broncos and that we *could* turn the season into a winning one. It was a very up feeling; everyone knew what we could accomplish.

There were about 40,000 people in the stadium and even though some were booing us, most of them were cheering us on. The Denver game was a big game and there was a lot of electricity in the stadium. Denver scored in the first quarter when quarterback John Elway hit Steve Watson on a 48-yard pass play. Elway didn't have one of his best

games, but he was dangerous. Denver didn't win 13 games and finish in first on luck.

Rich Karlis, Denver's kicker, hit a field goal in the second quarter to put them up 10-0. A few minutes later Chiefs quarterback Bill Kenney hit Carlos Carson for a touchdown. So at the half it was 10-7 Denver.

Our guys on defense had a good game. Denver had that big pass play in the first quarter for a touchdown, but after that they were shut down pretty well. Karlis hit another field goal in the third quarter and that was it for them. They were leading 13-7 after three quarters, but it wasn't like they had control of the game. We knew that if our offense put a few good plays together we could either get into the end zone or get within field-goal range.

I missed a long field goal during the game, a 55-yard attempt, but I didn't miss in the fourth. Kenney was moving the offense and got us within field-goal range early in the quarter. I hit a 46-yarder about three minutes into the period to pull us within three points. A few minutes later I tied the game with a 28-yarder.

Most of the action stayed around midfield for the next few minutes. It was getting to the point where people were starting to think about overtime. I was on the sideline getting ready physically and mentally because I figured I'd either get a shot at a field goal with only a couple of minutes left in the game or in overtime. When the game gets down to that point, I'm concentrating on nothing but putting the ball between the uprights. There are no distractions, just concentration.

As it turned out, Kenney moved the offense within range with less than two minutes to play. I hit a 42-yarder and put us on top for the first time, 16-13.

Denver still had a good shot at tying the game. Elway moved them down to our 25 with about 10 seconds to play. The week before, Denver was almost in the exact same position. They were down 27-24 to Seattle and had a shot to tie it with a few seconds left. But Rich hit the upright and Denver lost.

I don't know what the odds are on this happening twice in two weeks, but Rich came out and hit the upright again! He was one of

Pride can be a big factor, especially when you're playing in front of your hometown fans. You want to show them that you haven't given up.

the best kickers in the league, but it just goes that way sometimes. Of course, that's hard to accept when it happens two weeks in a row.

We won the game and afterward I ran over to Rich and put my arm around his shoulder. I told him not to let it get him down, that he shouldn't lose his confidence. Kickers are a closeknit fraternity, and even though we compete against each other, we look out for one another when the situation calls for it. Hey, if kickers don't look out for one another, who else is going to?

The win over Denver gave us a lot of confidence for the rest of the season. The next week Seattle came in and we blew them out, 34-7. On the last week of the season we went into San Diego and beat them. We finished 8-8, which didn't get us into the playoffs but did earn us a great deal of respect. We could have rolled over when we were 5-8, but we didn't. We got tough.

—As told to Barry Janoff

Nick "Dr. Toe" Lowery got into only two games with the New England Patriots in 1978 before catching on with the Kansas City Chiefs in 1980. He stayed for 14 seasons, racking up franchise single season and career records for field goals and points. Lowery retired after three seasons with the New York Jets (1994–96), with a career average of 99 percent on convert attempts. He kicked 383 career field goals and amassed 1,711 points.

In my first eight seasons with the Rams, we had reached the playoffs three times, but had never advanced beyond the first

DECEMBER 29, 1974
MINNESOTA VIKINGS 14, LOS ANGELES RAMS 10
METROPOLITAN STADIUM, BLOOMINGTON, MINNESOTA

SCORING

LA	0	3	0	7	**10**
MIN	0	7	0	7	**14**

MIN   Lash, 29-yard pass from Tarkenton (Cox kick)
LA   Ray, 27-yard field goal
MIN   Osborn, 1-yard run (Cox kick)
LA   Jackson, 44-yard pass from Harris (Ray kick)

TEAM STATISTICS	LA	MIN
First Downs	15	18
Rushes-Yards	33-121	47-164
Passing Yards	219	105
Passes	13-23-2	10-20-1
Punts-Average	5-43.3	6-39.2
Fumbles-Lost	3-3	5-2
Penalties-Yards	7-70	2-20

INDIVIDUAL STATISTICS
Rushing
LA   Bertelsen 14 rushes for 65 yards; McCutcheon 12-32; Harris 3-17; Cappelletti 3-8; Baker 1-minus 1
MIN   Foreman 22-80; Osborn 20-76; Tarkenton 4-5; Marinaro 1-3
Passing
LA   Harris 13 completions, 23 attempts, 248 yards, 2 interceptions
MIN   Tarkenton 10-20-123-1
Receiving
LA   Bertelsen 5 receptions for 53 yards; Jackson 3-139; McCutcheon 2-20; Snow 1-19; Klein 1-10; Cappelletti 1-5
MIN   Voigt 4-43; Lash 2-40; Gilliam 2-33; Marinaro 1-6; Osborn 1-1

ATTENDANCE: 46,444

round. The fourth time was a charm. We won our division title for the second straight year in 1974 and we beat Washington 19-10 in the opening round of the playoffs.

We had lost to the Redskins, 23-17, three weeks earlier in a Monday night game. By winning that game Washington qualified as the NFC's wild-card team instead of Dallas. Subconsciously, I think we wanted to face Washington rather than Dallas in the playoffs. We had lost to the Cowboys in the playoffs the previous year. We knew a lot more about the Redskins—they had a lot of former Rams on their team and their coach, George Allen, had been our coach through the 1970 season.

It was on to Minnesota to play for the title. We were just one step from reaching the Super Bowl. We beat the Vikings 20-17 earlier in the season and we believed we could do it again.

We played Minnesota up there for the NFL's Western Conference championship in 1969 and they won, 23-20. One play I'll never forget in that game was when the Vikings' Alan Page intercepted a slant-in pass thrown by Roman Gabriel when we were driving late in the game. Page was made out to be the hero for making a spectacular play, but that wasn't exactly the true picture. The play was a pass over the middle. Our center, Ken Iman, and I double-teamed Page on the block; we fired out and knocked him three yards off the line of scrimmage. He kept his balance and straightened up and Gabe threw the ball right to him. Ken and I did our job and we turned the guy into a hero. We knocked him right back into the interception.

I was looking forward to playing against Alan again. For some reason, I always seemed to have pretty good games against him. Alan always seemed to come up with the big play in a game. He had outstanding speed—he would catch a guy from behind and make him fumble 20 yards from where he had lined up. He was a fantastic hustler.

It was an atypically beautiful late December day in Bloomington, around 30 degrees with the sun shining. Minnesota scored first in the second quarter on a Fran Tarkenton touchdown pass. We came back to pull within 7-3 at half on a field goal by David Ray.

The biggest sequence of events for us happened well into the second half and, unfortunately and unfairly, I was involved. We had the ball on Minnesota's 25-yard line when Harris called a pass play. He dropped back and began scrambling. He broke away from two Minnesota tacklers and threw to Harold Jackson, who ran to the two-yard line before he was forced out of bounds.

Tommy Bell was the head referee that day and, after that pass play was over, he turned to me and Joe Scibelli and said, "That's the greatest play I've ever seen a quarterback make in terms of ad-libbing." He didn't know how Harris did it. That, to me, was a fantastic comment, coming from a guy who had pretty much seen everything during his many years associated with the game.

On the first play after that 73-yard gain, we moved the ball to the six-inch line. Harris called a quarterback sneak and I knew it was going to work. With the way our defense was stopping Minnesota, we were going to be tough to beat.

The first mistake we made on the quarterback sneak call was making it a long count. Harris called the snap count on two and he held it for a long time, going through a set, an audible system, then a non-rhythmic count. The whole process took around five seconds and that's tough on your linemen when they all have their weight forward and are just itching to fire out.

The Vikings were playing a gap defense and Gary Larsen was on my inside. With the long count, Gary jumped, but not offside. When that happened, Page charged forward and knocked me over backwards. Alan immediately began pointing and yelling, "He moved! He moved!" One official threw his flag and immediately signaled the Vikings offside; then this side judge, I don't remember his name, raced in and overturned the other official. He said that somebody in the Rams' interior line had moved and that it must have been the guard. Those were his

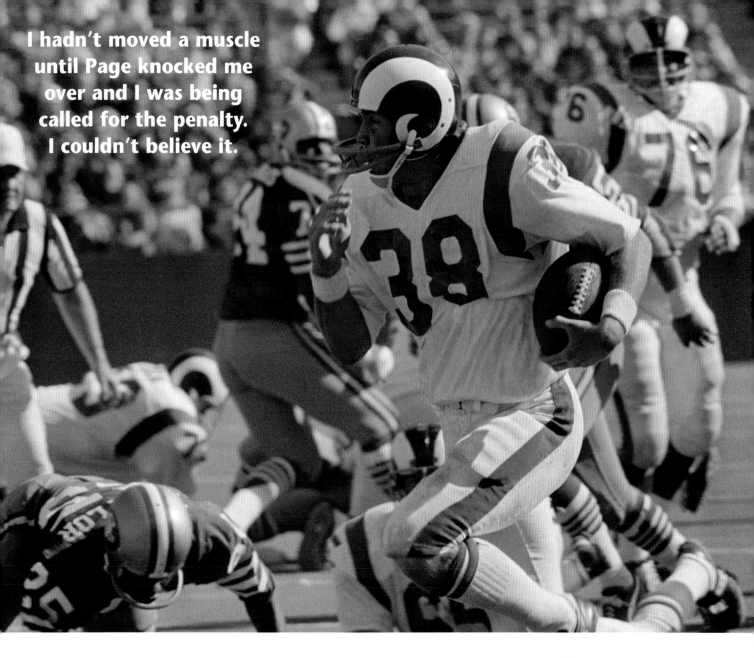

I hadn't moved a muscle until Page knocked me over and I was being called for the penalty. I couldn't believe it.

exact words. I hadn't moved a muscle until Page knocked me over and I was being called for the penalty. I couldn't believe it.

As it turned out, we came up empty on the series. On third down from the two-yard line, Harris threw a pass into the end zone that deflected off Wallace and into the arms of Wally Hilgenberg for an interception.

That really seemed to take the wind out of our sails, especially for the defense, which had played so well up until that point. The Vikings took the ball at their 20 and drove for a touchdown and a 14-3 lead. I can still picture Chuck Foreman ripping off big chucks of yardage on that drive.

Interestingly, we came right back and stuck it to them when we scored on a pass from Harris to Jackson. There were still more than five and a half minutes left in the game and I knew we were going to score again and

win the game. We had moved the ball against them the last two series and all we needed now was for our defense to get the ball back and we would take it from there.

But it never happened. We were the ones who were all charged up after getting that score, yet the Vikings, to their credit, managed to run out the clock. We had what I feel was one of the finest defenses in the league. The fact that Minnesota was able to control the ball on them those final precious minutes made it all the more frustrating for those of us standing on the sidelines.

It was a tough defeat because we left Minnesota knowing we were the best football team, but it didn't reflect on the scoreboard. Minnesota was going to the Super Bowl and we were heading home.

—As told to Dave Payne

Offensive guard **Tom Mack**, shown above running with a recovered fumble, completed a rare feat in a remarkable career. Mack never missed a single game in his 13 NFL campaigns (1966–78), all with the Los Angeles Rams. Although the Rams had nine seasons with 10 or more victories during his years with the team, Mack never made it to the Super Bowl. He was elected to 11 Pro Bowl games, however, and joined the Pro Football Hall of Fame in 1999.

I was laying in the end zone after diving across the goal line with three seconds remaining in my first NFL game, in 1971

with New Orleans. My one-yard scamper around the left end had capped a dramatic last-minute march down the field, giving us a 24-20 victory over the Los Angeles Rams.

Maybe this win would send u toward a Cinderella season. Maybe I would be carried off the field by my teammates. Maybe this was a defining moment for me and the team. Or maybe not.

Lying there, I happened to notice a few referees, talking about the play. As they were discussing whether I had had possession and scored—or whether it was a fumble and we were about to lose—I thought to myself, "You can't take this moment away from us. Please don't take the touchdown away from us." We had worked too hard and come too far to lose like this.

I joined the Saints that season when they made me the second pick overall in the draft. During the offseason, the Saints had traded veteran quarterback Billy Kilmer to make room for me to take over the starting job. Coming from the Bayou—being drafted out of Ole Miss—I naturally was viewed as the hometown boy who would be a savior of sorts. The Saints hadn't had a winning season in their first four years of existence, and I was supposed to change all that.

While I could see we weren't going to go out and win the Super Bowl, I thought we had the makings of a pretty good team, despite the fact that not one guy on the squad was older than 30. In fact, we had 13 rookies on the roster, and many other players were in their second or third seasons.

While we may have been short on experience, we had plenty of enthusiasm. We were upbeat entering the 1971 season opener against the Rams. They were one of the best teams in the league during that period, led by Roman Gabriel, who was a smart, strong-armed quarterback. Whether he was handing off to 1,000-yard rusher Willie Ellison or throwing to Lance Rentzel or Jack Snow, Gabriel was a superb field general.

The Rams defense was downright scary. On the front line, the team had Deacon Jones, Merlin Olsen and Coy Bacon starting, with a young guy named Jack Youngblood—who eventually became an All-Pro himself—coming in to spell them.

As if it weren't bad enough having those guys breathing down your neck, it was an oppressively hot day in New Orleans for that season opener. The teams traded field goals in the second quarter, but we broke out on top in the third quarter. I hit tight end Dave Parks with a 6-yard touchdown pass, then Gresham added a 2-yard touchdown run.

We were sky-high at that point, leading the Rams 17-3. But they weren't about to tuck their tails between their legs. Gabriel rallied his team, and the result was a field goal, a 29-yard TD pass to fullback Les Josephson, and a one-yard scoring run by Josephson. Suddenly, our big lead had evaporated into a 20-17 deficit.

Doubt could have easily seeped in, but we just went out there determined to win the game. Starting at our 30 on our final drive, we methodically moved down the field. Mixing mostly passes with a few runs to keep the Rams honest, we got the ball down to the one-yard line.

There was enough time left for just one more play. We called a play where I would roll out to my left and would have the option of throwing the ball or tucking it under my arm and running into the end zone. As I took the ball from center and began to roll, I saw an opening. I told myself that I couldn't throw it—I had to run it. I put my head down and bowled into the end zone, with the ball coming loose at one point.

Was it a touchdown or a fumble? I sat and waited for the call for what seemed like an eternity. When the refs raised their hands into the air to signify a touchdown, it set off a celebration. Our players and coaches hugged, and the fans went wild. We had stolen a 24-20 victory from the mighty Rams.

So, was it really a touchdown? Did I fumble before I crossed the goal line? I honestly don't know—and looking back, I don't really care.

—As told to Chuck O'Donnell

SEPTEMBER 19, 1971

NEW ORLEANS SAINTS 24, LOS ANGELES RAMS 20

TULANE STADIUM, NEW ORLEANS, LOUISIANA

SCORING

NEW	0	3	14	7	**24**
LA	0	3	3	14	**20**

NEW Butler, 32-yard field goal
LA Ray, 31-yard field goal
NEW Parks, 6-yard pass from Manning (Butler kick)
NEW Gresham, 2-yard run (Butler kick)
LA Ray, 27-yard field goal
LA Josephson, 29-yard pass from Gabriel (Ray kick)
LA Josephson, 1-yard run (Ray kick)
NEW Manning, 1-yard run (Butler kick)

TEAM STATISTICS	LA	NEW
First Downs	11	21
Rushes-Yards	26-118	41-112
Passing Yards	144	154
Passes	11-30-0	16-29-1
Punts-Average	7-45.4	5-41.6
Fumbles-Lost	1	0
Penalties-Yards	124	36

INDIVIDUAL STATISTICS

Rushing
LA Smith 5 rushes for 23 yards; Ellison 13-43; Josephson 6-26; Rentzel 1-21; Klein 1-5
NEW Gresham 21-42; Granger 8-33; Manning 4-14; Strong 5-25; Ford 2-minus 2; Parks 1-0

Passing
LA Gabriel 11 completions, 30 attempts, 164 yards, 0 interceptions
NEW Manning 16-29-218-0

Receiving
LA Rentzel 3 receptions for 42 yards; Klein 1-10; T. Williams 1-8; Ellison 2-35; Josephson 2-37; Snow 2-32
NEW Newland 3-33; Parks 3-45; Strong 1-2; Abramowicz 5-73; Gresham 3-51; Burchfield 1-14

ATTENDANCE: 70,915

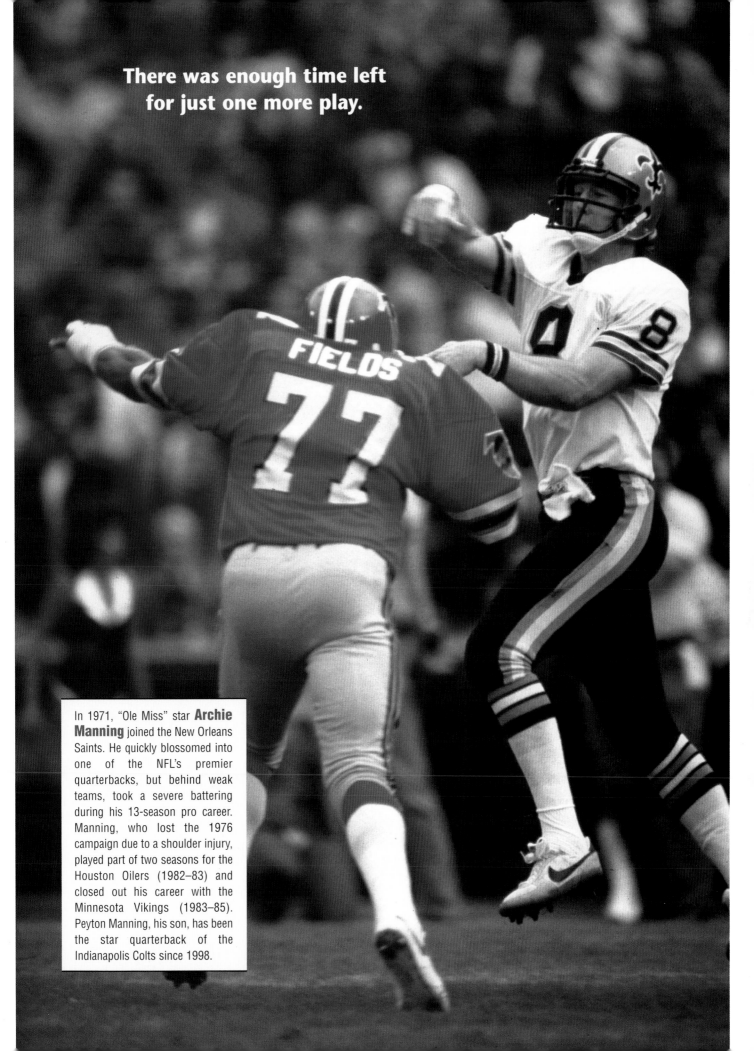

**There was enough time left
for just one more play.**

In 1971, "Ole Miss" star **Archie Manning** joined the New Orleans Saints. He quickly blossomed into one of the NFL's premier quarterbacks, but behind weak teams, took a severe battering during his 13-season pro career. Manning, who lost the 1976 campaign due to a shoulder injury, played part of two seasons for the Houston Oilers (1982–83) and closed out his career with the Minnesota Vikings (1983–85). Peyton Manning, his son, has been the star quarterback of the Indianapolis Colts since 1998.

1990 NFC CHAMPIONSHIP GAME

The buildup toward the 1990 NFC Championship game with the San Francisco 49ers started several years

earlier for me. I broke my wrist sacking St. Louis Cardinals quarterback Neil Lomax in 1987, so 1988 was going to be my comeback year. I wanted to prove to myself and to the Giants that I was worthy of another Pro Bowl.

Well, I had eight sacks in 1988, a disappointing total for me, so 1989 was going to have to be another year to regroup. Again I wanted to prove to myself, our coaches and my teammates that I could still make plays. I had nine and a half sacks and 59 solo tackles in '89, so it wasn't a bad year. We did lose to the Rams 19-13 in overtime in the playoffs, though, and after their receiver caught the winning pass and kept running through the end zone into the tunnel, I ran for home in Florida.

I did some soul-searching there. The pressure got to me at times in New York. The area has so many major newspapers, it seems even your best effort is never good enough for everyone. When the 1990 summer camp opened, I didn't think I'd be a New York Giant. Both Lawrence Taylor and I sat out that camp. I thought of how I didn't make the Pro Bowl, and I honestly felt I was a better player than the Washington Redskins' Charles Mann, who did go.

Finally, I was tired of doubting myself. I decided to be successful. A funny thing happened, though: Head Coach Bill Parcells said I wasn't ready to play and instead started John Washington ahead of me. I always felt that Bill wanted to play me but still wanted to teach me a lesson after my contract holdout. This was in 1990, when coaches could choose where they worked but players could not.

My season started to come together when we played Indianapolis on *Monday Night Football* in November. I was happy to showcase my talents on national television, and I wanted to perform to the best of my ability. I ended with seven tackles and two sacks, and we won the game 24-7.

We played the 49ers in San Francisco several weeks later. We played well, but not

well enough to win, losing 7-3. On their touchdown pass, Joe Montana slipped by me and hit Jerry Rice in the end zone.

That loss became our driving force the rest of the season. We kept a chip on our shoulders, knowing we would see that team again somewhere. Bill instilled a confidence in us to keep thinking like street ballplayers—a certain toughness you get when you're a kid and you play football in the streets. We were ready to play the 49ers anywhere, even if it was in the parking lot for a six-pack of Pepsi and cookies.

After we beat the Chicago Bears 31-3 in a divisional playoff game, I saw the rematch with the 49ers as another opportunity. I also figured San Francisco was scared to play us again after its earlier narrow win. I knew this would be the game of my life.

I decided on game day that I would make this the most miserable day in Joe Montana's life. I would spit on him, hit him and sack him two to three times if I had to. We kept hearing how the 49ers said they were destined to win their third championship and were already making plans for Tampa Bay and Super Bowl XXV. They believed they were the only team that would match up with Buffalo.

The first half was a defensive battle, with four field goals making it a 6-6 tie. Our backup quarterback Jeff Hostetler, who had replaced the injured Phil Simms, performed like a true warrior that day. He'd get hit, beaten and still get up and make things happen. On one particular play, 49ers tackle Jim Burt—a former teammate of mine with the Giants—busted through the line and hit Jeff on his throwing leg right below the knee, while his foot was still planted. Burt hit him late, trying to end Jeff's career. I almost came on the field after him for that. The Giants always played hard but clean.

We gathered and told one another we had to make plays and win the game, but not try to hurt anyone. I decided I wanted to win this game more than anything.

Early in the third quarter, San Francisco scored the game's only touchdown when John Taylor's 61-yard pass reception gave the 49ers a 13-6 lead. I don't remember who was guilty, but that was a blown coverage. The defensive players all said, "OK, that hurt, but

---

JANUARY 20, 1991
NEW YORK GIANTS 15, SAN FRANCISCO 49ERS 13
CANDLESTICK PARK, SAN FRANCISCO, CALIFORNIA

SCORING

NYG	3	3	3	6	**15**
SF	3	3	7	0	**13**

SF	Cofer, 47-yard field goal
NYG	Bahr, 28-yard field goal
NEG	Bahr, 42-yard field goal
SF	Cofer, 35-yard field goal
SF	Taylor, 61-yard pass from Montana (Cofer kick)
NYG	Bahr, 46-yard field goal
NYG	Bahr, 38-yard field goal
NYG	Bahr, 42-yard field goal

TEAM STATISTICS	NYG	SF
First Downs	20	13
Rushes-Yards	36-152	11-39
Passing Yards	159	201
Passes	15-29-0	19-29-0
Punts-Average	3-41.3	5-40.0
Fumbles-Lost	0-0	3-1
Penalties-Yards	5-45	9-63

INDIVIDUAL STATISTICS
Rushing
NYG Anderson 20 rushes for 67 yards; Meggett 10-36; Reasons 1-30; Hostetler 3-11; Carthon 2-8
SF Craig 8-26; Montana 2-9; Rathman 1-4
Passing
NYG Hostetler 15 completions, 27 attempts, 176 yards, 0 interceptions; Meggett 0-1-0-0; Cavanaugh 0-1-0-0
SF Montana 18-28-190-0; Young 1-1-25-0
Receiving
NYG Ingram 5 receptions for 82 yards; Bavaro 5-54; Baker 2-22; Meggett 2-15; Anderson 1-3
SF Rice 5-54; Rathman 4-16; Jones 3-46; Craig 3-16; Taylor 2-75; Sherrard 2-8

ATTENDANCE: 65,750

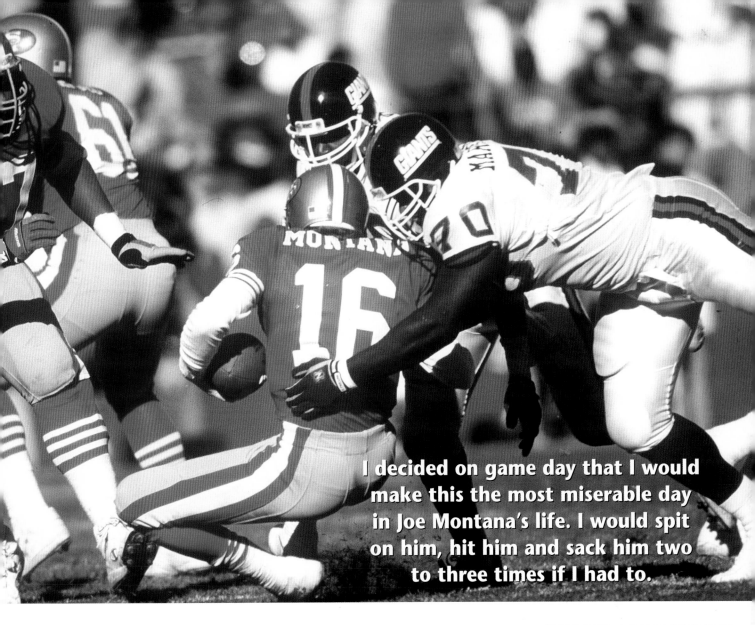

I decided on game day that I would make this the most miserable day in Joe Montana's life. I would spit on him, hit him and sack him two to three times if I had to.

our backs aren't broken." We regrouped.

With San Francisco leading 13-9 early in the fourth quarter, I made the biggest play of my life, one that changed the outcome of the game. On the snap, I slipped, got blocked by Bubba Paris, cut by Tom Rathman and leg-whipped by Paris—but then I got up to see Montana waving Rice downfield. I sacked Montana, who fumbled—it was recovered by the 49ers—and was done for the day with a broken finger. There were just over nine minutes left in the game.

We drove the field on our next possession, and Matt Bahr kicked another field goal to make it 13-12 San Francisco. I then knocked the ball loose from running back Roger Craig, on the 49ers' first play from scrimmage following our field goal. They recovered again, but several plays later they ran a play they never should have: a 35-sprint, right at me. I saw it coming and stacked Paris into the ground. Roger ran up Bubba's back because he

had nowhere else to go. I punched Roger in the belly, our nose tackle Erik Howard punched the ball loose, and Taylor recovered it.

I remember telling Bahr before the game that he was going to win it for us. It was going to be a low-scoring, defensive game, and the team that liked to hit the hardest, the longest, would win. San Francisco is too soft; we come from the snow, the cold and the wind.

We drove the ball 33 yards, Bahr kicked a 42-yard field goal and we won the game 15-13. I remember the celebration after the game. One of my favorite entertainers and people, Gregory Hines, was in the locker room. Two other great Giants fans were Billy Crystal and rock singer Jon Bon Jovi. Jon traveled with us the whole season, wearing my jersey under his sweatshirt.

That day was special. It was one of the best of my life.

—As told to John Nixon

Giants' defensive end **Leonard Marshall** (70), above, hits San Francisco quarterback Joe Montana (16) during New York's 1990 NFC Championship victory. The Giants went on to Super Bowl XXV victory the following week. Marshall won his first ring in Super Bowl XXI. He also went to two Pro Bowls during his 10 years (1983–92) with the Giants. Marshall played single seasons for the New York Jets (1993) and Washington Redskins (1994) before retiring. He finished his career with 399 solo tackles, 163 assists and 83.5 sacks.

I think that any professional athlete looks at his career as if he's improving all the time. I felt I was getting better every

DECEMBER 24, 1977
OAKLAND RAIDERS 37, BALTIMORE COLTS 31
MEMORIAL STADIUM, BALTIMORE, MARYLAND

SCORING

OAK	7	0	14	10	0	6	**37**
BAL	0	10	7	14	0	0	**31**

OAK Davis, 30-yard run (Mann kick)
BAL Laird, 61-yard interception return (Linhart kick)
BAL Linhart, 36-yard field goal
OAK Casper, 8-yard pass from Stabler (Mann kick)
BAL Johnson, 87-yard kickoff return (Linhart kick)
OAK Casper, 10-yard pass from Stabler (Mann kick)
BAL R. Lee, 1-yard run (Linhart kick)
OAK Banaszak, 1-yard run (Mann kick)
BAL R. Lee, 13-yard run (Linhart kick)
OAK Mann, 22-yard field goal
OAK Casper, 10-yard pass from Stabler

TEAM STATISTICS

	OAK	BAL
First Downs	28	22
Rushes-Yards	47-167	50-187
Passing Yards	324	114
Passes	21-40-2	12-26-0
Punts-Average	8-46.8	13-33.7
Fumbles-Lost	4-2	1-0
Penalties-Yards	7-65	8-82

INDIVIDUAL STATISTICS

Rushing
OAK van Eeghen 19 rushes for 76 yards; Davis 16-48; Banaszak 11-37; Garrett 1-6
BAL Mitchell 23-67; R. Lee 11-46; Leaks 8-35; Jones 6-30; McCauley 2-9

Passing
OAK Stabler 21 completions, 40 attempts, 345 yards, 2 interceptions
BAL Jones 12-26-164-0

Receiving
OAK Biletnikoff 7 receptions for 88 yards; Branch 6-113; Casper 4-70; van Eeghen 2-39; Davis 2-35
BAL Mitchell 3-39; Scott 2-45; R. Lee 2-22; McCauley 2-11; Chester 1-30; Doughty 1-20; Pratt 1-minus 3

ATTENDANCE: 60,783

season and I always looked forward to playing my best game.

I was in two Super Bowls with Oakland and I had good games in both. But my most unforgettable game was when we beat the Baltimore Colts in sudden-death overtime during the 1977 playoffs.

We had a great team that year. It was the season following our first Super Bowl win—32-14 over Minnesota in Super Bowl XI—and I feel we should have gone to the Super Bowl again that season. It didn't work out that way, but we still had a great year.

Oakland made the playoffs as a wild-card team in 1977 and we faced Baltimore in the opening round. The Colts had won their division that season—the last time they did that well for a while. The game was on their home field—in Memorial Stadium—and what I vividly remember is that there wasn't a single blade of grass on the field. It was so cold and barren looking that I felt as if I was playing on the surface of the moon.

Physically and emotionally, that was a tremendous game. There were so many great plays. Our quarterback, Ken "Snake" Stabler, had a great game. Clarence Davis had a great game. And so did Dave "Ghost" Casper. He caught only four passes, but three of them were for touchdowns. He had two especially tremendous catches: one right near the end of regulation time, and one in the second overtime that won the game.

The game was being billed as a shootout between the Snake and Colts quarterback Bert Jones. But we scored our first touchdown when Davis ran in from the 30, and their first 10 points came off an interception and a field goal. The score was 10-7 at the half, and it seemed like neither team wanted to take charge.

Ghost caught his first touchdown pass in the third quarter to give us the lead, but their kick returner, Marshall Johnson, took the kickoff all the way back to give them the lead again. Ghost caught his second touchdown

pass that quarter to give us the lead.

I don't remember ever thinking that we were going to lose, even when we were losing late in the fourth quarter. I remember thinking that if I do my job and everyone else does theirs, we will win.

It was toward the end of the game and we were trailing when Ghost made one of those great catches I mentioned before. He was running toward the end zone and looking over his left shoulder when he saw the ball coming over his right shoulder. So he twisted around in mid-air at the last second to make the catch.

That is a famous play . . . in fact, there's a painting of Casper making that catch called *The Ghost to the Post*, which was the name of the play because Casper heads for the goal post.

Errol Mann kicked a field goal a few plays later to tie the score and send the game into overtime. We held Baltimore scoreless in the first overtime quarter, but we didn't score either, which set up Ghost's tremendous catch in the second overtime.

We were about 10 yards out when Snake put up a pass toward the left corner of the end zone. It looked like it was going out. But Ghost leaped up and just grabbed it over his shoulder, like an outfielder would catch a ball if he were running toward the wall with his back to the plate. I remember after the game Ghost told some reporters, "Any stiff could have done it." But I don't think so.

I had some nice plays that game. Our entire defensive line was playing very well. We sacked Jones six times, which was special to me because getting after Bert Jones was one of my favorite things. He was a great competitor. My job was to get to the quarterback, and I seemed to get pumped up a little more when I played against him.

We played Denver after we beat Baltimore and I remember that was a tough game. We had a rivalry going with the Broncos and that game—a 20-17 AFC title match defeat—was a bitter loss. I still feel we should have gone to the Super Bowl that year. We would have had a great chance against Dallas. Dallas beat Denver 27-10 in Super Bowl XII.

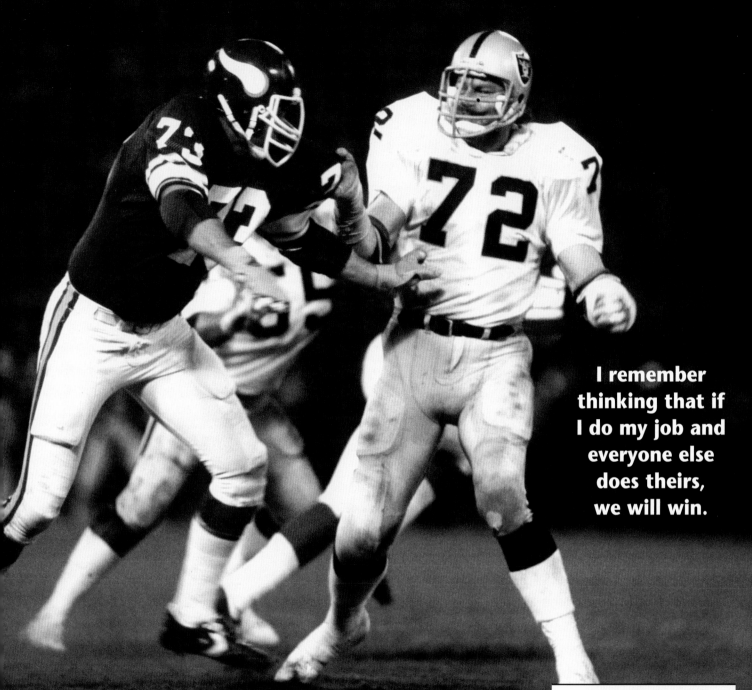

I remember thinking that if I do my job and everyone else does theirs, we will win.

One play that stands out in the Denver game was a great hit that Oakland's Jack Tatum put on Rob Lytle. That was one of the hardest hits I've ever seen or heard; Lytle got the crap knocked out of him and fumbled the ball. Phil Villapiano had one of the hardest hits I've ever seen when he was with Oakland. But Tatum had the best hit I've ever seen. We were playing Los Angeles and Terry Nelson caught a pass and made a great move on Tatum to get past him. But Tatum caught him near the sideline, picked him up and threw him at the Rams coaches.

I remember a great game against Pittsburgh in 1977, the same season we beat Baltimore in overtime. We were playing the Steelers in Pittsburgh and Raider coach John Madden told us before the game, "These people are going to be yelling and screaming at you all game. They'll be against you. But go out there and pretend they're yelling for you." We went out on the field and I heard the crowd yelling obscenities at us. But I thought of what Madden had told us and I said to myself, "Isn't it great how all of these people are cheering for us?"

We won that game, 16-7. That was a great game, but the overtime win against the Colts has to be the most unforgettable one of my career.

—*As told to Barry Janoff*

Six-foot-eight, 280-pound defensive lineman **John Matuszak** (72), above, found his niche during six seasons (1976–81) with the Oakland Raiders and was a key to wins in Super Bowls XI and XV. A stormy rookie year with the 1973 Houston Oilers led him to try, unsuccessfully, to jump to the World Football League. Dealt to Kansas City in mid-1974, he briefly entered the ring as a pro boxer before returning to the Chiefs in 1975. In 1976, Matuszak was traded to—and then waived by—the Washington Redskins before ending up in Oakland.

1960 NFL CHAMPIONSHIP GAME

When we opened the 1960 season with a 17-point loss to the Cleveland Browns and a nail-biting, two-point win over the

expansion Dallas Cowboys, people were saying the Philadelphia Eagles should start building for next year.

Who could blame them? We certainly didn't come into the season with the most talented team. We had guys like Norm Van Brocklin and Sonny Jurgensen at quarterback, Pete Retzlaff at receiver and Chuck Bednarik at center, but there were several teams that easily had more talent than us.

In the Western Conference, Vince Lombardi's Green Bay Packers were loaded with Hall of Famers. By the end of the decade, they'd be winning Super Bowls. The Browns had a couple of guys named Jim Brown and Bobby Mitchell in their backfield.

What happened in between that embarrassingly narrow win over the Cowboys and our victory over the Packers in the 1960 Championship Game could almost be called a miracle. We somehow went from woeful to world champions.

A big part of the reason for the transformation was the guts the team had. What we lacked in talent, we would make up for in desire and hustle. We had guys who would bite, kick, scratch, gouge—whatever it took to win, they would do it.

For instance, when Peaks got hurt, rookie Ted Dean came out of nowhere and carried the rushing load. He finished with 304 yards rushing that year. When the linebackers got hurt, Bednarik stepped up and said, "I'll play there." He played both ways for the last part of the season. Van Brocklin was playing in his twelfth year in the NFL. A lot of other quarterbacks would have thrown in the towel by then and taken up selling insurance or real estate. But he had guts. That year, he looked like a fresh-faced rookie, throwing for almost 2,500 yards and 24 touchdowns.

I only caught 39 balls in 1960, but I was still proud. Thirteen of them went for touchdowns. Today, guys catch 100 balls and maybe score 10 touchdowns. My catches were primarily for big gains. Our team was really built around the big play.

We eked out a 31-27 win over the Cardinals in the third game of the season, and never looked back. Before we lost to Pittsburgh in the second to last game of the year, we won nine straight games.

Our 10-2 record was good enough to win the Eastern Conference and send us into the title game against the mighty Packers. This team had everything. It had a star in the making at quarterback in Bart Starr. It had a star halfback in Paul Hornung, who scored a record 176 points that year. It had a star fullback in Jim Taylor, who ran for 1,100 yards and 11 touchdowns that season. It had offensive linemen like Jerry Kramer, Fuzzy Thurston, Jim Ringo and Forrest Gregg. It had defensive terrors like Ray Nitschke, Willie Wood and Henry Jordan. They should have called this team the Canton Packers because that's where almost all of them ended up.

What we had going for us was that we didn't know much about them. We didn't play them in the regular season, so all we knew of them was what we saw on the highlight reels. This was an advantage because we weren't intimidated by them.

At the start of the game, we played like we were intimidated. On our very first play from scrimmage, we fumbled the ball away on our own 14-yard line. But our defense was equal to the test, stopping Green Bay on downs.

We got the ball back and turned it over to them again. This time the Packers took the ball over on our 22 and eventually kicked a field goal to take a 3-0 lead.

In the second quarter, we took the lead. Van Brocklin found me on a 35-yard touchdown throw. As I was going into the end zone, one of the Packers shoved me in the back and I went into snow. They had so many people in the stadium, they let them put seats on the field. That's where I went— right into the people. Everyone wanted the ball. They were yelling, "Get him up! Get him up! Get the ball! Get the ball!"

Later we added a field goal and felt good about our 10-6 lead going into halftime.

The Packers weren't about to quit. They took the lead back in the fourth quarter when Max McGee caught a 7-yard

---

DECEMBER 26, 1960
PHILADELPHIA EAGLES 17, GREEN BAY PACKERS 13
FRANKLIN FIELD, PHILADELPHIA, PENNSYLVANIA

SCORING

PHI	0	10	0	7	**17**
GB	3	3	0	7	**13**

GB — Hornung, 20-yard field goal
GB — Hornung, 23-yard field goal
PHI — McDonald, 35-yard pass from Van Brocklin (Walston kick)
PHI — Walston, 15-yard field goal
GB — McGee, 7-yard pass from Starr (Hornung kick)
PHI — Dean, 5-yard rush (Walston kick)

TEAM STATISTICS

	PHI	GB
First Downs	13	22
Rushes-Yards	32-99	42-223
Passing Yards	197	178
Passes	9-20-1	21-35-0
Punts-Average	3-39.5	5-45.2
Fumbles-Lost	3-2	1-1
Penalties-Yards	0-0	4-27

INDIVIDUAL STATISTICS

Rushing
PHI — Dean 13 rushes for 54 yards; Barnes 13-42; Van Brocklin 2-3
GB — Taylor 24-105; Hornung 11-61; McGee 1-35; Moore 5-22; Starr 1-0

Passing
PHI — Van Brocklin 9 completions, 20 attempts, 204 yards, 1 interception
GB — Starr 21-34-178-0; Hornung 0-1-0-0

Receiving
PHI — McDonald 3 receptions for 90 yards; Walston 3-38; Retzlaff 1-41; Dean 1-22; Barnes 1-13
GB — Knafelc 6-76; Taylor 6-46; Hornung 4-14; McGee 2-19; Moore 2-9; Dowler 1-14

ATTENDANCE: 67,325

What we lacked in talent, we would make up for in desire and hustle. We had guys who would bite, kick, scratch, gouge—whatever it took to win, they would do it.

touchdown pass from Starr.

But like I said, we had guts, and those guts helped us win the game with five minutes remaining. They kicked off to us after taking the lead and Dean returned it to their 39. We used our running game, not our big-play passing game, to drive it downfield. Finally, Dean took it the last five yards for a touchdown.

Green Bay tried to come back again, but time ran out on them with them holding the ball on our 9-yard line.

I would never have imagined it because there were so many teams with more talent. To me, our win proved that hustle and desire could compensate for a lot of things.

The only other game in my career that

would come close was in 1959. I had my jaw broken in the first game of the year against the San Francisco 49ers. I played the next week against the Giants because they said to me, "You're going to play. We need you."

They wired my jaw shut. I had to live on a diet of chocolate shakes. I thought there was no way I was going to last the whole game because I was losing weight like crazy. I must have been down to 141 pounds. I couldn't even talk. But, as it turned out, I scored four touchdowns against the Giants. I caught three touchdown passes and ran back an 81-yard punt.

—As told to Chuck O'Donnell

Tommy McDonald runs with the ball, above, during Oklahoma's victory over Maryland in the 1956 Orange Bowl. McDonald joined the Philadelphia Eagles in 1957 and the five-foot-seven, 175-pound wide receiver tallied 278 receptions for 5,499 yards and 64 touchdowns before he was traded to Dallas in 1964. McDonald was dealt to the Los Angeles Rams in 1965 and concluded his Pro Football Hall of Fame career with the 1967 Atlanta Falcons and the 1968 Cleveland Browns.

I figured there was no way I was going to play in Super Bowl I against the Kansas City Chiefs. Vince Lombardi kept me and

JANUARY 15, 1967
GREEN BAY PACKERS 35, KANSAS CITY CHIEFS 10
MEMORIAL COLISEUM, LOS ANGELES, CALIFORNIA

SCORING

GB	7	7	14	7	**35**
KC	0	10	0	0	**10**

GB   McGee, 37-yard pass from Starr (Chandler kick)
KC   McClinton, 17-yard pass from Dawson (Mercer kick)
GB   Taylor, 14-yard run (Chandler kick)
KC   Mercer, 31-yard field goal
GB   Pitts, 5-yard run (Chandler kick)
GB   McGee, 13-yard pass from Starr (Chandler kick)
GB   Pitts, 1-yard run (Chandler kick)

TEAM STATISTICS

	KC	GB
First Downs	17	21
Rushes-Yards	19-72	33-130
Passing Yards	228	250
Passes	17-32-1	16-24-1
Punts-Average	7-45.3	4-43.3
Fumbles-Lost	1-0	1-0
Penalties-Yards	4-26	4-40

INDIVIDUAL STATISTICS
Rushing
KC   Dawson 3 rushes for 24 yards; Garrett 6-17; McClinton 6-16; Beathard 1-14; Coan 3-1
GB   Taylor 16-53; Pitts 11-45; D. Anderson 4-30; Grabowski 2-2
Passing
KC   Dawson 16 completions, 27 attempts, 211 yards, 1 interception; Beathard 1-5-17-0
GB   Starr 16-23-250-1; Bratkowski 0-1-0-0
Receiving
KC   Burford 4 receptions for 67 yards; Taylor 4-57; Garrett 3-28; McClinton 2-34; Arbanas 2-30; Carolan 1-7; Coan 1-5
GB   McGee 7-138; Dale 4-59; Pitts 2-32; Fleming 2-22; Taylor 1-minus 1

ATTENDANCE: 61,946

Paul Hornung on the Green Bay Packers roster all year because he thought we kept the team loose; he liked to keep me around because he figured, in a pinch, he could trust me to go out and get the job done. But I hardly played that season. By then I was 34 and had caught only three passes all year, so I had no reason to think I'd start playing now.

They didn't need me much anyway. We'd had a strong season, winning the NFL title for the fourth time in six years. We had a great team, with guys like quarterback Bart Starr, fullback Jim Taylor, offensive linemen Forrest Gregg and Jerry Kramer, linebacker Ray Nitschke and defensive back Herb Adderley, just to name a few.

Those are the guys who led us into the inaugural NFL-AFL title game against the AFL-champion Kansas City Chiefs. Some of the writers covering the game began to call it the "Super Bowl," although it wasn't as big of a deal then as it is now.

We got to southern California a week early to practice, and our team was staying in Santa Barbara. Well, Santa Barbara is primarily a retirement community, so there wasn't much of anything to do at night. I felt like I was being kept in a cage.

The day before the game, they moved us into Los Angeles. We were itching to have some fun. I had spoken with a few airline stewardesses before curfew and told them that I'd meet up with them in Beverly Hills later on that night. I went back to the hotel the team was staying at and was in bed under the sheets with my clothes on when they came around for bed check. As soon as they finished checking my room, I checked out.

It was like getting out of jail. I met up with those stewardesses and had a good time. I wasn't a heavy drinker; I was just out enjoying myself. I must have been out until 4 or 5 a.m.

The next day, when we got to the stadium, I still figured there was no way in the world I was going to play. I didn't even

bother to stretch out too much because I figured I'd just be sitting around watching anyway.

The game had just started, and I was sitting on the bench with Hornung. We were sitting there planning his bachelor party when I heard Lombardi yell out in his gravely voice, "McGee! McGee!" Boyd Dowler had gotten injured on the first series of downs, and Lombardi was yelling for me to go in. I had to scramble to my feet. I grabbed a helmet—I'm pretty sure it was someone else's; I don't think I could find mine—and I went in. Little did I know it would end up being the game I'll never forget.

In the second quarter, I scored the first touchdown in Super Bowl history on a 37-yard pass from Starr. But Kansas City refused to quit, even though everyone thought that because we were from the more established league, we'd win easily. We took a slim 14-10 lead into halftime.

In the third quarter, however, we broke it open. Elijah Pitts scored on a five-yard run to give us a 21-10 lead, and then I caught my second touchdown pass of the game—a 13-yarder from Starr—to really lock things up. I finished the game with seven catches for 138 yards and two scores. It was one of the best days of my career, one of those days when I couldn't do anything wrong. And I didn't show any signs of rustiness. I guess once you're a well-conditioned athlete, you can return to that state in a pinch.

The only game that comes close to that Super Bowl in my memory was the 1960 NFL Championship Game against the Philadelphia Eagles. It was a real seesaw battle. We had an early lead on two Hornung field goals, but Eagles quarterback Norm Van Brocklin threw a touchdown pass to Tommy McDonald to put them ahead.

They were leading 10-6 in the third quarter when we came up with a big defensive stand, stopping the Eagles on our 4-yard line. We got the ball back but were forced to punt. I was doing the punting in those days. I used to fake the punt and take off with the ball fairly regularly before Lombardi took over the season before; he took me aside and said not to do that

By then I was 34 and had caught only three passes all year, so I had no reason to think I'd start playing now.

Green Bay Packer **Max McGee** snares a pass in the end zone, above, for one of his two touchdown receptions in Super Bowl I. McGee played his first season for the Packers in 1954—at end and punting—but missed the following two seasons serving in the military. He returned to Green Bay for 11 more seasons (1957–67), hitting career highs in 1961 with 51 receptions, 883 receiving yards, and eight touchdowns. McGee retired with 345 receptions for 6,346 yards and 41 touchdowns.

anymore. But on this one formation, I saw that I had plenty of room to run. Something inside me took over, and I tucked the ball under my arm and took off. I got the first down and would have gotten more had I not slipped on a patch of ice. But it kept the drive alive. We drove the ball inside their 10, where Starr found me on a slant pattern for a seven-yard touchdown pass.

Our lead didn't last long. The Eagles' Tom Dean ran the ensuing kickoff back 58 yards. A few plays later, Dean scored on a five-yard run to put them ahead for good.

In the locker room after the game, I didn't want to face Lombardi. I was sure he was going to be steamed with me for faking that punt. A reporter immediately asked him about the play. Lombardi said it was a great call, and that in that situation he didn't want to give up the ball. He said, "A guy with McGee's experience has the option of running it in that situation." Boy, did I laugh. I thought I was going to be exiled for faking that punt.

—*As told to Chuck O'Donnell*

In Super Bowl XX, the Chicago Bears beat New England 46-10. The Bears lost only one game that season, and we had a lot of

NOVEMBER 10, 1991
PHILADELPHIA EAGLES 32, CLEVELAND
   BROWNS 30
MUNICIPAL STADIUM, CLEVELAND, OHIO

SCORING

PHI	0	17	6	9	**32**
CLE	16	14	0	0	**30**

CLE   Stover, 50-yard field goal
CLE   Turner, 42-yard interception return (Stover kick)
CLE   Hoard, 65-yard pass from Kosar (kick failed)
CLE   Slaughter, 18-yard pass from Kosar (Stover kick)
PHI   K. Jackson, 16-yard pass from McMahon
         (Ruzek kick)
PHI   Barnett, 70-yard pass from McMahon (Ruzek kick)
PHI   Ruzek, 21-yard field goal
CLE   Langhorne, 24-yard pass from Kosar (Stover kick)
PHI   Ruzek, 37-yard field goal
PHI   Ruzek, 24-yard field goal
PHI   Ruzek, 19-yard field goal
PHI   Williams, 5-yard pass from McMahon (kick failed)

TEAM STATISTICS

	PHI	CLE
First Downs	24	16
Rushes-Yards	28-97	11-25
Passing Yards	341	246
Passes	26-43-1	14-33-1
Punts-Average	4-46.8	5-48.6
Fumbles-Lost	0-0	1-1
Penalties-Yards	10-72	7-86

INDIVIDUAL STATISTIC
Rushing
PHI   Joseph 20 rushes for 89 yards; Sherman 2-6;
         Byars 5-3; McMahon 1-minus 1
CLE   Mack 10-23; Hoard 1-2
Passing
PHI   McMahon 26 completions, 43 attempts, 341
         yards, 1 interception
CLE   Kosar 14-33-246-1
Receiving
PHI   Barnett 8 receptions for 146 yards; Williams
         6-76; Keith Jackson 6-76; Johnson 2-13;
         Sherman 1-9; Green 1-9; Byars 1-7; Joseph 1-5
CLE   Slaughter 5-74; Langhorne 4-73; Brennan 2-22;
         Hoard 1-65; Galbraith 1-13; Mack 1-minus 1

ATTENDANCE: 72,086

players who were totally dedicated to winning, winning, winning and not stopping until we won the Super Bowl. That whole season stands out for me because so many things happened—so many good things as well as strange things.

When it comes to a particular game, though, there was one in 1991 with Philadelphia that stands out simply because it shouldn't have happened the way it did, and maybe we should have lost. But we won when we came back to beat Cleveland 32-30 after trailing 23-0.

Football is a challenge. You pit your best against their best, and if everything goes according to plan your best will beat their best. But that's the challenge—to see that your best can beat their best.

On that day, there were moments when it didn't seem as if we could do what we needed to do to win. Let me rephrase that: There were moments when it didn't seem as if I could do what I needed to do to win. A lot of guys on the team showed me that day that no obstacle was too big to overcome. They were giving me a lot of credit for the win after the game, but they were the ones who inspired me.

My right elbow had bothered me all season. I had a tendonitis problem that began in training camp. I knew that I could deal with the situation, but I ended up having to use it a lot more and a lot sooner than was anticipated after Randall Cunningham went down with a season-ending injury in the opening week. The pain wasn't going to stop me, but the elbow got worse as the season went along until it reached a point where using my arm was a big problem.

On the Friday before the Browns game I got an injection of painkiller in my elbow. Early Saturday morning I woke up nauseous and with my elbow throbbing and feeling about the size of a watermelon. I figured, "Man, someone is playing a number on me." But it wasn't the pain so much because if you can't play through the pain you don't belong

in this league. The problem was that I couldn't use my arm. The swelling hadn't gone down by Sunday morning, and I even had to have tackle Ron Heller tie my ponytail for me before we left for the game.

Our trainer, Otho Davis, spent several hours working on my elbow, and just before the game, team physician Dr. Vincent DiStefano drained the fluid out of it. Coach Rich Kotite kept asking me how I felt. After Davis and DiStefano worked on me for four or five hours, I got some movement back. So I told the coach that we should go for it.

I regretted the decision for the whole first quarter, which might have been the worst of my career. Browns safety Eric Turner intercepted my second pass of the day and ran it back for a touchdown. Browns quarterback Bernie Kosar threw a touchdown pass a few minutes after that, and then threw another one a few seconds into the second quarter. So we were down 23-0 and getting our butts kicked.

The game was being played in Cleveland, and the Browns fans were having a great time. At that point some other coaches might have replaced their quarterback, but coach Kotite was behind me all the way. I told him that my elbow actually felt better and that my arm had more mobility. And, to be honest, I didn't want to come out at that point. The other guys on the team weren't quitting. Wide receiver Fred Barnett kept coming back to the huddle saying, "I can beat that guy." And the other guys were saying, "They aren't better than us. We can take them."

I figured that if we got one touchdown, we could turn the situation around. We put a good offensive drive together early in the second quarter, and I hit Keith Jackson with a pass for our first score about five minutes into the quarter. Our defensive guys started to put their game together at that point, and the Browns didn't score when they got the ball back. On our next possession, I hooked up with Fred on a 70-yard touchdown pass. On the sidelines, I said to him, "You were right. You could beat that guy."

We scored again on a Roger Ruzek field goal, and Bernie threw another touchdown pass before the half, so we went into the locker room trailing 30-17. Making up the 13

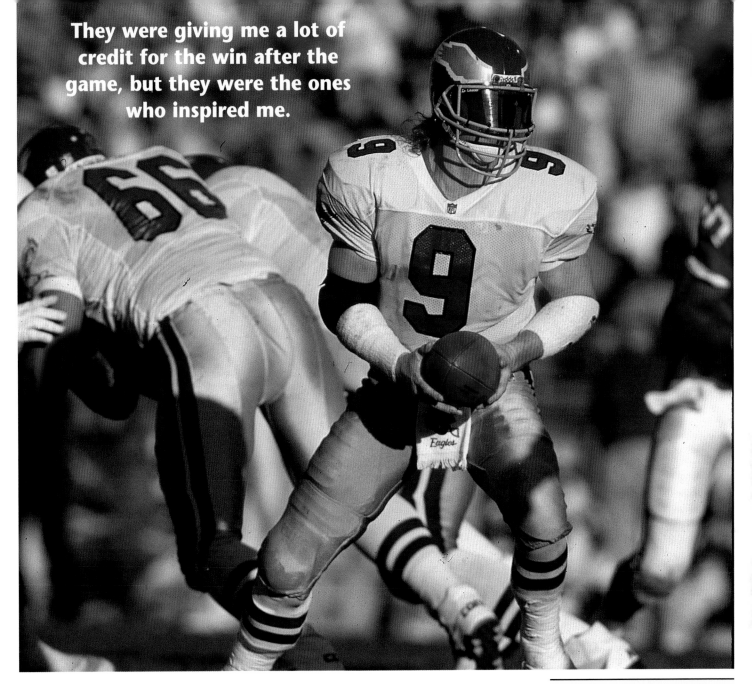

They were giving me a lot of credit for the win after the game, but they were the ones who inspired me.

points was possible, especially since we had been down by 23 just a few seconds into the second quarter. The feeling was upbeat. Every one of us firmly believed that we could meet the challenge and pull out a win.

My elbow began to swell and tighten up a bit, but Otho worked on it during halftime. I called a lot of audibles in the second half, and that seemed to keep Cleveland's defensive guys off balance. Ruzek kicked a couple of field goals in the third quarter, and then another a few minutes into the fourth quarter to put us within four points, 30-26.

We weren't overpowering on offense in the second half, but our defensive guys were amazing, and we were able to keep the ball away from Kosar for a very long time. About five or six minutes into the fourth quarter,

we went on a drive that I felt had touchdown written all over it. I was still calling a lot of audibles, and their defensive guys seemed to be back on their heels rather than being aggressive. We got down to about Cleveland's five, and then I hit wide receiver Calvin Williams with what turned out to be the winning touchdown pass.

The point after was blocked, so we were up by only two with about five minutes to play. Our defensive guys played super tough to shut down Cleveland. The Browns couldn't even get within field-goal range.

There were a lot of heroes for us that day, but we ended up giving game balls to Otho and Dr. DiStefano.

—As told to Barry Janoff

Quarterback **Jim McMahon** starred with the Chicago Bears for seven seasons (1982–88). His best year proved to be 1985: McMahon went to the Pro Bowl after completing 313 passes for 2,392 yards. More important, he led the Bears to victory in Super Bowl XX. After leaving Chicago, McMahon bounced to the San Diego Chargers (1989), the Philadelphia Eagles (1990–92), the Minnesota Vikings (1993), the Arizona Cardinals (1994) and the Minnesota Vikings (1995–96). He retired after completing 1,492 passes for 18,148 yards and 100 touchdowns.

1982 AFC FIRST-ROUND PLAYOFF GAME

The Freeman McNeil who tossed and turned in bed the night before taking on the Cincinnati Bengals in the 1982 season's

first round of the playoffs wasn't the same running back who walked off the field victorious the next day. After that game—after rushing for 202 yards, scoring a touchdown and throwing another TD strike in the New York Jets' 44-17 win over Cincinnati—I was changed.

That was a strange season because the players went on strike after two games. The leaders on the Jets kept the players close during that period by holding practices; they talked to younger guys like me about what was happening and explained why it was important for us to be on strike.

When the season resumed after a seven-game hiatus, we had a strong year. Powered by a lethal offense consisting of quarterback Richard Todd and an offensive line anchored by Marvin Powell, we won our first four games after the strike. I finished the season with a league-leading 786 rushing yards, a yards-per-carry average of 5.2, and six touchdowns. Although our defense was hurt by a knee injury to Joe Klecko, "the New York Sack Exchange" still was fantastic, thanks to Mark Gastineau, Marty Lyons and Abdul Salaam.

It all added up to a second straight trip to the playoffs. This time we were going to face the Bengals, who had assembled a powerhouse offense that included quarterback Kenny Anderson, running back Pete Johnson, wide receivers Cris Collinsworth and Isaac Curtis and tight end Dan Ross.

As we flew to Ohio, I was really nervous. I knew that a lot of things would fall on my shoulders, even though our plan was to throw the ball a lot. Our offensive coordinator, Joe Walton, had instituted a new passing system with plays we called "waggles." It sounded kind of corny to me. I didn't really understand the scheme—and neither did half the team—but that's what we were going to use.

The night before the game, I sat in the locker room at a table and listened to the other guys talk about the significance of this match-up. They were saying that everything was starting to come together under coach Walt Michaels. As I sat back and listened, I began to worry. Here was this big game, and they were telling me that it would be nationally televised.

I looked across the room and saw the coaches convene. Michaels had a habit of kicking all the players out because he didn't want them to know what the coaches were going to talk about. I was the last one left in the room, and I walked over to Michaels and said, "I really need to talk to you." To my amazement, he dismissed all of his coaches. I then sat down and talked to him about his playing days, about what it was like to be in championship games.

Coach Michaels felt pretty much the way I did. He told me about a teammate of his on the Cleveland Browns, a guy named Jim Brown. Michaels had asked Brown the same questions: How do you approach a big game? What do you do? Brown, maybe the greatest football player ever, said he approached each play as if it were his last because you never knew what might happen next.

The next day, as the first quarter ended, I found myself looking at a scoreboard that read: "Bengals 14, Jets 3." The Bengals fans were rocking in Riverfront Stadium—and our team was on its heels. Michaels, however, knew what was going on; he was an ex-player who had been in a lot of situations, and he could counteract anything. He told Walton to cease on that waggle stuff because the players didn't know it very well. He said we had an offensive line and a young running back—we needed to run. So we went to the running game.

In the second quarter, we ended up moving the ball well on the ground, which set up our first touchdown. We had a trick play designed to look like a sweep: I got the pitchout, but I wasn't running—I was throwing. Derrick Gaffney was wide open, and I hit him with a 14-yard touchdown pass. We put 10 more points on the board and went into the locker room at halftime with a 20-14 lead.

When we came back out to start the second half, the assistant coaches were

JANUARY 9, 1983
NEW YORK JETS 44, CINCINNATI BENGALS 17
RIVERFRONT STADIUM, CINCINNATI, OHIO

SCORING

NYJ	3	17	3	21	**44**
CIN	14	0	3	0	**17**

CIN	Curtis, 32-yard pass from Anderson (Breech kick)
NYJ	Leahy, 32-yard field goal
CIN	Ross, 2-yard pass from Anderson (Breech kick)
NYJ	Gaffney, 14-yard pass from McNeil (Leahy kick)
NYJ	Walker, 4-yard pass from Todd (Leahy kick)
NYJ	Leahy, 24-yard field goal
NYJ	Leahy, 47-yard field goal
CIN	Breech, 20-yard field goal
NYJ	McNeil, 20-yard run (Leahy kick)
NYJ	Ray, 98-yard interception return (Leahy kick)
NYJ	Crutchfield, 1-yard run (Leahy kick)

TEAM STATISTICS

	NYJ	CIN
First Downs	27	23
Rushes-Yards	34-234	21-62
Passing Yards	283	333
Passes	21-29-1	26-36-3
Punts-Average	0-0.0	2-43.0
Fumbles-Lost	2-1	2-1
Penalties-Yards	12-95	7-60

INDIVIDUAL STATISTICS
Rushing

NYJ	McNeil 22 rushes for 202 yards; Dierking 3-11; Harper 1-9; Newton 2-6; Todd 3-3; Augustyniak 2-2; Crutchfield 1-1
CIN	Johnson 9-26; Alexander 7-14; Anderson 2-5; Griffin 3-17

Passing

NYJ	Todd 20 completions, 28 attempts, 269 yards, 1 interception; McNeil 1-1-14-0
CIN	Anderson 26-35-354-3; Schonert 0-1-0-0

Receiving

NYJ	Walker 8 receptions for 145 yards; Augustyniak 1-4; J. Jones 2-22; Gaffney 4-50; Harper 2-35; McNeil 1-9; Dierking 2-9; Barkum 1-9
CIN	Griffin 3-14; Collinsworth 7-120; Curtis 3-63; Ross 6-89; Harris 1-20; Kreider 3-41; Johnson 3-7

ATTENDANCE: 57,560

We had a trick play designed to look like a sweep: I got the pitchout, but I wasn't running—I was throwing.

talking to Michaels, who was staring out at the field. Walton ran up to him and began talking; he was trying to tell Michaels that he had fixed the problem with the new passing offense, but Michaels just looked right through him.

I happened to be standing there while Walton talked to Michaels. Suddenly, Michaels looked at Walton, looked at me, and pushed Walton aside. Michaels asked me point-blank: "What do you want to do?" I was so scared at first that I couldn't answer him. A lump in my throat made it difficult to breathe, and I almost passed out. Then it just came to me, and I said: "I want to run the

ball, Coach." With that, everyone got quiet and shrank away.

We dominated the Bengals in the second half, outscoring them 24-3. We wound up with 234 rushing yards, capped by my 20-yard touchdown run in the fourth quarter. That game left a big impression on me. Michaels handed me a tremendous responsibility, and that always has stayed with me. From then on, I approached every game as if it were my last. It was the best advice anyone has ever given me.

—*As told to Chuck O'Donnell*

New York Jets running back **Freeman McNeil** led the NFL in the strike-shortened nine-game 1982 campaign, when he rushed for 786 yards. He went to the Pro Bowl that season, and again in 1984 and 1985. McNeil, drafted in the first round out of UCLA, played 12 seasons (1981–92) for the Jets, amassing 8,074 yards and 38 touchdowns from 1,798 carries. He also made 295 receptions, for an additional 2,961 yards and 12 touchdowns.

I suppose it is traditional, when one reflects on the single game he best remembers, to recall some big win in

DECEMBER 11, 1960
DETROIT LIONS 23, DALLAS COWBOYS 14
BRIGGS STADIUM, DETROIT, MICHIGAN

SCORING

DET	0	16	7	0	**23**
DAL	0	7	0	7	**14**

DET	Pietrosante, 43-yard run (Martin kick)
DET	Safety, center pass went out of end zone
DET	Pietrosante, 40-yard run (Martin kick)
DAL	Dupre, 1-yard run (Cone kick)
DET	Cogdill, 7-yard pass from Morrall (Martin kick)
DAL	Howton, 31-yard pass from LeBaron (Cone kick)

TEAM STATISTICS	DET	DAL
First Downs	17	24
Rushes-Yards	50-213	30-114
Passing Yards	130	172
Passes	12-14-0	18-27-1
Punts-Average	2-44.5	3-33.0
Fumbles-Lost	3-1	3-2
Penalties-Yards	8-86	8-117

INDIVIDUAL STATISTICS

Rushing

DET   Barr 1 rush for minus 7 yards; Lewis 12-58; Morrall 8-20; Pietrosante 21-142; Webb 8-0

DAL   Babb 2-18; Dupre 15-83; Kowalczyk 7-4; LeBaron 3-5; McIlhenny 3-4

Passing

DET   Morrall 12 completions, 14 attempts, 145 yards, 0 interceptions

DAL   LeBaron 18-27-195-1

Receiving

DET   Cassady 5 receptions for 63 yards; Cogdill 2-21; Gibbons 5-61

DAL   Doran 2-23; Dugan 6-73; Dupre 2-17; Howton 6-84; Kowalczyk 1-6; McIlhenny 1-minus 8

ATTENDANCE: 43,272

which he had an outstanding day. Or maybe even one of the most disappointing defeats. Frankly, I can't come up with one in either category at the moment.

But there's one I vividly recall. The last game of that 1960 season, our first in the league—I'll never forget it. It was the final defeat we would suffer in a 0-11-1 season.

We were in Detroit to play the Lions and there was no way I was going to get into the game. Eddie LeBaron was still our quarterback then. He had been playing well and I was dead certain he would go all the way. So, I decided the night before the game would be as good a time as any to get acquainted with the Motor City. That was the first time in my football career I had ever made a complete night of it. But, shoot, I wasn't worried.

In fact, by the time the sun came up I wasn't even feeling the cold anymore.

That Sunday was unbelievable. It was well below the freezing mark and there was a 17-mile-per-hour wind ripping off the icy river. Why in the world 43,000 people would come out to watch a game in weather like that was beyond me. They were even building fires in the stands. All I could figure was that they knew they were all but guaranteed to see their Lions beat us. Everybody else had.

Anyway, I reported to the dressing room that afternoon in a pretty good frame of mind. Wasn't worried about a thing. Until Tom Landry came up to me and told me I was going to be the starter.

I was sitting there with my pads on, my jersey, my socks and shoes, trying my darndest to figure out how I was going to make it through the day when Nate Borden, the former Green Bay defensive end who had been picked up by the Cowboys that year, came over. He looked down at me and said, "Boy, you're gonna need a lot of help today."

I grinned at him and told him, shoot, I was ready. He started laughing his head off and then said, "Well, then, maybe it would

be a good idea if you put your pants on before we go out. Which I understand we're going to be doing in just a very few minutes. It's a little chilly out there today."

The biting cold on the field performed a minor miracle. As we went through the pregame warm-ups I began to return to the living and, in fact, was getting pretty excited over the prospect of getting to start. Then we went back into the dressing room before the kickoff and I had a major sinking spell. As soon as I got warm all I could think about was some nice, cozy place to lie down and sleep for a couple of days.

But once we got back outside I made another comeback. Then Landry came up to me right before the kickoff and told me that he'd changed his mind; that he had decided to start LeBaron after all. But I was supposed to warm up and be ready.

So all through the first quarter I stood over on the sidelines, warming up. LeBaron threw an interception. And I continued to warm up. LeBaron got his hand stepped on and time-out was called. But he stayed in and I continued to warm up. That went on through the whole first half. Never got in for a single play. And then we had to go back into that warm dressing room again. I'm still not sure how I made it back onto the field for the second half, but I do recall Landry telling me to warm up again and be ready as the third quarter got underway.

It was even colder by then and had begun to snow. I had decided that Detroit was not one of my favorite places.

Midway through the third quarter Eddie got his hand stepped on again and for a few minutes they thought something might be broken. But he stayed in and I kept warming up, until the third quarter finally ended. Then I went over and sat down on the bench next to Don Heinrich. He always carried a pack of cigarettes in one of his socks so I bummed one, put on one of those big sideline jackets, and had a smoke. Why not? Landry had obviously forgotten about me.

But then, late in the fourth quarter, he came over to me and told me to warm up again. I couldn't believe it. I was worn out from warming up and didn't see any

He looked down at me and said, "Boy, you're gonna need a lot of help today."

In a nine-season (1960–68) career with the Dallas Cowboys, **Don Meredith** threw 1,170 completions for 17,199 yards and 135 touchdowns. Although "Dandy Don" helped lift the Dallas Cowboys to the top of the NFL's Eastern Conference and went to the Pro Bowl in each of his last three seasons, he retired at the age of 31. In 1970, the creation of *Monday Night Football* opened the perfect spot for Meredith, who amused and instructed football fans as a color analyst for 12 seasons.

legitimate reason in the world to do it again what with the game being almost over. I told Tom I'd just as soon not.

We lost that day, 23-14. I didn't play any football, but I learned a couple of things:

First, I found out that all-night partying is okay if you don't have to play a football game the next day. And it was on that afternoon that I first began to realize that Tom and I were going to really have a lot of fun together.

—As told to Carlton Stowers

A lot of great things happened to me after I joined the Redskins in 1980. Washington had been to the Super Bowl three times

NOVEMBER 26, 1989

WASHINGTON REDSKINS 38, CHICAGO BEARS 14

RFK STADIUM, WASHINGTON, D.C.

SCORING

WAS	0	14	10	14	**38**
CHI	0	14	0	0	**14**

WAS   Warren, 3-yard pass from Rypien (Lohmiller kick)
WAS   Clark, 5-yard pass from Rypien (Lohmiller kick)
CHI   Sanders, 96-yard kickoff return (Butler kick)
CHI   McKinnon, 12-yard pass from Tomczak (Butler kick)
WAS   Lohmiller, 28-yard field goal
WAS   Monk, 18-yard pass from Rypien (Lohmiller kick)
WAS   Monk, 9-yard pass from Rypien (Lohmiller kick)
WAS   Byner, 5-yard run (Lohmiller kick)

TEAM STATISTICS	CHI	WAS
First Downs	13	35
Rushes-Yards	19-59	37-102
Passing Yards	132	390
Passes	13-24-2	30-47-1
Punts-Average	5-37.2	1-55.0
Fumbles-Lost	1-1	2-1
Penalties-Yards	9-108	5-50

INDIVIDUAL STATISTICS

Rushing
CHI   Anderson 13 rushes for 27 yards; Gentry 1-13; Tomczak 2-10; Muster 3-9
WAS   Byner 20-82; Morris 12-20; Dupard 1-7; Rypien 3-minus 3; Sanders 1-minus 4

Passing
CHI   Tomczak 13 completions, 24 attempts, 137 yards, 2 interceptions
WAS   Rypien 30-47-401-1

Receiving
CHI   McKinnon 3 receptions for 48 yards; Gentry 3-28; Morris 2-26; Anderson 2-13; Boso 1-9; Davis 1-7; Muster 1-6
WAS   Monk 9-154; Clark 8-124; Sanders 6-67; Byner 5-45; Morris 1-10; Warren 1-3

ATTENDANCE: 50,044

and had won two of those games. Unfortunately, I was injured during the 1982 playoffs and didn't participate in our victory over Miami in Super Bowl XVII. And I was out with an injury during the last month and for most of the playoffs of the 1987 season, so I only saw limited action in our victory over Denver in Super Bowl XXII.

Washington always had a total team concept, especially under head coach Joe Gibbs. Winning the two Super Bowls was a great thrill, but I felt my contribution to those specific games was limited because of my injuries. I have to look at a game in 1989 to see one that stands out for me, not only because it was a total team victory, but also because I was happy with my production.

We were playing the Chicago Bears in Washington, and any time we met the Bears it seemed to become a great game. They wanted to beat us, and we wanted to beat them; it was a great rivalry. We were 5-6 going into that game, and they were 6-5, and it was a major turning point for us. We didn't make the playoffs, but we finished the year very strong at 10-6. Chicago ended up having a bad season—their first in a lot of years—and I think they were 6-10.

I don't know if I felt anything special before the game, or that anything special was going to happen. But I felt good, and I felt that if we stuck to our game plan we could beat them, especially with our home crowd behind us. We wanted to give them a good game because we had lost a couple of games earlier that we felt we should have won.

The defense geared its game toward stopping Chicago running back Neal Anderson. Our offense was geared toward spreading out their secondary and to keep them from focusing too much on one or two of our guys. We figured to throw a lot of passes and to vary our pass routes.

Our quarterback, Mark Rypien, had a great game, which certainly went a long way toward reaching our goal. But our receivers

were sharp all day. Gary Clark had more than 100 yards receiving, and I had nine catches for more than 150 yards. But I think five or six guys caught passes that day.

Actually, the first quarter didn't really tell much about the game—it was a defensive quarter with no scoring. In the second quarter, Rypien hit tight end Don Warren with a touchdown pass and Gary with another touchdown pass, and we were up 14-0 with about five minutes gone in the quarter.

The Bears came right back and tied the score before the quarter was over. Right after our second touchdown, Thomas Sanders took the kickoff and ran it back for a touchdown, which put a damper on our emotions. About eight minutes into the quarter Bears quarterback Mike Tomczak hit Dennis McKinnon with a pass that tied the score.

The locker room was noisy during the half, but the overall feeling was the same, I believe. We knew that we had to take charge of the game and take charge of the season if we wanted to come away with a victory. The Bears weren't the type of team that rolled over; you had to keep playing tough, hard football and keep them off their game or they'd do the same thing to you.

We seemed to have an extra step or two on their defenders for most of the second half. Either that, or our guys were able to put in more than 100 percent on almost every play. It wasn't the best half of football that I've seen our team play, but it was a great half.

Most of the play was back and forth at midfield, but we put a drive together around the 10-minute mark, and Chip Lohmiller hit a field goal that put us ahead 17-14. Some of our defensive guys went out onto the field to cover the kickoff, yelling, "No return, no return," because of what Sanders had done in the second quarter. I don't remember exactly what happened on the kickoff, but I do know the Bears didn't score.

I had been running my pass routes pretty well all day, and I was getting double coverage at times. Toward the end of the third quarter we put a pretty strong offensive drive together, and Rypien hit me with an 18-yard pass for a touchdown. That was a great feeling because I wanted to get into the end

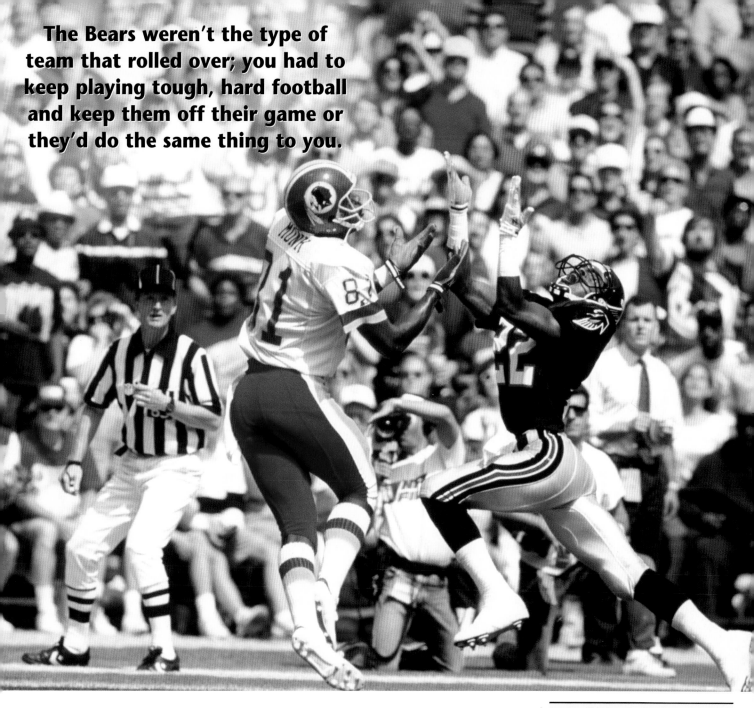

The Bears weren't the type of team that rolled over; you had to keep playing tough, hard football and keep them off their game or they'd do the same thing to you.

zone to get some points on the board for us.

Our defensive guys shut down the Bears for the entire second half, which was a great boost to the offense. Part of the total team concept we played was that the offense boosts the defense and the defense boosts the offense, and that really worked well that day.

I scored again, in the fourth quarter, and running back Earnest Byner also scored in the fourth, so the final score, 38-14, may have looked more lopsided than it actually was. The Bears played us tough, and it was an extremely close game until I scored that touchdown at end of the third quarter.

Part of the joy of playing pro football is that you get some time to savor every

victory. Not a lot of time, because you need to concentrate on the next game, but enough time in the locker room or on the way home or wherever to make each victory feel special. Beating the Bears was a definite boost for us because our season was less than special up to that point.

It's hard to put a regular-season victory in the same category as winning a championship game or the Super Bowl, but that was a special game. It gave our fans a lot to cheer about, and it went a long way toward boosting our team confidence. We carried that for the rest of the season.

—*As told to Barry Janoff*

Washington Redskins wide receiver **Art Monk**, above left, and Atlanta Falcons defensive back Tim McKyer look for the ball in a 1992 game. Monk won his third title ring the previous season in Super Bowl XXVI, in which he caught seven passes for 117 yards. Elected to three Pro Bowl games during his 14 campaigns (1980–93) with the Redskins, Monk also played for the New York Jets (1994) and the Philadelphia Eagles (1995). He retired with 940 career receptions for 12,721 yards and 68 touchdowns.

Unforgettable games? There have been a few that stand out. The Super Bowl victories, of course. Many more. But I don't

think of these games in terms of individual honors; I think of them in terms of how important they were to the team and what kind of impact these games had on the team as a whole. There were impact games when I was at Notre Dame, and there were impact games throughout my years with San Francisco.

Maybe the one that set the tone for so many things that followed was the NFC Championship Game against Dallas in the 1981 playoffs. A lot of guys on our team found themselves during that game, and what I mean is that we played a tough team in a pressure game, we were up against it in the last minute, and we won. If we had lost that game, we would have gone home and Dallas would have gone to the Super Bowl. But we won 28-27, then beat Cincinnati in Super Bowl XVI, and things took off from there.

That wasn't a one-man game, it was a team effort. It had an impact on us all. After the game, sitting in the locker room, there was a special feeling among the players. It was as if we had faced our biggest challenge, met the problem head on and come out on top. It was a physical victory, but it also was a mental victory.

About "The Catch"—the pass was intended for Dwight Clark all along. We set it up exactly that way in the huddle, including the fact that Dallas defensive end Ed "Too Tall" Jones was supposed to knock me to the ground as I released the ball. (Of course, I'm joking.)

Actually, that's the one play I get asked about more than any other. But that play came at the end of a long drive that involved the entire offensive unit. We were trailing 27-21 and were on our 11 with less than five minutes to play. That was a long 89 yards, but there was never a doubt in my mind that we could cover the distance and score the touchdown.

Dallas had a solid defensive unit, and they were in a nickel defense at that point. Our head coach at the time, Bill Walsh, and I knew we had time to move the ball with short-

yardage plays underneath Dallas' coverage, which is what we did. Lenvil Elliot, who hadn't been activated until a week before the Dallas game, gained six yards on a draw play. Then wide receiver Freddie Solomon caught a six-yard pass to give us a first down on the 23. Then we called a bob-18, which had offensive guards Randy Cross and John Ayers opening a gap on the right side of the line for Elliot, who ran through for about 11 yards.

Our guys were getting more and more charged with every play. The fact that we were successful on running plays and on pass plays during that drive was a great confidence booster because everyone was involved. Every man on the field was in on the action. It was very intense; it took total concentration from everyone.

We were near midfield at the two-minute warning. There was a lot of activity on the sideline, a lot of people running around. But my focus was on Bill and the upcoming plays. The fact that our home crowd was roaring and that our guys on the sideline were cheering us on was a great feeling, but not a distraction. My concentration was on the next play, the next moment I would be on the field.

We like to keep things interesting, so coming out of the two-minute warning we had Freddie run a reverse, which gained about 14 yards. That was the only time he ran the ball all day, but it helped to keep Dallas' defenders back on their heels rather than up on their toes. Every edge helps, and that was a big one.

We called Dwight's number on an out pattern on the next play, and he made a super catch after defensive back Everson Walls tipped the pass. Then Freddie made a great catch in heavy coverage that put us on their 13 with about a minute and 20 to play. We called a time-out and set up a couple of plays on the sideline, the first one of which was a 29-scissors. Freddie ran his pattern— cutting in and then cutting out toward the left corner of the field—but I rushed the pass a bit and it went over his head. We came back with a 19-bob, with Elliot following the offensive line on a sweep to the left. That picked up seven to put us on their six with less than a minute to play.

JANUARY 10, 1982

SAN FRANCISCO 49ERS 28 , DALLAS COWBOYS 27

CANDLESTICK PARK, SAN FRANCISCO, CALIFORNIA

SCORING

SF	7	7	7	7	**28**
DAL	10	7	0	10	**27**

SF	Solomon, 80-yard pass from Montana (Wersching kick)
DAL	Septien, 44-yard field goal
DAL	Hill, 26-yard pass from White (Septien kick)
SF	Clarke, 20-yard pass from Montana (Wersching kick)
DAL	Dorsett, 5-yard run (Septien kick)
SF	Davis, 2-yard run (Wersching kick)
DAL	Septien, 22-yard field goal
DAL	Cosbie, 21-yard pass from White (Septien kick)
SF	Clark, 6-yard pass from Montana (Wersching kick)

TEAM STATISTICS

	DAL	SF
First Downs	16	26
Rushes-Yards	32-115	31-127
Passing Yards	135	266
Passes	16-24-1	22-35-3
Punts-Average	6-39.3	3-35.7
Fumbles-Lost	4-2	3-3
Penalties-Yards	5-39	7-106

INDIVIDUAL STATISTICS

Rushing

DAL Dorsett 22 rushes for 91 yards; J. Jones 4-14; Springs 5-10; White 1-0

SF Elliott 10-48; Cooper 8-35; Ring 6-27; Solomon 1-14; Easley 2-6; Davis 1-2; Montana 3-minus 5

Passing

DAL White 16 completions, 24 attempts, 173 yards, 1 interception

SF Montana 22-35-286-3

Receiving

DAL J. Jones 3 receptions for 17 yards; DuPree 3-15; Spring 3-13; Hill 2-43; Pearson 1-31; Cosbie 1-21; Johnson 1-20; Saldi 1-9; Donley 1-4

SF Clarke 8-120; Solomon 6-75; Young 4-45; Cooper 2-11; Elliott 1-24; Shumann 1-11

ATTENDANCE: 60,525

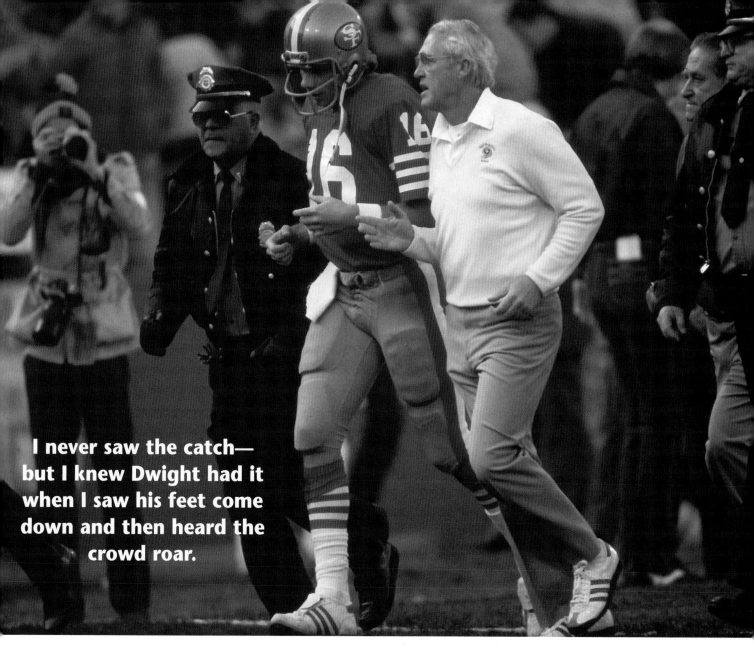

I never saw the catch—but I knew Dwight had it when I saw his feet come down and then heard the crowd roar.

We called another time-out at that point to set up the proper play. We didn't want anything fancy, just a solid play that would put us in the end zone. And, of course, everything was perfect, right down to the last step. (I'm kidding again.)

Actually, the call was a sprint-right option, which was the call when Freddie scored our first touchdown. Freddie was lined up on the right, and Dwight was on the right. Freddie goes into the end zone, then cuts left; Dwight goes into the end zone, cuts left, then cuts back right. I drop back, then roll right. I'm checking the options, and I pump two or three times. Freddie is covered, but Dwight gets a step on Walls. Walls had intercepted me twice in the game in addition to recovering a fumble, but I figured that a pass up and toward the right would lead Dwight just enough and keep Walls behind him and away from the ball.

One of the options on this play is to throw the ball away. Too Tall was in my face with his long arms up, so I passed it off the wrong foot toward Dwight, then took a solid hit from Jones and went down. I never saw the catch—but I knew Dwight had it when I saw his feet come down and then heard the crowd roar.

Dallas only needed a field goal to win after that, but our defensive guys came out and stopped them on a couple of key plays. That win put us into the Super Bowl and had a great impact on the entire franchise. I feel we would have been successful even if we had lost the game, but I'm glad we won. I'm glad that Dwight jumped higher than he ever had to jump in his playing career to pull down my "perfect" pass.

—As told to Barry Janoff

Pro Football Hall of Fame quarterback **Joe Montana** was voted to the Pro Bowl eight times and won three MVP awards in four San Francisco Super Bowl victories in the 1980s. A 49er from 1979–92, Montana hit a personal best in 1990 with 3,944 passing yards, but missed the 1991 season and all but the final 1992 game due to injury. He concluded his career with two seasons (1993–94) with the Kansas City Chiefs, bringing his totals to 3,409 completions for 40,551 yards and 273 touchdowns.

There are about three or four games I think I could talk about, but I'll go back a long ways to a game between the Detroit

DECEMBER 4, 1960
DETROIT LIONS 20, BALTIMORE COLTS 15
MUNICIPAL STADIUM, BALTIMORE, MARYLAND

SCORING

DET	3	0	0	17	**20**
BAL	2	6	0	7	**15**

BAL   Safety, Lary punt blocked by Shields
DET   Martin, 20-yard field goal
BAL   Moore, 80-yard pass from Unitas (kick failed)
DET   Cassady, 40-yard pass from Morrall (Martin kick)
DET   Martin, 47-yard field goal
BAL   Moore, 38-yard pass from Unitas (Myhra kick)
DET   Gibbons, 65-yard pass from Morrall (Martin kick)

TEAM STATISTICS

	DET	BAL
First Downs	18	19
Rushes-Yards	32-133	23-54
Passing Yards	169	333
Passes	12-28-2	22-40-3
Punts-Average	5-51.4	4-33.7
Fumbles-Lost	2-1	4-2
Penalties-Yards	6-35	4-50

INDIVIDUAL STATISTICS

Rushing
DET   Lewis 12 rushes for 47 yards; Ninowski 2-minus 18; Pietrosante 12-69; Lary 1-19; Webb 5-16
BAL   Ameche 3-15; Hawkins 6-13; Moore 8-18; Unitas 1-0; Walsh 1-0; Pricer 4-8

Passing
DET   Ninowski 8 completions, 22 attempts, 82 yards, 2 interceptions; Morrall 5-6-151-0
BAL   Unitas 22-40-357-3

Receiving
DET   Cogdill 3 receptions for 24 yards; Gibbons 3-83; Cassady 3-69; Webb 1-15; Junker 2-20; Pietrosante 1-22

ATTENDANCE: 57,808

Lions—when I was with the Lions—and the Baltimore Colts.

This game is something special to me for a lot of reasons. The Baltimore Colts were the number-one power in football, the defending champions. They beat the New York Giants for the title in that overtime game in 1958, and then beat them again in 1959.

Now it was a year later. They were still the same Colts, with John Unitas and all those great players, but over at Green Bay Vince Lombardi was doing things with the Packers, and in Detroit we were trying to ride to the top on the strength of our great defense. Our problem was putting a consistent offense together.

Jim Ninowski started at quarterback for us and we had some trouble moving the ball. We were pushed back until Yale Lary had to punt from our own end zone. The Colts wanted to force a break early so they put on a big rush. It worked. One of their big linemen came crashing through right up the middle and Lary kicked the ball squarely into his chest. The ball bounced right out of the end zone for a two-point safety for the Colts.

Late in the quarter Ninowski got a drive going and worked the ball down to the Baltimore 13-yard line. But the Colts dug in and Jungle Jim Martin had to back up and kick a 20-yard field goal. At least we had the lead.

I really can't say too much about our defense in that game. They were really great. Unitas completed more than 20 of 40 passes, but they made the big stops when they had to. The front four put on a terrific rush all day. They deflected about five passes and forced him into three interceptions—one at our 19, another at our 24—and forced him into a fumble on our 12-yard line.

You can't stop a team like that forever, though. In the second quarter Unitas and Lennie Moore electrified the huge crowd. You knew something was coming when Moore went out and lined up on the right flank. At the snap he ran a hard angle over the middle and Unitas hit him right in front of the safetyman. A missed tackle and goodbye. The pass went about 15 yards and Moore did the rest himself, 80 yards overall for the touchdown.

They missed the extra point, and the score stood like that, 8-3, through the half and through the third quarter. Our coach, George Wilson, must have thought it was time for a change. At the start of the fourth quarter he sent me in to replace Ninowski. My second pass found Hopalong Cassidy all alone down the sideline for a 40-yard touchdown and the lead for the first time that day.

A fierce line charge forced Unitas to bobble the ball on fourth and two at our 25-yard line. Now we had to sit on the ball as much as we could and run out the clock. That called for a more conservative approach. We ran and ran and ran, and inched the ball into Colt territory. When Jim Martin boomed home a field goal from the Colt 47-yard line to move us ahead 13 to 8, there was only one minute and 15 seconds left to play.

The Colts needed a touchdown and with the way our defense was playing we felt pretty comfortable. Baltimore, though, was driven by desperation, and that can be the greatest incentive in the world. They took the kickoff and started to march. There were no interceptions or fumbles now. Unitas was cool and masterful and everything at once that anyone has ever said about him. He was in perfect control, working the sideline to Berry, the quick hitch to Jim Mutscheller; using Moore as a decoy and always finding the weakness in our defense. Sometimes I think that John liked to get into those situations because it was only then that he really came alive.

He was perfect this time, working the ball down to our 34-yard line. Then came the quick strike to Moore, who made a sensational diving catch in the end zone. That stadium absolutely went nuts. It was 15-13 Baltimore.

The fans started running out on the field, players started pushing each other. Fights broke out. Cops and ushers were running around screaming and hollering and the public address announcer kept shouting into

We were pushed back until Yale Lary had to punt from our own end zone. The Colts wanted to force a break early so they put on a big rush. It worked.

his microphone, "Please clear the field! The game isn't over yet!"

And it wasn't. The clock showed there were still 14 seconds left to play.

The kickoff used up some of that. It went into the end zone, but Steve Junker figured we had nothing to lose now so he came out with it. He made a good run back to the 35. All I was thinking of was trying to move it into position for a long field-goal try. I knew I only had time for one, maybe two plays, but three points would be enough to win.

I figured they'd play their cornerbacks a little wide to keep us from getting out of bounds with the ball, but I thought if I could hit a quick one over the middle we had a chance for the long field goal shot.

I told Jim Gibbons to run a slant. I threw just as he was moving in front of the safetymen. There was a big tangle of bodies on about the 50. Gibbons got the ball and the two Baltimore safeties collided, knocking each other out of the play. He started to run for the

sideline, but when he saw he had an open field he turned toward the Baltimore goal.

Gail Cogdill had run a deep pattern down the sidelines and he wiped out one cornerback with a block. Our fullback, Ken Webb, had circled out of the backfield. There was only one Colt with a chance to catch Gibbons now—Bobby Boyd coming across the field—but Webb turned upfield and the three of them, Gibbons, Boyd and Webb, came together on about the Colt 20. Webb put a shoulder into Boyd and Gibbons was home free. Detroit 20, Baltimore 15.

Time had run out about then, and if Boyd had managed to make the tackle the game would have ended right there.

The Baltimore crowd, thinking they had the game won a few minutes before, was stunned into silence. It was a game none of them will ever forget either.

—*As told to Bob Billings*

Quarterback **Earl Morrall**'s 21-season pro career began with the San Francisco 49ers in 1956. He joined the Pittsburgh Steelers the following year—and went to the Pro Bowl—but was traded to the Detroit Lions early in the 1958 campaign. Morrall played three seasons (1965–67) for the New York Giants and four (1968–71) for the Baltimore Colts. He was elected to the 1968 Pro Bowl and relieved Johnny Unitas to help win Super Bowl V. Morrall won two more Super Bowl rings during five seasons (1972–76) with the Miami Dolphins.

Any veteran player in the NFL will have a number of games that stand out in his mind. I was part of a lot of big games with

**JANUARY 3, 1987
CLEVELAND BROWNS 23, NEW YORK JETS 20
MUNICIPAL STADIUM, CLEVELAND, OHIO**

SCORING

CLE	7	3	0	10	0	3	**23**
NYJ	7	3	3	7	0	0	**20**

NYJ Walker, 42-yard pass from Ryan (Leahy kick)
CLE Fontenot, 37-yard pass from Kosar (Moseley kick)
CLE Moseley, 38-yard field goal
NYJ Leahy, 46-yard field goal
NYJ Leahy, 37-yard field goal
NYJ McNeil, 25-yard run (Leahy kick)
CLE Mack, 1-yard run (Moseley kick)
CLE Moseley, 22-yard field goal
CLE Moseley, 27-yard field goal

TEAM STATISTICS	NYJ	CLE
First Downs	14	33
Rushes-Yards	31-104	27-75
Passing Yards	183	483
Passes	17-30-0	34-65-2
Punts-Average	14-38.0	8-39.0
Fumbles-Lost	0-0	2-0
Penalties-Yards	10-94	4-40

INDIVIDUAL STATISTICS
Rushing
NYJ McNeil 25 rushes for 71 yards; O'Brien 3-22; Paige 3-11
CLE Mack 20-63; Fontenot 3-8; Dickey 3-4; Kosar 1-0
Passing
NYJ O'Brien 11 completions, 19 attempts, 134 yards, 0 interceptions; Ryan 6-11-103-0
CLE Kosar 34-64-489-2; Brennan 1-1-5-0
Receiving
NYJ Toon 5 receptions for 93 yards; Shuler 4-43; McNeil 4-35; Walker 2-49; Paige 1-10; Sohn 1-7
CLE Newsome 6-114; Slaughter 6-86; Fontenot 5-62; Mack 5-51; Brennan 4-69; Langhorne 4-65; Holt 2-42; Weathers 1-3; Dickey 1-2

ATTENDANCE: 79,720

the Washington Redskins, including our Super Bowl XVII win against Miami. The game I'm thinking about now, however, was when I was with the Cleveland Browns and we played the New York Jets in the playoffs. I kicked a field goal with less than a minute to play to send the game into overtime, and then I kicked the game-winning field goal in the second overtime.

The main thing about that game is that I didn't let my teammates down and I didn't let myself down. People had said I didn't belong in the league anymore, but the Browns had confidence in my abilities.

I had better games than that one. I missed three field goals, including one in the first overtime that would have given us the victory. I remember walking to the sidelines after that, thinking, "What if I cost the team a game with my last kick?" I didn't want to finish up like that. So when I kicked the game-winning field goal, it was with a tremendous feeling of accomplishment for me and for the team.

The 1986 season was a strange one for me. I had been cut by the Redskins after 14 years. I wasn't sure what direction my career would take, but I always had a desire to work on television. I hooked up with CBS and was doing some work on *NFL Today* when I got a call from the Browns. I was at the studio and someone told me that I had a call from Ernie Accorsi, the Browns' general manager. I didn't take it seriously; I figured it was a crank call or something. But they called me again the next day and we worked everything out.

I joined the team after midseason, and we had a good campaign to win the division title. We had the first week of the playoffs off, but then had to face the Jets after they'd beat Kansas City. We matched up pretty well against the Jets, but they were a hard team to figure because of the strange season they had. At one point they were 10-1, then lost their last five games. But they looked strong

in beating the Chiefs, so in the week prior to our game we knew we were going to be in for a good, tough fight.

Kickers prepare for games differently than the rest of the team. I had my confidence level way up; I wanted the game to come down to my kicking a game-winning field goal. I knew I wasn't going to choke.

I missed a 46-yard field goal in our first possession of the game, but I kicked a 38-yarder in the second quarter. Both teams spent the first half trying to get some kind of an edge, but it turned into a back-and-forth affair: They scored a touchdown, then we scored one. We kicked a field goal, then they kicked one. I think everyone was happy with the results at the half.

We didn't talk about anything special in the locker room during the break at halftime. Mainly we had to keep playing our game on offense and try to keep the Jets from playing their game on offense. I wasn't thrown off by that missed field goal in the first quarter, but anytime I miss one I try to see if there is anything I should do to adjust for the next time. After 16 years in the league, I figured there was still room for improvement.

The Jets kicked a field goal on their first possession of the second half. I missed one from the 44 on our next possession, and the rest of the quarter was played mostly around midfield, with neither team scoring. In the fourth quarter, the Jets' defensive unit made some great plays, including a couple of interceptions off of Browns' quarterback Bernie Kosar. After their second interception, they were on our 25 and needed only one play to score a touchdown: Jets quarterback Ken O'Brien handed off to Freeman McNeil, and he ran in for the score.

There were only four minutes left, and the Jets were up by 10. But our guys hung tough and scored on the next possession. Kosar hit Brian Brennan with a couple of key passes. On one play, the Jets' Mark Gastineau came in on Kosar and was hit with a roughing-the-passer penalty. Kevin Mack went in from the one for the touchdown, then I hit the extra point to bring us within three with less than two minutes to play.

On the sidelines, the entire offensive unit was cheering the defense on. The important thing was to stop their drive and to get the ball back. The Jets went one-two-three and kicked, and we ended up with the ball on our 33, but with not much time remaining in the game.

On first down, Kosar threw an incomplete pass to Brennan, but Carl Howard was called for pass interference, so we had the ball first-and-10 on the Jets' 42. Then Kosar connected with Webster Slaughter for a 37-yard pass to the Jets' five. The next play was an incomplete pass, so I got the call with less than 10 seconds to play. Everything want nice and smooth, and I kicked a 22-yarder to tie the game.

I didn't feel any extra pressure going into overtime. I had been in that situation before—knowing that if the team got anywhere within field-goal range, I would get the call. What I was thinking, however, was that I *wanted* the opportunity to win the game.

The Jets had to punt on their first possession, and our offense followed with a great drive deep into the Jets' end, which set up what would have been a 23-yard field goal for me. Normally, I make those shots. But for some reason I was off balance and falling away from the ball. I barely hit it, and it went wide to the right. Walking off the field, I felt like I was carrying the weight of 80,000 people on my shoulders. You can be a hero or a heel in those situations, and I was on my way to being a heel.

On the sidelines, guys were encouraging me, saying things like, "We'll get another shot at it." My confidence was still up, and I knew that if I had another opportunity, I would be successful.

Our defense was solid in overtime and held the Jets' offense to short-yardage gains. They never got close to field-goal range, and the game went into a second overtime. Our offense put another good drive together to open up the second overtime, and it came down to a situation where the ball was just a few yards farther out from where I had missed the field goal in the first overtime. As I was heading onto the field, coach Marty Schottenheimer said to me, "Make it. It's time to go home." There was no problem; I knew the field goal was good right from the instant I hit it.

Things go bad out there sometimes. It's a question of who can handle it, who can come back. People say kickers are a strange breed. Some guys could go out there and miss the second shot because they were still

I got the call with less than 10 seconds to play. Everything went nice and smooth, and I kicked a 22-yarder to tie the game.

thinking about the first one they missed. People tend to remember kickers for their last kick. After missing the first one in overtime, everyone on the team—to a man—came over and said not to worry about it. After that I knew if I had a second opportunity to win the game, I would do it.

—As told to Barry Janoff

Place kicker **Mark Moseley** was waived by the Philadelphia Eagles after his 1970 rookie campaign, and cut by the Houston Oilers after two seasons (1971–72). His career took off with the Washington Redskins in 1973. Moseley won the 1983 NFL MVP award—he was the only kicker ever to do so—and went to two Super Bowls and two Pro Bowls. He concluded his career in 1986 with the Cleveland Browns, retiring with 482 extra points, 300 field goals and 1,382 total points.

I was drafted by the Houston Oilers in 1982, long before they became the Tennessee Titans. The team was rebuilding

at that time. The "Luv Ya Blue" years had ended, and coach Bum Phillips was gone. The great runner Earl Campbell was still in Houston, but there weren't many good players around him. So when I first arrived, we were 2-14, 3-13 or 5-11 every season.

It was a tough situation, but our lousy finishes also meant that we were able to acquire a lot of great players through the draft. We had running back Mike Rozier, and we drafted offensive linemen Dean Steinkuhler and Bruce Matthews and wide receiver Ernest Givins. And, of course, we brought in Warren Moon to play quarterback.

Little by little, we improved—and in 1987, we made a run at the playoffs. That was a strange year because there was a strike. The strike lasted four weeks, but we came back and put our season back together.

We played over our heads just to get into the playoffs, earning a wild-card berth at home against the Seattle Seahawks. That was the game I'll never forget.

After starting my career the way I did—I had been to a couple of Pro Bowls but never had been on a winning team—the 1987 season was fantastic. We finally turned the corner and got a little respect as a team. It's all about winning and getting to the playoffs. That gives some validity to what you've accomplished, and you can say, "Hey, we are becoming a good team, and we're doing something right here."

So here we were, in the playoffs. It was a new feeling for us, a new situation. I remember what a thrill it was to have the game at the Astrodome. The place was sold out; it was rocking in there. It was like the old days for Houston after all those years of rebuilding.

The Seahawks came in with a really good team. They had some great defensive players at the time, guys like linemen Jacob Green. And on offense, the Dave Krieg–to–Steve Largent connection was something you

always had to be prepared for. In fact, Largent caught a couple of touchdown passes in that game—he caught anything thrown near him.

Still, we seemed to dominate the whole game. The Seahawks were playing without their big running back, Curt Warner, so they didn't have much of a rushing attack that day.

Warren was having a good game for us, but Seattle's defense wouldn't break. Despite the fact that we had the clear advantage, the Seahawks kept things close and wound up tying the score, 20-20, in the final minute of the fourth quarter. To say the least, we were stunned that we were headed for overtime in a game we had dominated.

Overtime is a really scary feeling: One play, and the game is over. That's all it takes. Anything can happen, and you can lose on one mistake. One little mistake, and your whole season goes up in smoke.

When we got the ball in overtime, we drove down the field. But then we were stopped. Everything was resting on the little shoulders of kicker Tony Zendejas. He had made a couple of real long field goals earlier in the game, a 47-yarder and a 49-yarder. But he also had hit the left upright and right upright on a couple of other tries. He was one of the best kickers in the league at that time, and most of us thought he was going to nail this 42-yard attempt. The team had come to put a lot of faith in him.

Of course, as he was lining up for the kick, the pressure in the building was almost tangible. Some guys couldn't even watch. They just put their heads down and listened for the fans' reaction.

Well, on this one, he was true. It went right through, and we won, 23-20. Unbelievable!

It was a great feeling. We had made it all the way from the bottom of the standings to the playoffs—and won a playoff game. We then went on a seven-year run of making the playoffs.

Unfortunately, we never reached the Super Bowl. But to see both sides of it—to be on a team that struggled at first and then became successful—was special.

—As told to Chuck O'Donnell

JANUARY 3, 1988
HOUSTON OILERS 23, SEATTLE SEAHAWKS 20
ASTRODOME, HOUSTON, TEXAS

SCORING

HOU	3	10	7	0	3	**23**
SEA	7	3	3	7	0	**20**

SEA Largent, 20-yard pass from Krieg (Johnson kick)
HOU Zendejas, 47-yard field goal
HOU Rozier, 1-yard run (Zendejas kick)
HOU Zendejas, 49-yard field goal
SEA Johnson, 33-yard field goal
SEA Johnson, 41-yard field goal
HOU Drewrey, 29-yard pass from Moon (Zendejas kick)
SEA Largent, 12-yard pass from Krieg (Johnson kick)
HOU Zendejas, 42-yard field goal

TEAM STATISTICS

	SEA	HOU
First Downs	11	27
Rushes-Yards	11-29	35-178
Passing Yards	221	259
Passes	16-36-0	21-32-1
Punts-Average	7-44.3	3-35.0
Fumbles-Lost	1-1	2-1
Penalties-Yards	3-20	4-25

INDIVIDUAL STATISTICS

Rushing
SEA Williams 7 rushes for 27 yards; Morris 4-2
HOU Highsmith 12-74; Rozier 21-66; Pinkett 11-29; Wallace 2-11; Moon 4-minus 2

Passing
SEA Krieg 38 attempts, 16 completions, 237 yards, 0 interceptions; Williams 1-0-0-0
HOU Moon 32-21-273-1

Receiving
SEA Largent 7 receptions for 132 yards; Butler 3-73; Skansi 2-13; Williams 2-5
HOU Givins 7-89; Hill 6-84; Drewrey 3-62; Highsmith 2-17

ATTENDANCE: 49,622

To say the least, we were stunned that we were headed for overtime in a game we had dominated. Overtime is a really scary feeling.

Guard **Mike Munchak** went to nine Pro Bowls during his 12 seasons (1982–93) with the Houston Oilers. The six-foot-three, 281-pound lineman was a devastating blocker, in both preventing quarterback sacks and in opening spots for the run. In 1990, Houston led the NFL in total offense and, in 1990 and 1991, also led in passing offense. Munchak retired due to years of chronic knee problems and immediately moved into coaching the Oilers' offensive line. He entered the Pro Football Hall of Fame in 2001.

CHUCK MUNCIE

When you played for the New Orleans Saints in the 1970s, you weren't used to being on *Monday Night Football*. But late

in the 1979 season, we played the Oakland Raiders on Monday night, and we built up a three-touchdown lead. I had more than 100 yards rushing that game, as well as a touchdown in the first half, and Howard Cosell was saying this was "Muncie Night Football."

Playing on Monday nights made your adrenaline run higher. As a player, you knew you were going to be on center stage. You got up for this game more than any other.

Aside from being on Monday night, this was a big game because we were battling for a playoff berth. We were trying to keep pace with the Los Angeles Rams in the NFC West. We were dying to make the playoffs.

Up until then, making the playoffs seemed like a distant dream. We went through a lot of losing seasons, and struggled to find a direction. But as we started to win in 1979, the fans were really getting behind us.

I think they were coming out to see our offense, which could put points on the board. Archie Manning was the quarterback, and we also had Wes Chandler, Henry Childs, Ike Harris, Tony Galbreath and me. In addition, we had brought in Conrad Dobler to strengthen the offensive line, and we had Garo Yepremian kicking. It was a lot of fun coming to the stadium every day because you knew we had a lot of good players and a lot of firepower. You knew it was only a matter of time before we started winning some games.

We had a great offense, but stopping the other team with our defense was another matter. We just didn't have a lot of great defensive players back then. Just didn't have 'em.

One thing we did have, however, was camaraderie. We were really a close-knit team. New Orleans is a big little town; whenever you went somewhere, you weren't by yourself. Usually four, five, six, seven or eight guys went out to dinner together.

That's one of the things I attribute to Hank Stram. When he was our coach, he really put an emphasis on camaraderie. He'd have little functions after practice—they would bring in big boxes of Popeye's chicken. Instead of guys bolting out the door, Hank would bring in some beer and some Popeye's fried chicken, and we would hang out in the locker room. Guys wouldn't have even gotten into the shower yet and they'd sit there for two, three hours together, just talking. So we got close, and I believe that by 1979, when Dick Nolan was coach, that made all the difference in our team.

Our attitude really helped us that year, and we thought we had that game against Oakland in the bag. But we should have known better. The Raiders never quit.

I'll tell you a story about how much the Raiders loved to compete. Later in my career,

---

DECEMBER 3, 1979
OAKLAND RAIDERS 42, NEW ORLEANS SAINTS 35
LOUISIANA SUPERDOME, NEW ORLEANS, LOUISIANA

SCORING

OAK	7	7	7	21	**42**
NEW	0	28	7	0	**35**

OAK Chester, 3-yard pass from Stabler (Breech kick)
NEW Galbreath, 2-yard run (Yepremian kick)
NEW Galbreath, 17-yard pass from Manning (Yepremian kick)
NEW Muncie, 1-yard run (Yepremian kick)
NEW Childs, 28-yard pass from Manning (Yepremian kick)
OAK Whittington, 1-yard run (Breech kick)
NEW Bordelon, 19-yard pass interception (Yepremian kick)
OAK van Eeghen, 1-yard run (Breech kick)
OAK Ramsey, 17-yard pass from Stabler (Breech kick)
OAK Branch, 66-yard pass from Stabler (Breech kick)
OAK Branch, 8-yard pass from Stabler (Breech kick)

TEAM STATISTICS

	OAK	NEW
First Downs	31	18
Rushes-Yards	36-142	32-162
Passing Yards	264	142
Passes	26-43-2	12-23-1
Punts-Average	3-40.0	5-37.0
Fumbles-Lost	4-1	2-1
Penalties-Yards	5-52	9-101

INDIVIDUAL STATISTICS

Rushing
OAK Whittington 14 rushes for 67 yards; van Eeghen 14-49; Russell 4-21; Jenson 2-9; Stabler 2-minus 4
NEW Muncie 21-128; Galbreath 6-18, Manning 4-9, Harris 1-7

Passing
OAK Stabler 26 completions, 43 attempts, 295 yards, 2 interceptions
NEW Manning 12-23-155-1

Receiving
OAK Branch 7 receptions for 126 yards; Casper 6-53, van Eeghen 5-41; Whittington 4-38; Chester 2-5; Russell 1-5; Ramsey 1-17
NEW Galbreath 7-106; Muncie 3-7; Harris 1-13; Childs 1-28

ATTENDANCE: 65,541

Up until then, making the playoffs seemed like a distant dream. We went through a lot of losing seasons, and struggled to find a direction.

when I was with the San Diego Chargers, the Raiders got a report that I had an injured ankle. It was the left one, but they got their report mixed up and thought it was my right one. So I got tackled, and on the bottom of the pile Lyle Alzedo had my right ankle and was grinding it and everything. I got up and pretended to limp. I looked back at him and said, "Hey, wrong ankle, asshole!" They were always a tough bunch of guys, from quarterback Ken Stabler on down.

And it was Stabler who began to lead the Raiders on a comeback on this Monday night. They kept closing the deficit, and we couldn't do anything to stop it.

Cliff Branch was the big problem for us that night. We were still ahead when he caught a little five-yard out and put a move on. Branch went all the way for a touchdown. Branch later caught another TD pass that wound up winning the game for the Raiders.

We got the ball back with just a minute or so to play, but we couldn't get anything going and their defense shut us down. After mounting a 28-14 halftime lead, we lost 42-35.

That was a really tough loss because not only did we blow a big lead, but we also fell a game behind the Rams in the NFC West. We didn't make the playoffs that year—we finished at 8-8—and that late-season loss may have been the key.

—As told to Chuck O'Donnell

San Diego Chargers running back **Chuck Muncie** (46), above, vaults over the Seattle Seahawks defense for a touchdown. Muncie broke into the league in 1976 with New Orleans. In 1979, he became the first Saint to run 1,000 yards in a season and went to his first of three Pro Bowls; he was the 1980 Pro Bowl MVP. Muncie, traded to San Diego early in the 1980 campaign, rushed for 1,144 yards and 19 touchdowns in 1981. Unfortunately, he ran into a drug problem that ended his football career in 1984.

There's no question that winning the Super Bowl in 1969 against Baltimore is the most memorable game I've been in. But if you're

DECEMBER 29, 1968
NEW YORK JETS 27, OAKLAND RAIDERS 23
SHEA STADIUM, FLUSHING, NEW YORK

SCORING

NYJ	10	3	7	7	**27**
OAK	0	10	3	10	**23**

NYJ Maynard, 14-yard pass from Namath (Turner kick)
NYJ Turner, 33-yard field goal
OAK Biletnikoff, 29-yard pass from Lamonica
NYJ Turner, 36-yard field goal
OAK Blanda, 26-yard field goal
OAK Blanda, 9-yard field goal
NYJ Lammons, 20-yard pass from Namath (Turner kick)
OAK Blanda, 20-yard field goal
OAK Banaszak, 5-yard run (Blanda kick)
NYJ Maynard, 6-yard pass form Namath (Turner kick)

TEAM STATISTICS

	OAK	NYJ
First Downs	18	25
Rushes-Yards	19-50	34-144
Passing Yards	401	266
Passes	20-47-0	19-49-1
Punts-Average	7-42.7	10-41.5
Fumbles-Lost	2-0	1-1
Penalties-Yards	2-23	4-26

INDIVIDUAL STATISTICS

Rushing
OAK Dixon 8 rushes for 42 yards; Banaszak 3-6; Smith 5-1; Lamonica 3-1
NYJ Snell 19-71; Boozer 11-51; Namath 1-14; Mathis 3-8

Passing
OAK Lamonica 20 completions, 47 attempts, 401 yards, 0 interceptions
NYJ Namath 19-49-266-1

Receiving
OAK Biletnikoff 7 receptions for 190 yards; Dixon 5-48; Cannon 4-69; Wells 3-83; Banaszak 1-11
NYJ Sauer 7-70; Maynard 6-118; Lammons 4-52; Snell 1-15; Boozer 1-11

ATTENDANCE: 62,627

looking for the toughest, most unforgettable game of my career, that would have to be the one prior to the Super Bowl, when the Jets beat Oakland for the AFL title. If we hadn't won that game—and we almost didn't—we wouldn't have gotten into the Super Bowl.

The Raiders seem to have a strong squad every year, going back to the '60s, before the leagues had merged. They had won the AFL title in 1967 and were going for their second straight crown. At that time, Daryle Lamonica was their quarterback, and they had guys like Ben Davidson, Jim Otto, Fred Biletnikoff, George Atkinson, George Blanda, Pete Banaszak . . . I'm leaving some good players out. But the point is, they were a strong team.

Things were a little different with the Jets. In 1967, it was the first time we finished over .500, and '68 was the first time we won our division and made the playoffs. We had some established players on the squad, but that experience playing for the title was new to us as a team.

We had our best season in the team's history in 1968 and finished 11-3, and won our division for the first time. But we weren't getting too cocky; we weren't thinking about the Super Bowl yet because we knew we had to win the AFL Championship first.

Oakland finished in a tie for their division lead with Kansas City and they had a one-game playoff to determine the champion. Oakland was awesome in that game and beat the Chiefs, something like 41-6. Kansas City was no pushover; they beat Oakland in the 1968 season and won the Super Bowl that year. But *that* season, it seemed like Oakland was not going to be stopped.

The AFL Championship Game was played on our home field, Shea Stadium. It was late December and I remember it was bitter cold and very windy. I remember the ground being very hard, solid. Anyone who hit the ground that day felt it for a week. I also remember the crowd; there were about 60,000 people and they were all yelling and

screaming for us. Maybe they were just trying to keep warm. Most of them were huddled together, all bundled up. But there were a few jokers running around without shirts! People say I've done some unusual things, but that . . . seems very unusual.

I had the honor of playing under two great coaches during my career: Bear Bryant at Alabama and Weeb Ewbank with the Jets. Weeb led us to the Super Bowl that season. He had been to the title game before—as coach of the Baltimore Colts—and he was a very great influence on us. He kept our minds on the game and boosted our confidence.

I guess it was a combination of the crowd rooting for us and the players wanting to win more than anything else, because we came out hitting and took a 10-0 lead in the first quarter. On one of our first possessions, we moved down to the Oakland 14 and I hit Don Maynard with a touchdown pass. Then we moved down to their 30 and Jim Turner hit a field goal.

Oakland came back hitting in the second quarter and pushed us back to our 29, where Lamonica hit Fred Biletnikoff with a touchdown pass. We traded field goals and the half ended, 13-10, in our favor.

The key to the first half wasn't the score, but the fact that both teams were fighting for every yard. No one was giving an inch and guys on both sides were hitting harder—and getting hit harder—than they had all season.

I haven't talked about this much, but in the locker room I was thinking of quitting. I was in a lot of pain and both my knees were killing me. But I didn't quit, because of my teammates. A lot of guys were hurting and in pain, and we all wanted to win. With that desire, I knew if we played together as a team, like we had all season, there was no reason we couldn't beat the Raiders.

During the half I took shots in both knees, which helped somewhat. The pain was still there, but the most important thing to me was to get on the field and play.

Oakland pushed down to our 10 early in the third quarter, but our defensive unit held them and Oakland had to settle for a field goal to tie the score. Up to that point, Maynard and George Sauer were my main

No one was giving an inch and guys on both sides were hitting harder—and getting hit harder—than they had all season.

targets, and both of them were getting a lot of attention from the Oakland secondary. So we called a play for Pete Lammons, who scored on a 20-yard pass play to give us the lead.

It was 20-13 in our favor going into the fourth, but Oakland scored the next 10 points to take the lead. Lamonica was having a great game and finished with more than 400 yards passing. But toward the end, I was matching him pass for pass, and our winning touchdown came on a pass from inside their 10 to Maynard, who was free in the end zone.

The game went down to the last minute. We were leading 27-23, and they were driving for another touchdown. But Lamonica tried a lateral to Charlie Smith and the ball rolled free. Ralph Baker, one of our linebackers, jumped on the ball and we were able to run out the clock.

Looking back, I think the keys to the victory were that we mixed our plays up so well, with Matt Snell and Emerson Boozer coming out of the backfield, and Maynard, George Sauer and Pete Lammons running our pass patterns. Also, our defense held their ground game to 44, 45 yards, which was fantastic.

The Super Bowl was another great game for us. But, hell, we wouldn't have gotten there if we hadn't played tough as a team and beaten the Raiders. The next season we could have won the Super Bowl again. But Kansas City beat us in the AFL playoffs, so we didn't have the chance to repeat.

—*As told to Barry Janoff*

New York Jets quarterback **Joe Namath** (12), above, prepares to pass against the Baltimore Colts defense in Super Bowl III. His MVP performance that day is most remembered, but "Broadway Joe" spent 12 superb seasons (1965–76) with the Jets. In 1967, he became the first quarterback to pass for more than 4,000 yards in a season. After four games with the Los Angeles Rams in 1977, Namath retired with 1,886 completions for 27,663 yards and 173 touchdowns. He entered the Pro Football Hall of Fame in 1985.

There were a lot of big games for me over the 14 seasons I spent with the Green Bay Packers. It seemed that from the moment

Vince Lombardi took over as head coach every game became a big one.

There was the thrill of our first World's Championship, in 1961, when we defeated the New York Giants, 37-0, in the first title game ever held in Green Bay. There was the tremendous satisfaction of winning three consecutive World Championships and the first two Super Bowl titles.

But the game I'll never forget, the game that means something *extra* special to me was the 1962 World Championship game against the New York Giants. They had something to prove. After we beat them, 37-0, in the championship game in Green Bay, the New York writers and fans got down on the Giants. They said they were "humiliated." That's not my word, understand, that's the word used by the fans and newspapermen.

The Giants had an excellent team, a team with outstanding personnel. Their quarterback was Y.A. Tittle, and for receivers he had Del Shofner, Frank Gifford and Joe Walton. Their running backs were big, strong and tough, Phil King and Alex Webster. They had an experienced offensive line anchored by center Ray Wietecha and tackle Roosevelt Brown.

The Giants had a tough defensive unit with Sam Huff, Andy Robustelli, Rosey Grier and Dick Modzelewski up front and Dick Lynch, Erich Barnes and Jim Patton in the secondary. This would be their fourth title game in five years.

The Packers had something to play for too. We were defending champions, and this was a sort of homecoming for coach Lombardi. Lombardi had been an assistant coach with the Giants before coming to Green Bay.

It seemed that both teams played through the season just to get it over with and get back at one another again. We sort of coasted to the Western Division Championship, winning 13 games and losing only one.

The Giants eased in with a 12-2 record. Finally, on Dec. 30 we got to the game. New York was wild with excitement. Everywhere we looked there were signs: "Beat Green Bay—Bushville U.S.A."

It was less than a perfect day for football. The frozen field forced us to change our cleated shoes for ripple soles. A howling wind of 40 to 50 miles an hour swept through Yankee Stadium, raising great brown clouds of dust. The temperature was down to about 15 degrees by kickoff time and the wind was numbing.

It was hard to change directions and we had to take short, choppy steps to keep from slipping. But our guys up front, Forrest Gregg, Jerry Kramer, Fuzzy Thurston, Jim Ringo and Norm Masters kept digging and Jimmy Taylor kept churning and about halfway through the first quarter we got it close enough for Jerry Kramer to kick a 26-yard field goal.

The Giants started coming upfield. Tittle couldn't throw long in the wind, but he was deadly with the short stuff and kept mixing in the runs. They got it down to our 15-yard line and then I got lucky. I knew Tittle liked to use his tight end, Walton, and I figured this might be the spot for one of his over-the-line quickies. So before the snap of the ball I cheated a little to my left and when he threw for Walton I made a desperation lunge for the ball.

I tipped it, and it landed right in the hands of our outside linebacker Dan Currie. That got us out of the hole and both teams exchanged a few punts until, with about four minutes left in the half, Currie hit King real hard and knocked the ball loose and I fell on it on the Giants' 34.

Bart Starr handed off to Paul Hornung running to his right. It looked like the old Packer sweep, but suddenly Paul slowed down, straightened up and hit Boyd Dowler for a 25-yard gain down to the Giant seven.

On the next play, Taylor rammed right through big Grier and Sam Huff for the touchdown.

We went into the locker room leading 10-0, and for the only time in my football life I was so miserable, numb and cold I didn't feel

---

DECEMBER 30, 1962
GREEN BAY PACKERS 16, NEW YORK GIANTS 7
YANKEE STADIUM, BRONX, NEW YORK

SCORING

GB	3	7	3	3	**16**
NYG	0	0	7	0	**7**

GB Kramer, 26-yard field goal
GB Taylor, 7-yard run (Kramer kick)
NYG Collier, recovered blocked punt in end zone (Chandler kick)
GB Kramer, 29-yard field goal
GB Kramer, 30-yard field goal

TEAM STATISTICS

	GB	NYG
First Downs	18	18
Rushes-Yards	46-172	25-94
Passing Yards	96	197
Passes	10-22-0	18-41-1
Punts-Average	6-25.5	7-42.0
Fumbles-Lost	2-0	3-2
Penalties-Yards	5-44	6-42

INDIVIDUAL STATISTICS
Rushing
GB Taylor 31 rushes for 103 yards; Hornung 8-34; Moore 6-31; Starr 1-4
NYG Webster 15-56; King 9-34; Starr 1-4
Passing
GB Starr 9 completions, 21 attempts, 75 yards, 0 interceptions; Hornung 1-1-21-0
NYG Tittle 18-41-197-1
Receiving
GB Dowler 4 receptions for 30 yards; Kramer 2-25; McGee 1-11; Taylor 3-30
NYG Gifford 4-32; King 3-18; Morrison 1-0; Shofner 5-70; Walton 5-77; Webster 1-5

ATTENDANCE: 64,892

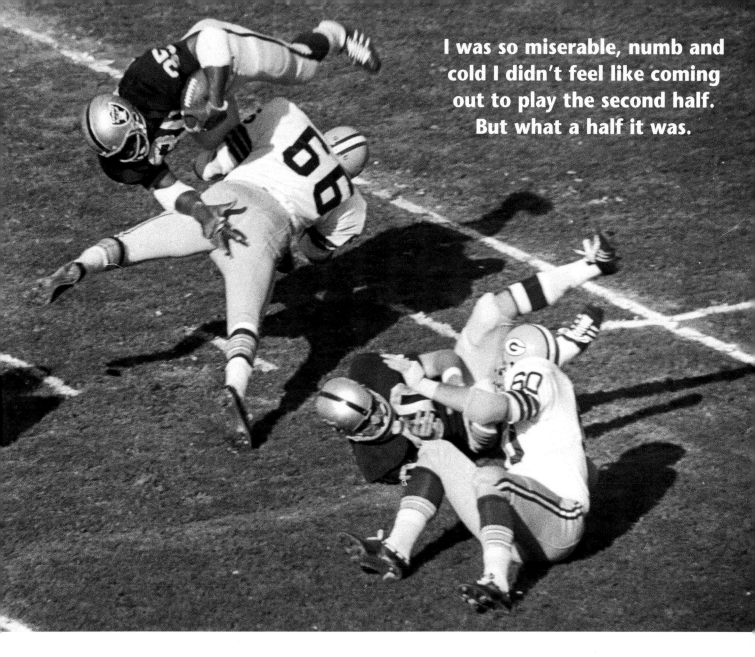

I was so miserable, numb and cold I didn't feel like coming out to play the second half. But what a half it was.

like coming out to play the second half. But what a half it was.

The Giants weren't dead and their backs were to the wall. Halfway through the third period they stopped us dead way down deep in our own territory. Max McGee had to punt from our end zone, but he never got it away. It was blocked, and Jim Collier fell on the ball for a touchdown.

The Giants must have smelled blood or revenge because they stopped us dead again. Then another break came our way. McGee punted to Sam Homer, but with the crazy wind and frozen fingers he couldn't hold the ball. I got a good start, and the ball took a Green Bay bounce. I fell on it at the Giants' 42. A few plays later Kramer kicked a 29-yard field goal and we had a little breathing room.

He kicked one about the same distance near the end of the game to make the final score 16-7.

It was a great win for us, defending our championship, and our defensive team wasn't scored on in eight consecutive quarters of championship play.

I was lucky enough to be chosen Most Valuable Player. It could have been any one of a number of players, and I looked upon the honor as a tribute to our entire defensive team.

But, anyway, nobody ever called us "Bushville U.S.A." anymore. From then on it was "Titletown U.S.A." And let's face it, it's got to give you a little extra kick for the smallest town in major league sports to knock off the biggest city in the nation. That's the game I'll never forget.

—As told to Bob Billings

Green Bay Packer **Ray Nitschke** (66), above, upends Oakland Raider Hewritt Dixon in 1968 action. Nitschke, named the NFL's all-time linebacker in 1969, played 15 seasons (1958–72) as the heart of a strong Packers defense. A hard-hitting tackler, he also had 25 career interceptions. Nitschke helped Green Bay win three NFL titles as well as the first two Super Bowls. In 1978, he became the first of that dynasty team of the 1960s to enter the Pro Football Hall of Fame.

If there ever was a game in which I just hoped to survive, it took place December 16, 1990, at home against the Seattle

Seahawks. I found myself floating around, simply trying to last from play to play.

I was eating before the game and suddenly became ill. After feeling extremely hot, I realized I was getting sick. Then I went to the bathroom and threw up. Dolphins coach Don Shula saw me and said, "We can't have this."

Despite my illness, my approach to football was that I wanted to play whenever possible, and Shula's plans were for me to be in the lineup. Since I was down on fluids, I had to get several IVs before the game. The temperature that day in Miami was 77 degrees, although it felt much hotter than that to me. During the game, I couldn't drink water, since I'd throw it up. As a result, there was no way for me to rehydrate myself.

Going into the Seahawks game, the Dolphins were 10-3 and battling for home-field advantage in the playoffs. At 7-6, Seattle simply was fighting for a postseason berth.

With Derrick Fenner and John L. Williams, we knew the Seahawks had a good running attack. Plus, Dave Krieg was an effective quarterback. After several years of mediocrity, our defense was starting to establish itself. Nevertheless, there still were questions about our ability, particularly in stopping the run. I put all of that on my shoulders; that's how I approached the sport.

At the end of the first half, we were up 17-10. I was thankful just to have lasted that long. I made a play here and there, which was great under the circumstances. For most of the game, the Seahawks banged on the door, but our defense made big plays to prevent them from scoring.

We led 24-10 going into the fourth quarter; that's when Seattle started to roll. Krieg used eight plays to drive the Seahawks to our 6-yard line. After an incomplete pass on first down, my number was called to blitz. The inside linebacker in our defense rarely blitzed. The play was designed for me to loop around the outside. Our defensive end sucked in Seattle's offensive tackle so that I could scoot around the corner. Seattle's tackle tried to scrape me off, but I ran by him and nailed Krieg for a 14-yard loss. Other teams used to laugh at us because they knew exactly what we were going to do.

At any rate, that play essentially killed their drive. Two plays later, Norm Johnson's 37-yard field-goal attempt bounced off the upright, preventing Seattle from scoring any points.

On their next possession, the Seahawks started from their own 28 and drove to our 30 with a little more than five minutes remaining in the game. I dropped back into my pattern reads and looked up; Krieg threw the ball right at me. The bullet hit me right between the eyes and stuck in my facemask. I grabbed the ball. How many times do you have an opportunity to make an interception from an inside position?

Anyway, I ran with the ball, and there was nobody in front of me. The only player with an angle on me was Seattle's behemoth offensive tackle, Andy Heck, who was six-foot-six and 295 pounds. I should have outrun him. I kept thinking, "I gotta get by this guy; I can't get caught." I passed Heck and started kicking straight up the field. Then I began thinking again: "What if he strips the ball from behind?"

Maybe I was being paranoid. After all, this was a guy who probably ran a 5.5 in the 40. At any rate, I decided to cover the ball with both hands, which caused me to run awkwardly. Amazingly enough, Heck leaped and caught my heel from behind. I fell down—bloop! That was pretty embarrassing since it had been an offensive lineman who had stopped me.

After I fell, my teammates jumped on me and started hugging me. I couldn't breathe. They dragged me back to our bench; I just felt so bad. I think I got a break for one series, but then I was ordered to get back on the field. I couldn't even stand up.

Seattle finally scored with less than two minutes left, but we still won 24-17. After the game, I yelled, "I made it!" Then I hit the road and sacked out at home for about two days. Although you'd like to, you simply don't forget those types of games.

—As told to John Nixon

DECEMBER 16, 1990
MIAMI DOLPHINS 24, SEATTLE SEAHAWKS 17
JOE ROBBIE STADIUM, MIAMI, FLORIDA

SCORING

SEA	3	7	0	7	**17**
MIA	3	14	7	0	**24**

SEA	Johnson, 24-yard field goal
MIA	Stoyanovich, 32-yard field goal
SEA	Fenner, 2-yard run (Johnson kick)
MIA	Pruitt, 4-yard pass from Marino (Stoyanovich kick)
MIA	Stradford, 6-yard run (Stoyanovich kick)
MIA	Edmunds, 11-yard pass from Marino (Stoyanovich kick)
SEA	Chadwick, 13-yard pass from Krieg (Johnson kick)

TEAM STATISTICS	SEA	MIA
First Downs	21	20
Rushes-Yards	22-83	31-105
Passing Yards	261	242
Passes	21-37-3	17-29-1
Punts-Average	3-46.0	5-45.8
Fumbles-Lost	2-1	3-2
Penalties-Yards	5-25	4-27

INDIVIDUAL STATISTICS
Rushing

SEA	Fenner 11 rushes for 15 yards; Williams 10-62; Krieg 1-6
MIA	Smith 17-51; Logan 5-20; Limbrick 3-10; Stradford 6-24

Passing

SEA	Krieg 21 completions, 37 attempts, 295 yards, 3 interceptions
MIA	Marino 17-29-250-1

Receiving

SEA	Kane 10 receptions for 162 yards; Blades 4-45; Skansi 1-17; Williams 1-3; Heller 2-34; Chadwick 3-34
MIA	Edmunds 5-76; Stradford 1-15; Smith 2-24; Pruitt 2-20; Martin 1-45; Limbrick 2-16; Jensen 2-24; Duper 2-30

ATTENDANCE: 57,851

Seattle's tackle tried to scrape me off, but I ran by him and nailed Krieg for a 14-yard loss.

Linebacker **John Offerdahl** was named to the Pro Bowl in each of his first five seasons, and started the game as a 1986 rookie. Unfortunately, injuries shortened his next three seasons. Offerdahl underwent knee surgery in 1991, abdominal surgery in 1992 and suffered torn biceps, a dislocated shoulder and a strained hamstring in 1993. After playing one exhibition game in 1994, he retired, realizing the injuries had taken too heavy a toll for him to continue.

I always liked Seattle. When we would come in from Kansas City to play the Seahawks—our AFC West rivals—I would

OCTOBER 8, 1989
KANSAS CITY CHIEFS 20, SEATTLE SEAHAWKS 16
KINGDOME, SEATTLE, WASHINGTON

SCORING

KC	3	0	7	10	**20**
SEA	7	9	0	0	**16**

SEA Jefferson, 97-yard kickoff return (N. Johnson kick)
KC Lowery, 39-yard field goal
SEA N. Johnson, 37-yard field goal
SEA N. Johnson, 26-yard field goal
SEA N. Johnson, 37-yard field goal
KC Okoye, 13-yard run (Lowery kick)
KC Lowery, 25-yard field goal
KC Roberts, 2-yard pass from Jaworski (Lowery kick)

TEAM STATISTICS	KC	SEA
First Downs	17	16
Rushes-Yards	40-199	19-52
Passing Yards	104	236
Passes	12-18-0	20-36-2
Punts-Average	5-42.0	5-37.0
Fumbles-Lost	2-1	1-0
Penalties-Yards	4-34	5-40

INDIVIDUAL STATISTICS
Rushing
KC Okoye 30 rushes for 156 yards; Heard 4-28; Saxon 4-15; McNair 1-0; Jaworski 1-0
SEA Krieg 3-29; Williams 9-22; Warner 7-1
Passing
KC Jaworski 12 completions, 18 attempts, 104 yards, 0 interceptions
SEA Krieg 20-36-252-2
Receiving
KC Harry 3 receptions for 41 yards; Saxon 2-13; McNair 2-11; Dressel 1-21; Paige 1-7; Mandley 1-5; Heard 1-4; Roberts 1-2
SEA Skansi 5-79; Williams 5-32; Blades 4-86; Kane 3-32; Clark 2-14; Tyler 1-9

ATTENDANCE: 60,715

get a chance to see a little bit of the city. Every time I went there, I liked it . . . except for two things. Number one: the artificial turf in the Kingdome. It was like playing on concrete. The turf was especially hard on a running back like me, who got tackled down to the ground on almost every play. Number two: we always lost there. Going into our match-up against the Seahawks in Seattle in week five of the 1989 season—the game I'll never forget—we had lost six straight in Seattle.

I don't know why we couldn't win there. When you play a team in your own division, your opponent seems to do some extra studying and scouting. You obviously want to beat all the teams in your division, so you put in a little more time and effort into your preparation. It almost feels like a playoff game.

The 1989 season turned out to be a big one for me, as I led the entire league in rushing yards, with 1,480. I had been in the league a few years and had had some success—some big games—but 1989 was my breakout year.

People ask me, "Why did you suddenly have such a big year?" The main reason was that Marty Schottenheimer came in as coach of the Chiefs that season. He was the type of coach who was prepared to run the ball a lot, and for me that was good news. If you were a big back, as I was, that meant the work would be there for you if you wanted it.

Carrying the ball is the one way you can do that. You can talk to any big back who has played in the league, and he'll say that catching the ball is OK but running it is what he likes to do. In 1989, I was given the ball a lot. I received the opportunities, and I made the most of them. I wanted to perform.

I remember one time Marty came up to me and asked, "Hey, how do you feel about all this work I'm giving you?" I guess some people were calling him and saying, "You're working Christian Okoye too hard." I told him, "I am perfectly fine with it."

Although I led the league in carries with 370, we actually had a pretty balanced offense. Steve DeBerg had a good year at quarterback, and some of our receivers, like Stephone Paige, had several big catches for us. That was the year we implemented the play-fake. It worked well; since I was running the ball a lot, we fooled the defense when we used the fake. Steve would look downfield and almost always find someone open to throw to. That was one of our biggest weapons.

But nothing, not even the play-fake, was working well against Seattle in that game in 1989. We fell behind early and were trailing 16-3 at halftime. It looked like we were on our way to yet another loss in Seattle.

In the second half, though, Marty decided we were going to control the ball. He gave me the ball more and more, and we began to move the chains and eat up the clock.

We got back into the game with a touchdown in the third quarter. I'll never forget this run—it might have been the best one of my career. We were 13 yards away from the goal line. It was noisy in the stadium—I mean *noisy*. If you had been there, your ears would have been ringing.

Anyway, Ron Jaworski, who was playing quarterback for us that game, was changing the play at the line of scrimmage, and I couldn't hear him. The fans were just too loud. He would sometimes call a play and then, once he got up to the line of scrimmage, tell you which way it was going to go. When he got to the line for this play, I didn't know which way he had called.

I went one way, and everybody else went the other. I was like, "Uh-oh. I'm in trouble now. What should I do now?" I had to cut back. I broke one tackle, then I broke free from another guy. I think I broke about seven tackles on my way to the end zone. That's one play I have at home on tape. It was just a great run, especially when you consider that it started as a broken play.

We really poured it on in the second half, just wearing down the Seahawks with our running game. We kept running, running, running. By the end of the game, I had rushed for 156 yards. I didn't really have any

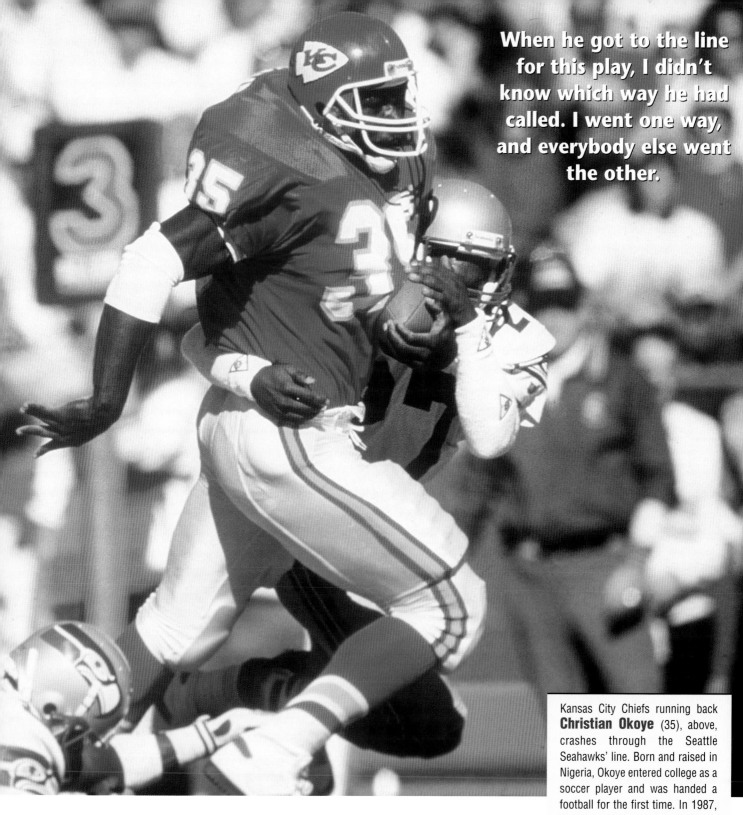

When he got to the line for this play, I didn't know which way he had called. I went one way, and everybody else went the other.

Kansas City Chiefs running back **Christian Okoye** (35), above, crashes through the Seattle Seahawks' line. Born and raised in Nigeria, Okoye entered college as a soccer player and was handed a football for the first time. In 1987, three years later, he was playing in the NFL. In 1989, the "Nigerian Nightmare" led the NFL with 370 carries and 1,480 yards. Although Okoye played only six pro seasons before a knee injury ended his career in 1992, he established a Kansas City franchise record with 4,897 rushing yards (since broken).

long runs, so the game was a workout for me. But I enjoyed it.

Our defense also stepped it up in the second half, shutting out the Seahawks. They couldn't get anything going offensively. The crowd quieted down a little, which was a big advantage for us. Between our second-half defense and our commitment to the run, we wound up winning 20-16.

Not only was it important to beat a divisional opponent, but we also finally won on the road in a place that had given us a lot of problems. It also was a big game for me personally. I had had some success up to that point, but that game really catapulted my career to the next level. It gave me a lot of confidence, made me feel like I could be a star in this league.

—As told to Chuck O'Donnell

There are many games that stick in my mind for a number of reasons. Sometimes you remember them for the wrong reasons,

or rather they stay with you for the wrong reasons. A loss can burn itself just as deeply into your memory as a big win. But the game I'll remember longest, the game that to me was the most exciting I've ever been in, was the game we played against the Green Bay Packers, December 9, 1967.

Let me set the stage for you: In 1967 the NFL was divided into four divisions—sixteen teams, four in each division. That was before the merger with the American Football League. Coming down the stretch we, the L.A. Rams, were locked in a close race with the Baltimore Colts for first place in the Coastal division. Baltimore had a 10-0-2 record. We were 9-1-2, one game behind the Colts.

If we could win our last two games, against Green Bay and Baltimore, we would be the division champions. In our first game with the Colts, in Baltimore, we had played a 24-24 tie. So, if we won the second game, even though we would have identical records we would win the division. But in order to set that up we first had to get by the Vince Lombardi Packers, the defending NFL and Super Bowl Champions.

You can talk about game plans all you want, but when you're down there in the pit it's the law of the fang and the jungle. They don't call it the pit for nothing. And when you were playing the Packers you knew they were going to come at you and keep coming at you until you cracked or you beat them into submission. We got so bruised and battered and tired we sometimes wound up playing in a kind of coma. By the end of the first half your instincts took over and by the end of the game you were an animal.

I've always said that it takes as many years to develop a defensive lineman as it does a quarterback. Intelligence, determination, confidence, concentration, quickness, deception and agility were my weapons as much as size and toughness. But what it really came down to was to give that

fellow across from you your best lick every single play.

The Packers' game plan was always a thing of beauty in its simplicity. "Attack the defense at its strongest point. Beat it there and your opponent is completely demoralized."

For the Rams that meant that the Pack would be coming right at us, trying to stuff the ball down our throats, because the strength of the Rams was in our front four, the outfit they called "the Fearsome Foursome"—Deacon Jones, Roger Brown, Lamar Lundy and me. We knew that before anything else we were going to have to stop the Packer running game.

Bart Starr, with the Green Bay running game choked off, got his team on the board first when he hit Carroll Dale, an ex-Ram, with a 30-yard pass for a touchdown. Roman Gabriel to Jack Snow evened that one up in the second quarter, but the Packers regained an edge when Don Chandler hit a 32-yard field goal to give them a 10-7 halftime lead.

We took the lead for the first time in the third quarter after Willie Ellison returned the kickoff 43 yards and Gabe hit Snow for another score. We upped that to 17-10 when Bruce Gossett, who had one blocked in the first quarter, hit a field goal from the Green Bay 23.

One lightning-like thrust was all the Packers needed to knot the score. Travis Williams, the Roadrunner, caught the following kickoff four yards deep in the end zone and went all the way—104 yards. That was no fluke—it was Williams' fourth TD kickoff return of the year.

Gabe engineered a long march that burned a lot of time off the clock in the fourth quarter. They didn't get it in, but Gossett was good on a field-goal try from the 16 to give us the lead, 20-17. The Packers used up most of the time remaining when Jim Weatherwax fell on a Dick Bass fumble on our 43-yard line and marched it in from there, with Chuck Mercein going the last four yards.

When Mercein scored there was a little more than two minutes and 50 seconds left in the game. The Packers kicked off and we weren't able to move the ball. On fourth

---

DECEMBER 9, 1967

LOS ANGELES RAMS 27, GREEN BAY PACKERS 24

MEMORIAL COLISEUM, LOS ANGELES, CALIFORNIA

SCORING

LA	0	7	10	10	**27**
GB	7	3	7	7	**24**

GB Dale, 30-yard pass from Starr (Chandler kick)
LA Snow, 16-yard pass from Gabriel (Gossett kick)
GB Chandler, 32-yard field goal
LA Snow, 11-yard pass from Gabriel (Gossett kick)
LA Gossett, 23-yard field goal
GB Williams, 104-yard kickoff return (Chandler kick)
LA Gossett, 16-yard field goal
GB Mercein, 4-yard run (Chandler kick)
LA Casey, 5-yard pass from Gabriel (Gossett kick)

TEAM STATISTICS

	LA	GB
First Downs	20	12
Rushes-Yards	34-102	32-98
Passing Yards	222	120
Passes	20-36-2	10-20-2
Punts-Average	2-38.5	6-28.3
Fumbles-Lost	2-1	0-0
Penalties-Yards	4-38	2-38

INDIVIDUAL STATISTICS

Rushing
LA Bass 11 rushes for 18 yards; Gabriel 4-11; Josephson 19-73
GB Anderson 7-20; Starr 2-23; Williams 12-26; Wilson 7-17; Mercein 4-12

Passing
LA Gabriel 20 completions, 36 attempts, 227 yards, 2 interceptions
GB Starr 10-20-138-2

Receiving
LA Bass 2 receptions for 5 yards; Casey 6-97; Josephson 5-51; Snow 4-48; Truax 2-14; Pope 1-12
GB Dale 2-43; Dowler 4-71; Wilson 2-4; Mercein 1-6; Williams 1-14

ATTENDANCE: 76,637

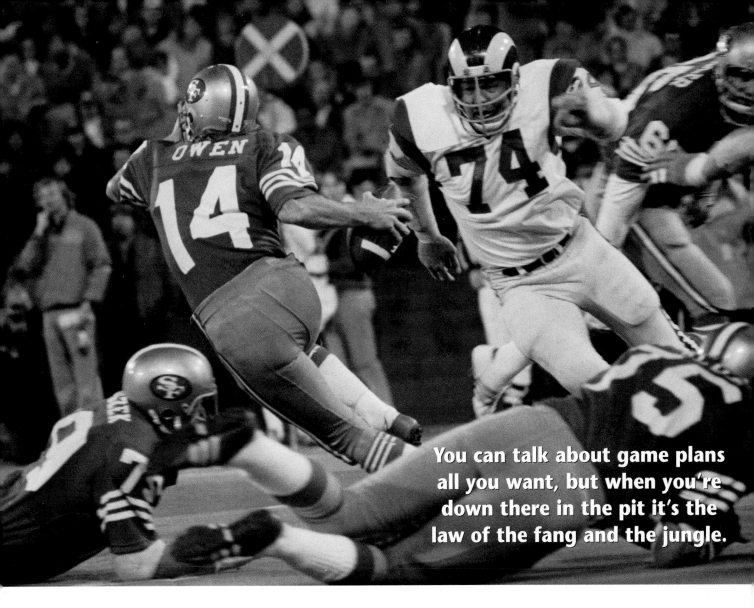

You can talk about game plans all you want, but when you're down there in the pit it's the law of the fang and the jungle.

down our coach, George Allen, sent in the punting team. That's when some of the crowd started to leave.

As the defensive team went back in, Allen told us that if we could hold we still had a chance to win.

Sweep was on my mind on first down— the old Packer sweep—and when Kramer made his move to pull I was ready. I shot through and caught Donny Anderson for a three-yard loss. They tried to run it again and this time the Deacon made a big play. On third and long we stopped them again.

There was only about a minute left on the clock when Anderson dropped back to punt. What do you do in a situation like that when you're behind and out of time-outs with only a minute left? You block the punt!

An all-out rush was on and Tony Guillory swept in from the left side and got to the ball just after it left Anderson's foot. It took a good bounce for us and Claude Crabb picked it up and ran it down to the five-yard line

before he was buried under an avalanche of Green Bay players.

Now we had plenty of time, but we had to get a touchdown. A field goal would leave us a point short. On first down, Gabe scrambled around under a heavy rush and then threw it into the end zone. Incomplete. About 20 seconds were burned off the clock.

Then he worked something to take advantage of the Packer heavy rush and quick pursuit. Gabe swung to his right, made a great fake to Tommy Mason on an inside handoff, then turned and threw across the field to Bernie Casey, standing all alone in the end zone.

Usually, during a game I'd get caught up in the feeling and intensity of the action, the movement and struggle of what was happening on the field. As soon as I walked off the field, though, I'd have a tremendous letdown. But that day, I stayed up in the clouds.

—As told to Bob Billings

The leader of the Los Angeles Rams' fabled "Fearsome Foursome," six-foot-five, 270-pound defensive tackle **Merlin Olsen** (74), above, prepares to sack San Francisco 49ers quarterback Tom Owen (14) in a 1974 game. Olsen was a Rams star from his 1962 rookie year until his retirement after the 1976 season. A model of consistency, Olsen played 198 consecutive games and was elected to 14 straight Pro Bowls. He entered the Pro Football Hall of Fame in 1982 and went on to a long and successful acting and voiceover career.

Some people might find it unusual that I go back to 1984 for the game that I'll never forget. That was my second season as

head coach of the New York Giants, and the game was our playoff victory against the Los Angeles Rams.

There are a number of reasons why I remember that particular game—reasons that are different from the ones why I remember our two Super Bowl victories or some of the other great games that the Giants had while I was head coach. We were just building our team at that time, and people were not expecting too much from us. In fact, we had come off a 3-12-1 campaign in 1983, and a lot of the forecasters didn't even think that we could make the playoffs.

But we had a plan that would lead us to the Super Bowl, and it had to start with the first steps. Some of the pieces were in place—Lawrence Taylor had been there since '81—but Leonard Marshall didn't join the team until 1983, Joe Morris' breakout year was '85 and Phil Simms didn't play a full season until 1984. That was his sixth season with New York, having missed all of 1982 and all but two games in 1983 due to injuries.

We gave up too many points in '83—347—and we only scored 267. Going into 1984, we knew we had to score more and give up fewer points. We accomplished that and we improved to 97 to make the playoffs as a wild-card team.

We had to fly out to Los Angeles to play a tough Rams team. Eric Dickerson was their main offensive weapon but they had a number of outstanding players. Dickerson was the key, though. We realized that we couldn't stop him; our plan was to keep him under control. He set an NFL record that season with 2,105 yards rushing, so we knew that he would be their go-to guy; he was going to carry the offensive load on his back.

Most of our guys had never been involved in an NFL playoff game, and this could have been a problem, but I figured that either way—win or lose—it would be a learning experience, something to build on for the

next season. Of course, I didn't go out to Los Angeles with the intention of losing. When I looked at the way our team matched up with theirs, I figured that we had a good shot to come out with a win.

We didn't have anyone on offense that we regarded as a big-game player. I knew that a lot of guys would have to have solid games for us to win. I also figured that if we could come out strong in the first quarter and score some points, we might force the Rams to alter their game plan.

That plan actually worked out better than I had anticipated. We opened the scoring when Ali Haji-Sheikh hit a field goal. Toward the end of the quarter, Taylor put a solid hit on Dickerson and forced a fumble. Then Phil Simms put a nice little drive together that included a three-yard scramble on a third-and-two and a six-yard pass to Bob Johnson on third-and-five. We ended up on their one, and Rob Carpenter went right in to give us a 10-0 lead.

Our defensive guys kept L.A. off the board for most of the half, but the Rams pushed downfield toward the end of the quarter and Mike Lansford put in a field goal from just inside the 40 to give them three points, making it 10-3.

We were still on an offensive roll going into the second half. After we took the kickoff, Simms moved us about 50 yards and Haji-Sheikh hit another field goal to put us up by 10. The L.A. crowd was getting restless, and so was Dickerson. About seven minutes into the quarter, L.A. went on a long drive that started on their 22 and ended with a 14-yard touchdown run by Dickerson. One big chunk of yardage for them—about 45 yards—came when Terry Kinard was called for pass interference. Whether it was interference or not . . . Well, the refs called it, and it was history.

We put another strong drive together toward the end of the quarter, which included a couple of clutch third-down passes from Simms to Lionel Manuel, one for 26 yards on third-and-13 and one for 20 yards on third-and-six. We ended up with a field goal instead of a touchdown, but that was a strong indication of things to come over the next few seasons. Now we were up 16-10.

DECEMBER 23, 1984

NEW YORK GIANTS 16, LOS ANGELES RAMS 13

ANAHEIM STADIUM, ANAHEIM, CALIFORNIA

SCORING

NYG	10	0	6	0	**16**
LA	0	3	7	3	**13**

NYG Haji-Sheikh, 37-yard field goal
NYG Carpenter, 1-yard run (Haji-Sheikh kick)
LA Lansford, 38-yard field goal
NY Haji-Sheikh, 39-yard field goal
LA Dickerson, 14-yard run (Lansford kick)
NYG Haji-Sheikh, 36-yard field goal
LA Lansford, 22-yard field goal

TEAM STATISTICS

	NYG	LA
First Downs	16	12
Rushes-Yards	27-40	26-107
Passing Yards	179	109
Passes	22-31-0	11-15-0
Punts-Average	4-38.8	4-37.8
Fumbles-Lost	3-0	2-2
Penalties-Yards	5-81	10-75

INDIVIDUAL STATISTICS

Rushing
NYG Morris 10 rushes for 21 yards; Carpenter 13-20; Simms 4-minus 1
LA Dickerson 23-107; Crutchfield 2-minus 2; Kemp 1-2

Passing
NYG Simms 22 completions, 31 attempts, 179 yards, 0 interceptions
LA Kemp 11-15-109-0

Receiving
NYG Mowatt 7 receptions for 73 yards; Carpenter 7-23; Manuel 3-52; Gray 2-20; Johnson 1-6; Galbreath 1-3; Morris 1-2
LA Brown 3-32; Barber 3-31; Ellard 2-22; J. McDonald 2-18; Da. Hill 1-6

ATTENDANCE: 67,037

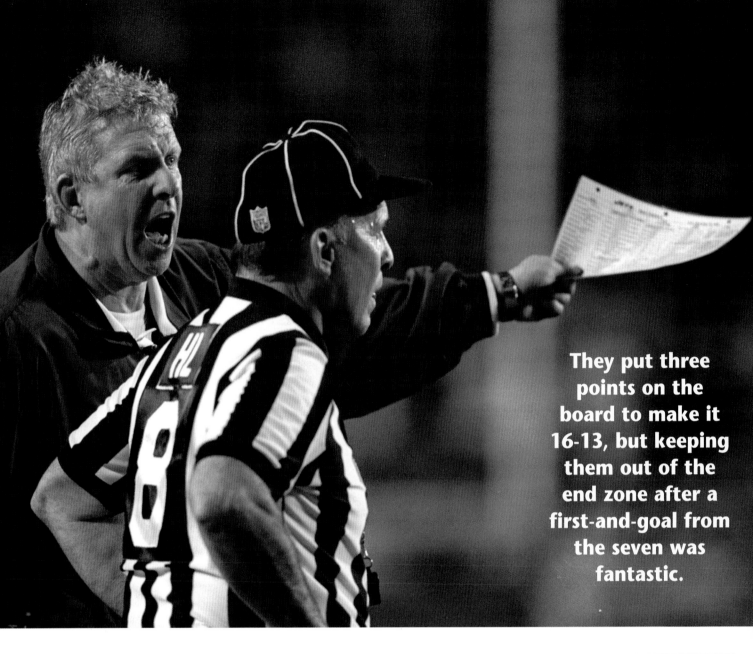

They put three points on the board to make it 16-13, but keeping them out of the end zone after a first-and-goal from the seven was fantastic.

Our defense made a strong statement on L.A.'s next drive. The Rams had a first down on their 42, and Dickerson took the handoff, jumped over defensive end Curtis McGriff and appeared to be headed for the end zone. But Kinard grabbed him from behind and pulled him down after a 24-yard gain.

A few plays later, they were in a first-and-goal situation on our seven. Dickerson took a pitchout and went for three to put them second-and-goal on our four. Then Leonard Marshall dropped Dwayne Crutchfield for a three-yard loss to give them third-and-goal back at the seven.

On third down, our defense forced Rams quarterback Jeff Kemp into a very-short-yardage pass that got them only two yards. They put three points on the board to make it 16-13, but keeping them out of the end zone after a first-and-goal from the seven was fantastic.

There was only about seven minutes left to play at that point, but both sides had other scoring opportunities. On a fourth-quarter drive, Joe Morris busted one for 61 yards to put us on L.A.'s three, but the play was called back when Kevin Belcher was called for holding. I didn't say anything, but I remember looking him dead in the eyes when he came off the field. Later, L.T. and George Martin hit Kemp and forced a fumble to end their final scoring opportunity, preserving our 16-13 win.

That victory was a confidence-booster. I remember thinking after the game, "Maybe we can win." That's what happened: The playoff success we had in following seasons began with that game.

—*As told to Barry Janoff*

Coach **Bill Parcells** has enjoyed a long and varied coaching career. His 83-52-1 record with the New York Giants (1983–90) included victories in Super Bowls XXI and XXV. In 1993, he took over the last-place New England Patriots and in 1996 took them to Super Bowl XXXI. He coached the New York Jets for three seasons (1997–99), getting them to the 1998 AFC Conference Championship. In 2003, after several seasons as a TV analyst, Parcells became the sixth coach of the Dallas Cowboys and immediately took them to the playoffs.

I was in quite a few unforgettable games during my career, and I suppose that everyone thinks of the "Hail Mary" game

in 1975 as being my most memorable one. But the one that really sticks out for me was a playoff game between Dallas and the Los Angeles Rams on December 23, 1973. It was my rookie season in the NFL, and that game against the Rams set the tone for my entire career.

I joined Dallas in 1973 as a free agent out of the University of Tulsa. I hadn't been selected in the NFL draft but, with help from my father-in-law Marques Haynes, I went to the Cowboys' preseason camp as a walk-on. It's funny, but I almost didn't get the opportunity to even try out for the squad until Dallas coach Tom Landry had Roger Staubach throw some passes to me. Roger and I became good friends almost immediately and apparently coach Landry liked my style because I played 11 seasons with the team.

I spent the early part of that season as a sub. But when Otto Stowe broke his ankle I got my first starting assignment. It was the tenth game of the season, and I was in the starting lineup on a regular basis after that.

The Cowboys had a well-balanced team that year, and a lot of the young guys were blending in very well with the established players. In addition to me, Billy Joe DuPree and Harvey Martin were in their rookie seasons, and Robert Newhouse and Benny Barnes were only in their second NFL seasons. We won our division and faced the Rams in the NFC Divisional Playoffs.

The Rams had an exceptional team that year, led by Jack Reynolds, Merlin Olsen, Jack Youngblood and Jim Youngblood, and their coach Chuck Knox took them to their divisional title. They had beaten us 37-31 earlier in the season, so everyone knew that the playoff game would be a good one.

We were really up for the game, especially since we were playing at home. There were 64,000 people at the Stadium, which added a great deal to the excitement and electricity.

We must have picked up on some of that

energy because we outscored the Rams 14-0 in the first quarter. Calvin Hill ran for the first touchdown and I scored the second on a short pass from Staubach.

In the second quarter Toni Fritsch kicked a field goal to extend our lead. But then the Rams started to come back. We were leading 17-6 at the half, but you could tell that they were picking up momentum. The Rams scored 10 points in the fourth quarter and, although we were still leading, we were playing flat. They definitely had the momentum going for them.

Their defense was containing our offense pretty well at that point and we knew we had to do something to get us going again. We had a third-and-13 situation and were getting ready to punt when Staubach called me on a post pattern. I ran up the side and cut across to the middle of the field, where he hit me with a perfect pass between two Ram defenders. I made one or two moves to avoid them and then took off for the end zone.

I had caught a pair of touchdown passes in our final game of the season—a 30-3 win over St. Louis—that helped us to clinch the division title. But the two I caught against the Rams were even more memorable. That second one turned into an 83-yard touchdown to put the game out of reach.

The first thing I remember was the crowd erupting as I scored that touchdown. The next thing I remember was standing in the end zone and seeing my teammates running over to mob me. These were guys that I had idolized—Staubach and Hill and Bob Hayes—and here they were coming over to congratulate me. It was just an awesome feeling.

We went on to win the game, but lost the next week to Minnesota in the conference final. However, as I mentioned, I feel that game against the Rams set the tone for my career. I was a rookie and many of the players and coaches were unsure of my abilities, especially since I had made the team as a free agent. I had caught some passes during the season, including the two touchdowns against St. Louis, but there was still a question about my ability to play consistently and under pressure.

DECEMBER 23, 1973
DALLAS COWBOYS 27, LOS ANGELES RAMS 16
TEXAS STADIUM, IRVING, TEXAS

SCORING

DAL	14	3	0	10	**27**
LA	0	6	0	10	**16**

DAL Hill, 3-yard run (Fritsch kick)
DAL Pearson, 4-yard pass from Staubach (Fritsch kick)
DAL Fritsch, 39-yard field goal
LA Ray, 33-yard field goal
LA Ray, 37-yard field goal
LA Ray, 40-yard field goal
LA Baker, 5-yard fun (Ray kick)
DAL Pearson, 83-yard pass from Staubach (Fritsch kick)
DAL Fritsch, 12-yard field goal

TEAM STATISTICS	LA	DAL
First Downs	11	15
Rushes-Yards	30-93	45-162
Passing Yards	99	136
Passes	7-24-1	8-16-2
Punts-Average	5-43.6	7-46.7
Fumbles-Lost	2-2	2-2
Penalties-Yards	2-20	5-44

INDIVIDUAL STATISTICS
Rushing
LA McCutcheon 13 rushes for 48 yards; Bertelsen 12-37; Hadl 2-10; Baker 1-5; Smith 2-minus 7
DAL Hill 25-97; Staubach 4-30; Garrison 10-30; Newhouse 6-5
Passing
LA Hadl 7 completions, 23 attempts, 133 yards, 1 interception; McCutcheon 0-1-0-0
DAL Staubach 8-16-180-2
Receiving
LA Snow 3 receptions for 77 yards; Smith 2-13; Jackson 1-40; McCutcheon 1-3
DAL Pearson 2-87; Hill 2-21; Fugett 1-38; Hayes 1-29; Garrison 1-3; DuPree 1-2

ATTENDANCE: 63,272

He hit me with a perfect pass between two Ram defenders. I made one or two moves to avoid them and then took off for the end zone.

When I came out of college a lot of people told me that I'd never make it in the NFL, that I'd never be able to play. But when I made that catch and then scored on what became an 83-yard pass play it was like me telling the world, "Hey, Drew Pearson can play in the NFL." I still get excited when I think of how I felt as I stood in the end zone after scoring that touchdown.

After that game, Dallas' coaches and players had more confidence in my abilities and started to use me more and more in clutch situations. They began to ask my advice in certain types of situations and what I could do on certain plays.

I remember a great game the next season, against Washington, when I caught a 50-yard bomb from Clint Longley to win a game on Thanksgiving Day. And in 1975 we beat Minnesota in the playoffs on their home field when I caught the "Hail Mary" pass with about 25 seconds to play. That game was unusual because I hadn't caught a pass all day. But on the final drive I caught four from Staubach, including the last one for a 50-yard touchdown.

We were trailing 14-10, and were 91 yards away from the end zone with time running out. But Staubach hit me with three quick passes to move us to midfield, and then tossed the "Hail Mary" pass that won the game for us. I remember that Viking cornerback Nate Wright matched me step for step, but as we neared the end zone I looked back and saw that Staubach's pass would be a little short. So I slowed down to reach back for the ball. That's when Wright and I collided. We both lost our balance, but I managed to catch the pass by holding on to it with one hand and squeezing it against my leg. As soon as the ref gave the touchdown signal, I tossed the ball into the stands.

—As told to Barry Janoff

Wide receiver **Drew Pearson** was a key player on a powerful Dallas Cowboys team. Over 11 seasons (1973–83), he made 489 receptions for 7,822 yards and 48 touchdowns. In 1974, Pearson was elected to his first of three Pro Bowls, after establishing personal bests with 62 receptions for 1,087 yards. He also went to three Super Bowls, winning a ring in Super Bowl XII.

The game I'll never forget was our victory against the Philadelphia Eagles in Super Bowl XV. Winning that game was a

JANUARY 25, 1981

OAKLAND RAIDERS 27, PHILADELPHIA EAGLES 10

LOUISIANA SUPERDOME, NEW ORLEANS, LOUISIANA

SCORING

OAK	14	0	10	3	**27**
PHI	0	3	0	7	**10**

OAK Branch, 2-yard pass from Plunkett (Bahr kick)
OAK King, 80-yard pass from Plunkett (Bahr kick)
PHI Franklin, 30-yard field goal
OAK Branch, 29-yard pass from Plunkett (Bahr kick)
OAK Bahr, 46-yard field goal
PHI Krepfle, 8-yard pass from Jaworski (Franklin kick)
OAK Bahr, 35-yard field goal

TEAM STATISTICS

	OAK	PHI
First Downs	17	19
Rushes-Yards	34-117	26-69
Passing Yards	260	291
Passes	13-21-0	18-38-3
Punts-Average	3-42.0	3-36.0
Fumbles-Lost	0-0	1-0
Penalties-Yards	5-37	6-57

INDIVIDUAL STATISTICS

Rushing
OAK van Eeghen 19 rushes for 80 yards; King 6-18; Plunkett 3-9; Whittington 3-minus 2; Jensen 3-12
PHI Montgomery 16-44; Harris 7-14; Harrington 1-4; Giammona 1-7; Jaworski 1-0

Passing
OAK Plunkett 13 completions, 21 attempts, 261 yards, 0 interceptions
PHI Jaworski 18-38-291-3

Receiving
OAK Branch 5 receptions for 67 yards; King 2-93; Chandler 4-77; Chester 2-24
PHI Krepfle 2-16; Montgomery 6-91; Harris 1-1; Spagnola 1-22; Carmichael 5-83; Smith 2-59; Parker 1-19

ATTENDANCE: 76,135

personal victory for me. It was also a special victory for the entire team because we came back to prove ourselves after being written off by many people early in the 1980 season.

That season wasn't my best, and our numbers were better overall in 1983 when we won Super Bowl XVIII. But 1980 is the season that typifies what the Raiders were all about. People had always written us off, but we continued to come back. Opposing teams thought they knew our weaknesses, but we went out and beat them. Critics talked about the Raiders being too old or too soft, and then we toughened up as a team and took care of business.

One of the best descriptions I've ever heard about the Raiders came from Gene Upshaw, who said: "People call us the halfway house of the NFL. Well, we live up to that image every chance we get." The team always featured a lot of players who had been either cut or traded by other teams, and the Raiders gave them the opportunity to be themselves and show that they could win. I'm speaking from experience, so I'm well aware of the feelings and emotions that made the Raiders special.

Dan Pastorini was our starting quarterback in 1980, but he broke his leg during the fifth game and was out for the year. We were 2-3 at that point and not playing as well as we should have been. After Dan went down, I became the starter for the rest of the season. We ended up going 9-2 in those 11 games and got into the playoffs as a wild-card team. It was just a matter of things falling into place for us; the guys sat down and said, "Let's get serious and show them what we're made of."

San Diego won the AFC West division title that season, but we beat them 34-27 in the AFC Championship Game. The conference championship game was a tough, hard-fought contest, but winning it gave us even more confidence going into the Super Bowl. We also had added incentive because

Philadelphia had beaten us 10-7 during the regular season.

People like to talk about the "bad boy" image of the Raiders, and they say we did all these awful things in New Orleans the week before Super Bowl XV. But we really had some tough workouts and were prepared both mentally and physically to beat Philadelphia. I think the worst thing that happened that week was John Matuszak breaking curfew one night—he had to pay a fine for that.

We were underdogs going into the game, which was fine with us. Philadelphia was being touted for its strong defense, but on the Eagles' first offensive series our defense set the tone for the game. Our linebacker Rod Martin intercepted quarterback Ron Jaworski's first pass of the game, returning it from midfield to the Eagles' 30-yard line. We stayed on the ground for a couple of plays, then I hit Cliff Branch with a pass on first down, and on third down I connected with him in the end zone for a touchdown. Philadelphia was defending against the run on that play, and we faked a running play to get them off-balance. But it was a pass to Branch all the way.

Two plays that occurred in the first quarter—both coming after we had scored—were the keys to the victory. Jaworski had moved the Eagles to our 40, and then he hit Rodney Parker with a pass that went the full 40 yards for a touchdown. However, Harold Carmichael was called for illegal motion on the play and the touchdown was called back. They ended up punting on that series, which had to be demoralizing for their offense. I know it was still just the first quarter, but when you lose the tying touchdown, it can have a negative effect on you for the rest of the game.

Then, with just over a minute left in the quarter, we started a drive from our own 14. We picked up about six yards in the first two plays and had a third-and-six situation on the 20. The play was supposed to be a short pass to Bob Chandler for a first down, but he was covered and I was forced to scramble out of the pocket. I knew I was running out of time with no place to go. Then I saw Kenny King downfield, waving his arms. He had gotten

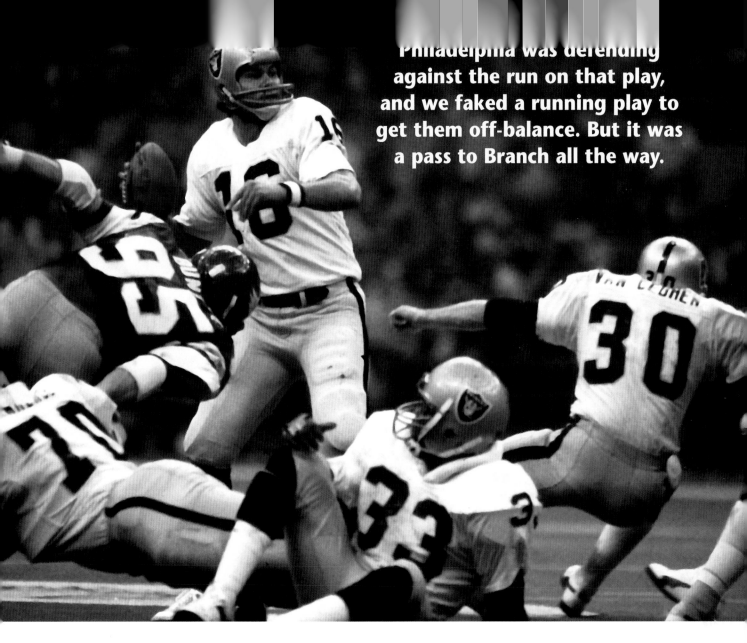

behind the secondary and all I had to do was get the ball over the hands of the cornerback covering him. He made a great catch at the 39 and went all the way for the touchdown.

That play really hurt the Eagles mentally. We were 14 points ahead, which isn't that wide a margin—especially with three quarters remaining—but the momentum definitely had shifted in our favor. The touchdown by King showed what the Raiders are made of, the fact that we could take a busted play and turn it into a touchdown.

Philadelphia scored on a field goal in the second quarter, so we had a 14-3 lead at halftime. We received the kickoff to begin the second half, and I knew right away that if we could score again we would really put the Eagles in a hole. There were two key plays on that drive, which started on our 14. The first was a 32-yard pass to Chandler that put us on the Philadelphia 33. Two plays later, I hit Cliff Branch with a pass that gave us our third touchdown.

We scored a couple of field goals in the second half, and Philadelphia scored a touchdown in the fourth quarter, but the way our guys were playing, the outcome had already been decided. As the game ended, I remember taking a few seconds on the sidelines to give thanks.

We came together as a team. And that game was a perfect example of the entire season: being the underdogs, completing the big passes, making the key plays. I was named the Super Bowl MVP, but the victory was a total team effort. I still look back on that season and think about all the things that got me to that point. There were times when I wanted to throw in the towel. But I didn't, and that's what the game is all about.

—*As told to Barry Janoff*

Quarterback **Jim Plunkett**, the 1970 Heisman Trophy winner, had an up-and-down 16-season (1971–86) NFL career. After four strong years with the New England Patriots, a disappointing 1975 campaign led Plunkett to request a trade. Two seasons later, he was released by the San Francisco 49ers. Plunkett signed with Oakland in 1978, but spent two years on the bench before winning MVP honors in Super Bowl XV. He led his team to another huge win in Super Bowl XVIII, and retired with 25,882 passing yards and 178 touchdowns.

NOVEMBER 22, 1981

When I look back at my career, there is an entire season that stands out for me: 1981, when I was with San Francisco and we

NOVEMBER 22, 1981
SAN FRANCISCO 49ERS 33, LOS ANGELES RAMS 31
ANAHEIM STADIUM, ANAHEIM, CALIFORNIA

SCORING

SF	3	7	17	6	**33**
LA	0	17	7	7	**31**

SF	Wersching, 47-yard field goal
LA	Corral, 44-yard field goal
LA	Tyler, 22-yard pass from Pastorini (Corral kick)
SF	Davis, 1-yard run (Wersching kick)
LA	Dennard, 7-yard pass from Gunman (Corral kick)
SF	Lawrence, 92-yard kickoff return (Wersching kick)
SF	Wersching, 34-yard field goal
SF	Lott, 25-yard interception return (Wersching kick)
LA	Arnold, 2-yard pass from Haden (Corral kick)
SF	Wersching, 32-yard field goal
LA	Tyler, 1-yard run (Corral kick)
SF	Wersching, 37-yard field goal

TEAM STATISTICS	SF	LA
First Downs	19	27
Rushes-Yards	28-71	47-203
Passing Yards	259	208
Passes	19-30-1	18-32-1
Punts-Average	2-44.0	4-45.0
Fumbles-Lost	1-1	4-1
Penalties-Yards	5-51	7-71

INDIVIDUAL STATISTICS

Rushing

SF	Davis 8 rushes for 23 yards; Patton 8-20; Hofer 5-16; Cooper 4-4; Lawrence 2-9; Montana 1-minus 1
LA	Tyler 23-97; Gunman 17-64; Pastorini 2-13; Bryant 2-4; Dennard 1-14; Haden 1-9; J. Thomas 1-2

Passing

SF	Montana 19 completions, 30 attempts, 283 yards, 1 interception
LA	Pastorini 8-18-79-1; Haden 9-13-122-0; Gunman 1-1-7-0

Receiving

SF	Solomon 5 receptions for 124 yards; Cooper 5-55; Clark 4-59; Hofer 2-20; Young 2-18; Shumann 1-7
LA	Dennard 5-56; Tyler 4-39; Gunman 3-28; Arnold 2-22; D. Hill 1-43; Waddy 1-8; Bryant 1-7; J. Thomas 1-5

ATTENDANCE: 63,456

won the Super Bowl. But there is one game from that season that is especially memorable, when we beat the Rams in Los Angeles on my birthday.

That was my first season with San Francisco after 11 years in Los Angeles, and I didn't exactly leave on good terms with the Rams. It's not something I like to talk about . . . Let's just say there was a difference of opinion between the Rams and me about how much money I was worth. So I joined the 49ers and had a few terrific seasons there. I ended up playing in three Super Bowls during my career: one with the Rams, when Pittsburgh beat us [Super Bowl XIV], and two with San Francisco, both of which we won [Super Bowls XVI and XIX].

That first season with San Francisco was the year we won our first championship. I have a lot of great memories from that season, but beating the Rams was an extra bonus for me. Actually, we beat the Rams twice that year. The first game was in San Francisco, and we won it by a field goal, 20-17. That game really set up our win in Los Angeles later in the season because it was the first time the 49ers had beaten the Rams since 1976; it was San Francisco's first win against L.A. in something like nine games. Of course, I had been on the winning side in all those games, playing with the Rams, so I wasn't going to stand around and all of a sudden be on the losing side in this series.

We were in first place by the time we went down to Los Angeles, and everyone on the team had the feeling that, hey, we could win the whole thing. The season before, the 49ers weren't exactly blowing away the opposition, and the Rams were making the playoffs, as usual. Then, one year later, we were running away with the division and defeating the teams that we had to beat.

I was really up for the game in Los Angeles. For one thing, it was my first game back on my old home turf as part of the enemy. And, like I said, it was my birthday

and I wanted to give myself a special present.

I remember being on the field before the game, warming up, and a few of the Rams players came over to me to talk. But on the field I'm all business. These guys came over and said, "Hey, lighten up." But I didn't want to fraternize; I just wanted to beat them.

This was one of those games where one team would get the lead, then the other would get it back, then the first team would get the lead again, et cetera. People watching at home on TV kept hearing, "The lead has changed hands eight times . . . nine times . . . 10 times . . . " It was the type of game where you get dizzy trying to keep up with the stats.

You don't get dizzy on the field, of course, but what a game like this does is keep all the players involved, on their toes all the time, until it's over. And even then you have to wait a few seconds to make sure the game really ended. It's the kind you want to play every week, especially if you win. And we won that baby.

The first half featured good football, but it was just the setup for a great second half. We led 3-0 after the first quarter. They tied the game, then went ahead by a touchdown. Then we tied the score. Then they went ahead on a weird option play, a seven-yard pass from running back Mike Guman to Preston Dennard. At the end of the half, the Rams were leading 17-10.

We had a good half, although not a great one, so I don't remember anything special being said in the locker room. I don't think anything special had to be said. I knew what I wanted the final outcome to be . . . I knew what the final outcome was going to be.

In the second half, things really got interesting. Amos Lawrence took the opening kickoff on our 8-yard line and ran the sucker back 92 yards for a touchdown. He ran right through their defense. Then Wersching put us ahead 20-17 with a field goal. Our defensive guys dug in. Ronnie Lott intercepted a pass off Pastorini on the Rams 25 and ran it back for a touchdown.

We were up by—check those stats, TV viewers—10 points now, but we knew the game was far from over. Toward the end of the quarter, Pastorini went out and Pat

We had a tough unit, but Los Angeles put on one hell of a drive.

Haden came in at quarterback for Los Angeles. He threw a touchdown pass to close the deficit. The lead didn't change hands, but we were up by only three after three quarters.

As we went into the last quarter, you could feel the excitement and tension building. You could *feel* it. Wersching kicked another field goal with about 10 minutes to play, so we were up by six. On the kickoff, Los Angeles was pinned back at its 10. As the defensive unit ran onto the field, I remember thinking, "Let's dig in; let's hold them."

We had a tough unit, but Los Angeles put on one hell of a drive. They would move the ball and we would stop them, but they'd get first-down yardage and keep the drive going. Eventually, they drove down to our one with less than two minutes to play, and Tyler went over the top of the line to tie the score. The crowd went nuts, then got quiet for a second, then went nuts again when Frank Corral

kicked the extra point to give them a 31-30 lead.

The next few minutes were frustrating for me because I wanted to be out on the field instead of on the sidelines watching our offense try to win the game. But quarterback Joe Montana led the offense on a super drive, moving from our 20 down to the Los Angeles 19. Then Wersching went out and kicked a field goal with no time left on the clock to give us the win.

I remember later seeing a photo of some of the guys out on the field celebrating, and I remember thinking it was a bit strange because I was out there celebrating in Anaheim Stadium but I wasn't wearing a Rams uniform. That feeling didn't last for long, though; it was more like I had said to the Rams, "I told you so."

—As told to Barry Janoff

Middle linebacker **Jack "Hacksaw" Reynolds** picked up his nickname after allegedly cutting in half a '53 Chevy in frustration over a 1969 University of Tennessee loss. Reynolds brought a similarly colorful intensity to his pro career. Over the course of 11 seasons (1970–80) with the Los Angeles Rams, he went to Super Bowl XIV and the 1975 and 1980 Pro Bowls. Reynolds joined the San Francisco 49ers for the next four campaigns (1981–84), winning rings in Super Bowl XVI and XIX.

The games that stand out most for me are the ones in which the whole team contributes and works together. Certainly

you would remember games in which individual players had exceptional performances, but that doesn't always win games for you.

Football is about winning and losing, and in that context, the game that stands out most for me was Super Bowl XXVI, when Washington beat Buffalo 37-24. We came in with a great team, we were playing a great team, and the game quickly turned into a memorable one—at least from our point of view.

Our whole team was focused in training camp on winning the Super Bowl. Coach Joe Gibbs was a great motivator and a great leader, but it seemed as if the whole team had the spirit right from the start. There are some years when you can feel that you can win it all and some years when you don't have that feeling. The 1991 season was a year in which we felt we could win it all.

I think the turning point of the season might have come in a game against the Giants, who had defeated Buffalo in Super Bowl XXV. We were trailing at halftime 13-0, but we came back to win 17-13. That was a great confidence booster for us, and I think it showed the guys that we were capable of coming back and winning big games.

Late in the season, Coach Gibbs added a no-huddle offense to our attack. It took some getting used to, but it proved to be very beneficial against Buffalo. We figured that they would try to disrupt our offensive flow by throwing several different defensive looks at us. They revamped their defensive line somewhat early on by shifting their nose tackle, Jeff Wright, a couple of yards off center and then dropping either defensive end Bruce Smith, linebacker Cornelius Bennett or linebacker Darryl Talley into the middle. But the way we countered that was to get to the line before they could set up or had time to make defensive adjustments.

Of course, it helped our case a great deal that our defensive guys played so tough and enabled the offense to open up that big lead in

the second quarter. I can't say enough about the way our offensive and defensive linemen played that game with such authority. Personally, I think Buffalo's defensive adjustments were a direct response to the way our offensive guys had been dominating people late in the season and in the playoffs.

There are a lot of stats that tell the tale of that game, but one of the most important to me was that I wasn't sacked all day. I had the time to find receivers and to set up plays—the offensive line was a major reason for that. Buffalo's defensive guys were able to knock me down during the game, but it always was after the fact.

A lot of people forget that we didn't get started on the right foot offensively. We had a strong drive in the first quarter that ended with Art Monk catching the ball in the end zone, but when the officials looked at the instant replay they ruled that one of his feet was out of bounds. We didn't get the touchdown, and we missed the field goal, which put the ball back into Buffalo's hands. On their next offensive play, though, Jim Kelly was picked off by Brad Edwards. But on the following series, I had a pass intercepted by Kirby Jackson.

We got on track in the second quarter. We drove the ball about 64 yards, which ended with a 34-yard field goal by Chip Lohmiller. Then we went about 50 yards and scored a touchdown on a 10-yard pass play when we sent Earnest Byner out of the backfield.

Our defensive guys continued to frustrate Jim on the next Buffalo offensive series when Darrell Green picked off a pass. In our offensive series, Gary Clark beat Kirby Jackson and moved the ball 34 yards. Ricky Ervins went 14 yards on a sweep, and Gerald Riggs went in from a yard out to give us our second touchdown of the quarter.

In the locker room at halftime, we knew that we were doing a lot of the things we wanted to do on offense and defense. Buffalo had to adjust to what we were doing, and we knew that Kelly would have to come out in the second half and really put the ball in the air. Our defense had pretty much shut down Thurman Thomas and the Bills ground game, so our secondary guys knew that they would

---

JANUARY 26, 1992
WASHINGTON REDSKINS 37, BUFFALO BILLS 24
HUBERT H. HUMPHREY METRODOME,
MINNEAPOLIS, MINNESOTA

SCORING

WAS	0	17	14	6	**37**
BUF	0	0	10	14	**24**

WAS	Lohmiller, 34-yard field goal
WAS	Byner, 10-yard pass from Rypien (Lohmiller kick)
WAS	Riggs, 1-yard run (Lohmiller kick)
WAS	Riggs, 2-yard run (Lohmiller kick)
BUF	Norwood, 21-yard field goal
BUF	Thomas, 1-yard run (Norwood kick)
WAS	Clarke, 30-yard pass from Rypien (Lohmiller kick)
WAS	Lohmiller, 25-yard field goal
WAS	Lohmiller, 39-yard field goal
BUF	Metzelaars, 2-yard pass from Kelly (Norwood kick)
BUF	Beebe, 4-yard pass from Kelly (Norwood kick)

TEAM STATISTICS

	WAS	BUF
First Downs	24	25
Rushes-Yards	40-125	18-43
Passing Yards	292	286
Passes	18-33-1	29-59-4
Punts-Average	4-37.5	6-35.0
Fumbles-Lost	1-0	6-1
Penalties-Yards	5-82	6-50

INDIVIDUAL STATISTICS

Rushing
WAS   Ervins 13 rushes for 72 yards; Byner 14-49; Riggs 5-7; Sanders 1-1; Rutledge 1-0; Rypien 6-minus 4
BUF   Davis 4-17; Kelly 3-16; Thomas 10-13; Lofton 1-minus 3

Passing
WAS   Rypien 18 completions, 33 attempts, 292 yards, 1 interception
BUF   Kelly 28-58-275-4; Reich 1-1-11-0

Receiving
WAS   Clark 7 receptions for 114 yards; Monk 7-113; Byner 3-24; Sanders 1-41
BUF   Lofton 7-92; Beebe 4-61; Davis 4-38; Reed 5-34; McKeller 2-29; Thomas 4-27; Edwards 1-11; Metzelaars 1-2; Kelly 1-minus 8

ATTENDANCE: 63,130

Late in the season, Coach Gibbs added a no-huddle offense to our attack.

be seeing a lot of action from that point on.

On the opening play of the third quarter, with Buffalo on its 20, Andre Collins came in on a blitz. Jim had to rush his pass, and he threw an interception to Kurt Gouveia, who took the ball down to Buffalo's two. Riggs ran in from there to give us a 24-0 lead.

Buffalo actually outscored us 24-13 from that point, and Jim had 58 pass attempts. But our defensive guys had him doing a lot of things he didn't plan to do.

Jim was sacked five times—including one sack in which he suffered a mild concussion and had to leave the game for a play—and intercepted four times. Buffalo wouldn't go away in the second half, even though our defensive unit did a good job containing the Bills running game and getting to Jim. They

scored on two long drives in the fourth quarter, but with less than four minutes to play they still needed two touchdowns to win. I had faith that our defensive unit would see that they didn't get those two touchdowns.

It was thrilling to be named MVP, especially since I didn't have the opportunity to play at all in Super Bowl XXII. That award may have had my name on it, but it was for the whole team. You don't get to the point of winning the conference title and then winning the Super Bowl behind just one man. I accepted the MVP on behalf of the entire team. That's what made the whole season, and Super Bowl XXVI in particular, unforgettable for me.

—*As told to Barry Janoff*

When healthy, quarterback **Mark Rypien** was hard to beat. After two years on injure-reserve, Rypien got nine starts for the Washington Redskins in 1989 and went to the Pro Bowl. In 1991— his first injury-free season— Rypien threw a career-best 3,564 yards and 28 touchdowns, won MVP honors in Super Bowl XXVI and went to another Pro Bowl. After leaving the Skins in 1993, he saw spot duty with the Cleveland Browns (1994), the St. Louis Rams (1995 and 1997), the Philadelphia Eagles (1996) and the Indianapolis Colts (2001) before retiring.

The toughest thing about being a pro rookie is that you're scared. You're scared all the time. And you worry about

OCTOBER 17, 1965

CHICAGO BEARS 45, MINNESOTA VIKINGS 37

METROPOLITAN STADIUM, BLOOMINGTON, MINNESOTA

SCORING

CHI	14	3	7	21	**45**
MIN	0	13	10	14	**37**

CHI	Bull, 33-yard run (LeClerc kick)
CHI	Morris, 14-yard pass from Bukich (LeClerc kick)
MIN	Cox, 28-yard field goal
MIN	Mason, 4-yard run (Cox kick)
CHI	LeClerc, 12-yard field goal
MIN	Cox, 14-yard field goal
MIN	Cox, 28-yard field goal
MIN	Brown, 40-yard run (Cox kick)
CHI	Sayers, 18-yard pass from Bukich (LeClerc kick)
MIN	Tarkenton, 2-yard run (Cox kick)
CHI	Sayers, 25-yard pass from Bukich (LeClerc kick)
MIN	Mason, 4-yard run (Cox kick)
CHI	Sayers, 96-yard kickoff return (LeClerc kick)
CHI	Sayers, 10-yard run (LeClerc kick)

TEAM STATISTICS

	CHI	MIN
First Downs	16	26
Rushes-Yards	30-182	46-304
Passing Yards	134	109
Passes	10-20-1	10-20-2
Punts-Average	6-37.2	2-43.0
Fumbles-Lost	0-0	5-3
Penalties-Yards	5-74	4-28

INDIVIDUAL STATISTICS

Rushing

CHI	Sayers 13 rushes for 64 yards; Bull 10-92; Livingston 5-1; Bukich 2-25
MIN	Brown 15-117; Tarkenton 8-71; Mason 18-90; Osborn 2-16; King 3-10

Passing

CHI	Bukich 9 completions, 19 attempts, 113 yards, 1 interception; Sayers 1-1-27-0
MIN	Tarkenton 10-20-121-2

Receiving

CHI	Jones 1 reception for 15 yards; Gordon 1-27; J. Morris 2-23; Sayers 4-63; Bull 2-12
MIN	Flatley 4-78; Brown 3-31; Mason 1-minus 8; Phillips 2-20

ATTENDANCE: 47,426

whether or not you can make it. You think about those great stars you've read about all your life–those giant linemen you have to run through, those vicious linebackers and those swift, hard-hitting defensive backs.

You worry that maybe the skills you've worked on ever since you were a boy won't be able to carry you through against stiffer competition. On the outside I might have shown confidence, but inside there was that question mark. It was there especially after some supposedly smart football men said I'd never make it as a running back in the National Football League.

Real confidence comes with doing it; and even when we arrived at Bloomington, Minnesota that sunny Sunday morning of October 17, 1965, I still didn't feel that I had done it yet, at least not to my satisfaction.

Coach George Halas broke me in slowly during the exhibition season, running back punts and kickoffs for starters. He was nursing me along slowly into the regular lineup.

The Bears, as we often did, got off to a slow start. The San Francisco 49ers really drubbed us and the Los Angeles Rams beat us out of a game we should have won. Then the Green Bay Packers gave us a lesson in fundamentals.

In the second half of that Packer game we started to come together and the following week we got back at the Rams. We beat them pretty good. I scored on an 80-yard pass from Rudy Bukich and I threw a touchdown pass myself, a 26-yard option pass to Dick Gordon.

We knew we'd be in for a tough afternoon with the Vikings because Fran Tarkenton always gave us a lot of trouble with his scrambling and passing. And there was Bill Brown, an ex-Bear who always did great things against his old team.

Right from the start, it looked like it was going to be our day. Ronnie Bull broke one up the middle and went 34 yards for a touchdown. Within 36 seconds, we had another. The Vikings' Tom Hall fumbled the kickoff and we recovered on the Minnesota 14. On the very first play, Bukich shot a pass to Johnny Morris for the score, Bears 14, Vikings 0.

We must have relaxed a little, though, because the Vikings came back with a field goal and touchdown to close the gap. Then we traded field goals to walk off the field with a 17-13 halftime lead.

Coming back on the field I started to feel real good. It was like a wave of confidence coming over me. I felt like I could do anything I had to do. I even felt that way after Cox kicked another field goal and Brown broke a 40-yard touchdown run to put them in the lead for the first time, 23-17. I just felt that no matter what they did we could come right back.

We took the kickoff and drove upfield. Bukich mixed up the runs and passes, and when we got to the Vikings' 18-yard line Rudy called a pass. The play put me one-on-one with a linebacker. I made a move to the inside and then veered quickly. The ball was right there and we had six more points, and the lead, 24-23.

A scrambling quarterback like Tarkenton can break down all your defensive keys and he was in rare form. He drove our guys crazy and marched the Vikings in for another score. They were on top again.

Back we came, and when we marched it down to the Minnesota 25, Bukich called a play similar to the one we had just scored on. It isolated me on a linebacker. When you get in that situation, no linebacker in football should be able to keep up with any running back if there is enough field to run in. Rudy laid it right in there and once again the Bears were back on top, 31-30.

Tarkenton took his team the length of the field, using as much of the clock as he could until finally he slipped the ball to Tommy Mason who drove the final four yards into our end zone. That put them six points up on us, 37-31.

I looked up at that clock as I trotted out to line up for the kickoff and saw there were only two minutes and 18 seconds left to go. I knew we could do it, though. I felt so good I felt like I was gliding, not even touching the ground.

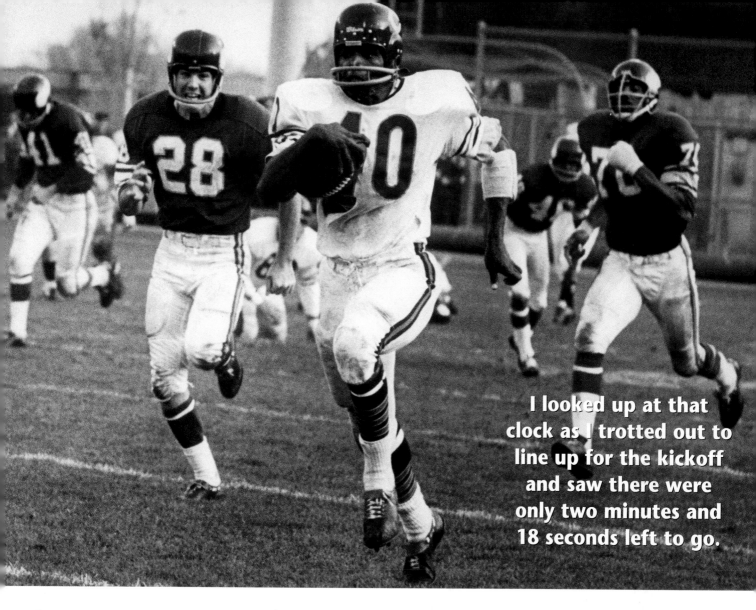

I looked up at that clock as I trotted out to line up for the kickoff and saw there were only two minutes and 18 seconds left to go.

I was just praying that they wouldn't squib it, that they'd kick it deep so I could get my hands on it.

Fred Cox hit the ball and I was so anxious to get it that it seemed to be drifting so slowly down to me. I kept telling myself not to get anxious, to wait for it, and don't start to run before I had it in my hands.

I caught it on the four. I started to move straight up the field and then Butkus and Seals blasted the Vikings aside. I cut to my left through a big hole and there was daylight.

I was running free. There were only two men with a chance to stop me, both angling over from the opposite side of the field. When they got close enough I gave them a head and shoulder fake to the inside. They were forced to break stride just slightly and I just turned it on down the sideline.

Touchdown! The only thing wrong was that Tarkenton still had enough time, about two minutes, to move his team into position for a field goal. We led by only a point.

Dick Butkus took care of that. He intercepted a Tarkenton pass on the Minnesota 45 and returned it down to the 10. On the first play they gave me the ball straight ahead and those linemen—Mike Pyle, Jim Cadile, Mike Rabold—really blew the Vikings out of there. I could have almost walked it in.

That was really great. I went on to have a bigger afternoon than those four second-half touchdowns. Later that year, I tied the pro record with six touchdowns in our second game with the 49ers. But it was a bigger thrill getting them against Minnesota because we really needed them.

After the game I heard coach Halas say to the reporters something about "Red Grange, George McAfee and Gale Sayers, and not necessarily in that order, gentlemen."

That's when I really knew I belonged, and that's why I'll never forget that game.

—As told to Bob Billings

On October 17, 1965, Chicago Bears running back **Gale Sayers** (40), above, runs a 96-yard game-breaking kickoff return against the Minnesota Vikings. By the end of that season, Sayers had set a rookie record (since broken) with 22 touchdowns. The 1997 Pro Football Hall of Fame inductee was MVP in three of the four Pro Bowl games he appeared in. Sayers suffered a knee injury in 1968 but came back in 1969 to lead the league in rushing (1,032 yards) for the second time. He retired after further injuries restricted him to two games in both 1970 and 1971.

When we came into Tampa Stadium prior to our divisional playoffs game against the Philadelphia Eagles in 1979—the first

DECEMBER 29, 1979
TAMPA BAY BUCCANEERS 24, PHILADELPHIA EAGLES 17
TAMPA STADIUM, TAMPA, FLORIDA

SCORING

TB	7	10	0	7	**24**
PHI	0	7	3	7	**17**

TB	Bell, 4-yard run (O'Donoghue kick)
TB	O'Donoghue, 40-yard field goal
TB	Bell, 1-yard run (O'Donoghue kick)
PHI	Smith, 11-yard pass from Jaworski (Franklin kick)
PHI	Franklin, 42-yard field goal
TB	Giles, 9-yard pass from Williams (O'Donoghue kick)
PHI	Carmichael, 37-yard pass from Jaworski (Franklin kick)

TEAM STATISTICS

	PHI	TB
First Downs	15	17
Rushes-Yards	18-48	55-186
Passing Yards	179	132
Passes	15-39-0	7-15-1
Punts-Average	5-44.3	5-42.6
Fumbles-Lost	2-1	0-0
Penalties-Yards	8-62	9-105

INDIVIDUAL STATISTICS

Rushing
PHI   Montgomery 13 rushes for 35 yards; Harris 4-13; Jaworski 1-0
TB   Bell 38-142; Eckwood 8-19; Williams 6-19; J. Davis 3-6

Passing
PHI   Jaworski 15 completions, 39 attempts, 199 yards, 0 interceptions
TB   Williams 7-15-132-1

Receiving
PHI   Montgomery 4 receptions for 35 yards; Carmichael 3-92; Smith 3-49; Krepfle 3-23; Harris 1-2; Campfield 1-minus 2
TB   Giles 3-43; Hagins 2-34; Mucker 1-34; Owens 1-21

ATTENDANCE: 71,402

playoff game in the history of the Tampa Bay Buccaneers—I had never seen the place in such an uproar. The energy and electricity that was flowing around the stadium was unbelievable. We looked around and said, "Wow! What's going here?" I think it inspired us to play that much harder. It was like a big-time college bowl game atmosphere, except all the fans were on our side. This was a bowl game with all *our* fans.

Considering where we had come from, no one would have thought we would be hosting a playoff game at this particular time. Ours was a worst-to-first story. We had won only five games in 1978, but that actually was a good year for us. In the first two years of our existence, we had won a total of only two games. So here was a team that had won just seven times in its first three years—and we suddenly were in the playoffs! Having gone through that made this moment much nicer.

Because I had been with the Buccaneers since their inception in 1976, I saw some hard, tough, painful times. It's an adjustment to get used to losing. Unless you're experienced at something like that, you don't know how you're going to respond as an individual and as a team.

Our coaches, especially Head Coach John McKay, set a tone that really allowed us to keep our spirit and morale up so that we could continue to do the work necessary to become better as a team. But every player, at some point in time, would hit rock bottom, where he'd say to himself, "How can this keep going on?" Or he'd have that one game where he'd say, "I'm sure. I believe this is the game we're going to win." But then we didn't win. To me, that was the kind of scenario that exemplified my lowest points because it would be games in which I would think, "We match up well. We're going to get our first win." And then it didn't happen.

Everyone went through that. But I think we all adjusted very well and understood that we had to continue to get better as a team if we expected to win, because we understood nobody was going to give us a win. It just wasn't going to happen; no one was going to feel sorry for us. So we knew we were going to have to cling together and keep working hard.

It was a great tribute to Coach McKay and the staff and players that we endured that building process. Slowly, we got a lot of good players together. On offense, we had guys such as Doug Williams, Jimmie Giles and Ricky Bell. On defense, we had David Lewis, Richard "Batman" Wood, Cecil Johnson, my brother Dewey and me. We kept adding pieces until we had the makings of a team.

The 1979 season started out great for us. A lot of people didn't see us coming; we surprised a lot of teams. We got on a roll, and it looked like we had the NFC Central title locked up. But then at the end of the season, we needed just one more win to clinch the division and couldn't get it.

I remember Coach McKay saying, "We can't win at home. We can't win on the road. We need to play at a neutral site." It came down to the last game. We played the Kansas City Chiefs at home in a torrential rainstorm and ended up winning 3-0. Neil O'Donoghue made the field goal, but don't ask me how he did it. After the game, there was pandemonium. Everyone was giddy, flopping around on the wet field. I remember the writers saying that all the rain that came down had created a neutral site.

That win got us into the divisional playoffs game against the Eagles. No one gave us much of a chance to win against Philadelphia, but I think everyone on our team was prepared to play. And like I said, the crowd gave us a lift right off the bat.

The opening possession set the tone for the game. We got the ball and started giving it to Ricky Bell. Ricky left, Ricky right, Ricky up the middle, Ricky off guard. Our offense took over at our 20 and spent more than nine minutes driving the ball downfield. Ricky, of course, ended up scoring. It was an incredible drive. And in the warm weather, the Eagles defense must have been dying. An 18-play drive—that's amazing. Our defense

It was an incredible drive. And in the warm weather, the Eagles defense must have been dying. An 18-play drive—that's amazing.

was just standing on the sideline, watching. About 10 plays into the drive, we started wondering, "Hey, is it our turn yet?"

That day, Ricky had a divisional-playoffs–record 38 carries for 142 yards. He was built for that type of workload. He was a big, tough guy and didn't mind being used that way. We certainly relied on him a lot. In the heat, he just wore the defense down; he kept pounding and pounding and pounding.

We also had a big day on defense, holding the Eagles to fewer than 50 rushing yards. That was huge because they had a really good running back in Wilbert Montgomery and a good offensive line with guys like Stan Walters, who was one of the better tackles in the league. I locked horns with Walters quite

a bit that day. Whenever you played him, it was a long afternoon. He was a huge guy, so you would try to home in using speed and technique. Overall, you would have to stick to your game plan and do things as a unit that gave you a chance to play well. So there was a little battle going on over there.

Mostly, though, the game belonged to Ricky. He wore down the Eagles until we won, 24-17. The crowd just went wild, and we were celebrating and savoring the win in the locker room. Like I said, after winning just five games in our first three years, this one was really sweet.

—As told to Chuck O'Donnell

The first draft pick in the history of the Tampa Bay Buccaneers, defensive end **Lee Roy Selmon** didn't disappoint. In his nine seasons (1976–84) with the Bucs, Selmon was voted All-Pro four times, All-NFC five times and went to six straight Pro Bowls. Unfortunately, he then suffered a back injury. After missing the entire 1985 season, Selmon retired. He had tallied 78.5 quarterback sacks and 380 quarterback pressures, forced 28.5 fumbles and recovered ten fumbles. Selmon entered the Pro Football Hall of Fame in 1995.

There are a lot of games I remember with the Raiders because of great moments or great team efforts. But one game

JANUARY 4, 1981

OAKLAND RAIDERS 14, CLEVELAND BROWNS 12

MUNICIPAL STADIUM, CLEVELAND, OHIO

SCORING

OAK	0	7	0	7	**14**
CLE	0	6	6	0	**12**

CLE	Bolton, 42-yard interception return (kick failed)
OAK	van Eeghan, 1-yard run (Bahr kick)
CLE	Cockroft, 30-yard field goal
CLE	Cockroft, 29-yard field goal
OAK	van Eeghan, 1-yard run (Bahr kick)

TEAM STATISTICS

	OAK	CLE
First Downs	17	19
RushES-Yards	38-76	27-85
Passing Yards	149	183
Passes	14-30-2	13-40-3
Punts-Average	9-38.3	6-39.5
Fumbles-Lost	2-1	6-1
Penalties-Yards	9-48	12-73

INDIVIDUAL STATISTICS

Rushing

OAK	van Eeghan 20 rushes for 45 yards; King 12-23; Plunkett 4-8; Whittington 1-1; Jensen 1-minus 1
CLE	M. Pruitt 13-48; Hill 2-23; Sipe 6-13; Miller 1-1; G. Pruitt 4-11; McDonald 1-minus 11

Passing

OAK	Plunkett 14 completions, 30 attempts, 149 yards, 2 interceptions
CLE	Sipe 13-40-183-3

Receiving

OAK	King 4 receptions for 14 yards; Chester 3-64; van Eeghan 3-23; Branch 2-23; Chandler 1-15; Whittington 1-10
CLE	Newsome 4-51; G. Pruitt 3-54; Rucker 2-38; Logan 2-36; Hill 2-4

ATTENDANCE: 78,245

stands out for me not only because of great moments and a great team effort, but because it was the coldest weather I've ever played in.

We were in Cleveland in January 1981 to meet the Browns in the AFC Divisional Playoffs. It was about one degree above zero, but with the wind blowing off Lake Erie and into the stadium I remember someone telling us that the windchill factor was about 37 below. The field was frozen and players were doing everything they could just to keep warm, but the game went on. For the Raiders, that game turned out to be very significant. We beat the Browns 14-12 and eventually won Super Bowl XV against the Philadelphia Eagles.

We entered the playoffs as a wild-card team, which meant we had to play a first round game, a divisional playoff game, and the AFC Championship Game to reach the Super Bowl. As a team, we were well prepared to work our way through the playoffs, but after every game you suck in your gut and try to extend your stamina another notch.

Cleveland had an exciting team that season; that's when it won a ton of games in the last minute of play and became known as "the Kardiac Kids." But the Raiders—we were still in Oakland at the time—also had a great tradition of winning tough, gritty games. I looked forward to playing the Browns because I knew it would be a tough, physical, well-played game. But I certainly didn't look forward to playing under those weather conditions.

It actually was funny prior to the game, watching all these grown men in the locker room—tough guys who would stand up to any players in the league—get ready to face the cold weather. We put on thermal underwear, we rubbed special cream on our skin, and we had special hand and body warmers. Gene Upshaw put on a plastic laundry bag under his thermals for extra protection.

During the game we had to sit on benches called Hot Seats, which Managing General Partner Al Davis got for us. They belonged to the Philadelphia Eagles, and they had used them the previous day in their playoff game. When the Browns found out we had Hot Seats they wanted them too. I think we ended up splitting the benches with them.

We went into the game knowing there probably wouldn't be a lot of scoring. That put some added pressure on the defensive guys because we knew that even one mistake could be costly. As it turned out there wasn't a lot of scoring, and we were able to compensate for any mistakes we made.

There were more than 77,000 people in the stands, and some of them really were fanatical. With the wind blowing in, though, it was hard to hear anything else.

The frozen field meant you really took a pounding when you hit the turf. A lot of guys were slipping around, too, like they were wearing ice skates. We didn't get a lot of yardage on the ground, but our guys came up with the big plays when we needed them.

Cleveland scored first when they intercepted a pass off of our quarterback, Jim Plunkett, and ran it in for a touchdown. We came back a few minutes later and scored a touchdown when running back Mark Van Eeghan went in from the one. Jim had a couple of great plays on that series. He hit Ray Chester with a 26-yard pass play on a third-and-13, and then he gave us a first down on a third-and-one, when he ran for a couple of yards after Van Eeghan had slipped trying to take the handoff.

I kept getting reminded all game how cold it was, not just because the wind was whipping up everywhere but also because cornerback Lester Hayes kept complaining that he couldn't use his stick-um, which he would put on his gloves to help him intercept passes. The stuff kept freezing up and turning into taffy, which really annoyed Lester. Still, he played a great game. He made two interceptions, and he was all over the place on other plays. He didn't need the stuff.

It was good to get into the locker room at the half, especially since we were leading.

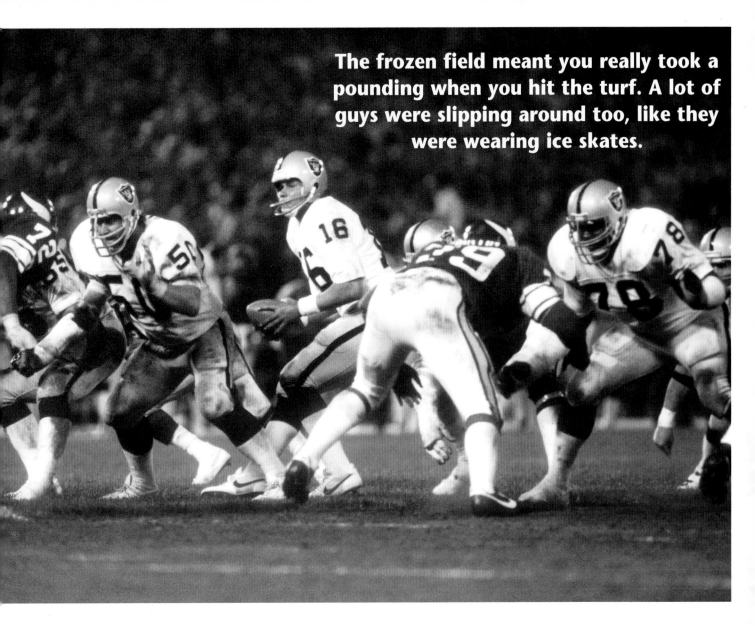

The frozen field meant you really took a pounding when you hit the turf. A lot of guys were slipping around too, like they were wearing ice skates.

Our coach, Tom Flores, was talking to us about second-half strategy, but mainly we wanted to get warm and stay warm for as long as possible.

The Browns defense contained our offense in the third quarter, and they took the lead on two field goals. But our defensive guys felt pretty good because we still had them held to only one touchdown. Going into the fourth quarter, though, we figured we needed to call up all our reserve energy to keep them off the scoreboard and to give our guys an opportunity to score some points.

The only scoring play of the quarter came about five minutes into the fourth. Jim directed an 80-yard drive, mostly with clean, sharp passes to van Eeghan, Cliff Branch and Kenny King. Van Eeghan closed out the drive with a one-yard run, but it was a great effort by everyone on offense.

Our defensive guys held Cleveland quarterback Brian Sipe pretty well in that quarter, but he led the Browns on a drive in the final minutes that almost won the game for Cleveland. They got down to our 13 with about a half-minute to play, and it seemed as if they might go for a game-winning field goal. But they lined up for a play, and Sipe let one go for Ozzie Newsome in the end zone. Mike Davis, who was covering Newsome for us, slipped, and I remember thinking, "Oh, no, Newsome is going to catch the ball." But Mike recovered and intercepted the pass, which effectively ended the game.

I can't speak for the Cleveland coaching staff, but I guess they looked at the frozen field, took into account the fact that they already had missed on a couple of field-goal attempts and a point-after attempt, and went for the pass. The way it turned out, I'm glad they did.

—As told to Barry Janoff

Tackle **Art Shell** (78), right, was one of the top offensive linemen through most of his 15-season (1968–82) career with the Oakland/Los Angeles Raiders. He played in 207 regular-season matches, 23 post-season games and eight Pro Bowls. A particular standout in Super Bowl XI, he won a second ring in Super Bowl XV. Shell entered the Pro Football Hall of Fame in 1989, the same year he became the first black head coach in modern NFL history. From 1989–95, he coached the Raiders to a 54-38 record and three playoff berths.

For me, an unforgettable game is one in which the entire team plays well, not one in which just one or two players stand out.

JANUARY 14, 1973
MIAMI DOLPHINS 14, WASHINGTON REDSKINS 7
MEMORIAL COLISEUM, LOS ANGELES, CALIFORNIA

SCORING

MIA	7	7	0	0	**14**
WAS	0	0	0	7	**7**

MIA Twilley, 28-yard pass from Griese (Yepremian kick)
MIA Kiick, 1-yard run (Yepremian kick)
WAS Bass, 49-yard fumble recovery return (Knight kick)

TEAM STATISTICS	MIA	WAS
First Downs	12	16
Rushes-Yards	37-184	36-141
Passing Yards	69	87
Passes	8-11-1	14-28-3
Punts-Average	7-43.0	5-31.0
Fumbles-Lost	2-1	0-0
Penalties-Yards	3-35	3-25

INDIVIDUAL STATISTICS

Rushing
MIA Csonka 15 rushes for 112 yards; Kiick 12-38; Morris 10-34
WAS Brown 22-72; Harraway 10-37; Kilmer 2-18; C. Taylor 1-8; Smith 1-6

Passing
MIA Griese 8 completions, 11 attempts, 88 yards, 1 interception
WAS Kilmer 14-28-104-3

Receiving
MIA Warfield 3 receptions for 36 yards; Kiick 2-6; Twilley 1-28; Mandich 1-19; Csonka 1-minus 1
WAS Jefferson 5-50; Brown 5-26; C. Taylor 2-20; Smith 1-11; Harraway 1-minus 3

ATTENDANCE: 90,182

Football is a team game. That's how I coached my players, and that's how you win games. It's not just one or two people, it's everyone working together.

I have to go back to 1972 for my most unforgettable season—when the Dolphins were undefeated—and then to the Super Bowl for an unforgettable game. That wasn't the best game we played that season, but it was the one in which we faced the most pressure and the one in which our guys showed how tough and dedicated they were. We were 14-0 that season, and then won two playoff games, against Cleveland and Pittsburgh; but if we had lost the Super Bowl, everything else we had accomplished would have been wasted. You're always remembered by your last game.

Miami had gone to the Super Bowl the year before, but we lost to Dallas 24-3. I don't base my decisions on what critics and outside observers say. I never have and I never will. But it was hard to ignore the fact that every time you heard the name Dolphins, people would label us "losers" and "chokers." That's something you never want, but it's especially annoying when you work your butt off and have a tough, dedicated bunch of players.

Coming into the '72 season, there was an attitude among all the players that if we played up to our potential, we could win the Super Bowl. I think the key that season was that we had a squad of team players—guys who would make sacrifices for the team. That's hard to find these days, but the teams that display that type of effort do extremely well.

We won some tough games during the season. We defeated Minnesota 16-14 in the final seconds, and had a tough game against Buffalo, 24-23. I remember thinking during the season that no matter how many games we won, we wouldn't be successful until we'd won that final game. It was a great moment when we won that 14th game and became the first NFL team to go undefeated. But I had mixed emotions. If we got to the Super Bowl and lost, and ended the season 16-1, it wouldn't have been good enough. We had to finish the season 17-0.

We were well prepared for the playoff games against Cleveland and Pittsburgh. Again we won because of a strong team effort. They had good squads, but we had the edge because of our determination to be the best.

Washington, under George Allen, had a good, solid team that year. They beat us in the preseason, but that didn't carry much weight with me by the time we got to the Super Bowl. My concerns were about how we would match up with them on offense and defense, and how we could best use our strengths to exploit their weaknesses.

One thing in our favor was that the Redskins were three-point favorites to win the game. That put some pressure on them, and took some of the edge off us trying to complete our season undefeated.

Bob Griese had been injured in the fifth game of the season, so Earl Morrall was our quarterback for the rest of the season. But Griese was healthy for the Super Bowl, and he was the one I wanted out there for us. I wanted to score early, and then keep them off balance as much as possible. We had a tough ground game with Larry Csonka, Jim Kiick and Mercury Morris, and we had a strong passing game with Griese and Paul Warfield. But, again, this was a strong team effort, and that included the entire defense and the offensive line that protected Griese and opened up holes for Csonka and Kiick.

Our defenders liked the fact that they had been labeled the "No-Name" defense, but they were far from unknown to the rest of the league. Guys like Nick Buoniconti and Manny Fernandez and Bob Matheson and Jake Scott were the backbone of our defensive unit. The teams we faced knew exactly who they were and what they could do.

Our first score was a good example of how our offense worked as a unit. Warfield had a key 14-yard gain, and Csonka and Kiick each had yardage on the ground. We started on our 37 and worked it down to their 28. We ran a pass play at that point, and their defense was keying on Warfield. But Howard Twilley cut across the middle and had a step on Pat Fischer. Griese hit Twilley on the

Garo should have fallen on the ball after his kick was blocked, but he picked it up and tried to throw a pass.

numbers, and he went in for the touchdown.

Washington, behind quarterback Billy Kilmer, tried to put together a couple of offensive drives after our score. But Scott intercepted a pass on one drive and Buoniconti intercepted a pass on the next drive. Buoniconti's interception actually set up our second score. He returned it 32 yards to the Redskins' 27. Griese hit Jim Mandich with an 18-yard pass, which gave us a first-and-goal on the two. Two plays later, Kiick went in to give us a 14-0 lead at the half.

We hadn't made any big mistakes in the first half, so what I emphasized in the locker room was maintaining our composure on the field. With a 14-0 lead, I knew we would be in good shape if our defensive guys played tough. And they did.

There were a couple of times late in the second half when it looked as if our guys had let Washington gain an edge. One play was stopped by Scott when he intercepted a Kilmer pass in the end zone and ran it back 55 yards. The other was a play late in the game when we should have gone up 17-0 but ended up giving them their only touchdown.

I watched the whole thing on the sidelines and I couldn't believe what I was seeing. Garo Yepremian was on the field to kick a field goal, but a low snap from center got the thing going wrong from the start. Garo should have fallen on the ball after his kick was blocked, but he picked it up and tried to throw a pass. Mike Bass intercepted whatever it was that Garo was throwing and ran it back 49 yards for the touchdown.

There were still two minutes to play, and we had to sweat out the time. The Redskins got the ball back with just over a minute to play, but our defense stopped them. Vern Den Herder and Bill Stanfill sacked Kilmer on the final play of the game. It was a perfect way to end the game.

There was a tremendous amount of excitement in the locker room afterward. I had my own feelings of excitement, knowing what we had accomplished as a team. That season, and that win in the Super Bowl, is something I'll never forget.

—As told to Barry Janoff

The Miami Dolphins carry coach **Don Shula**, above, off the field after a 1993 victory over Philadelphia that made Shula the winningest coach in NFL history. Shula, a defensive back and halfback in the 1950s with the Cleveland Browns (1951–52), Baltimore Colts (1953–56) and Washington Redskins (1957), tallied a record 328 wins as head coach of the Colts (1963–69) and the Dolphins (1970–95). He went to six Super Bowls, winning twice, including in 1972, when Miami completed the only undefeated season (17-0) in league history.

Without a doubt, the entire 1986 season will be one that I'll always remember. Not just because of what happened, but also

DECEMBER 1, 1986

NEW YORK GIANTS 21, SAN FRANCISCO 49ERS 17

CANDLESTICK PARK, SAN FRANCISCO, CALIFORNIA

SCORING

NYG	0	0	21	0	**21**
SF	3	14	0	0	**17**

SF	Wersching, 30-yard field goal
SF	Rice, 11-yard pass from Montana (Wersching kick)
SF	Rice, 1-yard run (Wersching kick)
NYG	Morris, 17-yard pass from Simms (Allegre kick)
NYG	Robinson, 34-yard pass from Simms (Allegre kick)
NYG	Anderson, 1-yard run (Allegre kick)

TEAM STATISTICS	NYG	SF
First Downs	20	26
Rushes-Yards	19-13	27-116
Passing Yards	384	251
Passes	27-38-2	32-52-1
Punts-Average	3-41.0	5-43.0
Fumbles-Lost	2-1	1-0
Penalties-Yards	1-5	6-25

INDIVIDUAL STATISTICS

Rushing

NYG	Morris 13 rushes for 14 yards; Carthon 1-1; Anderson 2-1; Simms 3-minus 3
SF	Tyler 13-59; Craig 10-43; Cribbs 2-11; Montana 1-2; Rice 1-1

Passing

NYG	Simms 27 completions, 38 attempts, 388 yards, 2 interceptions
SF	Montana 32-52-251-1

Receiving

NYG	Bavaro 7 receptions for 98 yards; Robinson 5-116; Moris 4-42
SF	Craig 12-75; Rice 9-86; Francis 5-39

ATTENDANCE: 59,777

because of the way things happened. There were some games we won that we might not have won in other seasons, but because of the way the Giants played as a team—and because we were building something solid all year long—the season became something special.

The culmination of the season, of course, had to be winning the Super Bowl. But there were several games that were special because they became confidence-builders for us as a team. Looking back, the game that convinced us we could win the whole thing was against the 49ers in San Francisco. We had just come off a series of tough games, and the 49ers were on a roll with quarterback Joe Montana in the lineup [after more than seven weeks away due to major back surgery].

We ended up getting blown out in the first half; we were trailing 17-0 at the half. But we put it all together in the second half and outscored them 21-0 to win the game 21-17. Not only was that a physical victory for us, but it was an emotionally and mentally uplifting win for us as well. After that—after coming all the way back against San Francisco—the feeling on the team to a man was that we could do whatever we had to do to win the Super Bowl.

We had a strong record going into the game against the 49ers, 10-2, and we were in first place in the NFC East division. We had won five in a row, but they weren't easy wins: We had beaten Denver the week before by three, Minnesota the week before that by two, Dallas and Philadelphia by three each and Washington by a touchdown. We were winning the games we had to win, but it seemed as if we were playing only well enough to win, rather than taking charge and really overpowering the opposition.

The victory against Denver the week before was at home, but the San Francisco game was our third road game in four weeks. At that point in the season, you try to get every little edge you can. So, naturally, it must have seemed to some that the 49ers

had the edge mentally and emotionally because they were at home and because they had their leader, Joe Montana, back.

I wouldn't say we were intimidated in the first half, but they had our number. Joe had something like 17 or 18 completions for 150 yards, and wide receiver Jerry Rice had scored two touchdowns. Also, their defense was stopping us on virtually every drive.

Even at that point, though, I don't think anyone on our team felt we were out of the game. We were down, but not out. In the locker room, Coach Bill Parcells put things into perspective. He wasn't yelling or ranting or raving. For him, and for us, it was simply a matter of everyone doing their job. I don't remember his exact words, but he told us that if our defense could stop them right away, our offense would score. His confidence was important.

The difference in the second half for us was our intensity. On our first possession we went right at the 49ers' defense and were successful. We moved from deep in our territory to their 48. Then I hit Mark Bavaro with a pass on the 40, and he ran another 23 yards with defensive guys hanging all over him. After the game, offensive guard Chris Godfrey came over to me and said, "That play turned it around. We told the Niners defense that the fun's over; we're going to run it right through you now." Right after that, I hit Joe Morris with a pass for our first touchdown.

On our very next possession, we had a fourth-and-one situation at the 50. The decision was to go for the first down, even though the 49ers would have had great field position if they stopped us. But the intensity was there, and there was no doubt that we should go for it. Joe got the call and ran through the defense for 16 yards, down to their 34. On the next play I hit Stacy Robinson with a pass for our second touchdown.

The intensity on the bench was incredible at that point. The defense came onto the field pumped up and stopped their offense without a first down. We came right out again and drove right at their defense, rather than trying to be cute about it. The key play of that drive came when we were at the 50 and I spotted Robinson open by a couple of steps

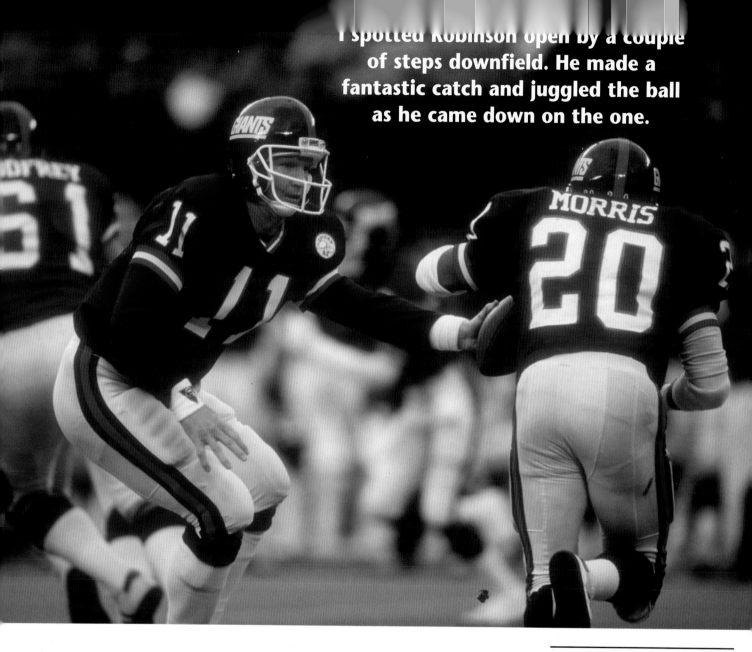

I spotted Robinson open by a couple of steps downfield. He made a fantastic catch and juggled the ball as he came down on the one.

downfield. He made a fantastic catch and juggled the ball as he came down on the one.

On the next play Ottis Anderson went in from the one to give us our third touchdown of the quarter.

The rest of the game really belonged to our defense. There were some close calls, but by that time everything seemed to be working for us and against San Francisco. On one play Rice had our secondary beaten by at least five steps at our 30, but Montana's pass was out of his reach. In the fourth quarter Rice caught a fourth-and-two pass at our 30, but he landed out of bounds. Then, with about five minutes to play, the 49ers were on our 22 or 23 on third-and-four, but Carl Banks got into the 49ers' backfield and downed Wendell Tyler for a three-yard loss.

I remember sitting in the locker room after the game thinking back to a time earlier in the season when my confidence level wasn't as high as it should have been. The team was 5-2 after seven games, and some of the fans were down on me; there were guys in the papers ripping my butt apart. But the coach pulled me aside one day and said, "Hey, I think you're great." He was convincing. I don't care who you are—sometimes you need that kind of support.

We went into Washington a week later and beat them by 10 points. That really solidified things for us, going into the playoffs. But I keep going back to that game against San Francisco. That's the one that put us over the top as a team, and that's the game I'll never forget.

—*As told to Barry Janoff*

Quarterback **Phil Simms** (11), above, hands off the ball to New York Giants teammate Joe Morris (20) in 1986. Simms won the Super Bowl XXI MVP award at the end of the season after completing 22 of 25 passes for 268 yards and three touchdowns. He won a second Super Bowl ring in 1990, after teammate Jeff Hostetler quarterbacked the team earlier in the post-season. After playing 168 games for the Giants between 1979 and 1993, Simms retired with 2,576 completions for 33,462 yards and 199 touchdowns.

Millions of dads and sons head to the backyard or the park on crisp autumn days to throw a football around, one generation

SEPTEMBER 24, 1979
CLEVELAND BROWNS 26, DALLAS COWBOYS 7
MUNICIPAL STADIUM, CLEVELAND, OHIO

SCORING

DAL	7	0	0	0	**7**
CLE	20	0	0	6	**26**

CLE   Logan, 23-yard pass from Sipe (kick failed)
CLE   Newsome, 52-yard pass from Sipe (Cockroft kick)
CLE   Darden, 39-yard interception return (Cockroft kick)
DAL   Hill, 48-yard pass from Staubach (Septien kick)
CLE   M. Pruitt, 2-yard run (kick failed)

TEAM STATISTICS

	DAL	CLE
First Downs	20	15
Rushes-Yards	30-123	33-82
Passing Yards	271	229
Passes	21-39-2	15-28-1
Punts-Average	5-42.8	8-36.4
Fumbles-Lost	3-3	1-0
Penalties-Yards	5-52	2-19

INDIVIDUAL STATISTICS
Rushing
DAL   Dorsett 14 rushes for 64 yards; Laidlaw 13-49; DuPree 1-minus 1; Staubach 2-11
CLE   Sipe 1-1; M. Pruitt 14-31; C. Hill 7-24; G. Pruitt 6-15; C. Miller 2-7; Feacher 1-minus 1; Moriarty 2-5

Passing
DAL   Staubach 21 completions, 39 attempts, 303 yards, 2 interceptions
CLE   Sipe 15-28-1-239

Receiving
DAL   Cosbie 1 reception for 7 yards; D. Pearson 5-109; T. Hill 3-70; P. Pearson 3-34; Laidlaw 3-9; Dorsett 1-9; DuPree 3-29; Saldi 1-15; Wilson 1-21
CLE   G. Pruitt 1-27; Rucker 5-57; Logan 2-42; C. Miller 3-55; Newsome 3-53; M. Pruitt 1-5

ATTENDANCE: 80,123

literally passing down its passion to the next. While my dad, Martin, couldn't get on the ground and wrestle with me for a fumble, few things could bond us like football.

My dad had been injured in the military as a young man, but we always talked about football. He was interested in developing my character and saw that, as a quarterback, I was put in a position of leadership. Our conversations revolved around how to get things done. He would always talk to me about staying cool under pressure. He saw that trait in me and tried to foster it.

I may have looked cool and composed before we played the Dallas Cowboys in week four of the 1979 season, but my stomach was doing cartwheels.

For one, this was a *Monday Night Football* game. In addition, the Cowboys had been picked by many NFL observers to go to the Super Bowl that year, and we had been tabbed to finish last in the AFC Central. Even though we were off to a surprisingly strong start, at 3-0, I was just hoping we wouldn't get embarrassed on national television.

Adding to the tension was that my dad was in the Municipal Stadium stands to see me play. He lived in Hawaii and didn't usually get to watch my games, but this was a special case. He was battling cancer, and he didn't know when he'd have another chance to see me.

I always prided myself on having tunnel vision on the field, on never letting my focus stray. But as I warmed up for that game, I thought of my dad. I slowly became overcome with emotion, choking back tears. I had to go to the locker room to regain my poise before kickoff.

When the game began, we got the ball and set out toward the open end of the stadium. It was difficult to throw in that direction because you had the wind in your face, but we moved the ball into the Cowboys' territory. That's when I hit sure-handed receiver Dave Logan for a 23-yard touchdown pass.

Our next series really sticks out in my mind. We had gotten to about midfield when we called a pass play designed to go to Ozzie Newsome. Ozzie was already developing into one of the best tight ends in the game, and I always knew I could find him open. On this particular play, Ozzie was supposed to watch the weak safety. If the weak safety began to inch up, Ozzie would break out of his pattern and head up the field.

As I dropped back, the blitz was in my face. This was Dallas' "Doomsday" defense, with Randy White, Harvey Martin and John Dutton up front, D.D. Lewis and Bob Breunig in the linebacking corps and Cliff Harris camping out in the secondary waiting to hit someone. With the rush all around me, I was trying to stay calm. I just let the ball go high and over the middle, hoping Ozzie had read the play.

As soon as I released the ball, I was knocked to the ground. As I lay there, I could hear the roar of the crowd; I knew Ozzie had caught it and run it in for a touchdown. We were winning 13-0 before the Cowboys knew what had hit them.

At that point, you could sense some urgency on the Cowboys' part, that they weren't going to stand for this, that they were getting just a little annoyed. But just when they thought they were going to get back into the game, our defense stepped up. Thom Darden, a free safety who had a great knack for intercepting passes, picked off Roger Staubach as he tried to throw the ball to running back Ron Springs. Staubach had thrown 150 consecutive passes without an interception up until that point.

With the ball tucked under his arm, Darden took off and ran 39 yards for a touchdown. The game was only about seven minutes old, but we already had a 20-0 lead. The Dawg Pound was howling, and our confidence started to soar.

Dallas cut into our lead with a touchdown pass from Staubach to wideout Tony Hill toward the end of the first quarter. The Cowboys kept the pressure on throughout the rest of the game, often dominating the action, but our defense came up with some big plays. It recovered three fumbles, Darden

I always prided myself on having tunnel vision on the field, on never letting my focus stray. But as I warmed up for that game, I thought of my dad.

picked off another pass, and Curtis Weathers blocked Rafael Septien's field-goal attempt. Later, Septien missed a 47-yard try.

We tacked on one final touchdown in the fourth quarter to put the game away. Mike Pruitt dove into the end zone from a few yards out to finish the scoring.

Our 26-7 victory that night made us 4-0 and capped an amazing string of games for us. In the season opener against the New York Jets, we tied the game with less than a minute left. The key play came when defensive lineman Joe Klecko was called for roughing the quarterback, keeping our drive alive. We eventually won in overtime on Don Cockroft's field goal. The next week, we beat the Kansas City Chiefs when I hit Reggie

Rucker with a touchdown pass with less than a minute to play. Then there was a three-point victory over the Baltimore Colts.

They were all great wins, but none was as sweet or as memorable as the one over Dallas. As the clock began to tick down and I realized the game was essentially over, I began to think about my dad again. I thought about how he wasn't always going to be there to see me play. But for as long as he lived, we shared that special night.

Even now, when I think of that game, I have to smile. That one was for you, Dad.

—*As told to Chuck O'Donnell*

In 1980, **Brian Sipe** accomplished several personal bests when he threw 337 complete passes for 4,132 yards and 30 touchdowns. He earned his first—and only—invite to the Pro Bowl and was voted league MVP. As quarterback for the Cleveland Browns for 10 seasons (1974–83), Sipe tallied a franchise record 1,944 completions for 23,713 yards and 154 touchdowns. In 1984, he signed with the USFL's New Jersey Generals. Traded to the Jacksonville Bulls the following season, Sipe finished one more injury-shortened campaign before retiring.

1974 AFC DIVISIONAL PLAYOFF GAME

We had lost to the Miami Dolphins in the two previous AFC Championship games and now we were coming up against them

DECEMBER 21, 1974
OAKLAND RAIDERS 28, MIAMI DOLPHINS 26
OAKLAND COLISEUM, OAKLAND, CALIFORNIA

SCORING

OAK	0	7	7	14	**28**
MIA	7	3	6	10	**26**

MIA N. Moore, 89-yard kickoff return (Yepremian kick)
OAK C. Smith, 31-yard pass from Stabler (Blanda kick)
MIA Yepremian, 33-yard field goal
OAK Biletnikoff, 13-yard pass from Stabler (Blanda kick)
MIA Warfield, 16-yard pass from Griese (kick failed)
MIA Yepremian, 46-yard field goal
OAK Branch, 72-yard pass from Stabler (Blanda kick)
MIA Malone, 23-yard run (Yepremian kick)
OAK Davis, 8-yard pass from Stabler (Blanda kick)

TEAM STATISTICS	MIA	OAK
First Downs	18	19
Rushes-Yards	17-213	32-135
Passing Yards	81	276
Passes	7-14-1	20-30-1
Punts-Average	6-32.2	7-42.7
Fumbles-Lost	0-0	0-0
Penalties-Yards	3-15	3-59

INDIVIDUAL STATISTICS
Rushing
MIA Malone 14 rushes for 83 yards; Griese 2-14; Kiick 1-2
OAK C. Davis 12-59; Hubbard 14-55; Banaszak 3-14; Stabler 3-7
Passing
MIA Griese 7 completions, 14 attempts, 101 yards, 1 interception
OAK Stabler 20-30-293-1
Receiving
MIA Warfield 3 receptions for 47 yards; N. Moore 2-40; Nottingham 1-9; Kiick 1-5
OAK Biletnikoff 8-122; Branch 3-84; B. Moore 3-22; C. Smith 2-35; C. Davis 2-16; Hubbard 1-9; Pitts 1-5

ATTENDANCE: 52,817

in the first round of the 1974 playoffs. There was a hell of a lot riding on this game—it was the first step to the Super Bowl for the winner and the last game of the year for the loser.

Our approach to this game was that it was no different than any other. The keys to success in the playoffs are a balanced attack and making as few mistakes as possible. We went into the game with all the respect in the world for the Dolphins. Anytime you played a Don Shula team, you were going against a well-coached, disciplined club; you knew you were going to have a battle on your hands.

Bob Griese was Miami's quarterback and I always enjoyed playing against him. Bob was a thinking man's quarterback—he threw when he thought it was time to throw and he used his running game exceptionally well. He's an intelligent guy who understood the running game—the Dolphins basically made their living on the ground with Larry Csonka, Jim Kiick and Mercury Morris packing the ball. Bob also had Paul Warfield and they could hook up and burn you with the long ball, too. A guy like Griese was hard to beat.

I remember this game as being one of the most fun and enjoyable of my career. I threw a lot of passes, we moved the ball well against a good Miami defense, and the crowd's enthusiasm made it all the more fun. It would have been an exciting game even if we hadn't won.

We had so much talent on our defense that I was like a kid with an erector set out there. I had a great line that gave me the time I needed to throw, I had outstanding receivers like Fred Biletnikoff and Cliff Branch, and Bob Moore was the tight end. That was Dave Casper's rookie year and he didn't play much then.

We drove the length of the field to win games in the final minutes so often that people came to expect it. But people don't realize how difficult it is to accomplish something like that, especially against the good teams. There is no room for error.

I enjoyed a game like that when it was done and we'd won. It gave you a great deal of satisfaction. On the other hand, if you had to do it every week that meant something wasn't going right. It might have meant our defense wasn't playing well, or maybe we were struggling on offense. It meant your team wasn't playing as a team.

Miami jumped on top 7-0, even before the fans were settled in their seats, when Nat Moore returned the opening kickoff 89 yards for a touchdown. That gave them early momentum, but I never really got excited or worried about anything that happened early in a game. There was a lot of time and football left and a lot of things could happen.

We'd made up many more than seven points in a game with a whole lot less time remaining. There was no reason to panic, but Moore's return made it all the more evident it was going to be a hell of a football game. We definitely were going to have a horse race on our hands.

We didn't do much on our first three offensive series—in fact we didn't even penetrate Miami territory. On our fourth possession, though, we moved to Miami's 31, where we had a first down. I threw for Charlie Smith and he made a fine catch at the goal line for the tying touchdown.

We took our first lead in the third quarter, 14-10, when Biletnikoff caught a 13-yard touchdown pass. It was without a doubt the greatest catch I've ever seen. Cornerback Tim Foley, who just as well could have been called for pass interference, was draped all over Freddie and had one of his arms pinned behind him. Yet Freddie still managed to go up and catch the ball one-handed and come down with his feet inbounds for the score.

Miami came back to take the lead on a 16-yard pass from Griese to Warfield. Early in the fourth quarter, Garo Yepremian added a field goal and they led 19-14.

On Miami's next possession, they didn't score, but they had a hell of a time-consuming drive that took more than five minutes. They punted and we took over on our own 17 with a little less than five minutes to play.

I threw an 11-yard sideline pass to

Freddie, then unloaded a long one to Cliff. Anytime you put one up for Cliff, there was a pretty good chance he was going to get it. We had a little luck on the play when the two defensive backs covering Cliff ran together. Cliff made a great catch just inside the Dolphins' 30-yard line and ran it in for a 72-yard play. George Blanda kicked the conversion and we led 21-19 with four and a half minutes to go.

Miami came right back and moved the ball from its own 32 to our 23, where they had a first down with a little more than two minutes remaining. All they needed was a field goal to go ahead and they were maintaining good ball control. Time was running out on us.

On their first play from the 23, Benny Malone ran a sweep around the right side and scored, putting them back in front 26-21. That left us two minutes to play with. There was talk after the game that Miami scored too quickly and left us with too much time to come back. That was ridiculous. The Dolphins got the touchdown and were in pretty good shape.

We had to accomplish the same thing Miami just did—move down the field in a short amount of time and get a touchdown. The thing I recall about that last drive was they never really put a heavy rush on me. A lot of teams in a situation like that will send their linebackers and really try to apply the heat. I remember Shula saying after the game that if he had it to do over, he would have put more pressure on me. The time I got allowed our receivers to run good routes. Freddie made a couple of good catches to get us down to where we were knocking on the door.

There were 35 seconds left when we had a first and goal at the Miami eight. We had just called our last time-out. I had time for four shots at the end zone. If the pass was incomplete, the clock would stop; if the pass was complete, we'd won. It was as simple as that.

I dropped back on first down and I spotted Clarence running toward the right corner of the end zone. He had his man beat and I knew we would have had it easy if I drilled the ball to him. As I began to throw, I was hit from behind by—as I learned later—their defensive end Vern Den Herder. I was falling forward when I released the ball and it kind of floated. I watched the flight of the ball and I knew Clarence had a shot at it, but so did two Dolphins. The ball was up for grabs. Clarence made one super catch as he out-wrestled two guys, 20 pounds heavier

I had time for four shots at the end zone. If the pass was incomplete, the clock would stop; if the pass was complete, we'd won.

than he was, for the ball.

We weren't out of the woods yet. Miami had the ball on its own 33 with 21 seconds left and could still win with a field goal. A couple of quick 20-yard completions by Griese and they would be well within Yepremian's range. Griese threw one about 20 yards on first down and Phil Villapiano picked it off.

Then the celebration began, on the field and in the stands. It was a great, exciting and satisfying victory.

—*As told to Dave Payne*

Quarterback **Ken "Snake" Stabler**'s beard and gunslinger demeanor personified the renegade Oakland Raiders of the 1970s. Although hardly used from 1970–72, Stabler established franchise records for passing—19,098 yards and 150 touchdowns—before the decade was over. The Raiders won Super Bowl XI and Stabler went to three Pro Bowls. After two years with the Oilers (1980–81) and three (1982–84) with the New Orleans Saints, Stabler retired with 2,270 career completions for 27,938 yards and 194 touchdowns.

JOHN STALLWORTH

Looking back, there are a lot of big games that stand out in my career. I have four Super Bowl rings, and there were a lot of

games that, when I think about them, were important to the team and important to me as an athlete.

But right now, the game I'll never forget was against the San Francisco 49ers on their home turf. We were underdogs, and we were losing late in the fourth quarter. But I scored the game-tying touchdown and we beat them 20-17.

That game is important to me for a few reasons. The 49ers went on to win Super Bowl XIX, so it's always a good feeling when you look back and know that you beat the champs. Also, Pittsburgh is known for winning the big games, and that was a big game for us because it solidified our hold on first place in the AFC Central, and turned out to be the 49ers' only loss of the year. So it was a great team victory.

But I look at that game on a personal level as well. I had a poor season in 1983—there were injuries and a few other factors—and there were people who felt I couldn't come back. But I had a good season in 1984, and that win over the 49ers was a great morale booster for me.

Going into the game, we knew that they were undefeated to that point. But we knew that we could beat them. They had established themselves as one of the top teams in the league. But people still weren't sure about us. That game received a lot of national attention, and it was important to us that we play our best as a team.

We really didn't have the type of rivalry with the 49ers that we had with Dallas, but there was a lot of intensity throughout the game. They had about 60,000 fans cheering for them, plus the momentum of being 6-0. But those things didn't faze us. Like I said, the Steelers were known for winning big games—and a lot of those games were on the road, under adverse conditions.

We knew going into the game that 49ers coach Bill Walsh mapped out their first 25 or so plays. So our plan was to catch them flat-footed and make them play catch-up. That might force them out of their game plan and put some extra pressure on them.

Mark Malone started at quarterback and he had the team moving from the outset. We were deep in the 49ers' territory when Rich Erenberg scored our first touchdown—on a two-yard run. We had been going to Frank Pollard on the ground for most of the game, but we used Erenberg as the second back. I think Frank rushed for more than 100 yards, but that set up a lot of key plays for Erenberg.

We scored on a field goal to open the second quarter, and were up 10-0 at that point. But we knew that the 49ers had an explosive offense and that their quarterback, Joe Montana, was an explosive player. He was going to his key receivers, and they were down inside our 10 when he scored on a quarterback keeper on an end run.

Our defense held them the rest of the half, and we went into the third quarter up 10-7. I don't remember anything special being said in the locker room, other than that we had to stay with our game plan and keep them off balance on offense and defense. The fact that we held them to one touchdown in the half was a boost for us, but we also knew that we could have made more of our scoring opportunities.

The 49ers showed us why they became champs that season when they held our offense down for the entire third quarter and then for most of the fourth. But our defensive guys were super too. San Francisco didn't score in the third, so it was still 10-7 going into the fourth. They tied the score in the fourth on a field goal, and then took the lead when Wendell Tyler scored on a run. They had two touchdowns in the game, but both of them were on the ground, and I think that was a great achievement by our secondary.

There were less than five minutes to play and we were down 17-10. We were going for the tie, at that point. But we felt that if we scored with enough time remaining, we could drive down into their territory again and we could win it with a field goal. Mark Malone and the coaching staff were mixing up the plays pretty well, and we were deep in their territory with just over three minutes to

---

OCTOBER 14, 1984

PITTSBURGH STEELERS 20, SAN FRANCISCO 49ERS 17

CANDLESTICK PARK, SAN FRANCISCO, CALIFORNIA

SCORING

PIT	7	3	0	10	**20**
SF	0	7	0	10	**17**

PIT	Erenberg, 2-yard run (Anderson kick)
PIT	Anderson, 48-yard field goal
SF	Montana, 7-yard run (Wersching kick)
SF	Wersching, 30-yard field goal
SF	Tyler, 7-yard run (Wersching kick)
PIT	Stallworth, 6-yard pass from Malone (Anderson kick)
PIT	Anderson, 21-yard field goal

TEAM STATISTICS

	PIT	SF
First Downs	23	22
Rushes-Yards	47-175	20-117
Passing Yards	149	241
Passes	11-18-1	24-35-1
Punts-Average	2-41.0	3-30.7
Fumbles-Lost	1-0	1-0
Penalties-Yards	11-68	8-57

INDIVIDUAL STATISTICS

Rushing

PIT	Pollard 24 rushes for 105 yards; Erenberg 11-44; Abercrombie 8-23; Malone 3-2; Veals 1-1
SF	Tyler 11-59; Craig 6-29; Montana 3-29

Passing

PIT	Malone 11 completions, 18 attempts, 156 yards, 1 interception
SF	Montana 24-34-241-1; Harmon 1-0-0-0

Receiving

PIT	Stallworth 6 receptions for 78 yards; Thompson 1-23; Kolodziejski 1-22; Erenberg 1-12; Capers 1-11; Garrity 1-10
SF	Craig 7-43; Cooper 6-50; Clark 5-67; Francis 2-50; Tyler 2-13; Wilson 1-14; Monroe 1-4

ATTENDANCE: 59,110

The 49ers showed us why they became champs that season.

play when Malone hit me with a six-yard touchdown pass. With the extra point, we were able to tie them.

Our defense really held tough on the next set of downs, and a 43-yard interception return by linebacker Bryan Hinkle set up our offense in great shape. The 49ers might have been thinking about overtime at that point, but we wanted to end the game in regulation. Mark moved us into position, and Gary Anderson kicked a 21-yard field goal that put us ahead.

The 49ers wouldn't quit, but neither did our defense. We held them to some tough yards and kept them out of the end zone. They marched 54 yards without any time-outs, and with about seven seconds to play they set up for a field goal that would have

tied the score. They went for a 37-yarder, but Ray Wersching's attempt was wide. When it missed, that was the first time we knew we had the game won.

It was a great feeling in the locker room afterwards, because it was a great team victory. I remember even Pittsburgh Coach Chuck Noll said it was the greatest victory of his coaching career, and that's something, because the man led us to four Super Bowl wins.

I think the main thing is that we played as a team and didn't fold, even when we could have folded. If we had lost, people would have said, "Well, they gave it a good try." We didn't want that. We wanted the victory—and that's what we got.

—*As told to Barry Janoff*

Wide receiver **John Stallworth** set the Pittsburgh Steelers' franchise records with 537 career receptions for 8,723 yards and 63 touchdowns. He won four Super Bowl rings during 14 seasons (1974-87) with the Steelers. His 73-yard reception for the fourth quarter go-ahead touchdown in Super Bowl XIV was particularly memorable. Stallworth went to the Pro Bowl in 1979 and 1982 as well as in 1984, when he set personal bests with 80 receptions for 1,395 yards and 11 touchdowns. He entered the Pro Football Hall of Fame in 2002.

To my mind there was no game quite like it, not because of how it ended, or how we were able to do it, but because of what it

DECEMBER 31, 1967
GREEN BAY PACKERS 21, DALLAS COWBOYS 17
LAMBEAU FIELD, GREEN BAY, WISCONSIN

SCORING

GB	7	7	0	7	**21**
DAL	0	10	0	7	**17**

GB Dowler, 8-yard pass from Starr (Chandler kick)
GB Dowler, 46-yard pass from Starr (Chandler kick)
DAL Andrie, 7-yard fumble recovery (Villanueva kick)
DAL Villanueva, 21-yard field goal
DAL Rentzel, 50-yard pass from Reeves (Villanueva kick)
GB Starr, 1-yard run (Chandler kick)

TEAM STATISTICS

	GB	DAL
First Downs	18	11
Rushes-Yards	32-80	33-93
Passing Yards	115	100
Passes	14-24-1	11-26-0
Punts-Average	8-29.0	8-39.0
Fumbles lost	2	1
Penalties-Yards	10	58

INDIVIDUAL STATISTICS
Rushing
GB Anderson 18 rushes for 35 yards; Mercein 6-20; Williams 4-13; Wilson 3-11; Starr 1-1
DAL Perkins 17-51; Reeves 13-42; Baynham 1-minus 1; Clarke 1-minus 8; Meredith 1-9
Passing
GB Starr 14 completions, 24 attempts, 191 yards, 1 interception
DAL Meredith 10-25-59-0; Reeves 1-1-50-0
Receptions
GB Dowler 4 receptions for 77 yards; Anderson 4-44; Dale 3-44; Mercein 2-22; Williams 1-4
DAL Hayes 3-16; Reeves 3-11; Clarke 2-24; Rentzel 2-61; Baynham 1-3

ATTENDANCE: 50,861

meant to us, to the Green Bay Packers. It gave us not just a championship, but our third consecutive championship, and no team had ever done that since the playoff system began in 1933.

Bright sunshine covered the field when we started and that belied the fact that it was 13 below when the game started, with an icy 15-mile-an-hour north wind.

Dallas had trouble moving after the opening kickoff because of our special defense, a five-two to cut off their wide stuff, and after a good punt we took over on our own 18-yard line.

Getting on the board was no problem. In 16 plays, we ended the drive by throwing a three-yard pass to Boyd Dowler in the end zone. On our next possession, the big play was a third and one call.

From their 43-yard line I faked an off-tackle play to Ben Wilson. He covered the ball well, but I pulled it back and spun deeper into the backfield. When I looked downfield I saw Dowler running free behind Mel Renfro and was able to hit him for the score.

Maybe we started to think about the cold and the conditions more than we thought about our own execution. But for whatever reason, we seemed to lose our momentum; and that can be fatal, because once you lose your momentum it is almost impossible to regain it. And football is nothing more than a game of momentum.

The Cowboys were a hungry and desperate team, but we put them in the game with our own mistakes. The first one was mine. I was back to pass and Willie Townes broke through and tackled me. I fumbled and Cowboy George Andrie scooped up the ball and trotted in for an easy touchdown.

Then, just before the half, Willie Wood fumbled a fair catch on a punt and Fred Clarke recovered for Dallas on our 17-yard line. Our defense did a great job, but they still got a 21-yard field goal to cut our lead to four points.

The Cowboys had a fine team and they certainly had something to do with what was going on out on that field. On the first play of the fourth quarter they stung us with one of our favorite maneuvers. With the ball on the 50, Dan Reeves took a handoff and bellied deep to his left as if he were running a sweep. As our cornerback Bob Jeter came up fast to stop the play, Reeves straightened up and arched a soft, high bomb to Bob Hayes. Hayes was in the clear and with his speed no one was going to catch him. Dallas had the lead.

For a long while it looked as though they also had the ball game. But it never looked that way to us. That's what made us the Green Bay Packers.

Four minutes and 15 seconds were left on the clock when Willie Wood ran back Danny Villanueva's punt nine yards to our 32-yard line. We opened with a pass to Dowler, then we came back with a little screen to Donny Anderson. He picked up six and then Chuck Mercein went off tackle for seven. These pecking tactics brought us to a first down on the Dallas 41-yard line, but Townes again broke through and tackled me for a 10-yard loss.

With second and 20 from our 49-yard line, the Cowboys dropped into a deep prevent defense. But we didn't try to make it all back with one play. We threw a swing out to Anderson that got us twelve yards. We threw to Anderson again, this time for nine yards and first down at the Cowboys' 30.

Now there was only a minute and 35 seconds to go. In the huddle, Mercein told me that if we ran the same formation and went to him he would be wide open because the deep backs and linebackers were dropping all the way back to guard against a touchdown pass. We did.

I looked deep to Dowler to look the defense off Mercein and then threw the ball out to him. Mercein moved downfield 19 yards to a first down at the 11, going out of bounds to stop the clock.

On first down we ran an influence play toward Bob Lilly, the Cowboys' great tackle. We knew Lilly got off the ball so quickly that we might be able to fool him with something like this at this stage of the game.

The Cowboys were a hungry and desperate team, but we put them in the game with our own mistakes. The first one was mine.

Our left guard, Gale Gillingham, pulled to his left as if we were running our bread-and-butter sweep. Lilly reacted on Gillingham's move. Mercein stepped to his left to influence the linebackers and then stepped back to take the ball and drive through the hole that Lilly vacated. He gained eight yards and we were down to the three.

There were 54 seconds left when we used our first time-out.

With three yards to go and three plays to make it we decided to go with our established play. That was a 31-wedge, Anderson driving between right guard and tackle; with a two-on-one block on the defensive tackle, Jethro Pugh, by our center, Ken Bowman, and our right guard, Jerry Kramer.

Anderson got two yards and a first down, but the play used up 14 seconds. We ran the same play again but the footing on the field was getting worse by the second. Donny was lucky to get back to the line of scrimmage.

We used our last time-out. With only 16 seconds left, I went over to talk to coach Vince Lombardi. A field goal would tie the game and force sudden-death overtime. But we never even discussed it.

Lombardi asked me about the footing and I told him that we were on the worst part of the field. He asked me if the linemen and backs could get any traction and I told him that I thought I would keep the ball, use the same blocking as on our lead play, 31-wedge, but instead of handing off I'd keep the ball.

In the huddle I told everyone what we wanted: 31-wedge, blocking on a sneak. At the snap, Bowman and Kramer got off real well and Forrest Gregg kept Townes from closing down and we were in the end zone.

We had our third consecutive championship. It literally came down to the very last chance in the game, but we did it. I think that no matter what, we just weren't going to lose.

—As told to Barry Janoff

In the 1967 NFL Championship Game, above, Green Bay Packers quarterback **Bart Starr** (15) passes against the Dallas Cowboys. Starr led Green Bay to five NFL titles, earned MVP honors and victories in the first two Super Bowls and went to four Pro Bowls. Although his team primarily relied upon the run for most of his 16-season (1956–71) career with the Packers, Starr entered the Pro Football Hall of Fame in 1977 with 1,808 completions for 24,718 yards and 152 touchdowns.

Several games come to mind in a hurry. But it's the 1972 Super Bowl game against Miami that I remember most.

JANUARY 16, 1972
DALLAS COWBOYS 24, MIAMI DOLPHINS 3
TULANE STADIUM, NEW ORLEANS, LOUISIANA

SCORING

DAL	3	7	7	7	**24**
MIA	0	3	0	0	**3**

DAL	Clark, 9-yard field goal
DAL	Alworth, 7-yard pass from Staubach (Clark kick)
MIA	Yepremian, 31-yard field goal
DAL	Thomas, 3-yard run (Clark kick)
DAL	Ditka, 7-yard pass from Staubach (Clark kick)

TEAM STATISTICS

	DAL	MIA
First Downs	23	10
Rushies-Yards	48-252	20-80
Passing Yards	119	134
Passes	12-19-1	12-23-0
Punts-Average	5-37.0	5-40.0
Fumbles Lost	1	2
Penalties-Yards	15	0

INDIVIDUAL STATISTICS

Rushing
DAL   D. Thomas 19 rushes for 95 yards; Garrison 14-74; Hill 7-25; Staubach 5-18; Hayes 1-16; Reeves 1-7; Ditka 1-17
MIA   Csonka 9-40; Kiick 7-40; Griese 1-0

Passing
DAL   Staubach 12 completions, 19 attempts, 119 yards, 1 interception
MIA   Griese 12-23-134-0

Receptions
DAL   D. Thomas 3 receptions for 17 yards; Alworth 2-28; Ditka 2-28; Hayes 2-23; Garrison 2-11; Hill 1-12
MIA   Warfield 4-39; Kiick 3-21; Csonka 2-18; Fleming 1-27; Twilley 1-20; Mandich 1-9

ATTENDANCE: 81,023

That was such an important game, not only for me but for the team. The Cowboys were tagged then as a team that couldn't quite make it. Imagine what it would have been like since then if we hadn't won. It would have been a disaster.

I recall it was the most excited I'd ever been before a game. I remember the pregame film sessions with coach Landry in his motel room. We all were so well prepared for that game. It made us confident rather than worried about whether we would win.

The only negative issue was Duane Thomas. He didn't show up for one practice back in Dallas. He also wasn't talking to the media, but that didn't bother anybody else.

Naturally, I was pretty nervous for a game like that. Everyone is. What reflected my nervousness was that I ran a couple of times on pass plays. I didn't get anywhere with it, though. The Dolphins pretty well contained me running.

On one of our early drives we got down to their two-yard line. It was third down. The irony was that in the Super Bowl the year before, in almost exactly the same situation, we had the same play called.

Craig Morton was the quarterback and he looked to the tight end too long before throwing to the halfback on a quick screen. The pass was knocked down.

What happened against Miami was that I never looked at the tight end at all. I threw to Thomas, who was stopped for no gain, and we had to kick a field goal. And Mike Ditka, our tight end, was wide open!

We got back to the bench and Mike was shook up and mad. Everybody was saying you should have done this or that. Right there the frustration left me. I just said, "To heck with this," and settled down.

The next time we got a drive working I threw probably two of the best passes of my life. The first was to Lance Alworth on third-and-seven down the middle. He was a secondary receiver and caught the ball over his shoulder for 17 yards to keep us going.

The other was a seven-yard touchdown toss to Alworth on a sideline route. I never threw a pass any harder. If I hadn't, Curtis Johnson, their cornerback, would have got it with a clear field in front of him.

We had pretty well dominated the game but still led only 10-3 at the half. We were confident with the way our defense was playing, but still, a lot of funny things sometimes happen.

Two things happened in the third quarter to give us some breathing room. We took the second-half kickoff and marched 71 yards for a touchdown that made it 17-3. I audibled the play Thomas scored on, and he went in behind a block by our tackle Tony Liscio, from the six-yard line. That was a big drive.

Then linebacker Chuck Howley intercepted one of Miami quarterback Bob Griese's passes and ran it back 41 yards to the Miami nine. That also was one of the funniest plays I've ever seen—only later, after the game was won—because Chuck flat tripped on his own feet and fell down. If he could have stayed up, he would have trotted over for a touchdown.

On third down from the Miami seven, I threw a TD pass to Ditka. Bob Hayes was the primary receiver and I was supposed to look toward Mike to draw attention away from Hayes. But when I looked at Mike he was open again.

I remember what Ditka said afterwards. He'd dropped a pass earlier so this was a big one for him. Mike said if he'd dropped that touchdown, he'd have kept going around the corner for a beer.

So we won Super Bowl VI, 24-3. I remember a feeling of complete satisfaction, not only for myself but for guys like Bob Lilly, Cornell Green and Mel Renfro who'd been through more than I had. They were beyond themselves.

I had only been with the team through two major disappointments, the 1969 playoff loss to Cleveland and the Super Bowl defeat by Baltimore the previous year.

Those guys had another Cleveland playoff loss in 1968, and two Green Bay games—in 1966 and 1967, for NFL titles—on their

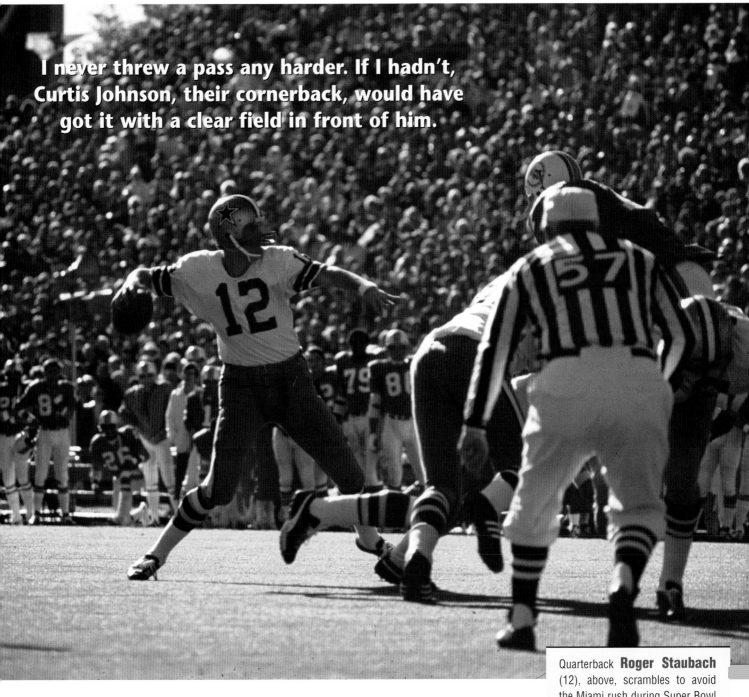

I never threw a pass any harder. If I hadn't, Curtis Johnson, their cornerback, would have got it with a clear field in front of him.

backs. The Cleveland game in '69 was the worst I'd ever seen coach Landry after a game, too. He was completely drained. So, to see that turned around was a pleasure.

I felt another emotion that's hard to express. Winning the Super Bowl is the epitome of professional sports for a team. Yet in my exhilaration, just when it seemed like I had everything, I noticed people who didn't have it so good.

I guess that's human nature, not any good-guy type thing. I hate to see or hear of people when bad things happen to them. I picked up the paper the next day and there was a story of a child getting run over by a car. I don't like all the negatives in the world.

It's a funny feeling. You have a lot personally, but you see all the tough things going on with other human beings. You wonder how they'd feel in your shoes.

—*As told to Frank Luksa*

Quarterback **Roger Staubach** (12), above, scrambles to avoid the Miami rush during Super Bowl VI. "Roger the Dodger" earned a ring and the MVP award that day, a highlight of the 1963 Heisman Trophy-winner's 11 campaigns (1969–79) with the Dallas Cowboys. He won a second ring in Super Bowl XII. Staubach, a six-time Pro Bowler who entered the league at age 27 after four years of military service, retired with 22,700 yards and 153 touchdowns passing, and 2,264 yards and 20 touchdowns rushing. He entered the Pro Football Hall of Fame in 1985.

It's hard for me to pick just one unforgettable game from my career, but I think one that really stands out in my

mind is the first game I played as a pro. Most people probably won't even remember this game. It was during the 1967 preseason when the Kansas City Chiefs played the Chicago Bears. I think we beat the Bears 66-24, but what was truly unforgettable was the electricity and intensity I felt that day.

The thing you have to remember is that this game took place prior to the merger between the AFL and the NFL. The season before, Kansas City was beaten in the first Super Bowl by Green Bay, so the game against Chicago was the first we were playing against an NFL team since that loss. The feeling between AFL and NFL teams was . . . it wasn't hatred, it was intense rivalry. The AFL players wanted to show that we were on par with the NFL players. Our guys had a lot of pride. And since many of them either were cut by NFL teams or were told that they weren't good enough to play in the NFL, they really wanted to show that they could play pro ball at least as well as the NFL players.

I was drafted by the Chiefs out of Montana State in 1966, but because I had a year of eligibility left to play college football, I didn't join them until 1967. The game against the Bears was my first as a pro and I was excited about everything that was happening. But as excited as I was, I couldn't match the emotions and intensity of the other players. I think it started the first day of training camp and kept building and building until the day of the game. For a couple of weeks before the game, it seemed, all everyone was talking about was playing the Bears and beating a team from the NFL.

In the locker room the day of the game everyone was getting really psyched up mentally, really building up the intense feelings that already existed. At that time we had a guy on the team nicknamed "The Hammer"—Fred Williamson, who later went into acting. I remember him before the Chicago game, walking around the locker room letting out these tremendous Tarzan

yells. The first time he let out a yell I jumped about two feet. But he was getting himself ready to play mentally, and he was getting everyone else into the spirit, as if the rest of the guys needed to get psyched up any more than they were. It was just an incredible scene, especially for a rookie such as me.

It helped a great deal that the game was being played in Kansas City. The fans there were great. The stadium was packed, and there was a tremendous amount of electricity in the air. People were on their feet, yelling and screaming, for three hours. I think they wanted to see their team beat a team from the NFL even more than we wanted it.

The Bears had some great players then: Gale Sayers, Dick Butkus . . . and Brian Piccolo was playing for them at the time. You're talking about athletes who play with a great deal of pride and emotion and who hate to lose, even in a preseason game like this one. But I have to tell you, I felt sorry for the poor Bears that day. There was no way their players could be as intense and emotional as we were. I'm sure they expected a tough battle, but there was no way they could have expected us to play with that degree of intensity.

We took control of the game right away and kept control of it till the end. Len Dawson, our quarterback, threw about four touchdown passes in the first half, Mike Garrett was having a good day running, and the team as a whole was playing superbly.

In the locker room at halftime, our coach, Hank Stram, told Dawson that he could sit out the second half. This was a preseason game, remember, when players are supposed to be getting in shape for the regular season. But when Stram told Dawson he could sit out the rest of the game, Dawson started pleading with the coach to let him stay in. He felt like the rest of us—he really wanted to go out there and beat the NFL players at their own game.

Things happened so fast that I really don't remember everything. I do remember my first field goal as a pro, though. Dawson had thrown a touchdown pass with just a few seconds to go in the first half. On the next kickoff, the Bears fumbled the ball and we recovered it in their territory. Since we had been scoring touchdowns all afternoon,

---

AUGUST 23, 1967
KANSAS CITY CHIEFS 66, CHICAGO BEARS 24
MUNICIPAL STADIUM, KANSAS CITY, MISSOURI

SCORING

KC	7	32	7	20	**66**
CHI	3	7	7	7	**24**

CHI	Alford, 35-yard field goal
KC	Taylor, 70-yard pass from Dawson (Stenerud kick)
KC	Burford, 11-yard pass from Dawson (Stenerud kick)
KC	Garrett, 1-yard run (McClinton pass from Dawson)
KC	G. Richardson, 11-yard pass from Dawson (Stenerud kick)
CHI	D. Gordon, 103-yard kickoff return (Alford kick)
KC	Taylor, 29-yard pass from Dawson (Stenerud kick)
KC	Stenerud, 22-yard field goal
KC	Thomas, 3-yard run (Stenerud kick)
CHI	Kurek, 32-yard run (Alford kick)
KC	G. Richardson, 80-yard pass from Beathard (Stenerud kick)
CHI	Piccolo, 1-yard run (Alford kick)
KC	Smith, 99-yard kickoff return (Stenerud kick)
KC	Beathard, 2-yard run (run failed)

TEAM STATISTICS	KC	CHI
First Downs	26	16
Rushes-Yards	36-182	32-122
Passing Yards	292	167
Passes	11-18-0	12-21-3
Punts-Average	5-39.8	6-42.0
Fumbles-Lost	0-0	4-1
Penalties-Yards	8-87	8-63

INDIVIDUAL STATISTICS

Rushing

KC	McClinton 8 rushes for 47 yards; Garrett 12-47; Taylor 1-32; G. Thomas 9-41; Coan 3-11; Stephens 1-2; Dawson 1-0; Beathard 1-2
CHI	Sayers 10-35; Kurek 7-49; Bukich 3-8; Piccolo 7-40; Bivins 2-0; Rakestraw 3-minus 10

Passing

KC	Dawson 10 completions, 15 attempts, 212 yards, 0 interceptions; Beathard 1-3-80-0
CHI	Bukich 5-8-40-1; Rakestraw 7-13-127-2

Receiving

KC	Taylor 4 receptions for 130 yards; Burford 2-27; McClinton 1-20; Richardson 2-91; Garrett 1-17; Arbanas 1-7
CHI	Morris 5-62; Allen 1-16; Gordon 2-31; Kurek 1-minus 7; Tones 2-53; Piccolo 1-6

ATTENDANCE: 33,041

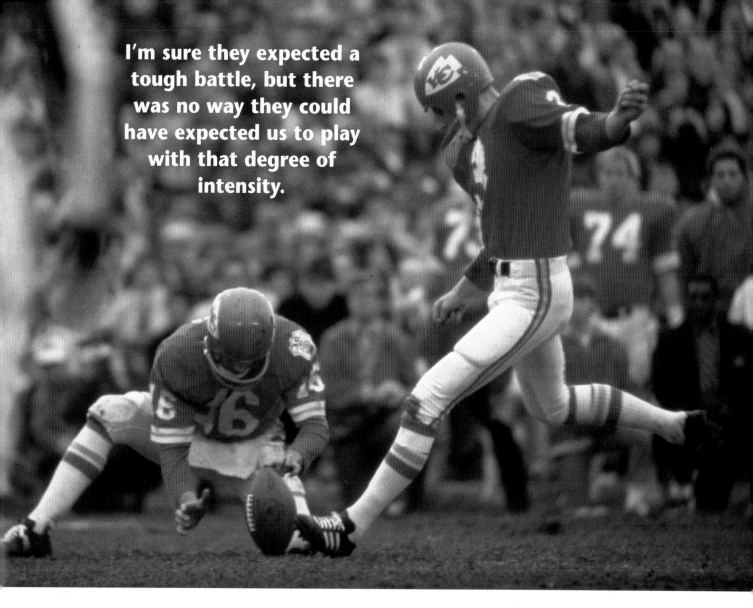

I'm sure they expected a tough battle, but there was no way they could have expected us to play with that degree of intensity.

there was no need for me to try a field goal. But in this situation, with just a second or two left, the coach sent me in to try one. I'll tell you, it was a great feeling watching the ball go through the uprights, and it's still a great feeling when I talk about it now.

Not everything went smoothly for us that day. On one play, Dick Gordon took a kickoff and ran something like 105 yards for a Chicago touchdown. But the negative plays were overshadowed that day. After I was successful on that field goal at the end of the half, for instance, we had to run across the field to the other side of the stadium to reach our locker room. As we ran across, the entire crowd rose to give us a standing ovation. They were yelling and cheering so loudly that it was hard to hear yourself think. Something like that you never forget.

We had a team mascot, a white horse named Old War Paint, take a victory lap around the stadium every time the Chiefs scored. A few weeks after the game I read an

interview with Dick Butkus, and he said that Kansas City had scored so often that day he thought the horse was going to die from having to take so many laps.

Aside from that being my first pro game, the reason it stands out for me is that it got my career off on a good foot. I was an inexperienced rookie, and that game was a confidence builder. I remember thinking after the game that if this is pro football, this is amazing. There was a special feeling—the emotions, the electricity, the bond that the players had for one another.

As a player, you try to capture that type of feeling every Sunday, for every game. You can't, of course. Even when we won Super Bowl IV a few seasons later, the feeling wasn't the same for me as it had been during that game against the Bears. As I said, that day was something special. Everything just came together for us.

—*As told to Barry Janoff*

Kansas City Chief **Jan Stenerud** (3), above, kicks a 48-yard field goal—a Super Bowl record at the time—to open Super Bowl IV scoring. He added two more field goals and two extra points, and the Chiefs defeated Minnesota 23–7. The first "pure" placekicker to enter the Pro Football Hall of Fame, Norwegian-born Stenerud went to Montana State on a ski scholarship and discovered football. After 13 seasons (1967–79) with Kansas City, he kicked for Green Bay (1980–83) and Minnesota (1984–85), tallying 1,699 career points on 580 converts and 373 field goals.

People say I had a smooth and graceful style on the football field, that I could make the hardest plays look easy. They say

JANUARY 18, 1976
PITTSBURGH STEELERS 21, DALLAS COWBOYS 17
ORANGE BOWL, MIAMI, FLORIDA

SCORING

PIT	7	0	0	14	**21**
DAL	7	3	0	7	**17**

DAL D. Pearson, 29-yard pass from Staubach (Fritsch kick)
PIT Grossman, 7-yard pass from Bradshaw (Gerela kick)
DAL Fritsch, 36-yard field goal
PIT Safety, Hoopes' punt blocked by Harrison
PIT Gerela, 36-yard field goal
PIT Gerela, 18-yard field goal
PIT Swann, 64-yard pass from Bradshaw (kick failed)
DAL P. Howard, 34-yard pass from Staubach (Fritsch kick)

TEAM STATISTICS

	DAL	PIT
First Downs	14	13
Rushes-Yards	31-108	46-149
Passing Yards	162	190
Passes	15-24-3	9-19-0
Punts-Average	7-35.0	4-39.8
Fumbles-Lost	4-0	4-0
Penalties-Yards	2-20	0-0

INDIVIDUAL STATISTICS

Rushing
DAL Newhouse 16 rushes for 56 yards; Staubach 5-22; Dennison 5-16; P. Pearson 5-14
PIT Harris 27-82; Bleier 15-51; Bradshaw 4-16

Passing
DAL Staubach 15 completions, 24 attempts, 204 yards, 3 interceptions
PIT Bradshaw 9-19-209-0

Receiving
DAL D. Pearson 2 receptions for 59 yards; P. Pearson 5-53; P. Howard 1-34; Young 3-31; Newhouse 2-12; Fugett 1-9; Dennison 1-6
PIT Swann 4-161; Harris 1-26; Stallworth 2-8; L. Brown 1-7; Grossman 1-7

ATTENDANCE: 80,187

I should have been wearing ballet shoes rather than a Pittsburgh Steelers jersey.

They always point to the catches I made in Super Bowl X in 1976 as some of the most acrobatic of my career. Well, football fans should know everything that was happening behind the scenes that day. Leading up to that match-up against the Dallas Cowboys, I wasn't even sure I would be able to play.

I had suffered a concussion two weeks earlier in the AFC Championship Game against the Oakland Raiders. In practices during the week before the Super Bowl, I was dropping passes left and right; my timing was off, and my concentration was awful. It didn't look as if the doctors were going to clear me to play, but shortly before the game I got the thumbs up.

I was excited because Dallas safety Cliff Harris had been talking trash during the week. He was a tough customer—a real vicious hitter—and he was saying that if I played, he would end my career with a big hit. Harris wasn't the only talented player in the secondary—the Cowboys also had Mel Renfro, Charlie Waters and Mark Washington.

The fact is, their team was filled with future Hall of Famers. The "Doomsday" defense had behemoths such as Ed "Too Tall" Jones and Harvey Martin, and the offense was under the command of Roger Staubach, who could hand the ball off to Preston Pearson or throw it to Golden Richards or Drew Pearson.

We had a strong field general of our own in Terry Bradshaw. Our offensive line was underrated, but Jon Kolb, Jim Clack, Ray Mansfield, Gordon Gravelle and Larry Brown opened holes for Franco Harris and gave Bradshaw time to get the ball to John Stallworth and me with his strong arm. The "Steel Curtain" defense was scary. With "Mean" Joe Greene, L.C. Greenwood, Jack Ham, Jack Lambert and Mel Blount, it was like having the Pro Bowl team on your side.

When we took the field at the Orange Bowl in Miami, I was questioning my own ability; I wasn't sure if I'd be able to perform, because of that brutal week of practice. What really helped me get into the game was a catch I made in the first quarter. Terry had called a play where I would go 10 or 15 yards and turn out, and when we lined up, the Cowboys covered me with Washington. I looked and saw the Cowboys were threatening to blitz; their linebackers were creeping up toward the line of scrimmage.

This wasn't the best play to run under those circumstances. I was almost expecting Terry to audible, but he stuck with the play. He threw the pass, and I just jumped over Washington, grabbed the ball, pulled it to my body and fell backward out of bounds for a 32-yard reception.

In the second quarter, I made a juggling, tumbling 53-yard catch while I was horizontal to the ground. I still don't know how I caught it; I don't know how I kept my concentration on the ball while I was going down.

After that, I started feeling my confidence return, and I was ready to have a big game. So were the rest of the Steelers. We fell behind 7-0 in the opening minutes, but tight end Randy Grossman caught a seven-yard pass from Terry to even the score. Dallas took a 10-7 lead in the second quarter and held it until the turning point in the game in the fourth quarter.

It was then that our defense stopped the Cowboys and forced them to punt from their own 16-yard line. Backup running back Reggie Harrison broke in from nowhere and blocked it, and the ball skipped through the back of the Cowboys end zone for a safety to make the score 10-9. We got the ball back, and Roy Gerela put us ahead for the first time with a 36-yard field goal. Soon after, he added an 18-yarder to give us a 15-10 edge.

Then I made one of the biggest catches of my career. It wasn't as fancy or difficult as some of my earlier ones that day but it meant a lot. I hauled in a 59-yard bomb from Terry and then trotted the final five yards into the end zone. Terry got absolutely hammered on the play, but he had the guts to stand in there and throw the ball. In fact, the hit sent him to the sidelines for the rest of the game. But his

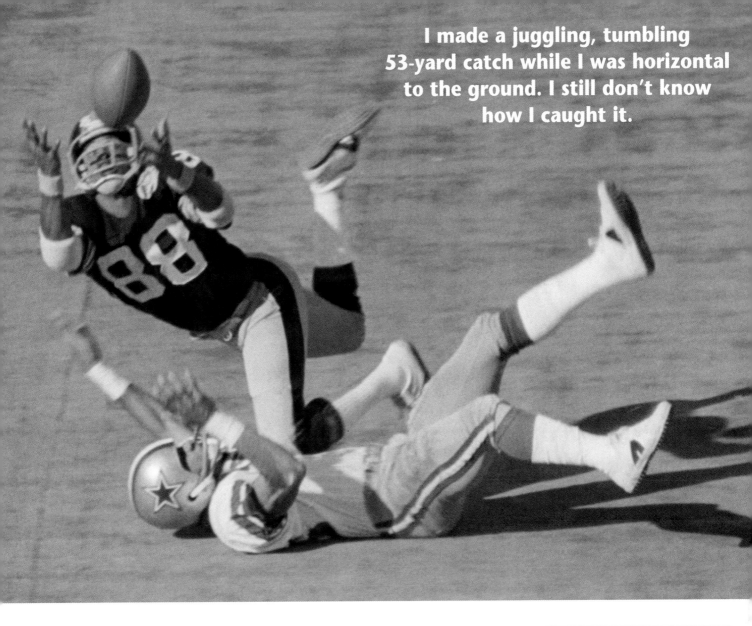

I made a juggling, tumbling 53-yard catch while I was horizontal to the ground. I still don't know how I caught it.

throw and my catch gave us some insurance, even though we missed the extra point.

As it turned out, we needed the breathing room. The Cowboys had this mystique of never quitting—they believed they could pull out a game no matter how dire the circumstances. With about two minutes remaining, Staubach—"Captain Comeback," as he was known—threw a 34-yard touchdown strike to Percy Howard, making the score 21-17.

Some scary moments followed. We stalled at the Cowboys 41 with about a minute and a half remaining, and coach Chuck Knoll faced a touch decision: Go for it or punt. A punt surely would go into the end zone, giving the Cowboys decent field position with a lot of time left. A first down, in contrast, would allow us to run out the clock.

Coach Knoll made a gutsy call, deciding to go for it. He conferred with Terry Hanratty who had replaced the woozy Bradshaw, and

drew up a running play. It netted a couple of yards, but fell short of the first-down marker. The Cowboys had the ball—and a flicker of hope. Staubach leaned under center with a minute and 22 seconds left on the clock and the belief that he could do the impossible. He completed a few passes, and for a moment it looked like this game would come down to the final seconds.

With the clock dwindling, Dallas was on our 38. I sat on the sideline and said, "Someone make a play. Please, someone do something." Glen Edwards did something: He intercepted Staubach's pass in the end zone, preserving the win and setting off a celebration.

After what I had been through, being named the Most Valuable Player of the game was special. I had caught four passes for a then-record 161 yards. Not bad for a guy who hadn't even thought he'd be able to play.

—*As told to Chuck O'Donnell*

Pittsburgh Steelers wide receiver **Lynn Swann** (88), above, makes a diving catch for 53 yards late in the second quarter of Super Bowl X. Swann was the MVP that day in 1976 and also helped Pittsburgh win Super Bowls IX, XIII and XIV. He retired after the 1982 season, having caught 315 career receptions for 4,991 yards and 51 touchdowns over nine campaigns (1974–82). Swann, one of football's greatest clutch performers, entered the Pro Football Hall of Fame in 2001.

There are a few games that I could single out when I think about my most memorable ones. Certainly I would have to

DECEMBER 11, 1989
SAN FRANCISCO 49ERS 30, LOS ANGELES RAMS 27
ANAHEIM STADIUM, ANAHEIM, CALIFORNIA

SCORING

SF	0	10	0	20	**30**
LA	17	0	7	3	**27**

LA	Bell, 3-yard run (Lansford kick)
LA	Johnson, 4-yard pass from Everett (Lansford kick)
LA	Lansford, 25-yard field goal
SF	Cofer, 19-yard field goal
SF	Taylor, 92-yard pass from Montana (Cofer kick)
LA	McGee, 13-yard pass from Everett (Lansford kick)
LA	Lansford, 22-yard field goal
SF	Wilson, 7-yard pass from Montana (Cofer kick)
SF	Taylor, 95-yard pass from Montana (kick failed)
SF	Craig, 1-yard run (Cofer kick)

TEAM STATISTICS

	SF	LA
First Downs	25	24
Rushes-Yards	25-63	31-106
Passing Yards	439	231
Passes	30-42-2	18-31-0
Punts-Average	4-34.8	4-40.3
Fumbles-Lost	2-0	2-2
Penalties-Yards	10-145	6-41

INDIVIDUAL STATISTICS

Rushing

SF   Craig 16 rushes for 48 yards; Montana 7-12; Rathman 2-3

LA   Bell 14-48; McGee 5-24; Delpino 8-23; Everett 2-9; Holohan 1-3; Anderson 1-minus 1

Passing

SF   Montana 30 completions, 42 attempts, 458 yards, 2 interceptions

LA   Everett 18-31-239-0

Receiving

SF   Taylor 11 receptions for 286 yards; Jones 7-85; Rice 5-38; Craig 4-31; Rathman 2-11; Wilson 1-7

LA   A. Cox 3-34; Holohan 3-31; McGee 3-25; Anderson 2-72; Ellard 2-38; Bell 2-11; Ro. Brown 1-27; Johnson 1-4; Delpino 1-minus 3

ATTENDANCE: 68,936

talk about the three Super Bowl wins that I have been part of with the 49ers. Super Bowl XXIII was unforgettable because my only catch that day was the game-winning touchdown against Cincinnati. And Super Bowl XXIV was great too, because I caught a touchdown pass in the blowout against Denver.

Probably the one game that stands out, though, was against the Los Angeles Rams during the 1989 season. We needed that game to clinch first place in the NFC West. The Rams were a tough squad, especially on their home turf, but I seemed to catch everything Joe Montana threw in my direction. I had 11 catches for 286 yards and two touchdowns, and we ended up beating the Rams 30-27 in a great come-from-behind win.

That's the type of game every receiver dreams of having. Playing on a team with super quarterbacks—especially stars such as Joe and Steve Young—is terrific for a receiver. These quarterbacks are guys who will get you the ball, and the coaches know that and design plays that way. But to say something about our receivers—me, Jerry Rice, Mike Sherrard, fullback Tom Rathman, running back Ricky Watters—we all busted our butts during a game, and it showed in the fact that the 49ers were among the best in the league.

In that game against the Rams—a Monday night game on national TV—there wasn't any thought on my part before the game that I would end up with 11 catches and almost 300 yards. It wasn't like our coach, George Seifert, came over and said, "We're going to call your number twice as much as usual in the huddle." But Jerry drew double- and triple-coverage, and we saw early on that I could run patterns that would free me up in the secondary.

Joe was really on target that game, so he made it a lot easier for me to pick up yards once I caught the ball. But it was a great team effort once we got it together after we fell behind 17-0 in the first quarter. I wasn't concerned at that point that they would

blow us out because it was much too early in the game and because our key guys had come back many times before. Still, it's no fun being down 17-0 on the road after the first quarter.

Toward the end of the first quarter we put a drive together that culminated in a second-quarter field goal. About 10 minutes into the second quarter, the Rams set up for a field-goal attempt but went for the first down instead and missed. They would have been up 20-3 if they had gone for and made the field goal. Instead, our offense got the ball. I remember our guys running out onto the field yelling, "Let's make something happen. Let's turn this around."

On second down, Joe hit me in the numbers with a short pass. I put a deke on the guy covering me and blew past the secondary. I knew I could beat their guys in the open field, and once I broke a couple of tackles I just turned it on and went 92 yards for a touchdown.

We were still down 17-10 when we got the ball back with about a minute to go in the half. We ended up moving from our 37 to the Rams' five. On a second-and-goal, Rams defensive end Kevin Greene sacked Joe back on the 17. Then a five-yard penalty for a false start pushed us back to the 22. With about 10 seconds to go, Joe hit Roger Craig with a touchdown pass, but the play was called back for offensive holding, which put us on the 32. That left about four seconds on the clock, so the coaches decided to go for a field goal. Mike Cofer hit a 49-yarder, but then that too was called back, for a false start. When he tried again from the 54 the ball hit the left upright.

The way the half ended was too unreal to cause a panic in our locker room. We felt more like we didn't have a great half and they had a good half. We went backwards from the five to the 37 in the last few seconds—we were lucky that time ran out on us or we could have been hugging our own goal line— but we still were down by only seven.

L.A.'s defense clamped down in the third quarter and into the fourth quarter, and they scored a touchdown and a field goal to take a 27-10 lead. We had to come back strong at that point, and we got seven back when Joe

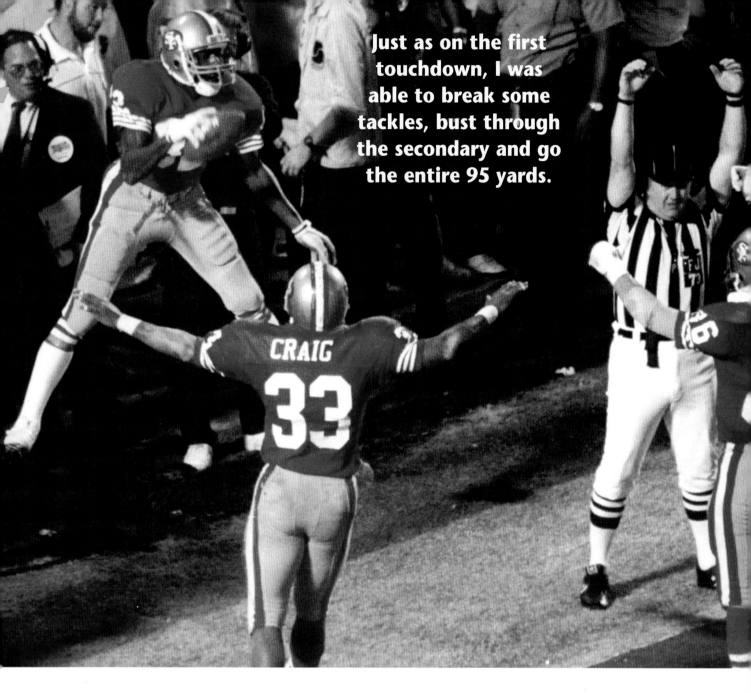

Just as on the first touchdown, I was able to break some tackles, bust through the secondary and go the entire 95 yards.

moved us downfield and then hit Mike Wilson with a touchdown pass.

We got a big break a few minutes after that. We were down 27-17 and the Rams had a first down on our five. But Jim Everett fumbled the snap, and Matt Millen recovered for us. On our first play, I slanted across the middle, caught a pass from Joe and headed for the right sideline. Just as on the first touchdown, I was able to break some tackles, bust through the secondary and go the entire 95 yards.

We missed the extra point, but we were only down 27-23. Then Ron Brown fumbled the kickoff and Keith Henderson recovered for us at the Rams 27. Five or six plays later Craig busted in from the one to give us the lead, which our defense held.

That was an incredible game, not just because we had to mount two big comebacks, but because we never felt as if we were out of the game. It always felt as if we could turn the thing around if one of our defensive guys made a big play or we put together a solid drive on offense.

That win put us at 12-2 and in the right frame of mind to close out the season and head into the playoffs. We ended up meeting the Rams in the championship game, but it wasn't even close this time as we won 30-3. That postseason drive was incredible for us. We outscored Minnesota, L.A. and Denver 126-26 and won Super Bowl XXIV. We were so overpowering as a team, that whole season was unforgettable.

—*As told to Barry Janoff*

With only 34 seconds remaining in the game, wide receiver **John Taylor** (82), above, celebrates his game-winning touchdown in San Francisco's 20-16 Super Bowl XXIII victory over Cincinnati. Taylor also won rings in Super Bowls XXIV and XXIX, highlights of his eight-season (1987–95) pro career with the 49ers. Although he played in the shadow of teammate and fellow wide receiver Jerry Rice, Taylor went to the 1988 and 1989 Pro Bowls. He set personal bests in the latter campaign with 1,077 receiving yards and 10 touchdowns.

Behind us was a win over the Dallas Cowboys in the 1982 NFC Championship Game, the most intense football game in

JANUARY 30, 1983
WASHINGTON REDSKINS 27, MIAMI DOLPHINS 17
ROSE BOWL, PASADENA, CALIFORNIA

SCORING

WAS	0	10	3	14	**27**
MIA	7	10	0	0	**17**

MIA	Cefalo, 76-yard pass from Woodley (von Schamann kick)
WAS	Moseley, 31-yard field goal
MIA	von Schamann, 20-yard field goal
WAS	Garrett, 4-yard pass from Theismann (Moseley kick)
MIA	Walker, 98-yard kickoff return (von Schamann kick)
WAS	Moseley, 20-yard field goal
WAS	Riggins, 43-yard run (Moseley kick)
WAS	Brown, 6-yard pass from Theismann (Moseley kick)

TEAM STATISTICS

	MIA	WAS
First Downs	9	24
Rushes-Yards	29-96	52-276
Passing Yards	80	124
Passes	4-17-1	15-23-2
Punts-Average	6-37.8	3-45.7
Fumbles-Lost	2-0	0-1
Penalties-Yards	4-55	5-36

INDIVIDUAL STATISTICS

Rushing
MIA   Franklin 16 rushes for 49 yards; Woodley 4-16; Nathan 7-26; Harris 1-1; Vigorito 1-4
WAS   Riggins 38-166; Harmon 9-40; Walker 1-6; Theismann 3-20; Garrett 1-44

Passing
MIA   Woodley 4 completions, 14 attempts, 97 yards, 1 interception; Strock 0-3-0-0
WAS   Theismann 15-23-143-2

Receiving
MIA   Cefalo 2 receptions for 82 yards; Harris 2-15
WAS   Brown 6-60; Warren 5-28; Walker 1-27; Riggins 1-15; Garrett 2-13

ATTENDANCE: 103,667

my years with the Washington Redskins. Ahead of us was a date with the Miami Dolphins in Super Bowl XVII, the *biggest* game of my career.

We were getting ready for a week of preparation . . . and some fun. I always describe the players on those Redskins teams of the early 1980s as characters with character.

Our linebackers called themselves "the Green Berets." As we arrived in Pasadena for the Super Bowl, they got off the plane dressed in army fatigues. My three wide receivers—Alvin Garrett, Virgil Seay and Charlie Brown—were called "the Smurfs," taken from the cartoon of the same name. During the middle of the week before the Super Bowl, those three guys got their pictures taken with the Smurfs. On Friday night, owner Jack Kent Cooke had a big party, and John Riggins, our bruising running back, showed up in a white tuxedo, tails and a top hat. Our offensive linemen, known as "the Hogs," were an entity to themselves; they were selling posters and popping up here and there.

It was a funny scene. We were getting ready to play in the Super Bowl, yet this was all going on. But when you threw these guys together, you had a great team.

In the NFC Championship Game, I was pumped up because we were playing Dallas. My first touchdown in the NFL came against the Cowboys; my first Monday night appearance was against them. So to play them in the NFC Championship Game was really special.

It was the first time I had a chance to be in that kind of situation, and everyone I talked to told me how the intensity of the play would be magnified in this game. Until you've been through it, it's hard to believe the game can actually get faster and players can get quicker and decisions have to get made even quicker. But that's exactly the way it was. It turned out to be just an incredible performance by a bunch of guys, and we won 31-17.

I remember some moments from that game vividly, such as Dexter Manley—a big, tough defensive end—flattening Danny White and knocking him out of the game. I remember scrambling to the sideline and throwing it back into the middle of the field for a reception and getting knocked into the cheap seats. I remember Darryl Grant returning an interception in the fourth quarter to put the game away.

But the thing that stands out the most in my mind about this particular game came late. There were 11 seconds to go, I was standing on the sideline and our fans were banging their feet so hard the ground was shaking beneath my feet. I got goose bumps. Someone came up to me and said, "Hey, we're going to the Super Bowl." I turned around and said to him, "No, don't say anything yet."

There were 11 seconds left and Dallas had to score two touchdowns, but to me it was such an incredible moment in my life that I couldn't fathom it going away. To hear the feet pounding and the screaming and the fans yelling, "We want Dallas! We want Dallas!" from the time we stepped on the field till the time the game was over three hours later made it the most intense football game I ever played in my life.

The next stop was the Super Bowl. The night before the game, I called Burt Reynolds, one of my best friends, and we talked for about an hour and a half. Then I decided it was time go to bed, but I only slept for about four hours. I woke up with my mind racing over a lot of things that were about to take place.

I arrived at the stadium early and walked the field to see what it was really like. You don't realize how big the Rose Bowl is until you're inside of it while it's empty.

When the game started, I guess I was so emotionally wrapped up in this thing that I don't remember the first five minutes. About two weeks after the game, I took my dad and sat down and watched it on film. As I was watching the tape, I couldn't remember the names of plays—nothing—until we ran a reverse and I got kicked in the head trying to throw a block. All of a sudden, the game came back to me. The first five minutes,

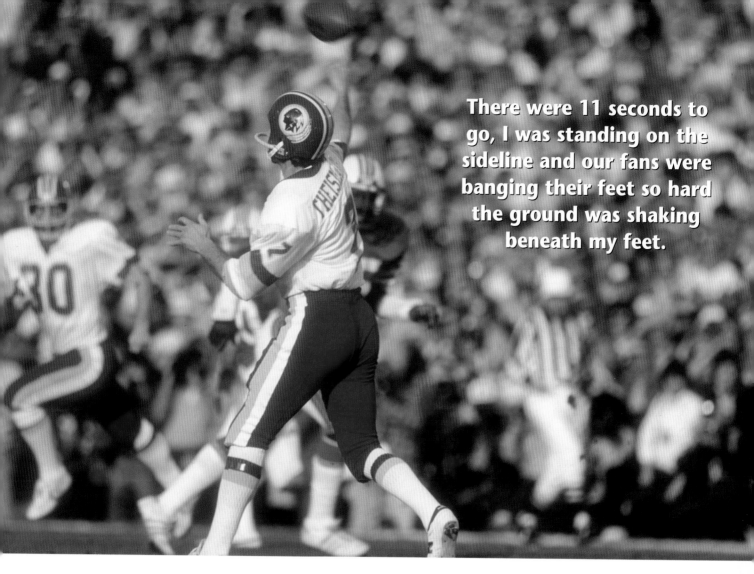

There were 11 seconds to go, I was standing on the sideline and our fans were banging their feet so hard the ground was shaking beneath my feet.

though, are lost somewhere in my memory.

In the third quarter, I had just finished throwing my second interception when a public service announcement I had done with the Cowboys' Drew Pearson, a high-school teammate of mine, was shown. It started with me saying, "Hi, I'm Joe Theismann." I thought, "Oh, what horrible timing."

There are a lot of moments that come back to me. I knocked the ball away from Dolphins lineman Kim Bokamper in what would have been an interception; I hit Charlie Brown for a touchdown. I'm not sure who the official was, but Charlie went up and got knocked out of bounds before his feet came down. We were waiting for the official to signal, but he turned toward the press box. He didn't signal touchdown while looking at the play—instead, he turned toward the press box and made the signal.

Then there was the memorable fourth-quarter, fourth-down touchdown by Riggins. Our whole game plan was to wear down the Dolphins. They didn't have a big front seven, and we had a huge line, so I figured we would get the first down. I had the best seat in the house. After I handed the ball to John, I saw Don McNeal go up and try to tackle him, and then I saw John strip away from him. After that, I saw Clint Didier, one of our tight ends, running down the sideline with John. I kept thinking, "Clint, don't clip anybody. Please, don't clip anybody." When John went into the end zone, it was just an incredible feeling.

At the end of the game, when we were up 27-17 and killing the clock, the last play I called was, "Winning Super Bowl formation on two." I barely got the words out of my mouth because I began to tear up. It was truly a dream come true for a kid from New Jersey who only wanted to play football and now had reached the top of the mountain.

I'm always reminded of that song by Whitney Houston, "One Moment in Time," when I think about the Super Bowl. Moments like that don't last, but very few people in life are able to experience that kind of a high.

—As told to Chuck O'Donnell

Washington quarterback **Joe Theismann**, above, heaves a pass during the Redskin's Super Bowl XVII victory over Miami. The 1970 Heisman Trophy runner-up with Notre Dame, Theismann played three seasons (1971–73) for the CFL's Toronto Argonauts before joining the Redskins. In addition to two Super Bowl games, he was the 1983 league MVP and 1984 Pro Bowl MVP. Playing in his 163rd consecutive game, Theismann suffered a career-ending broken leg in 1985. He retired with 25,206 yards and 160 touchdowns passing, and 1,815 yards and 17 touchdowns rushing.

When I look back on the unforgettable games of my career, I think about three games during the 1985 playoffs. New

JANUARY 12, 1986
NEW ENGLAND PATRIOTS 31, MIAMI DOLPHINS 14
ORANGE BOWL, MIAMI, FLORIDA

SCORING

NE	3	14	7	7	**31**
MIA	0	7	0	7	**14**

NE   Franklin, 23-yard field goal
MIA   Johnson, 10-yard pass from Marino (Reveiz kick)
NE   Collins, 4-yard pass from Eason (Franklin kick)
NE   D. Ramsey, 1-yard pass from Eason (Franklin kick)
NE   Weathers, 2-yard pass from Eason (Franklin kick)
MIA   Nathan, 10-yard pass from Marino (Reveiz kick)
NE   Tatupu, 1-yard run (Franklin kick)

TEAM STATISTICS

	NE	MIA
First Downs	21	18
Rushes-Yards	59-255	13-68
Passing Yards	71	234
Passes	10-12-0	20-48-2
Punts-Average	5-40.0	4-41.0
Fumbles-Lost	2-2	5-4
Penalties-Yards	2-15	4-35

INDIVIDUAL STATISTICS
Rushing
NE   C. James 22 rushes for 105 yards; Weathers 16-87; Collins 12-61; Tatupu 6-9; Eason 3-minus 7
MIA   Carter 6-56; Davenport 3-6; Nathan 2-4; Bennett 1-2; Marino 1-0
Passing
NE   Eason 10 completions, 12 attempts, 71 yards, 0 interceptions
MIA   Marino 20-48-248-2
Receiving
NE   Morgan 2 receptions for 30 yards; D. Ramsey 3-18; Collins 3-15; Tatupu 1-6; Weathers 1-2
MIA   Nathan 5-57; Hardy 3-52; Duper 3-45; Clayton 3-41; Davenport 3-23; Johnson 1-10; Moore 1-10; Rose 1-10

ATTENDANCE: 75,662

England had to win three games on the road to reach the Super Bowl, and we ended up gutting it out and winning them all against tough teams. We lost the big game—Super Bowl XX against Chicago—but in the playoffs we showed our true character as a team.

Because we were playing on the road, a lot of people didn't give the Patriots much of a chance to reach the Super Bowl. But we went to New York and beat the Jets, then to Los Angeles and beat the Raiders, then to Miami and beat the Dolphins.

Each game was important because a loss would mean elimination from the playoffs, but the Miami game stands out the most because the AFC championship was on the line. The Dolphins and the Raiders were favored that season to meet in the AFC Championship Game, so when we beat the Dolphins—after having beaten the Raiders the week before—we all felt a great sense of accomplishment.

We had a strong team that season, and our coach, Raymond Berry, had us thinking about winning a title right from the first day of training camp. But the AFC East had a number of tough teams, so we knew that we'd have to play well all season just to make the playoffs. As it turned out, we finished with an 11-5 record, one game behind the Dolphins and tied with the Jets in the East. The Jets got to host the wild-card game, so we had to win three road games to get to the Super Bowl. People had us written off even before we stepped onto the field.

Much of our success had to do with our position that it was us against them. We had problems in the front office and problems on the field all year, and that made it hard to concentrate at times. But those problems helped to bring the team together, because we developed the attitude that if we didn't take care of ourselves, no one else would do it for us. Then, once we hit the playoffs and the critics came out from everywhere putting down the team, we were more determined than ever to prove what we could do on the field.

The first playoff game against the Jets set the tone for us. We scored in every quarter, held a good offensive team to 14 points and won the game 26-14. The game against the Raiders was tough because we were behind at halftime against one of the top offensive teams in the NFL. But we shut them out in the second half and won the game 27-20, after our defense recovered a fumble in the end zone.

We played the Dolphins twice during the season and were well aware of their strengths and weaknesses. They were undefeated at home that year and we had only been 4-4 on the road, but none of that mattered in the playoffs, especially after the confidence we gained in beating the Jets and Raiders on the road.

As a linebacker, my job was to stop Miami quarterback Dan Marino and to disrupt their offensive game plan. For the most part, we stayed with five linebackers and switched off to double-team Mark Duper and Mark Clayton. We also had someone shadowing Marino all the time so that no matter where he went someone was in his face.

Miami's strength was the passing game, and its running game was weak by comparison. So, if we could establish a lead and then cut off Marino's passing lanes, we had a good chance to win. For the most part, that's how the game went. We held them to 68 yards rushing and kept Marino to 248 yards passing, which was amazing considering that he usually broke 300 yards without even working up a sweat.

Our defense played a great game but our offense came through with some key plays, especially running back Craig James and quarterback Tony Eason. James rushed for over 100 yards and Eason had three touchdown passes. Eason had missed about half the season and Steve Grogan stepped in for him and did a great job, but then Tony came back for the playoffs.

We took the lead in the first quarter on a field goal, but Miami put together a good drive toward the end of the quarter and then scored at the beginning of the second quarter. They had about 75,000 fans who figured the game was over right there and

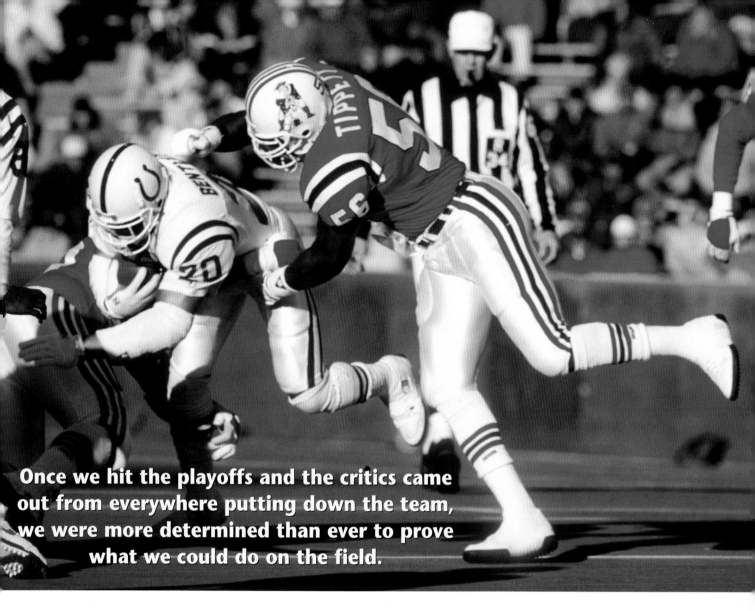

Once we hit the playoffs and the critics came out from everywhere putting down the team, we were more determined than ever to prove what we could do on the field.

then, but I knew that our game plan was better than theirs. Eason threw two touchdown passes in the quarter, and our defense kept them off the board and didn't let Marino establish any rhythm to his offense. We had his receivers covered for the most part, and our defensive linemen played right in Marino's face. He was sacked only once, but we covered his receivers both long and short, which upset his timing. He threw 48 passes and completed only 20. Some quarterbacks consider that a good day's work, but in Miami's offensive game plan, which depended so much on the passing game, that was not a successful day.

We were up 17-7 at the half, but we knew Marino could hit his receivers quickly and blow us out. We knew we could beat them, but we knew we had to concentrate on doing more of the things we'd established in the first half to win. We were confident that our offense would score some more points, but on the defensive side the key was to prevent

Marino from getting his passing game in gear. At that point, leading by 10, if our defense could hold them in the second half, we'd be headed for the Super Bowl.

As it turned out, they scored a touchdown early in the fourth quarter, but that was their only major drive in the half. Our offense scored a touchdown in each quarter, but I'd have to say that our defensive effort in the second half was even more important. Marino was getting frustrated that we had his receivers so well covered, and that caused him to get out of his game plan and to force his passes too much.

It was a great feeling when the game ended, partly because we were headed for the Super Bowl, but mostly because I knew that it was a total team effort that got us there. It was as if the rest of the league had said to us, "Show us what you're made of"—and that's exactly what we did.

—As told to Barry Janoff

New England Patriots linebacker **Andre Tippett** (56), above, brings down Indianapolis Colts running back Albert Bentley. Tippett, a six-foot-three, 241-pound second-round draft pick out of Iowa, joined the Patriots in 1982. In 1984, he notched a personal-best 18.5 quarterback sacks and went to his first of five straight Pro Bowls. After losing the entire 1989 campaign to injury, Tippett returned for four more seasons. He retired in 1993 with 100 career sacks.

My most memorable game wasn't what I would call the most gratifying of my career, but it was my finest individual

OCTOBER 28, 1962
NEW YORK GIANTS 49, WASHINGTON REDSKINS 34
YANKEE STADIUM, BRONX, NEW YORK

SCORING

NYG	7	14	21	7	**49**
WAS	7	6	7	14	**34**

WAS	Mitchell, 44-yard pass from Snead (B. Khayat kick)
NYG	Morrison, 22-yard pass from Tittle (Chandler kick)
NYG	Walton, 5-yard pass from Tittle (Chandler kick)
WAS	Dugan, 24-yard pass from Snead (kick failed)
NYG	Morrison, 1-yard pass from Tittle (B. Khayat kick)
WAS	Mitchell, 60-yard pass from Snead (B. Khayat kick)
NYG	Shofner, 32-yard pass from Tittle (Chandler kick)
NYG	Walton, 26-yard pass from Tittle (Chandler kick)
NYG	Gifford, 63-yard pass from Tittle (Chandler kick)
NYG	Walton, 6-yard pass from Tittle (Chandler kick)
WAS	Snead, 1-yard run (B. Khayat kick)
WAS	Junker, 35-yard pass from Snead (B. Khayat kick)

TEAM STATISTICS	NYG	WAS
First Downs	25	19
Rushes-Yards	28-97	19-58
Passing Yards	505	346
Passes	27-39-0	17-40-3
Punts-Average	4-47.0	6-31.0
Fumbles-Lost	3-0	1-1
Penalties-Yards	7-127	3-35

INDIVIDUAL STATISTICS

Rushing

NYG	Webster 16 rushes for 54 yards; King 8-24; Dudley 3-18; Tittle 1-1
WAS	Barnes 12-39; Boessler 3-19; Cunningham 2-9; Snead 1-1, Dugan 1-minus 9

Passing

NYG	Tittle 27 completions, 39 attempts, 505 yards, 0 interceptions
WAS	Snead 17-40-346-3

Receiving

NYG	Shofner 11 receptions for 269 yards; Walton 6-63; Gifford 4-127; Morrison 2-24; Webster 2-11; King 1-7; Dudley 1-4
WAS	Mitchell 5-158; Barnes 3-45; Dugan 3-36; Boessler 3-32; Jouker 1-35; Cunningham 1-23; Anderson 1-17

ATTENDANCE: 62,844

game. I threw for seven touchdowns and 505 yards in 1962 during a win over the Washington Redskins at Yankee Stadium. The seven TDs still have me tied with a number of others in the NFL record book, and the 505 yards was then the second most passing in a pro game.

The interesting thing about that game is I nearly didn't play at all and, even though I did start, I was about one or two incomplete passes away from being taken out.

It all started the week before when we played the Detroit Lions. We were at home in what I'm sure some of the old-time Giants fans will remember as one of the most bruising, physically tough games ever played by the Giants. It was one of those eyeball-to-eyeball, man-to-man battles and we came out of it with a very satisfying 17-14 win. During the game I took a shot to my right arm and hurt my bicep. Blood drained from my bicep to my elbow and, when Monday rolled around, I couldn't even lift my arm. I took treatment all week but couldn't throw. I tried the day before the Washington game, but I could hardly get the ball in the air. It was decided at that time I would try it again just before the game to see if I could perform.

I wanted to play very badly because some friends of mine had come all the way to New York from San Francisco to watch me and I didn't want to disappoint them. Allie Sherman was our coach and he knew how much starting meant to me.

After I warmed up before the game, I told Allie I could play. I could throw pretty well, at least on short patterns. I also wanted to play because, as you probably know, in those days players were always holding on, not holding out like many of them do today. If I hadn't been able to play, the rookie from Notre Dame, Ralph Guglielmi, would have been in there.

I missed on my first eight or nine passes of the game and I knew Allie was close to taking me out. Norm Snead, who passed for four touchdowns that day, had already moved the Redskins ahead and it was a game we couldn't afford to lose. Then, all of a sudden, it was as if the Red Sea had opened up. I hit on my next 12 passes, a Giants' record for consecutive completions. I couldn't miss. And they weren't short passes, either. My receivers, Joe Walton and Del Shofner in particular, were getting wide open. It was like shooting fish in a barrel. Walton caught three of my scoring passes.

I had a chance to get an eighth touchdown pass for the all-time record, but I didn't go for it. A lot of people thought I passed up the opportunity because I was modest. But that wasn't the reason at all. We were in the fourth quarter and weren't that far ahead at the time. I didn't want to chance them picking off one of my passes and running it back for six. I preferred to keep the ball on the ground to kill the clock rather than jeopardize our lead for an individual record. We ended up winning 49-34.

Another reason that was a memorable day for me was because of what happened after the game. First, I appeared on *The Ed Sullivan Show*, which was a tremendous thrill. Later that evening I went to Toots Shore's for dinner and Jackie Gleason invited me over to his table for a cup of coffee. While we were talking, three kids came up and asked me for my autograph and asked who the guy was sitting next to me. Gleason replied, "I'm a big, fat tackle, what does it look like?'

In the last game of that season I threw six touchdown passes against Dallas, three of them to Walton.

My most memorable moment in Baltimore, I suppose, would be the day I played my first pro game and threw four touchdown passes against the Yankees.

My most memorable play was against the Detroit Lions during a 1957 league game when I was with San Francisco. We were behind 31-27 with something like 18 seconds left and pretty well backed up in our territory. My high, towering alley-oop passes to R.C. Owens were already prominent by then and that's what Jack Christensen and the rest of the Lions' secondary was looking for at the time. While they were

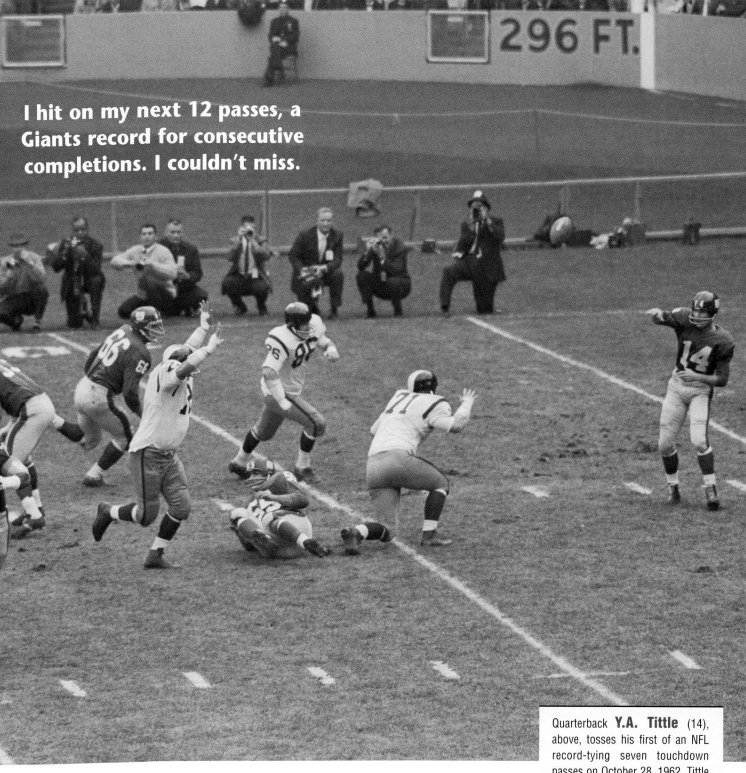

296 FT.

I hit on my next 12 passes, a Giants record for consecutive completions. I couldn't miss.

Quarterback **Y.A. Tittle** (14), above, tosses his first of an NFL record-tying seven touchdown passes on October 28, 1962. Tittle spent two pro seasons with the Baltimore Colts in the All-America Football Conference before the club joined the NFL in 1950. He played 10 seasons for the San Francisco 49ers (1951–60) and guided the New York Giants to the NFL title game in each of his last four seasons (1961–64). Tittle, a two-time league MVP, was inducted into the Pro Football Hall of Fame in 1971.

concentrating on R.C., I completed two straight passes to Billy Wilson and Hugh McElhenny to get out around midfield, where I had to get the ball so I could reach the end zone with a pass. There was time for one more play.

Everyone in Kezar Stadium was standing—the place was sold out with more than 59,000 on hand—and the Lions had three guys covering R.C. I dropped back and let it fly; the gun went off while the ball was in the air. R.C. went high over the Lions'

defenders in the end zone and came down with the ball. The place went absolutely crazy. It was one of the most unbelievable and exciting moments of my career.

There were a lot of thrilling games and plays for me. I enjoyed every moment of my football career. There is nothing I would rather have done. I'll always treasure those years.

—*As told to Dave Payne*

The older I get, the madder I get that I didn't receive the proper credit and accolades from Super Bowl III. But I

JANUARY 12, 1969
NEW YORK JETS 16, BALTIMORE COLTS 7
ORANGE BOWL, MIAMI, FLORIDA

SCORING

NYJ	0	7	6	3	**16**
BAL	0	0	0	7	**7**

NYJ Snell, 4-yard run (Turner kick)
NYJ Turner, 32-yard field goal
NYJ Turner, 30-yard field goal
NYJ Turner, 9-yard field goal
BAL Hill, 1-yard run (Michaels kick)

TEAM STATISTICS

	NYJ	BAL
First Downs	21	18
Rushes-Yards	43-142	23-143
Passing Yards	195	181
Passes	17-29-0	17-41-4
Punts-Average	4-38.8	3-44.3
Fumbles-Lost	1-1	1-1
Penalties-Yards	5-28	3-23

INDIVIDUAL STATISTICS

Rushing
NYJ Snell 3 rushes for 121 yards; Boozer 10-19; Mathis 3-2
BAL Matte 11-116; Hill 9-29; Unitas 1-0; Morrall 2-minus 2

Passing
NYJ Namath 17 completions, 29 attempts, 206 yards, 0 interceptions; Parilli 0-1-0-0
BAL Morrall 6-17-71-3; Unitas 11-24-110-1

Receiving
NYJ Sauer 8 catches for 133 yards; Snell 4-40; Mathis 3-20; Lammons 2-13
BAL Richardson 6-58; Orr 3-42; Mackey 3-35; Matte 2-30; Hill 2-1; Mitchell 1-15

ATTENDANCE: 75,389

also have to remind myself that I was on a team with such a super sports personality as Joe Namath. It was Joe who predicted all week we would beat the Baltimore Colts, which really drew the attention of the press, so naturally it was Joe who drew all the attention after we won.

Joe was a fantastic football player. There has never been anyone I'd rather have on my side on a football field than Joe Namath. He was a leader. He believed in us players, and we believed in him.

But it still burns me up that more credit didn't go to some of the other people on our team for that win. I kicked three important field goals, Matt Snell rushed for more than 100 yards, George Sauer caught eight passes for more than 100 yards, our offensive line did one hell of a job against one of the best front fours in football and our defense was outstanding against a pretty fair offense.

The press said Joe won the game; that's not true. We all won it. Even Joe will tell you that today. But with each year that passes since that game was played, the more people seem to remember that Joe Namath was the only player on the field for the Jets that afternoon.

Still, we won it over that arrogant NFL bunch from Baltimore. I'll never forget the oddsmakers making us an 18-point underdog. And there were writers in Miami that week who picked the Colts to win by as many as 60 points.

Baltimore had a great, great team and we had all the respect in the world for them. Heck, they had just buried Cleveland 34-0 for the NFL Championship. The New York Jets also were a great, great team, but the Colts didn't respect us. We were the American Football League's number-one team on offense. And we had made it to the Super Bowl by upsetting an outstanding Oakland Raider team 27-23.

People didn't believe in us because they didn't believe in the AFL. The Green Bay Packers had won by big scores over Kansas City [35-10] and Oakland [33-14] in the two previous Super Bowls, so everyone figured Baltimore would continue that domination.

I still recall the disdain the Colts showed for us in pregame warm-ups in the Orange Bowl. They weren't wearing pads or helmets. And, except for some Jets fans who were in the stands, I had that feeling everyone was against us. Why waste time pulling for a team that is going to be obliterated, right?

But we weren't intimidated. We knew what we could do and we knew we could do it against Baltimore. And we realized the importance of this game to the AFL. If our league had been blown out for a third consecutive year by the established NFL, it might have been over for the Super Bowl and maybe TV for the AFL, which would have killed the league. Curt Gowdy calls Super Bowl III the single most important professional football game every played because of what it led to [the NFL-AFL merger], and I agree with him all the way.

The Colts kicked off to us and we moved the ball about 20 yards, picking up one first down before we were forced to punt. Baltimore moved well against us the first time and reached our 19, where they had a first down. We stopped them there and got a break when Lou Michaels missed a 27-yard field-goal attempt. That is an easy-appearing field goal to the guy sitting in the stands with a hot dog and beer, but when you are the one doing the kicking with all that pressure on you, it isn't that easy, believe me. We stopped Baltimore again early in the second quarter after we gave them the ball on a fumble on our 12-yard line. On a third down from our six, Morrall tried a pass into the end zone and it was intercepted by Randy Beverly. That was the play that swung the momentum in our direction.

Starting from our 20, Joe began mixing up his calls well with handoffs to Snell and passes to Sauer while taking us to a touchdown in 12 plays. Snell scored on a four-yard run around the left side. Was that ever pretty. It was the first time an AFL team had led in the Super Bowl.

When I was coming off the field after kicking the conversion, I could really feel a change in the attitude of the crowd. More people seemed to be moving over to our side.

There was no more scoring in the first half. Michaels missed a 46-yard field-goal try and I missed one from 41 yards. The Colts nearly tied it late in the half when they reached our 15 after a long run by Tom Matte. But we stopped them when Johnny Sample intercepted a pass on our two. By now the crowd was sensing an upset; they knew they were sitting in on a classic.

The Colts fumbled on the first play from scrimmage in the second half and we recovered on their 33. We moved to the 11, but then the Colts pushed us back outside the 20. So I came in and kicked a 32-yard field goal. That was big. Now they had to score at least twice to overtake us.

Joe passed us into field-goal range again on our next possession and I kicked one from 30 yards. We had the ball most of the quarter. The Colts only ran seven plays and didn't get one first down.

Late in the third quarter Joe hit Sauer with a pass for a 39-yard gain to the Colts' 10. We failed to punch it in, so I kicked a nine-yard field goal for a 16-0 lead. Now the Colts would have to score at least three times to beat us with only about 12 minutes left to play. The Orange Bowl was going crazy.

I missed a 42-yard field-goal try about midway through the fourth quarter. The Colts then took over at the 20 and began their last-ditch attempt at winning. With Johnny Unitas at quarterback, they drove to a touchdown. But the possession took several plays while wiping about three more minutes off the clock.

There were only a little more than three minutes left in the game, so naturally we were looking for the onside kick. That's what they did and they got away with it. Unitas immediately passed them down to inside our 20. But we stopped them on downs and were able to keep the ball until we punted with about 15 seconds left. All Joe did on that last possession was hand the ball to Snell.

The celebration on the field and in the locker room was fantastic. But our team party that night was even more emotional. A lot of the players from other AFL teams dropped by, including a bunch of the Kansas City Chiefs. Many of them, even big Buck Buchanan, broke down and cried, they were so happy. It was really something.

There will never be another Super Bowl played with the importance and tension of this one. I played in Super Bowl XII with Denver against Dallas and, compared to

People didn't believe in us because they didn't believe in the AFL.

Super Bowl III, the thrill just wasn't the same. The game missed the flavor of the AFL-NFL rivalry that made it so great.

I was in the AFL when everyone said the league stunk, and I'm proud to have been a part of pro football history when the AFL won the respect and recognition it deserved. I'll never forget the American Football League.

—As told to Dave Payne

New York Jets kicker **Jim Turner** booted a record (since broken) 34 field goals in 1968, and tallied a career-best 145 total points. He kicked two more field goals in the AFC Championship Game and three in the Jets' victory in Super Bowl III. Turner played seven seasons (1964–70) for the Jets before he was traded to the Denver Broncos. He retired after the 1979 season with 521 converts, 304 field goals and 1,439 total points.

I'll never forget the sight of Lennie Moore's flashing white spats, veering and cutting and flying over the frozen turf in

Baltimore's Memorial Stadium. That was the run that made the Baltimore Colts. It gave us our first Western Division title and set us up for our first World Championship a couple of games later—the sudden-death overtime game against the New York Giants.

To be honest, I suppose most people would expect me to pick that World Championship game, which some have called "the greatest game ever played." But my own favorite came a couple of weeks earlier, on November 30, 1958.

We went into that game a hot team, 8-1, with our only defeat at the hands of the Giants a couple of weeks earlier, 24-21. We were up against the San Francisco 49ers, a great team with some of the most outstanding players in the game. A Colt victory assured us at least a tie for the division championship.

They had Y.A. Tittle at quarterback; Joe Perry and Hugh McElhenny at running back; Leo Nomellini, Bob Toneff, Gordy Soltau and Bob St. Clair up front.

The first half was a Baltimore nightmare. Almost 60,000 fans were there to cheer us to our first title and we stunk the joint out. Tittle drove his team 80 yards for a score after the opening kickoff. They ate it up in 11 plays with Y.A. sneaking in for the score.

We couldn't move the ball, and back came the 49ers. Milt Davis broke up their drive with an interception, and then we got fired up enough to move in for the tying touchdown. But that was all we could do. Bert Rechichar missed a field goal from the Frisco 38 and they came storming back. Tittle, Perry and McElhenny gobbled up that yardage and it was 13-7 so fast, I was back on the field before I could catch my breath.

They had us bottled up deep. On third down I dropped back to pass, but big Toneff hit me into the nickel seats and the ball was rolling free. Alex Sandusky fell on it for us on the one, but then Ray Brown punted it out only to the 27.

Tittle made the most of his chance. He hit

Clyde Connors with a pass to the three and McElhenny took it over from there. Now we were down 20-7. There was at least some hope because Ordell Braase blocked Soltau's try for the extra point after the second 49ers touchdown. That at least gave us something to shoot for.

But we only fell deeper into the hole. Usually sure-handed, Lennie Lyles fumbled the kickoff and had to fall on it on our six-yard line. I dropped back to pass and Nomellini broke through, came in high and deflected the ball. It sailed right into the hands of the 49ers linebacker, Matt Hazeltine, and he walked in for the score as I lay buried under a ton of Nomellini.

Mercifully, the gun sounded for the half. It was a dismal offensive performance. I completed only five of 17 passes for something like 25 yards, and we only managed about another 60 or so rushing.

I can talk about it now and not make it sound like an alibi, but I was playing with some fractured ribs, and the aluminum and rubber harness they had me in was causing me some problems. But there is no excuse for the kind of performance we put on. When you're out there you either do it or you don't. You don't look for alibis.

We got the second-half kickoff and started moving. On the 49ers side of midfield, we started to bog down a little, and then came one of those plays everybody likes to call turning points. We had a fourth and one on the 49ers 41.

We had no choice. We had to go for it. I handed the ball to Alan Ameche, and "The Horse" got us that big yard. That wound us up again and a couple of plays later I hit Moore with a pass down on the three and Ameche took it over.

Our defense was really coming on now. You can talk about great defense and great front fours just about forever, but I'll still go with ours: Gino Marchetti, Art Donovan, "Big Daddy" Lipscomb, Don Joyce up front; Bill Pellington, Leo Sanford and Don Shinnick behind them; and Carl Taseff, Johnny Sample, Milt Davis and Andy Nelson in the secondary.

We should have sliced up that ball and given each of those guys a piece of it. They earned it.

NOVEMBER 30, 1958
BALTIMORE COLTS 35, SAN FRANCISCO 49ERS 27
MEMORIAL STADIUM, BALTIMORE, MARYLAND

SCORING

BAL	7	0	7	21	**35**
SF	7	20	0	0	**27**

SF   Tittle, 1-yard run (Soltau kick)
BAL Unitas, 4-yard run (Myhra kick)
SF   Tittle, 3-yard run (kick failed)
SF   McElhenny, 1-yard run (Soltau kick)
SF   Hazeltine, 13-yard interception return (Soltau kick)
BAL Ameche, 1-yard run (Myhra kick)
BAL Ameche, 1-yard run (Myhra kick)
BAL Moore, 73-yard run (Myhra kick)
BAL Berry, 7-yard pass from Unitas (Myhra kick)

TEAM STATISTICS

	BAL	SF
First downs	24	22
Rushes-Yards	39-219	30-155
Passing Yards	196	158
Passes	17-33-1	15-29-5
Punts-Average	3-28.0	3-40.0
Fumbles-Lost	5-1	5-0
Penalties-Yards	5-46	4-50

INDIVIDUAL STATISTICS
Rushing
BAL Ameche 17 rushes for 78 yards; Dupre 9-15; Moore 8-114; Unitas 5-12
SF   McElhenny 11-36; Perry 14-113; Tittle 5-6

Passing
BAL Unitas 17 completions, 33 attempts, 229 yards, 1 interception
SF   Tittle 15-29-168-5

Receiving
BAL Moore 5 receptions for 38 yards; Berry 9-114; Mutscheller 3-77
SF   Connor 3-37; Owens 2-29; McElhenny 2-13; Wilson 4-48; Perry 4-41

ATTENDANCE: 57,557

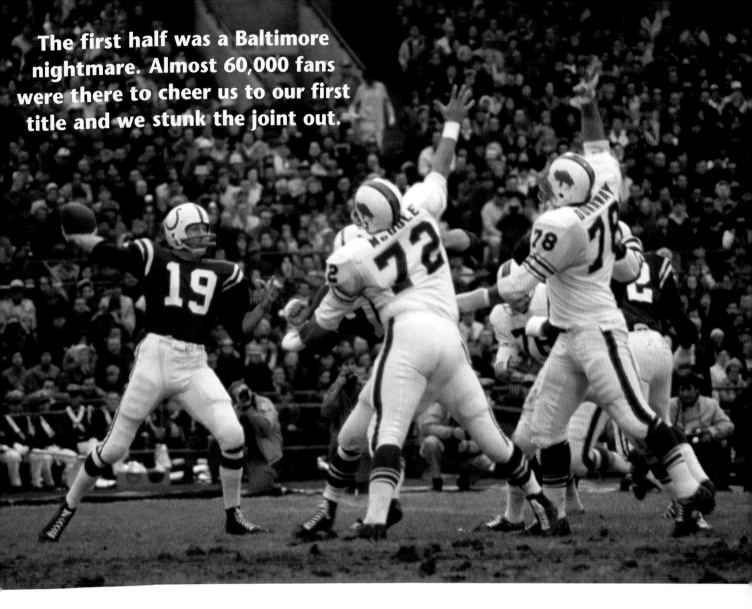

The first half was a Baltimore nightmare. Almost 60,000 fans were there to cheer us to our first title and we stunk the joint out.

We got out of the hole when Jim Mutscheller made a great catch and run for a 59-yard gain. On third down I found Ray Berry, good old third-down Ray Berry, on the 49er 16. A couple of plays later Ameche took it over and we had the score down to 27-21.

Then came another of those great, turning-point, key defensive plays. The 49ers had it third-and-one on their own 40. They gave the ball to McElhenny and it looked like he got mobbed by 11 Colts. They had to punt and the ball rolled dead on our 27.

I lined Moore up at halfback and called a sweep to the left. Lennie took the handoff and bellied back a little to let the blocking form. The left guard and tackle, Art Spinney and Jim Parker, collapsed the 49er line. Ameche threw a block. Moore turned the corner and started upfield. Then Berry threw a block. Lennie twisted away from the cornerback and with the pursuit coming heavy, cut back sharply toward the middle of the field.

I was just another spectator now, cheering him on. Looming up ahead of him was our big right tackle, George Preas. Together they went all the way, 73 yards for a touchdown. The place was bedlam when Steve Myhra booted home the extra point to put us in the lead, 28-27.

After that it was anti-climactic. We drove in for another touchdown. I threw an eight-yarder to Berry that tied me with Cecil Isbell's record of having thrown at least one touchdown pass in 23 consecutive games. To tell you the truth, I didn't even care. I knew we had the title, the first championship any Baltimore team had won since John McGraw played in town.

The fans boiled down out of the stands and went hysterical. They carried every player off the field right to the locker room. I sure was happy for the defense. It was the only rest they had that day. And as for me, well, I'll never forget it.

—*As told to Bob Billings*

Legendary quarterback **Johnny Unitas** (19), above, broke virtually every significant NFL passing record during his 17 seasons (1956–72) with the Baltimore Colts. His record of 47 consecutive games with at least one touchdown pass still stands. Voted NFL Player of the Year three times, Unitas was named MVP three times in 10 Pro Bowls. He concluded his career in 1973 with the San Diego Chargers. Unitas entered the Pro Football Hall of Fame with 2,830 completions for 40,239 yards and 290 touchdowns.

The rivalry between the New York Jets and Miami Dolphins is a strong one, so whenever the two teams meet, the game is intense and exciting. But one game in the series stands out for me—when we beat the Dolphins at home in 1986. Not only was the game thrilling, but for me it was the type of game a player waits his whole career to have.

It was very early in the season, but our victory over the Dolphins helped establish us as one of the top teams in the league. We had our problems toward the end of the year, but for the first two thirds of 1986 the Jets probably were the best team in the NFL.

We beat the Dolphins in overtime, 51-45. The guys on offense had a great time, but I'm sure our defensive players were a little disappointed about giving up so many points. From a personal standpoint, it was a day I'll never forget: four touchdowns, including the winning TD in overtime, and 194 yards receiving. After the game the guys were kidding our wide receiver Al Toon, saying, "Too bad you didn't have such a great game," and, "Too bad you can't keep up with an old guy like Walker." The thing is, Toon had a great day as well, catching seven passes for 111 yards.

Going into the game, I think we expected to see a lot of scoring, but we figured something like 28-21 or 30-24. Kenny O'Brien, the Jets quarterback, can air out the ball, and you know their quarterback, Dan Marino, is going to put points on the board. But even with all that scoring, our defense made a couple of key plays that enabled us to win.

Actually, the first quarter only featured two scores; we had a field goal and they had a touchdown. In the second quarter, though, we were able to exploit their weaknesses in the secondary. We scored four touchdowns, and I had two of them in the last few minutes of the half.

The key for our offense in the second quarter was consistency. Our offensive line had a lot to do with that. I think Kenny was sacked only three times in the game, as he had time to find his receivers. We mixed up our plays pretty well, too, and that kept the Dolphins defense off balance. Johnny Hector scored our first two touchdowns. The two touchdowns I had in the second quarter were both long-pass plays. The first one covered 65 yards when I beat a couple of their defensive backs. On the second one, which occurred about three minutes later, I was able to isolate defensive back Don McNeal and beat him for a 50-yard touchdown.

Even though we were up at the half, we knew we had to maintain our success on offense and try to apply more pressure on defense. Their two key receivers, Mark Clayton and Mark Duper, were having a super game. I think they ended up with 300 yards receiving, and Marino had six touchdown passes.

Everything we tried to do in the third quarter didn't work. They scored a couple of touchdowns, plus a field goal; and we didn't score at all. The amazing thing about the game was that we had a strong second quarter and a strong fourth quarter, but only three points in the first period and none in the third. Marino was burning our secondary in the third quarter, and Miami had the lead [38-31] by the time the period ended. Our defensive backs were banged up going into the game, but we wouldn't use that as an excuse. Like I said, we knew before the game began that Marino was going to air it out. And in addition, our defense shut down their running game so completely that Marino had to go to the air even more than he wanted to.

Going into the fourth quarter, we knew we had to put together some consistent drives. Kenny had a great quarter; I think at one point he completed nine or 10 passes in a row. We scored to tie the game, then Marino threw a short pass to Clayton to give them the lead again.

There were less than three minutes to play when Miami scored the go-ahead touchdown, and when I took the field I could see their defensive guys digging in. I found out later that some of our fans had left the stadium. I guess they figured we wouldn't pull it out.

We couldn't do anything on our drive after Miami's touchdown, but then our defensive guys dug in and we got the ball back with just over a minute to play. The big

---

SEPTEMBER 21, 1986
NEW YORK JETS 51, MIAMI DOLPHINS 45
GIANTS STADIUM, EAST RUTHERFORD,
NEW JERSEY

SCORING

NYJ	3	28	0	14	6	**51**
MIA	7	14	17	7	0	**45**

NYJ Leahy, 32-yard field goal
MIA Pruitt, 6-yard pass from Marino (Reveiz kick)
NYJ Hector, 1-yard run (Leahy kick)
NYJ Hector, 8-yard run (Leahy kick)
MIA Johnson, 1-yard pass from Marino (Reveiz kick)
MIA Duper, 13-yard pass from Marino (Reveiz kick)
NYJ Walker, 65-yard pass from O'Brien (Leahy kick)
NYJ Walker, 50-yard pass from O'Brien (Leahy kick)
MIA Duper, 46-yard pass from Marino (Reveiz kick)
MIA Reveiz, 44-yard field goal
MIA Hardy, 1-yard pass from Marino (Reveiz kick)
NYJ Bligen, 7-yard run (Leahy kick)
MIA Clayton, 4-yard pass from Marino (Reveiz kick)
NYJ Walker, 21-yard pass from O'Brien (Leahy kick)
NYJ Walker, 43-yard pass from O'Brien

TEAM STATISTICS	MIA	NYJ
First Downs	27	32
Rushes-Yards	17-50	34-132
Passing Yards	435	449
Passes	30-50-2	29-43-1
Punts-Average	6-37.0	4-38.0
Fumbles-Lost	2-1	5-3
Penalties-Yards	9-82	5-33

INDIVIDUAL STATISTICS
Rushing
MIA Nathan 4 rushes for 36 yards; Bennett 4-7; Hampton 6-6; Davenport 3-1
NYJ Hector 22-82; Bligen 7-30; Paige 3-10; Toon 1-2; O'Brien 1-8

Passing
MIA Marino 30 completions, 50 attempts, 448 yards, 2 interceptions
NYJ O'Brien 29-43-479-1

Receiving
MIA Duper 7 receptions for 154 yards; Clayton 8-174; Hampton 5-46; Pruitt 2-16; Johnson 2-12; Nathan 2-19; Bennett 1-8; Hardy 3-19
NYJ Toon 7-111; Klever 5-64; Walker 6-194; Hector 3-46; Shuler 6-44; Sohn 1-14; Paige 1-6

ATTENDANCE: 71,025

On the final play of the game, from Miami's 21, I ran a pattern down the sideline and then cut across the middle of the field.

thing, of course, was scoring the tying touchdown, but a key play came earlier in the drive on a hook-and-lateral play. We were on our 33-yard line and Kenny connected with Mickey Shuler for a big completion. Mickey then lateraled to Johnny Hector, who ran the ball to Miami's 39.

On the final play of the game, from Miami's 21, I ran a pattern down the sideline and then cut across the middle of the field. I had a couple of steps on Bud Brown, and Kenny hit me with a pass for the touchdown. That put us down by one point, and Pat Leahy kicked the extra point with no time left in regulation to tie it up.

Going into overtime, I had two things on my mind: Don't turn the ball over, and try to get open for a big play. I figured we had the momentum going into overtime because the Dolphins had to be somewhat down; they had the game won with just a few seconds to play, only to have us score and force

overtime. Also, we were confident because we were playing on our home field.

The key in overtime was our offensive line. The guys gave Kenny enough time to set up and to look for me downfield. The game-winning play was similar to the one at the end of the first half when I beat McNeal for a touchdown. Their defensive backs were set up in a prevent defense, but I was able to isolate on McNeal and go one on one. I got a couple of steps on him at the Miami 43, and Kenny hit me with a perfect pass.

When I scored the touchdown, I remember that a lot of emotions hit me at once. I was glad the game was over and that we had won. But when you're having a good game, when you feel like everything you do is going to work out in a positive way, you don't want those feelings to end. It was a great game for me and for the team—a game I'll never forget.

—As told to Barry Janoff

Although he was legally blind in one eye, speedy New York Jets wide receiver **Wesley Walker** enjoyed a productive 13-season (1977–89) NFL career. He got off to a strong start, averaging 21.1 yards per reception in his rookie season. As a 1978 sophomore, he went to his first of two Pro Bowls after tallying a personal best—and league-leading—1,169 receiving yards. His 12 touchdowns in 1986 were another career high. Walker retired with 438 career receptions for 7,748 yards and 71 touchdowns.

From the time I started playing football when I was nine, I had never been on a team that won the big game. As many of

you may have noticed after seeing the highlight clip a thousand times, I was the Dallas Cowboys cornerback trailing Dwight Clark when he made "The Catch" in the 1981 NFC Championship Game, ending our hopes of reaching the Super Bowl.

Even playing Pop Warner football as a kid growing up in Dallas, I couldn't get a break. I remember one year my team lost a crucial game on something called penetration. In a tie game, they used the number of first downs to determine the victor, and it turned out I gave up the last first down, which cost us the game.

But as a member of the New York Giants in Super Bowl XXV on January 27, 1991, I had a chance to redeem myself, to finally win the big one.

With seconds left, we had played what experts would later say was the perfect game, keeping the ball away from the Buffalo Bills' high-powered offense. We had turned our ball-control offense and bend-but-don't-break defense into an art form, not to mention a 20-19 lead. Redemption would either rise or fall on the foot of Scott Norwood, who had come on the field to attempt a 47-yard field goal with only four ticks remaining.

On that play, my job was to position myself behind the line and watch for anything tricky. I didn't want to end up on another highlight film chasing the holder down the field as he scored the winning touchdown, so I kept an eye on everything until the ball was kicked. Then I became a spectator. As I watched the ball sail over my head, I knew the Bills were in trouble. I was not lined up at the center of the field, yet the ball went right over my head. I knew this could finally be my moment to win it all.

When the Giants signed me prior to the 1990 season, they felt they were one big-play defensive back away from going to the Super Bowl. At the press conference to introduce me, people were talking about how the Giants had lost in the playoffs the year before when the Los Angeles Rams' Flipper Anderson had

caught the winning touchdown in overtime. The Giants and their fans were hoping I was going to be the guy to stop those big plays and come up with some turnovers.

Although the secondary needed a shot in the arm, the front seven was one of the most dominant units I had ever seen. Lawrence Taylor was a terror, whether he was blitzing a quarterback or pursuing a runner. About the only linebacker in the league in the same class as him was the guy on the opposite side, Carl Banks. Pepper Johnson was a tremendous run-stopping inside linebacker; Leonard Marshall was a good pass-rushing end; and Gary Reasons, Eric Dorsey and Erik Howard never seemed to make a mistake.

Against the Bills, our coach Bill Parcells and defensive coordinator Bill Belichick knew we had to come up with something different to stop quarterback Jim Kelly, running back Thurman Thomas, wideout Andre Reed and the rest of the offense. Simply put, the Bills were lethal. They scored 44 points in their opening playoff game against the Miami Dolphins, then trounced the Los Angeles Raiders 51-3 in the AFC Championship Game. Based on the Bills' play, the oddsmakers had tagged us about a touchdown underdog, even though we had beaten Buffalo 17-13 late in the regular season.

Parcells and Belichick came up with an unorthodox lineup in which we would use two defensive linemen, three linebackers and six defensive backs for most of the Super Bowl, and I was in charge of calling the defenses for the first time in my life. Having all those defensive backs on the field gave us the mobility we needed to cope with the Bills' no-huddle offense. It also allowed us to play up tight on the receivers and prevent them from getting a free release from the line of scrimmage.

Our strategy seemed to work early in the game. We traded field goals in the first quarter, but the Bills took a 12-3 lead in the second quarter, on Don Smith's touchdown and Bruce Smith's sack of quarterback Jeff Hostetler in the end zone for a safety. However, Stephen Baker's touchdown catch sent the teams into the locker rooms at halftime engaged in a tight 12-10 contest.

By the second half, a pattern was

JANUARY 27, 1991
NEW YORK GIANTS 20, BUFFALO BILLS 19
TAMPA STADIUM, TAMPA, FLORIDA

SCORING

NYG	3	7	7	3	**20**
BUF	3	9	0	7	**19**

NYG Bahr, 28-yard field goal
BUF Norwood, 23-yard field goal
BUF D. Smith, 1-yard run (Norwood kick)
BUF Safety, Hostetler tackled in end zone by B. Smith
NYG Baker, 14-yard pass from Hostetler (Bahr kick)
NYG Anderson, 1-yard run (Bahr kick)
BUF Thomas, 31-yard run (Norwood kick)
NYG Bahr, 21-yard field goal

TEAM STATISTICS	BUF	NYG
First Downs	18	24
Rushes-Yards	25-166	39-172
Passing Yards	205	214
Passes	18-30-0	20-32-0
Punts-Average	6-38.8	4-43.8
Fumbles-Lost	1-0	0-0
Penalties-Yards	6-35	5-31

INDIVIDUAL STATISTICS
Rushing
BUF Thomas 15 rushes for 135 yards; Davis 2-4; Mueller 1-3; D. Smith 1-1; Kelly 6-23
NYG Anderson 21-102; Meggett 9-48; Carthon 3-12; Hostetler 6-10

Passing
BUF Kelly 18 completions, 30 attempts, 212 yards, 0 interceptions
NYG Hostetler 20-32-222-0

Receiving
BUF Reed 8 receptions for 62 yards; Lofton 1-61; Thomas 5-55; McKeller 2-11; Davis 2-23
NYG Cross 4-39; Ingram 5-74; Baker 2-31; Anderson 1-7; Bavaro 5-50; Carthon 1-3; Meggett 2-18

ATTENDANCE: 73,813

I thought to myself, "Man, I finally won the big one. I can finally die in peace."

developing: Our offense was eating up the clock and keeping the ball away from the Bills. And although Thomas was having a big day rushing, Kelly and the receivers were knocked out of sync. Much to everyone's surprise, we took a 17-12 lead heading into the fourth quarter, thanks to Ottis Anderson's one-yard touchdown run. Anderson's TD capped a 14-play, 75-yard workmanlike drive that took nine and a half minutes off the clock.

Even though the Bills regained the lead on the first play of the fourth quarter—when Thomas scored on a 31-yard run—we didn't stray from our game plan. It was working too well to change now.

The offense, behind the blocking of Jumbo Elliott, William Roberts, Hart Oates, Eric Moore and Doug Riesenberg, went back to work. This time it mounted a 14-play, 74-yard drive, eating up chunks of time along the way. When the drive finally stalled, Matt Bahr hit a 21-yard field goal that put us up 20-19.

The Bills weren't about to let the game end there, though. They finally got on track in the final two minutes, driving from their own 10 to deep into our territory on quick hits to Reed and Thomas. But even though we were bending, we didn't break.

Then Norwood came out to try that 47-yarder. Giants fans everywhere huddled together to hope against all hope. As everyone inside Tampa Stadium held their breath, as millions of people watched throughout the world, my thoughts went back to "The Catch" and that Pop Warner loss. I thought to myself: "Man, am I going to have the prize snatched out of my hands again?" Not this time. Norwood made contact with the ball, and I turned and watched it fly wide right of the uprights.

We had done it. I jumped in the air and ran over to where my family and a group of Giants fans were sitting. I was screaming and yelling and hugging any teammate I could find. I thought to myself, "Man, I finally won the big one. I can finally die in peace."

—As told to Chuck O'Donnell

Cornerback **Everson Walls** (28), above, during the New York Giants' victorious trip to Super Bowl XXV. Walls spent his first nine seasons with the Dallas Cowboys (1981–89) before joining the Giants in 1990. Traded to the Cleveland Browns midway through the 1992 campaign, Walls retired a year later with 57 career interceptions and 504 yards returned.

The Dallas Cowboys were not even expected to make the playoffs in 1980, my first full season as a starter. So when we

made it to Atlanta that season to face the Falcons in a divisional playoff game, we were just happy to be there–even if it was a cold, miserable day and Atlanta-Fulton County Stadium was full of Falcons fans, all wearing red and constantly stomping their feet.

We'd finished the regular season at 12-4, which tied us with the Philadelphia Eagles for the best mark in the NFC East. The Eagles owned a tie-breaker advantage over us, however, so we finished second in the division. The Falcons also had finished 12-4, best in the NFC West and good for their first division title.

The Falcons had two good running backs that year—William Andrews and Lynn Cain, who combined for more than 2,000 yards rushing during the regular season—plus quarterback Steve Bartkowski. What I remember most about that game is the last six minutes of the fourth quarter. We hadn't done much offensively up to that point. Meanwhile, Bartkowski was throwing bombs and had led the Falcons to a 27-17 lead with six minutes and 37 seconds left in the game.

We got this feeling in the huddle that this was it. We can all get on the plane, fly home and watch the rest of the playoffs on TV, or we can do something now. Basically, we worked our two-minute offense, and as I look back on it now, Atlanta probably should have changed its defense. The Falcons stayed in a prevent defense and only rushed three linemen at me. Problem is, the two-minute offense is designed to attack the prevent defense—the cornerbacks don't roll up, so sideline patterns are usually wide open.

We started at our own 38-yard line. I connected on three of four passes to give us a first down at the Atlanta 14. On the next play, the Falcons blitzed their safety, but we picked it up. The touchdown pass I threw to Drew Pearson was a busted play. I rolled right, stopped, looked and pointed to Pearson to run toward the left side of the end zone. Well, most of the Falcons defenders

went left, but Drew stayed put. Fearing an interception, I threw that ball high in the air—I was afraid I overthrew him—and Pearson leaped up and grabbed the ball while surrounded by three Falcons.

This scoring drive fired up our defense, which limited Atlanta to three plays and a punt. We took over at our 30-yard line with just under two minutes to play. I threw a 20-yard sideline pass to Butch Johnson, then found Pearson over the middle for another 14 yards. The crowd was noisy—I was calling plays at the line of scrimmage—but I managed to complete a pass to Tony Dorsett that put us at the Atlanta 23. Tony Hill caught a ball out of bounds, but another pass to Pearson over the middle went for a TD to give us the lead with 49 seconds left. I'll never forget the dead silence that echoed through the stadium.

Our defense then shut Atlanta down when Harvey Martin sacked Bartkowski and Bartkowski's next three passes failed to get a first down. The defense allowed the Falcons 27 points, but it did stop them when it had to and gave us the chance to win the game. Our defense also held Andrews and Cain to a combined 86 yards rushing.

We were like a wounded animal in a corner those last six minutes. I give credit to guys like Drew Pearson, Bob Breunig, Charlie Waters, Jethro Pugh, Robert Newhouse—all players near the end of their careers, but all among the most competitive guys I've ever played with. If you beat guys like this, you'd better get on the bus and get out of town, because they are coming after you. That kind of attitude helped us win that game in the closing minutes of the fourth quarter.

You play for moments like that, to play a role that affects so many people. Part of the reason was for the money, but we were also a step closer to the Super Bowl. The whole city of Dallas was affected by that win. It was an indescribable feeling—as great a feeling as I ever had playing football.

—As told to John Nixon

JANUARY 4, 1981
DALLAS COWBOYS 30, ATLANTA FALCONS 27
ATLANTA-FULTON COUNTY STADIUM,
ATLANTA, GEORGIA

SCORING

DAL	3	7	0	20	**30**
ATL	10	7	7	3	**27**

ATL   Mazzetti, 38-yard field goal
ATL   Jenkins, 60-yard pass from Bartkowski (Mazzetti kick)
DAL   Septien, 38-yard field goal
DAL   DuPree, 5-yard pass from White (Septien kick)
ATL   Cain, 1-yard run (Mazzetti kick)
ATL   Andrews, 5-yard pass from Bartkowski (Mazzetti kick)
DAL   Newhouse, 1-yard run (Septien kick)
ATL   Mazzetti, 34-yard field goal
DAL   Pearson, 14-yard pass from White (Septien kick)
DAL   Pearson, 23-yard pass from White (kick failed)

TEAM STATISTICS	DAL	ATL
First Downs	22	18
Rushes-Yards	24-112	27-86
Passing Yards	310	285
Passes	25-40-1	18-33-1
Punts-Average	4-38.8	4-36.0
Fumbles-Lost	4-1	1-1
Penalties-Yards	6-72	4-48

INDIVIDUAL STATISTICS
Rushing
DAL   Dorsett 10 rushes for 51 yards; Newhouse 6-31; D. Pearson 1-9; White 4-1; P. Pearson 1-11; DuPree 1-5; Newsome 1-4
ATL   Andrews 14-43; Cain 13-43
Passing
DAL   White 25 completions, 39 attempts, 322 yards, 1 interception; Springs 0-1-0-0
ATL   Bartkowski 18-33-320-1
Receiving
DAL   Hill 4 receptions for 53 yards; DuPree 3-29; Springs 3-39; P. Pearson 4-51; D. Pearson 5-90; Dorsett 5-40; Johnson 1-20
ATL   Miller 3-48; Francis 6-66; Jenkins 4-155; Jackson 1-12; Andrews 2-19; Cain 2-20

ATTENDANCE: 60,022

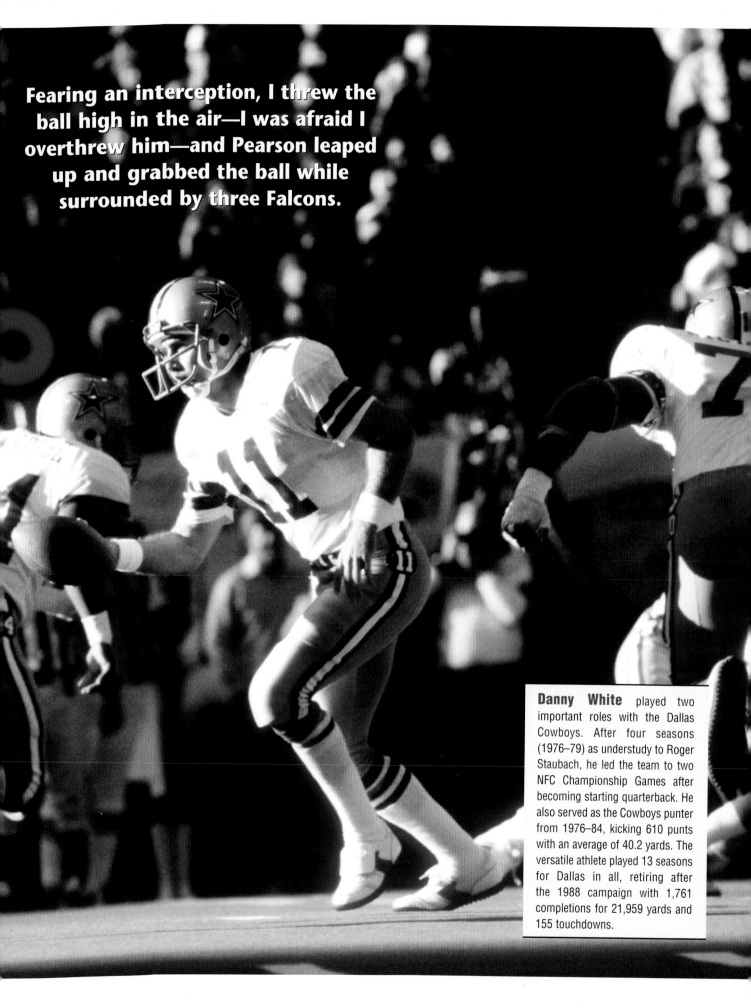

Fearing an interception, I threw the ball high in the air—I was afraid I overthrew him—and Pearson leaped up and grabbed the ball while surrounded by three Falcons.

Danny White played two important roles with the Dallas Cowboys. After four seasons (1976–79) as understudy to Roger Staubach, he led the team to two NFC Championship Games after becoming starting quarterback. He also served as the Cowboys punter from 1976–84, kicking 610 punts with an average of 40.2 yards. The versatile athlete played 13 seasons for Dallas in all, retiring after the 1988 campaign with 1,761 completions for 21,959 yards and 155 touchdowns.

There are games that I'd rather remember, and there is one that I'd like to forget, but I can't. So why don't we just call it the

game I'll never get rid of. It's a game that will never leave my mind.

I do know we were winning the game 28-16 with about two minutes to go and we lost it. In a situation like that, with that kind of lead, you should be able to stop the other fellows. But we didn't. Obviously, we made some mistakes. But that is not to take anything away from the Dallas Cowboys, because in those last two minutes they did everything they had to do and made some great plays. Everything they did was right, and everything we did was wrong.

For them it was a million-to-one shot and they pulled it off. For us it was a one-in-a-million and we lost. The game I'm talking about was the December 23, 1972 Playoff Game.

The week before, we beat the Minnesota Vikings in the last few seconds to win our division, and now we were up against the defending Super Bowl champions. We might not have finished right, but we certainly got off strong. Vic Washington took the opening kickoff and ran it back 97 yards for a touchdown. From then on we kept up intense defensive pressure. We forced the Dallas quarterback, Craig Morton, into repeated mistakes. We picked off two of his passes and we forced him to fumble under a heavy pass rush.

We were ready for Dallas. They fooled us a little the year before with all the motion and moving around they do. But basically they were really a simple team. The "I" was their basic formation and they liked to run Calvin Hill about 20 to 30 times a game. And coming out of the deep back spot in the "I" he could hit any hole along the line of scrimmage. They liked to give you all that motion and movement to get you to follow it and make a move with it, and then they just attacked where you should have been all along.

This time we didn't seem to be as bothered by the motion and we were really playing aggressive defense. So aggressive that

Hill fumbled a couple of times and we turned three of those turnovers into touchdowns, all on one-yard plunges by Larry Schreiber. When you work like that you really have a great team feeling. The defense gets the ball and the offense puts it in for the score. Both units feel they are really contributing and you are a complete team.

We were so effective that at one time we led 21-3. They narrowed that slightly to 28 to 13, then they switched quarterbacks and brought in Roger Staubach. He hadn't played too much all year because he was hurt in the preseason and then couldn't get his job back from Morton.

He wasn't exactly a ball of fire either. We were solving the problems he created as easily as we did when Morton was in the game. We sacked Staubach four times and another time we got to him and forced a fumble, which we recovered. He did manage, though, to get his team in position for another field goal. But with only two minutes and 2 seconds to go in the game, we still led 28-16.

Then I don't know what happened. Maybe we thought we had the game won and we lost a little of our concentration. And when you've lost a little concentration, you've lost it all. But, suddenly, everything they did was perfect.

They had the ball at their own 45-yard line. We knew Staubach was going to pass. Our rush was good and so was our coverage. Roger was forced to dump the ball off to his fullback, Walt Garrison. The next play it was the same thing and again he was forced to dump it off to Garrison.

On those two plays they gained about 15 yards, but we didn't mind that so much because it was taking up time and they didn't have any time to waste. Then Staubach hit Billy Parks with about a 20-yard curl-in and quickly called time-out. There was a minute and a half left now and they still had 20 yards to go for a score. Staubach came right back to Parks on a post from the left side of their formation. Now it was suddenly tight, 28-23.

Dallas' only chance now was an onside kick. We were ready for it. We had all backs and ends, fellows who are used to handling

---

DECEMBER 23, 1972
DALLAS COWBOYS 30, SAN FRANCISCO 49ERS 28
CANDLESTICK PARK, SAN FRANCISCO, CALIFORNIA

SCORING

DAL	3	10	0	17	**30**
SF	7	14	7	0	**28**

SF	V. Washington, 97-yard kickoff return (Gossett kick)
DAL	Fritsch, 37-yard field goal
SF	Schreiber, 1-yard run (Gossett kick)
SF	Schreiber, 1-yard run (Gossett kick)
DAL	Fritsch, 45-yard field goal
DAL	Alworth, 28-yard pass from Morton (Fritsch kick)
SF	Schreiber, 1-yard run (Gossett kick)
DAL	Fritsch, 27-yard field goal
DAL	Parks, 20-yard pass from Staubach (Fritsch kick)
DAL	Sellers, 10-yard pass from Staubach (Fritsch kick)

TEAM STATISTICS

	DAL	SF
First Downs	22	13
Rushes-Yards	31-165	37-105
Passing Yards	237	150
Passes	20-41-2	12-22-2
Punts-Average	6-41.8	6-37.3
Fumbles-Lost	4-3	5-1
Penalties-Yards	3-35	7-56

INDIVIDUAL STATISTICS

Rushing

DAL Hill 18 rushes for 125 yards; Staubach 3-23; Garrison 9-15; Horton 1-2

SF V. Washington 10-56; Schreiber 26-52; Thomas 1-minus 3

Passing

DAL Staubach 12 completions, 20 attempts, 174 yards, 0 interceptions; Morton 8-21-96-2

SF Brodie 12-22-150-2

Receiving

DAL Parks 7 receptions for 136 yards; Garrison 3-24; Alworth 2-60; Sellers 2-21; Montgomery 2-19; Hayes 1-13; Ditka 1-9; Hill 1-6; Truax 1-2

SF Riley 4-41; G. Washington 3-76; Schreiber 3-20; V. Washington 1-8; Kwalick 1-5

ATTENDANCE: 61,214

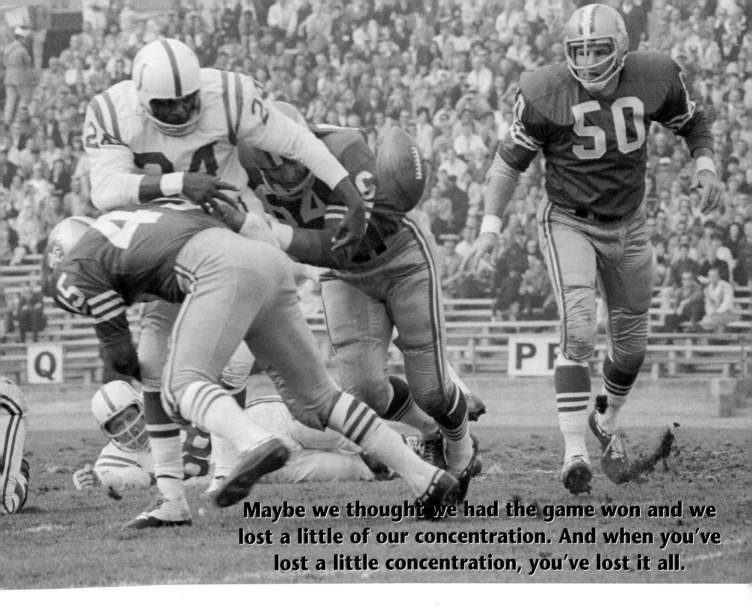

Maybe we thought we had the game won and we lost a little of our concentration. And when you've lost a little concentration, you've lost it all.

the ball, up front to grab the kick. They kicked it right to one of our men at midfield. The only trouble was he couldn't hold it. Mel Renfro, once a college teammate of mine, fell on it for the Cowboys right on the 50-yard line. I didn't feel like singing the old school song with Mel right about then.

Now they had both time and field position. On first down we put on a tremendous pass rush, but somehow Staubach wiggled free and he was running loose. Before we could come up from our passing zones and tackle him he had turned a near-disastrous play into a gain of 21 yards. There was still about a minute left.

Again Roger went to Parks. He hit him along the sideline at our 10-yard line to kill the clock with 52 seconds left. Now it was really hairy. They needed a touchdown to win and they didn't have too much field for fancy maneuvering.

To get the initiative and momentum back, we decided to blitz our middle linebacker,

Frank Nunley. But Staubach read it perfectly and hit Ron Sellers right over the middle for the touchdown.

Suddenly, with less than 50 seconds left, we were behind for the first time in the game. It felt like we had just stepped into a large, dark hole.

Our offense didn't give up. All we needed was a field goal. John Brodie worked it down to the Dallas 38-yard line, but then we got hit with a holding penalty and that was it. We lost.

I think we all learned something. For one thing, it taught us that you have to play for 60 minutes, not 58, or 59. It also taught us, me anyway, that if you just keep going, you just hang in there, sooner or later one of these days you're going to get that big break. Never, never quit, no matter how hopeless it appears.

Sometimes you don't learn that even if you win the Super Bowl.

—*As told to Bob Billings*

In a 1965 game, above, San Francisco 49er **Dave Wilcox** (64) and teammate Elbert Kimbrough (45) force a fumble from Baltimore Colts running back Lenny Moore. Wilcox—nicknamed "The Intimidator" for his aggressive style of play—missed only one game over the course of his 11-season (1964–74) career with the 49ers. Voted All-NFL five times, the six-foot-three 241-pound linebacker went to seven Pro Bowls. Wilcox entered the Pro Football Hall of Fame in 2000.

It's easy for me to say that the highlight of my career and the game I'll never forget was Super Bowl XXII. But that's not so

much because of what I accomplished as because of what the team accomplished. You can have a great game and still lose. I was named the MVP, but that was a team award because it was a team victory.

When I think back on that game, I remember a lot of feelings and emotions, perhaps more than the actual plays. The team kept coming back from adversity that whole season. The 1987 season was unusual from the outset. There was the players' strike, and there were a lot of guys coming and going. I was the number-two quarterback on the chart, behind Jay Schroeder. People kept putting us down and writing us off, but we took up the challenge on a personal level. To a man, we all wanted to prove to ourselves that we were the best team in the NFL. In that season, under those conditions, I know that we were.

People ask me how I feel about being a role model. In some ways, I don't see myself as one. I'm no Jackie Robinson, but I am in a position to be a model for kids because I worked hard and reached my goals. I never let anyone put limitations on what I could or couldn't do.

Super Bowl XXII was a good example. People came in talking about how the Denver Broncos would overmatch us and how John Elway was going to take charge of the game. Elway is a great player, but we knew we were the team to beat, not the other way around. And we went out and did our job and reached our goal—to be champions of the NFL.

The game didn't start out well for the Redskins. The Broncos opened on offense, and on their first play from scrimmage they isolated wide receiver Ricky Nattiel on Washington cornerback Barry Wilburn. Nattiel had about five yards on Wilburn upfield, and Elway hit him with a perfect pass for a 56-yard touchdown. On their next possession, they got down to our 13-yard line. Elway called a draw play on a third-and-

five, but Dave Butz put him down for about a 10-yard loss. They kicked a field goal and were up by 10.

Our offense was off by a step or two in that quarter. I think we were too emotional. When it looked as if Denver might blow it open early, there was a lot of yelling and shouting on our sideline. But that didn't last long. Guys were going over to one another and telling themselves to relax, to focus our energy in the right direction.

I had had emergency root-canal work done the day before the game, and my mouth was sore. But what put me out of the game, for one play, was a twisted knee I suffered toward the end of the first quarter. What really upset me more than having to leave the field, though, was the fact that we lost 10 yards on the play. All that happened, really, was that I slipped on the turf and hyperextended the knee. I was in pain, but when head coach Joe Gibbs came over to see how I was, I told him I had played in pain before and this time wouldn't be any different.

Physically and emotionally, we went into the second quarter determined to take control of the game. We stayed with our game plan and emphasized the things we knew we could do best. We made the adjustments we had to make in order to win the game.

Our first offensive play of the quarter was a short pass to Ricky Sanders. He got behind Denver cornerback Mark Haynes at midfield, and I hit him with a pass for our first touchdown. At that point, the team's confidence level went way up. And maybe Denver's confidence was shaken a bit. A couple of minutes later we shook it some more on the same call, but this time to Gary Clark. We were at about Denver's 30 and Clark was supposed to run a short-yardage pattern. But he got bumped at the line and adjusted by going deeper. He had a few steps on Steve Wilson, which was all the space I needed to hit him for our second touchdown.

Our third touchdown was off a play the Redskins had been running for years, a counter gap, which is a trap play based on misdirection. The idea is to get the defense

---

JANUARY 31, 1988

WASHINGTON REDSKINS 42, DENVER BRONCOS 10

JACK MURPHY STADIUM, SAN DIEGO, CALIFORNIA

SCORING

WAS	0	35	0	7	**42**
DEN	10	0	0	0	**10**

DEN   Nattiel, 56-yard pass from Elway (Karlis kick)
DEN   Karlis, 24-yard field goal
WAS   Sanders, 80-yard pass from Williams (Haji-Sheikh kick)
WAS   Clark, 27-yard pass from Williams (Haji-Sheikh kick)
WAS   Smith, 58-yard run (Haji-Sheikh kick)
WAS   Sanders, 50-yard pass from Williams (Haji-Sheikh kick)
WAS   Didier, 8-yard pass from Williams (Haji-Sheikh kick)
WAS   Smith, 4-yard run (Haji-Sheikh kick)

TEAM STATISTICS

	WAS	DEN
First Downs	25	18
Rushes-Yards	40-280	17-97
Passing Yards	322	230
Passes	18-30-1	15-39-3
Punts-Average	4-37.0	7-36.0
Fumbles-Lost	1-0	0-0
Penalties-Yards	6-65	5-26

INDIVIDUAL STATISTICS

Rushing
WAS   Smith 22 rushes for 204 yards; Bryant 8-38; Clark 1-25; Rogers 5-17; Griffin 1-2; Williams 2-minus 2; Sanders 1-minus 4
DEN   Lang 5-38; Elway 3-32; Winder 8-30; Sewell 1-minus 3

Passing
WAS   Williams 18 completions, 29 attempts, 340 yards, 1 interception; Schroeder 0-1-0-0
DEN   Elway 14-38-257-3; Sewell 1-1-23-0

Receiving
WAS   Sanders 9 receptions for 193 yards; Clark 3-55; Monk 1-40; Bryant 1-20; Warren 2-15; Smith 1-9; Didier 1-8
DEN   Jackson 4-76; Nattiel 2-69; Sewell 4-41; Kay 2-38; Winder 1-26; Elway 1-23; Lang 1-7

ATTENDANCE: 73,302

I told him I had played in pain before and this time wouldn't be any different.

moving in one direction while your play goes in the opposite direction. In this case we got Denver's people moving toward the right, with linemen Joe Jacoby and Raleigh McKenzie actually leading the blocking in toward the left. Smith followed them and tight end Clint Didier, who had a key block, and ran in for a 58-yard touchdown. We used that play a lot that day, with Jacoby and McKenzie the lead blockers on the left and Mark May and R.C. Thielemann the lead blockers on the right. We called Smith's number at least three times on the counter gap that quarter, and he ended up with a touchdown and a lot of yardage.

We were up 21-10, but the quarter was far from over. Sanders came over during one of our next possessions and said he could beat Tony Lily deep, so we called his number on a slant-in and he caught the pass for a 50-yard score. A couple of minutes later we had the

ball back when Wilburn intercepted a pass from Elway. We were inside Denver's 10, and I hit Didier over the middle for an eight-yard touchdown.

The key to that quarter was that everyone on our team did his job. The offensive guys gave me plenty of time to find receivers, and the receivers were beating their men in almost every situation. It wasn't as if we planned to score five touchdowns in the quarter, but after Sanders scored we said, "Let's get another." We ended up with five. Amazing.

That game is the highlight of my career, not because I was named MVP, but because we played in the Super Bowl and won. A lot of guys never get there, and many who do come up short. On that day, I was quarterback for the best team in pro football. That's a feeling you never forget.

—*As told to Barry Janoff*

Washington quarterback **Doug Williams** (17), above, wrenched his knee in Super Bowl XXII. Yet after coming off the bench in the last game of that 1987 season, he led the Redskins through the playoffs and garnered Super Bowl MVP honors. After five strong seasons (1978–82) with the Tampa Bay Buccaneers, Williams sat out the 1983 campaign. He played two seasons (1984–85) in the USFL before the rival league folded. In 1986, he joined the Redskins as a backup. Williams retired in 1989 and began a successful coaching career.

REGGIE WILLIAMS

I played for 14 years in the NFL, all of them with the Cincinnati Bengals. So, of course, I have a lot of memories—some

more unforgettable than others. We won two AFC championships and went to the Super Bowl twice, and we played and won a lot of big games throughout the years. I also met a lot of people who helped me and who helped to make my career a rewarding experience.

The most unforgettable game for me was the AFC Championship Game against the Buffalo Bills in 1988. That was our second conference title, but I'd say that victory was somewhat sweeter than the first, mainly because of the events that led up to it. We were 4-11 in 1987, and a lot of people figured that the team had run its course, that we were not title contenders anymore. Entering the 1988 season, a lot of people had written us off. They figured we weren't going anywhere.

To a man, we went into training camp in 1988 with the determination that we would work hard as a team, win games and win the conference title. Pride is a big motivating factor, and we certainly were motivated that year.

As it turned out, a lot of guys on the team had super years. We won the AFC Central and tied Buffalo for the best record in the conference. Eddie Brown, Tim McGee and Eric Thomas had great seasons, and so many people played so well that it was hard to believe we were 4-11 the year before.

There were certain factors in 1987 that split the team apart and had us working against one another instead of working together. The players' strike seemed to take a lot of heart and soul away from the Bengals. But that was something we had to work out internally, which we did.

One important thing that happened was that even when we were winning games, we never let it go to our heads. We never said, "Hey, this is easy. We can take any team." We always were focused on the task at hand: prepare for the next game, play our best and work together as a team. There was a change in attitude throughout the roster—one for the betterment of the Bengals. I feel that

even if we hadn't won the AFC title that season, it would have been a successful one, simply because we came together as a team.

In the playoffs that season we had to face the Seattle Seahawks first. They had a strong, young team, and they won their division that year. We came in well prepared for them, but it was a close game, 21-13.

The championship game was in Cincinnati, which made all of us feel more confident. The people there are extremely supportive of the Bengals, and playing at home in that type of pressure game was a big plus.

Prior to the game we had to make some adjustments to the offense our coach, Sam Wyche, had been employing during the year. Basically, your offense goes from one play to the next without a huddle, which means the defense can't substitute with the degree of intensity it would like. It can't bring in more defensive backs for a nickel defense, for example, because it doesn't have the time or opportunity.

Coach Wyche also liked to use quick snaps on offense, which the NFL said he couldn't use in the game against Buffalo. I don't remember the specifics, but Coach Wyche was upset about it. However, he used that as a motivation for us, in effect setting it up as the Bengals against the NFL. It motivated the coach, at least.

As a member of the defense, my job was to help stop Buffalo's offensive weapons, such as Jim Kelly, Thurman Thomas and Andre Reed. It wasn't a fluke that Buffalo won 12 games that year; they had a strong team, solid coaching by Marv Levy and a winning attitude. The championship game was a good match-up of clubs whose entire seasons had been focused on playing well as a team and achieving success.

The game began as a defensive struggle. There were three interceptions and several good defensive plays by both teams in the first quarter. Toward the end of the quarter we were right on Buffalo's goal, and Ickey Woods ran it in to give us the lead. But the Bills came back with a couple of solid drives in the second quarter. They scored a touchdown about a minute and a half into

---

JANUARY 8, 1989
CINCINNATI BENGALS 21, BUFFALO BILLS 10
RIVERFRONT STADIUM, CINCINNATI, OHIO

SCORING

CIN	7	7	0	7	**21**
BUF	0	10	0	0	**10**

CIN   Woods, 1-yard run (Breech kick)
BUF   Reed, 9-yard pass from Kelly (Norwood kick)
CIN   Brooks, 10-yard pass from Esiason (Breech kick)
BUF   Norwood, 39-yard field goal
CIN   Woods, 1-yard run (Breech kick)

TEAM STATISTICS

	BUF	CIN
First Downs	10	23
Rushes-Yards	17-45	50-175
Passing Yards	136	74
Passes	14-30-3	11-20-2
Punts-Average	6-45.1	6-36.8
Fumbles-Lost	0-0	2-0
Penalties-Yards	5-50	4-45

INDIVIDUAL STATISTICS
Rushing
BUF   Mueller 8 rushes for 21 yards; Kelly 2-10; Thomas 4-6; Riddick 1-4; Byrum 1-3; Harmon 1-1
CIN   Woods 29-102; Wilson 5-29; Esiason 7-26; Jennings 2-12; Brooks 7-6

Passing
BUF   Kelly 14 completions, 30 attempts, 163 yards, 3 interceptions
CIN   Esiason 11-20-94-2

Receiving
BUF   Reed 5 receptions for 55 yards; Riddick 3-28; Harmon 3-18; T. Johnson 2-48; Metzelaars 1-14
CIN   Holman 4-38; Brooks 2-21; Riggs 2-16; McGee 2-14; Collinsworth 1-5

ATTENDANCE: 59,747

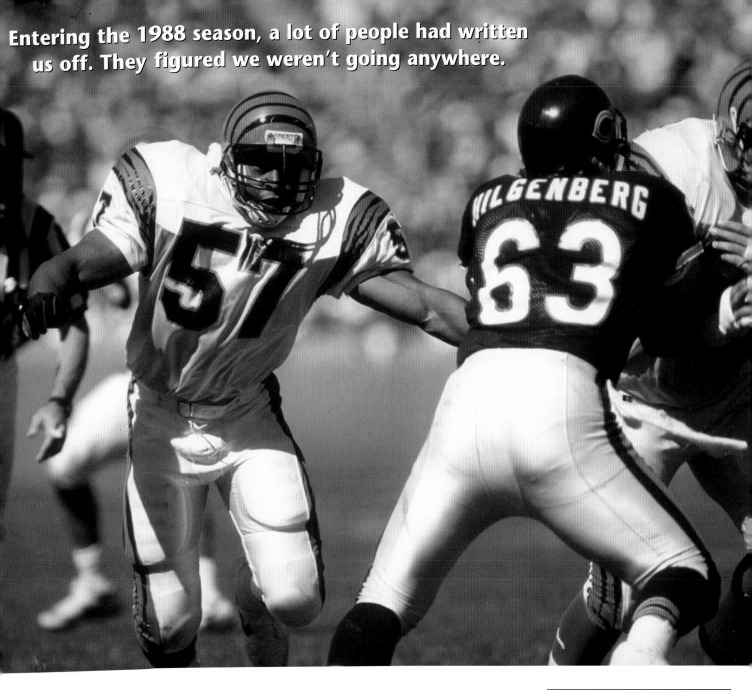

Entering the 1988 season, a lot of people had written us off. They figured we weren't going anywhere.

the quarter to tie the game, but our quarterback, Boomer Esiason, came back less than a minute later to hit James Brooks with a touchdown pass from about 10 yards out.

There was a flurry of scoring early in the second quarter, but then nothing happened again until late in the first half when the Bills hit a field goal to make it 14-10 at halftime. We didn't score again until the fourth quarter, but more important was the fact that we shut Buffalo down in the second half. I even had a quarterback sack, which was monumental for me at that time because I only had two or three all year. What happened was that we were able to disrupt Buffalo's offensive flow for most of the second half.

The key in this sport is playing a team game. We did ourselves proud that season because of all the positive things we made happen. We didn't win the Super Bowl, but we played a strong game. San Francisco played a stronger game, though, and won 20-16, but it was only a matter of inches that separated the two teams at the end.

No one has an easy time in life, but hard work and determination can go a long way. Whenever I talk to kids or adults, I stress those things. Being an ex-athlete, I know that also works on the football field. We worked hard in 1988 and earned our reward, which was winning the AFC Championship. That's why the game against Buffalo was unforgettable.

—As told to Barry Janoff

In 1989 action, above, Cincinnati Bengals linebacker **Reggie Williams** (57) rushes past Chicago Bears center Jay Hilgenberg (63). Williams missed only seven games during his 14-season (1976–89) career with the Bengals, racking up 16 interceptions and 41 sacks. He went to Super Bowls XXIII and XVI but lost to the San Francisco 49ers both times. Williams, a tireless worker with numerous charities, received the NFL's 1986 Man of the Year Award and, in 1988, was appointed to the Cincinnati city council.

1975 NFC DIVISIONAL PLAYOFF GAME

I guess what people look for in a game you remember the most is the big play—the scoring plays, the sacks, the fumbles and

DECEMBER 27, 1975
LOS ANGELES RAMS 35, ST. LOUIS
CARDINALS 23
MEMORIAL COLISEUM, LOS ANGELES,
CALIFORNIA

SCORING

LA	14	14	0	7	**35**
STL	0	9	7	7	**23**

LA	Jaworski, 5-yard run (Dempsey kick)
LA	Youngblood, 47-yard interception return (Dempsey kick)
LA	Simpson, 65-yard interception return (Dempsey kick)
STL	Otis, 3-yard run (kick failed)
LA	Jackson, 66-yard pass from Jaworski (Dempsey kick)
STL	Bakken, 39-yard field goal
STL	Gray, 11-yard pass from Hart (Bakken kick)
LA	Jessie, 2-yard fumble recovery (Dempsey kick)
STL	Jones, 3-yard run (Bakken kick)

TEAM STATISTICS	STL	LA
First Downs	22	26
Rushes-Yards	27-95	50-237
Passing Yards	268	203
Passes	22-41-3	12-23-0
Punts-Average	6-42.7	5-31.6
Fumbles-Lost	3-2	5-3
Penalties-Yards	6-70	5-38

INDIVIDUAL STATISTICS
Rushing

STL	Otis 12 rushes for 38 yards; Jones 6-28; Metcalf 8-27; Latin 1-2
LA	McCutcheon 37-202; Scribner 4-16; Bryant 3-12; Jaworski 6-7

Passing

STL	Hart 22 completions, 41 attempts, 3 interceptions, 291 yards
LA	Jaworski 12-23-0-203

Receiving

STL	Metcalf 6 receptions for 94 yards; Otis 4-52; Gray 3-52; Harris 2-33; Latin 2-23; Jones 2-19; Cain 2-17; Smith 1-1
LA	Jessie 4-52; McCutcheon 3-8; Jackson 2-84; Bryant 2-28; Nelson 1-33

ATTENDANCE: 72,650

recoveries. The way I look at it is that all of these things are gravy, at least for a defensive end. It's how well you perform your job within the structure of the defense that's important to me, even if it doesn't appear spectacular to the guy in the stands. I've had a lot of what I feel were good games from that standpoint.

The game I would have to choose as my most memorable was the opening round of the 1975 playoffs against the St. Louis Cardinals. I did happen to make a big play or two in that one, and we also played a good all-around game that day against a very good St. Louis team.

We had plenty of momentum going into that game. We had just completed the league season by beating Pittsburgh 10-3 for our sixth straight win. We were a relatively young team, yet we still went 12-2 in league games.

This was going to be only my second game against St. Louis since I came to the Rams in 1971. We had lost to them 24-14, late in the 1972 season, in a game that knocked us out of first place in our division and opened the door for the San Francisco 49ers to sneak in and win the title.

Preparing for a Don Coryell–coached team wasn't easy. The Cardinals had a lot of weapons: Terry Metcalf and Jim Otis at running backs, Jimmy Hart at quarterback and receivers like Mel Gray, J.V. Cain and Jerry Smith. The key, of course, was applying pressure on Hart, because he'd pick you apart if he was given time. We went into the game with the reputation for having a good pass rush, and the Cardinals' offensive line had a reputation for providing excellent pass protection. We had Fred Dryer and me at the ends and Merlin Olsen and Cody Jones at tackles; they had Dan Dierdorf and Roger Finnie at tackles, Bob Young and Conrad Dobler at guards and Tom Banks at center.

My opponent was Dierdorf. He was one of the top four tackles I faced in my career. (The others? Rayfield Wright, Russ Washington and

Ron Yary.) Dan was always a real challenge for me. He had all the attributes necessary to be a super tackle: size, strength, quickness and intelligence. He was a great pass blocker. And, I'd like to add, he's a super person. He and I came into the pros the same year and became friends. But you forget that friendship within the framework of the game when you're out there competing against each other. It becomes more of a respect thing for each other.

Merlin was an intense, clean player, and he didn't care for some of the things Dobler pulled. But Merlin handled himself—and Dobler—just fine. Merlin, in essence, wrote the book on how to play on the defensive line. It was an honor playing next to him for six years; he taught me a lot of basic things you don't pick up in college.

Our offense didn't waste any time getting us on the board. We took the opening kickoff and drove about 80 yards for a touchdown. I recall Lawrence McCutcheon carried about nine times on that march. He rushed for over 200 yards that day. Ron Jaworski scored on a five-yard run to give us the lead.

About a minute later, it was my turn. On the Cardinals' second play from scrimmage, we called a dog blitz and I stayed back to spy. I stepped outside and the tackle came on me okay, but the back flared too close to me. Hart hurried his throw intended for Otis and the ball came right to me. I returned it 47 yards for a touchdown. It all happened so fast I didn't have time to be surprised; once I got the ball, I wanted to hang onto it and get as far downfield as I could. I didn't want to get caught from behind by some offensive tackle because I would have never been able to live that down. Everything falls into place; you know what you're doing out there, no matter what the situation.

It was my second career interception. I ran the other one back for a touchdown too. It was in a preseason game against Steve Spurrier of the 49ers. Spurrier and I went to the same school: Florida.

The Cardinals were having a tough time getting untracked. On the first play after the next kickoff, they fumbled and Dryer recovered. We didn't turn that into any

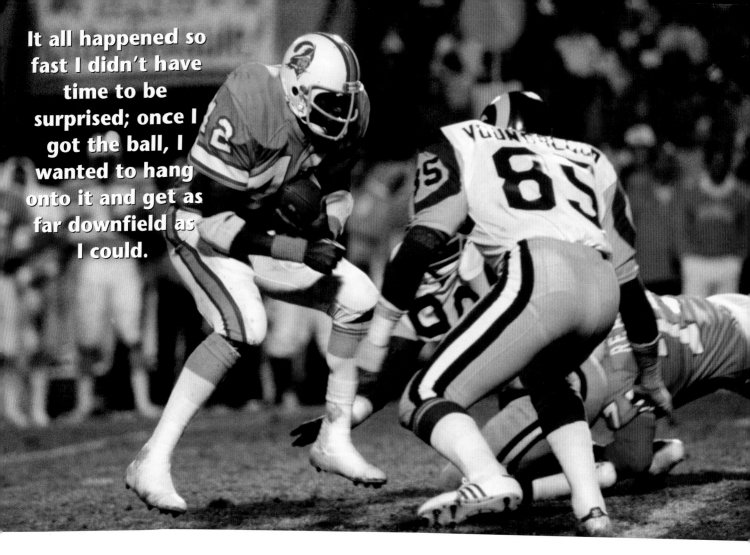

It all happened so fast I didn't have time to be surprised; once I got the ball, I wanted to hang onto it and get as far downfield as I could.

points, but it bought a few more minutes of rest for the defense.

We struck again defensively early in the second quarter when our free safety, Bill Simpson, intercepted a Hart pass and returned it 65 yards for a touchdown. That gave us a 21-0 lead.

St. Louis came back to score a touchdown a few minutes later, but I blocked Jim Bakken's extra point attempt. That can be a demoralizing thing. It meant that they would now have to score more than two touchdowns to overtake us.

We demoralized them even more about a minute later when Jaworski hit Harold Jackson for a 66-yard touchdown to give us a 28-6 lead. Bakken kicked a field goal later in the quarter. We led 28-9 at the half.

The Cardinals weren't about to give up. We kicked off to them to start the second half and they shoved the ball down our throats on an 80-yard touchdown drive.

Both defenses took over from that point on until well into the fourth quarter. I sacked Hart in the third quarter and Dryer got him early in the fourth quarter. Even though our defense put good pressure on him, those were the only two sacks we got.

Midway through the fourth quarter, Hart tried to throw to Cain and Simpson got his second interception of the game. We scored a lucky touchdown with around four minutes left to play when McCutcheon ran about nine yards before fumbling at the Cardinals' four. Our wide receiver, Ron Jessie, alertly picked up the ball at the two and scored. That put us out of reach, 35-16.

St. Louis scored again with less than a minute to play on a time-consuming drive. We gave them the short stuff and they took it. They spent something like 12 plays to drive 68 yards to score. The game ended: 35-23.

That win put us into the NFC Championship Game against Dallas the following week in Los Angeles. They struck fast and upset us 37-7. It was a disappointing thing, naturally, at the time; but when I look back on it now, I think of it as an excellent season for a young, developing team. We won 13 games and lost only three. Not bad.

—As told to Dave Payne

In 1979 action, Los Angeles Rams defensive end **Jack Youngblood** (85), above right, blocks Tampa Bay running back Ricky Bell (42). Youngblood earned entry to the Pro Football Hall of Fame in 2001 based on 14 consistently outstanding seasons (1971–84) with the Rams. The six-foot-four, 247-pound lineman went to his first of seven consecutive Pro Bowls in 1973. Youngblood played a team-record 201 consecutive games, and missed only one match—in his last season.

INDEX

PHOTO CREDITS

front cover:	© Al Tielemans/Sports Illustrated
back cover	© Al Messerschmidt
title page:	© Al Messerschmidt
6 (top)	© Al Messerschmidt
6 (bottom)	© Al Messerschmidt
7 (top)	© Stephen Dunn/Getty Images
7 (middle)	© Sports Illustrated
7 (bottom)	© Bettmann/CORBIS/Magma
9	© Walter Iooss Jr/Sports Illustrated
11	© Al Messerschmidt
13	© Al Messerschmidt
15	© Al Messerschmidt
17	© Al Messerschmidt
19	© NFL Photos
21	© Bettmann/CORBIS/Magma
23	© NFL Photos
25	© Bettmann/CORBIS/Magma
27	© Bettmann/CORBIS/Magma
29	© Bettmann/CORBIS/Magma
31	© John Iacono/Sports Illustrated
33	© Al Messerschmidt
35	© Al Messerschmidt
37	© Al Messerschmidt
39	© Bettmann/CORBIS/Magma
41	© Walter Iooss Jr./Sports Illustrated
43	© Al Messerschmidt
45	© John Iacono/Sports Illustrated
47	© Al Messerschmidt
49	© Bettmann/CORBIS/Magma
51	© Al Messerschmidt
53	© Bettmann/CORBIS/Magma
55	© Bettmann/CORBIS/Magma
57	© Al Messerschmidt
59	© Bettmann/CORBIS/Magma
61	© Wally McNamee/CORBIS/Magma
63	© Bettmann/CORBIS/Magma
65	© Bettmann/CORBIS/Magma
67	© Bettmann/CORBIS/Magma
69	© Al Messerschmidt
71	© Heinz Kluetmeier/Sports Illustrated
73	© Al Messerschmidt
75	© Bettmann/CORBIS/Magma
77	© Bettmann/CORBIS/Magma
79	© Al Messerschmidt
81	© Wally McNamee/CORBIS/Magma
83	© Al Messerschmidt
85	© Al Messerschmidt
87	© Al Messerschmidt
89	© Al Messerschmidt
91	© Heinz Kluetmeier/Sports Illustrated
93	© Al Messerschmidt
95	© Bettmann/CORBIS/Magma
97	© Al Messerschmidt
99	© Al Messerschmidt
101	© Al Messerschmidt
103	© Al Messerschmidt
105	© Al Messerschmidt
107	© Stephen Dunn/Getty Images
109	© Al Messerschmidt
111	© Bettmann/CORBIS/Magma
113	© Richard Mackson/Sports Illustrated
115	© John W. McDonough/Sports Illustrated
117	© Al Messerschmidt
119	© Bettmann/CORBIS/Magma
121	© Bettmann/CORBIS/Magma
123	© Richard Mackson/Sports Illustrated
125	© Al Messerschmidt
127	© Al Messerschmidt
129	© Al Messerschmidt
131	© Andy Hayt/Sports Illustrated
133	© Al Messerschmidt
135	© Al Messerschmidt
137	© Al Messerschmidt
139	© Al Messerschmidt
141	© Bettmann/CORBIS/Magma
143	© Bettmann/CORBIS/Magma
145	© Al Messerschmidt
147	© Damian Strohmeyer/Sports Illustrated
149	© Bettmann/CORBIS/Magma
151	© Andy Lyons/Getty Images
153	© James Drake/Sports Illustrated
155	© Walter Iooss Jr/Sports Illustrated
157	© Al Messerschmidt
159	© Al Messerschmidt
161	© Bettmann/CORBIS/Magma
163	© Al Messerschmidt
165	© Al Messerschmidt
167	© Neil Leifer/Sports Illustrated
169	© T.G. Higgins/Getty Images
171	© Al Messerschmidt
173	© Getty Images/Staff
175	© Al Messerschmidt
177	© Bettmann/CORBIS/Magma
179	© Walter Iooss Jr./Sports Illustrated
181	© Neil Leifer/Sports Illustrated
183	© Bettmann/CORBIS/Magma
185	© Al Messerschmidt
187	© Getty Images/Staff
189	© Al Messerschmidt
191	© Bettmann/CORBIS/Magma
193	© Al Messerschmidt
195	© James L. Amos/CORBIS/Magma
197	© Al Messerschmidt
199	© Al Tielemans/Sports Illustrated
201	© Al Messerschmidt
203	© Bettmann/CORBIS/Magma
205	© John Biever/Sports Illustrated
207	© Jonathan Daniel/Getty Images
209	© Wally McNamee/CORBIS/Magma

ACKNOWLEDGMENTS

Special thanks go to Lionel Koffler, Michael Worek and Brad Wilson from Firefly Books Ltd. Your enthusiasm for *The Football Game I'll Never Forget* is much appreciated. Brad in particular played a huge role in shaping this book and looked after myriad details. I also want to acknowledge the entire Firefly crew, from reception to publicity to sales to shipping. At every point, despite hectic schedules, you maintain good cheer while making the books and successfully getting them out to readers. I'm indebted to you all.

Of course, this book owes everything to the talented stars of the National Football League who agreed to reminisce about their most meaningful games. Thank you for sharing your incredible stories. And this collection would not exist if the *Football Digest* writers who gathered these tales had not done such an excellent job. Special kudos go to George Vass and Chuck O'Donnell. Thank you also to Will Wagner, Editor in Chief at Century Publishing Co., for obtaining permissions and ensuring this volume could be born.

Joanne Richter has been the kind of editor all writers like to work with. She asked good questions that helped me and the guys at Football Digest help our athletes tell their stories well, without distorting their individual voices. Joanne also put her keen eye to work on the statistical game summaries that we've included, catching some errors and omissions. Likewise, Anna Filippone has done an excellent job proofreading. Any mistakes that may remain are mine.

Designer Christine Gilham has done a wonderful job for me again, remaining open to suggestion while putting her own stamp on the book. I'm really pleased with how everything looks. The outstanding photos we've used came from a variety of sources. Al Messerschmidt diligently pored over his vast archive and provided me with great choices. Prem Kalliat at Sports Illustrated, Howie Burke at Getty Images and Joanne, Lucie, Tina and the rest of the team at Magma Photo also supplied great shots. Thank you all.

To ensure we had correct and complete statistical information, Chad Reese of the Pro Football Hall of Fame was of great help. Likewise, many NFL teams dug into their archives on my behalf. I would like to especially acknowledge Roger Hacker of the Chicago Bears, Dino Lucarelli and Nathan Boudreaux of the Cleveland Browns, Deanna Caldwell and Cletus Lewis Jr. of the Detroit Lions, Avis Roper of the New York Giants, Aaron Staenberg of the St. Louis Rams, Mike Kane of the Washington Redskins and the public relations staff of the Tennessee Titans and San Francisco 49ers.

I also made use of *The New York Times* archives at the University of Western Ontario and *The 2002 National Football League Record and Fact Book*. The Pro Football Hall of Fame website (*www.profootballhof.com*) was also helpful, and I mined a lot of NFL information from two other sites that I highly recommend: *www.jt-sw.com/football* by John Troan and *www.pro-football-reference.com* by Doug Drinen.

My family, as always, continues to be supportive of my work. A special note of gratitude goes to my parents, Alanson and Nora McDonell, who generously anchor so many gatherings while maintaining a lively interest in the individual lives of an increasingly large family. My sisters Anne, Carolyn, Marjorie, Barbara and Janet and my brother Kevin, along with their respective spouses, always offer genuine encouragement and warm and frequent hospitality. Thanks. I am also blessed with wonderful in-laws. Randy and Nancy Gordon frequently go out of their way to support our family, as does their daughter Karen. My mother-in-law Mary Gordon stays connected despite living in British Columbia, and we always feel her present in spirit. Eric and Eileen Gordon are unstintingly generous, bridging the geographical gap between us in a loving way. Thank you for all that you do to enrich my life.

My deepest appreciation goes to Sue Gordon. Sue is the rock in my life, the person I can turn to for consolation and inspiration, for a hug or a nudge and for a good laugh. I am blessed to be her life partner. Our children, Quinn, Tara and Isaac, keep me rooted in the workaday world while simultaneously helping ease me through it. Their astonishing growth as beautifully developing individuals reminds me that life is a short trip and to treasure the time we have together. Thank you, with all my love.

— Chris McDonell